Against the Stream

To the British Bolsheviks,
supporters of the International Left Opposition,
in admiration

Against the Stream

A History of the Trotskyist Movement in Britain, 1924-38

Sam Bornsten and Al Richardson

MERLIN PRESS

First published 1986

Reprinted 2007 by The Merlin Press Ltd. in association with Socialist Platform Ltd.

Merlin Press Ltd.
96 Monnow Street
Monmouth
NP25 3EQ
Wales

www.merlinpress.co.uk
www.revolutionary-history.co.uk/socplat.htm
www.revolutionary-history.co.uk

ISBN. 978-0-85036-600-6

British Library Cataloguing in Publication Data
is available from the British Library

Printed in Great Britain by
Lightning Source UK, Milton Keynes

Errata

Page 41 Note 29 1975 is incorrect and should be 1925.

Page 43, notes 88 and 91. Both refer to Trotsky's 'What we Gave and What We Got'. Note 88 gives a date of 23 September 1927 but note 91 gives a date of 23 September 1926. It is in fact 1927.

Page 73 there are 2 notes numbered 71. The second 71 should be numbered 72. And note 71 (on page 73) should be deleted. This will square up with notes on page 93.

Page 78 It says that the British Section of the ILO was formed on 19 December 1932. This should be 1931.

Page 82 second para line 1 't' should be added to 'Trotskyis'.

Page 85 there are 2 notes numbered 141. The second should be 144.

Page 93 note 78 the date should be 1932.

Page 95 note 116 the date of the publication of Labour Monthly should be included. It is 1929.

Page 155 note 4 the page number should be included. It is page 111.

Contents

Illustrations *(between pages 148 and 149)*

The authors are grateful to the following for the loan of photographs: Rita Dewar (2), Margaret Johns (7), Daisy Groves (8) and Julian Harber (9).

Foreword

Anyone who has had to read the policy documents, books and journals of the more severe and intransigent political sects will know the immense weariness of mind and spirit it can inflict upon the researchers. Only those acquainted with their story and who know it from the inside can appreciate the problems raised by the inacessibility of material, the often incomplete minutes of meetings, the scattering of records, and the uneven value of individual recollections.

It is pleasing to report that the authors of this study of 'Trotskyism' in Britain have come through this ordeal, if not completely unscathed, at least with their tolerance and judgement intact. Readers can trust their narrative, their conclusions and their summaries of the origins, activities and internal conflicts of the various groups. Some damage, it is true, was done to their patient researches by the destruction or loss of files, minute books, journals and membership lists during the war, but it is partly repaired by the personal recollections of those who survived.

Other difficulties arose from the nature of the events themselves. The obscurity of the earlier attempts to correct the course of the British Communist Party lay in the fact that they were immediate responses to the changes in the policies and purposes of the Communist International. Its tighter discipline was only slowly recognised by some as the increasing imposition of the Russian Party's absolute control over a supposedly representative international body. Major breakaways did come from this, but there was still the problem of purging the influence of Social Democracy, which remained substantial despite the bloody war, and the subsequent restoration of pre-war capitalist power everywhere. Nonetheless, up to the General Strike of 1926 the C.P.G.B. grew steadily, and Trotsky's book issued shortly before it made a profound impression in working class and intellectual circles. But by the end of 1926 most of them had left, and in the party an atmosphere of excessive sloganisation grew, stemming from a more or less literal translation of Russian material.

Unlike most of those who call themselves Trotskyists today — and the term has become so loose as to be almost meaningless — we in the Balham Group were from working class families, mainly skilled working class with the exception of some who were unemployed. We were not intending to encourage 'breakaways' or set up new parties: our aim was to be part of a world effort to free the Comintern from its rôle as a mere instrument of the foreign policy of the Russian government. We sought to alert the International Labour movement to the dangers of the policy of the Communist International in Germany by raising the demand for a United front between the Communist Party and the Social Democratic Party and its trade unions to crush the menace of Fascism. We began the publication of *The Communist*, which was not immediately traced back to us, with a lengthy article by Trotsky warning of the growing crisis in Germany and its portent for the world Labour movement, and indeed the Soviet Union itself. In due course we were expelled. The numbers concerned were few, but we attracted some rare birds indeed, and like all such, were ignored, save by a few fanatical specialists. It took the subsequent 'Treason Trials' in Moscow to force many to realise the factional corruption of Russian power politics and the extent to which it stretched beyond the territory of the Soviet Union.

One minor point needs emphasising. It was old Henderson's red-and-gold painted bookshop in Charing Cross Road that was the source of our discovery in the early thirties that there were at least two breakway Communist Parties in the United States, one of them of a 'Right' character led by Jay Lovestone, and the other to the Left, Trotskyist in policy, led by James Cannon and Arne Swabeck. and publishing *The Militant*. Through this we were brought into contact with the International Left Opposition.

The authors of this unique history have made it concise, coherent and tolerable without reducing its usefulness and intrinsic interest. It is factual and unsectarian, though they must have spent many hours of their research listening to partisans. The result is a valuable saver of time for many students of history, and a 'must' for the shelves of Universities and the libraries of Polytechnics, etc. More to the point, it will be of interest to many people in the Labour and Trade Union movement, who must wonder from where the word 'Trotskyism' comes, now that it has become a synonym for all protesters.

What remains from the struggle before the war is contained in this book, and our thanks are owed, not only to the resourcefulness of Al and Sam, but to all the collaborators who aided them with the project. Congratulations!

6th October 1985. Reg Groves

Preface

Dr. Johnson once remarked that he who writes books for any reason other than money must be a fool, and probably most people would agree with him. When whole forests are being cut down for books and magazines, each book must have at least some justification for appearing.

In this case we could plead public interest. Never before have the media been as fascinated by what is called 'Trotskyism' as at the moment. Hardly a week goes by without some mention of it in the newspapers; and its use by broadcasters, reporters and politicians has eclipsed the traditional bogey of the Communist Party. That a movement should have such an influence out of all proportion to its numbers and implantation is something of a minor miracle — were it not for the fact that it has many times been proved that ideas have the power to affect the lives of millions.

However, when we examine the majority of organisations in Britain laying claim to Trotskyism — upwards of a dozen of them — we find little ideological coherence, and wide differences in methods of work, spheres of activity, slogans and programme. When we compare such groups with those which claimed the same allegiance forty years ago we see a void of difference. A whole thought world separates them. Whatever the differences then, there was a general consensus about the superiority of United Front over Popular Front; of the crucial role of the working class in the struggle for socialism; and of the primacy of questions of class over those of sex or colour. Today we see a blurring of the differences between Trotskyism and Stalinism; the two have found a common environment in what is called the 'New Left'. Now that principled positions — particularly class issues — have become secondary, a new unity of theory has emerged. Since Stalinism has limited its concessions to dropping the name itself and taking its distance from Moscow, the real concessions have come from the Trotskyists. Much of what passes for Trotskyism now is a rehash of Third Period or Popular Front Stalinism, or even an odd combination of the two.

Such theoretical confusion has prevented the groups that now exist from dealing with Trotskyist history in a coherent way. Instead, rival groups produce selected snippets of history designed to justify their current practice. Yet the experiences of the Trotskyists in the past are a rich store of lessons for today. Many of the problems of revolutionaries in the labour movement were first encountered then. They include: how the broad labour movement is to be approached; how trade union work must be carried on; what should be the attitude of socialists to the intelligentsia, to liberalism, to Soviet Russia, to war and disarmament and to a multitude of other questions. All these were hotly debated in the period covered by this book, and the seriousness with which they were treated cannot fail to be of use to socialists today.

In a previous book, which described the role of the Communist Party in the 1930s and 1940s,[1] we asked whether that now redundant party could survive for much longer.[2] That question has now been answered, as the Communist Party is about to split in two. But paradoxically, though the C.P. political machine is about to shatter, its ideological legacy remains pervasive. The anti-working class attitude promoted by the Communist Party during the Popular Front of the Thirties has now been taken up by the 'Trotskyists' and by others in the 'Broad Left', who have failed to see the connexion between those views and the new alliance openly preached by the Communist Party, between Labour, Liberal and S.D.P. Perhaps the threat of a new Popular Front is now even greater, since Attlee certainly would never have allowed himself to be 'advised' by any Stalinist theorist in the way that Kinnock is alleged to be by Hobsbawm. The only antidote to such policies is to go over, yet again, the experiences of the past and to draw lessons from them. If conscious socialists have any function, surely it is to act as a reservoir of these past lessons and to hand them on for future use. Otherwise, history will repeat itself as an endless cycle of catastrophe.

One lesson stands out like a sore thumb, and it is so obvious as to be surprising that anyone should have missed it. At no time during the lifetime of L. Trotsky was there any warrant at all for a small group of a few hundred comrades standing outside the rest of the Labour movement and calling itself a 'party'. When Trotskyism began in Britain, it was as a faction inside the Communist Party; this was followed by the experiences of entry into the I.L.P. and the Labour Party. If independent groups arose, they did not have the sanction of the International Secretariat. Neither did groups that were half 'open' and half 'entrist'. Entry work was the total passing of the whole organisation into the larger party with the intention of winning over large sections to revolutionary politics. Entry was simply the form taken by the 'United Front' where the revolutionaries had no forces of their own to bring to the class alliance, the 'United Front From Within'. Short-term 'smash and grab' raids were a feature of Stalinism during this period, not of Trotskyism. These simple propositions, baldly stated, disqualify almost all of the organisations claiming to be Trotskyist today at one or another phase of their development.

The work for this book and its following volume has occupied the writers for a dozen years, and it is with some relief that we now place our first results before the public. In the course of the research we heard that John Archer and Martin Upham were also at work on books of a like scope; and just before we went to press, a book from an academic writer appeared under a similar title.[3] We began to wonder whether our own efforts would be made redundant. However, the book that has appeared proves to be a sociology of the post-1960s middle-class groups, with a distinct bias towards those whose contact with the working class and its movement are most tenuous. Our view remains that far more fruitful lessons are to be gained from the history of those organisations that were, or aspired to be, part of the Labour movement. We still feel that the true home of revolutionary ideas is the trade union or Labour Party meeting rather than the salon or the seminar room. So in spite of the disbelief of our more jaundiced critics,[4] we have gone ahead, and hope that our rashness will encourage Martin Upham and John Archer to do the same. Different approaches to the subject can only sharpen our critical sense and increase our understanding of the struggle of the Trotskyists during those dark years.

Since so much of the history of the Trotskyist movement at that time is so little known, we have felt justified in sacrificing analysis to factual detail whenever there was a conflict between them. Space alone has prevented us from making more than occasional reference to the general history of the broader labour movement. We have been obliged to refer to its organisations and their prominent figures without any further explanation. Those who did not live through the period, or who find that their memories no longer serve them adequately, can easily gain the necessary background knowledge from a number of general Labour history books. Our own view of these events has already appeared in *Two Steps Back*, and the references we make to it absolve us of any need to repeat that analysis. As the aim of this present book is to fill a real gap in information, we felt it must include as much of the basic documentation as is feasible, leaving it to the reader to use his own judgement. In any case, those whose concept of socialist theory is a mish-mash of bourgeois feminism, sexual liberation and Third Worldism with the occasional genuflection in the direction of Gramsci or *New Left Review* will have already realised that this book is not written for them, and will seek such high theory elsewhere.

Questions of theory inevitably lead on to method. The nature of our subject imposed on us a need to combine oral and documentary sources. Theoretical discussion is most accurately embodied in written documents, as those who took part in the disputes inevitably modified their memories either through factional considerations or in the light of subsequent experience. On the other hand, documents do not adequately reflect the inner life of the movement, nor the real experiences of its supporters as they fought its cause within the unions and political parties, or from street-corner platforms. Only by tapping the seam of oral reminiscence are we able to look beyond the writings and doings of the leadership to the rich life of the movement below them. 'Theory is always grey, but the tree of life is ever green.'

Our gratitude to all those who helped us in this way — listed in Appendix I below — must be obvious to all. If this book speaks authentically of the work of the Trotskyists in the twenties and thirties, it is because they speak directly through it.

Our thanks go to all those, too numerous to mention, whose donations have allowed this book to appear; to our typist, Mrs. Linda Finn, who with unfailing patience has typed and retyped the manuscript until she is better acquainted with it than we are. Bruce Robinson has done sterling service by providing us with an index. Finally, and belatedly, we extend our thanks to Mr. Christopher Matthews, who proof-read our previous book several times over, and whose name was omitted from the acknowledgements of *Two Steps Back* by an inadmissible lapse of manners.

Notes

1. S. Bornstein and A. Richardson, *Two Steps Back*, London, 1982.
2. Ibid., p. 141.
3. J. Callaghan, *British Trotskyism*, Oxford, 1984.
4. W. Hunter, 'Handraisers for the Bureaucracy', in *Labour Review*, January 1983, p. 44.

Chapter One

The Stalin–Trotsky Conflict in the British Communist Party, 1924–29

The first member of the British Communist Party to regard himself as a Trotskyist was the lawyer A.E. Reade, who was a member of the London District Committee and business manager of R. Palme Dutt's *Labour Monthly*. It is difficult at this stage in time, without access to the correspondence, to establish whether Dutt allowed (or encouraged) him to put forward his views, flying a kite, as it were, since Dutt was to continue to express guarded approval of some of Trotsky's ideas after the fashion had become to condemn them. But a two-part article appearing in his journal [1] summarised for the first time the 'Discussion in the Russian Communist Party' in terms that expressed a favourable view of Trotsky, describing him as 'particularly outspoken in his denunciation of bureaucracy',[2] and noting that 'the position at present is that the rigid central control of the party has tended rather to the development of bureaucracy'.[3] It defended the Russian Opposition against the accusations of forming an illegal fraction against the party; 'the "opposition" have denied this charge,' it noted, 'and there does not seem to be any serious basis to it.' The views of the Opposition and of the 'defenders of the Party machine, particularly Stalin' were summed up fairly in selected quotations, but the article was careful to cover its tracks by adding that 'the mass of polemics is already so vast and so recondite' that it was 'almost impossible to disentangle the real truth of the matter'.[4] A similar article from Tom Bell appearing at the same time in *The Communist Review* also gave Trotsky a favourable press.[5]

Some interest appears to have been raised by these articles in Scotland, where the Dundee branch of the Party rejected an amendment to prevent a 'Comrade Douglas' from explaining 'the attitude of Trotsky and the others in regard to their advocacy of increased democracy within the Russian Party'.[6] But at the same time it did not take long for the Communist Party to make up its mind and come down on the other side, without even formally discussing the issue. The April issue of *The Communist Review* printed the resolution of the 13th Congress of the Communist Party of the Soviet Union condemning the Opposition, and at the Fifth Comintern Congress of June 1924 the British delegation voted along with the majority to accept it as a decision of the Communist International. They signed the resolution to condemn the Opposition along with the parties of France, Germany and the United States, and did not see fit to add their support to the protests against the personal attacks on Trotsky that were made by other national sections (for example, those from France and Poland).

The simple truth of the matter was that the British Party did not understand the issues involved. As MacFarlane notes, 'the Communist Party of Great Britain never intended to put themselves at loggerheads with the dominant faction led by Stalin'; they were 'unaware of the seriousness of the crisis in the Russian Party and the relative strength of the opposing factions.'[7] They continued, without any apparent hostility, to print Trotsky's articles on a variety of subjects,[8] just as they had always done with both him and the other prominent Russian leaders. Indeed, they could be forgiven for believing that the whole affair had been a regrettable incident, a momentary problem, which had now been dealt with, whilst they turned to their not inconsiderable difficulties in building up a party at home.

A.E. Reade had some advantages over the others, because he had arrived at his opinions through a very careful study of both Communist and opposing literature in German and other languages, which were not widely understood by the average party rank-and-filer. He gave a summary of the information he had gained in a course on Marxism for the Young Communist League branch in Battersea, which stirred the interest of Harry Wicks, among others.[9] As yet there was no ban on discussions of this nature, and there were no excesses of hostility against those who raised such issues.

The reopening of the conflict in a sharp form in Russia made it necessary for the British Party to consider it again. As a preface to the edition of his writings of 1917, Trotsky published an essay under the heading of *Lessons of October*, which drew uncomfortable parallels between the behaviour of Zinoviev, Stalin and Kamenev in that year and the erratic policies of the Communist International at crisis points in other countries since. The Central Committee of the Communist Party of the Soviet Union censured him for starting the conflict again after it had been closed, and released a notice in *Pravda* which began another spate of speculation in the world press about an imminent split. On the one hand there was interest in what the British Party had to say about the affair, and on the other the Stalin group needed the support of the International Communist movement for its internal struggle. Comintern sections in other countries were obliged to pronounce upon it, and that included the British Party as a matter of course.

The Party Council met in the public library at Bethnal Green on 30th November 1924, to hear a discussion introduced by Tom Bell, who had the responsibility for liaison with the International. As one of its sections, he pointed out, the British Party was obliged to express an opinion 'on a question which so vitally affected another section', especially one affecting 'party discipline', on which they 'must take a strong line'.[10]

Then he moved a resolution offering support to the position of the Political Bureau of the Russian Party, even though as yet the British C.P. only had a summary of Trotsky's article to go on, and not the thing itself.[11]

> The Party Council of the Communist Party of Great Britain sees in the Preface to Comrade Trotsky's book on '1917' an attempt not only to reopen the discussion closed by the decision of the 13th Congress of the R.C.P.[12] and the 5th Congress of the Communist International, which, in the opinion of the C.P.G.B., will not only definitely encourage the British imperialists, the bitterest enemies of Soviet Russia, but will also encourage the lackeys of the Second International and those other elements who stand for the liquidation of the C.I.[13] and the C.P. in this country.
>
> The Party Council and Executive Committee of the C.P.G.B. records its solidarity with and implicit faith in, the Communist Party of Russia and the Executive Committee of the Communist International. Especially is this most necessary in this most critical period, when the world situation demands the closest co-operation of every member of the Communist International in carrying out the accepted policy of the International.[14]

It is of interest that the condemnation of the Russian Opposition should have been demanded out of loyalty to the Communist International — a loyalty not shared by Stalin himself, when he reduced its congresses and finally dissolved it in 1943. Even more strange was the expression of 'implicit faith', an attitude that ill becomes an assembly of militant atheist revolutionaries.

But this motion to close the discussion in the Russian Party had the effect of opening it in Britain. The Party here had not yet suffered the programme of 'Bolshevisation', which made the membership endorse automatically the decisions of their leading bodies without a hearing of other points of view. At the prompting of A.E. Reade, the London District Committee questioned the decision and asked for further information.[15] It was decided to call a London aggregate meeting for early January 1925, and in the meantime a spate of slanted articles began to appear in the Party press. Tom Bell ascribed Trotsky's support to 'the bureaucrats and the Nepmen' (the reverse of the truth),[16] while an unsigned article dismissed reports that Trotsky had been 'prohibited from writing' or that there had been a split 'or the likelihood of there being a split' as 'fantastic rubbish'. Trotsky's 'illness' had been the reason why he had not 'ventured to answer the case' against his 'grave breach of discipline', not as a result of 'an arbitrary or even disciplinary act'.[17] This was before a single word of Trotsky's side of the case had appeared, though underneath the article was an advertisement for Stalin's *Foundations of Leninism*, which was 'just out'.[18]

The London aggregate met on 17th January 1925, when some 200 comrades were called upon by J.T. Murphy to endorse the decisions of the Party Council. He argued ingenuously that 'few of our party members could have thought of disassociating Lenin from Trotsky' because of the 'general ignorance of international affairs prevailing amongst the membership in Britain'. Now they were let in on the secret that they 'had been in continuous opposition for 25 years', that the 'sudden love for Trotsky' shown by the capitalist press went along with 'a concentration of the petty bourgeoisie' at a difficult period of the N.E.P. which 'meant that extraordinary methods had to be adopted to safeguard the revolution'. He answered 'those who criticised the action of the Political Bureau for their haste in bringing it before the membership' with the assertion that 'the mere fact that Trotsky's action was a challenge to the international leadership was a sufficient justification'.

Nowhere was it said that the almost indecent haste to secure a condemnation was due to Stalin's need in the internal struggle to use the weight of the foreign parties to strike a blow at the Left Opposition, and the appeal to capitalist pressure and the emergency of the situation was to become an old chestnut raked out whenever it was necessary to justify the infringement of the rights of the rank and file, in both Britain and Russia.

A.E. Reade got up to move an amendment defending the London District Committee's demand for more information before such a condemnation was acceptable:

> This aggregate meeting of the London District membership of the C.P.G.B. joins with the D.P.C. in regretting the hasty vote of the Party Council in condemning Comrade Trotsky without full information, and this meeting at the same time takes the

> opportunity to express the London membership's most emphatic support both to the Left Wing Minority's fight in the Russian Party and against divergencies from Leninism in the French, German, Bulgarian, and other sections of the international.

Reade now made a summary of what evidence there was to hand. He supported Trotsky's critique of the vacillations of Stalin, Zinoviev and Kamenev in 1917, and its relevance to the current international situation, pointed out that *Inprecorr* and the other official press had given full publicity to the Stalin group's version of the clash, but that 'Trotsky's side had been suppressed', and ended with a reference to Lenin's 'Testament', also suppressed.

Rothstein answered that 'the talk of suppression was all rot', because Trotsky 'had made, at his own request, private arrangements for publishing his book', but 'special arrangements had been made to circulate very cheap editions throughout the party membership'. This might have been true of *Lessons of October*, but it was certainly not the case with the other documents of the Opposition, particularly Lenin's 'Testament'. Rothstein described it as 'a document not intended for publication', available only in a 'garbled and distorted account published in the Menshevik press in Germany', and said that it was 'characteristic of Reade's anti-party attitude' for him to read it.[20] It was oddly illogical to claim that documents had not been suppressed, and then blame someone for going to what sources there were in order to consult them.

R. Page Arnot then made a personal attack on Reade as a 'romantic', and forgot his own education in his urge to maintain that 'Trotsky's supporters were not to be found among the working class, but amongst the University students who had become divorced from actualities'.

This appeal to the anti-intellectualism (or shall we say anti-theory) of the members had the desired effect, for a motion to adjourn the discussion pending the receipt of further information fell by 81 votes to 65, and the main resolution was passed with only 15 votes against, one of them cast by Harry Wicks, who to this day remembers the violence of Murphy's and Rothstein's tirades against Trotsky.[21]

It was the first — and in fact the fullest — discussion of the conflict between Stalin and Trotsky that the British Communist Party ever had. A bad pointer for the future cropped up in the article with which 'C.M. Roebuck' (apparently Andrew Rothstein) gave the fullest description of the meeting, in which Trotsky's proposals for an economic plan were described as 'anti-party, anti-Bolshevik', 'the outlook of the petty-bourgeois intellectual, subjectively prompted by an enormous desire to assert his own individuality', whose supporters 'played the game of Menshevism' and were supported by the capitalist class. Those who opposed the condemnation of Trotsky without a hearing 'only show that they have a terrible deal to learn yet before they become real communists', but it was to be '*hoped that any comrades who have made such mistakes will realise the anti-Communist anti-Party, and anti-revolutionary path they have been treading, before it is too late, and before they have irretrievably reached the point at which it leads out of the Party and out of the Communist International.*' [22]

Time has passed a stern verdict on these proceedings. It took thirty years for the British Communists to realise that the cult of the personality was Stalin's, not Trotsky's; only four years for Stalin to adopt the Opposition's own plan and force it through at break-neck pace; and less than a year after that for the first expulsions to come.

From this time a harsher note crept into the Party's publications when the Trotskyist question was raised. For though the leadership of the Russian Party should have been satisfied with the British Party's standpoint, they were disturbed at the low-key way in which it was expressed, and the fact that there had not been enough build-up before the condemnation. One of the papers seized by the British authorities at the time of the arrest of the C.P. leaders in October 1925 was an unsigned letter from the chief of the Agitation and Propaganda Department of the Executive of the Communist International to the Central Executive of the C.P.G.B. listing the faults of the party's theoretical journal, *Communist Review*. 'The discussion of matters of urgent importance for the development of the party have been placed somewhat in the background,' it affirmed. 'Here we refer especially to the struggle against the Trotskyist deviation . . .'[23] What they probably had in mind here was an article in the magazine by Tom Bell, describing how 'the party has been forced to more or less transform itself into such an apparatus, and the state bureaucracy has accordingly become associated with the party', and 'the Party lost necessarily to a certain extent, its proletarian character'.[24]

This meant that Bell had to show that his article was a mistaken lapse into idolisation. Bukharin provided the occasion at the Tenth Session of the Enlarged Executive Committee of the Comintern on 3rd April 1925, where Bell was present, when he spoke of 'sentimental Communists', 'good fellows' who 'say that we ought not to ill-treat a comrade like Trotsky'.[25] Bell explained how the British party had 'followed the whole discussions around what is called Trotskyism and has no hesitation in allying itself with the Central Committee of the R.C.P. and the E.C. of the C.I.' 'Comrade Trotsky is a fine fellow,' he went on, 'in England and in Western Europe he is regarded as a romantic figure and particularly among the intellectual sections of our movement in England as well as in other countries, there is a feeling that he should have special privileges, a certain amount of scope and criticism. They all agree that he is a wonderful leader, a wonderful fighter for the world revolution. But why, therefore, should the Party be so severe on Comrade Trotsky? I will tell you the substance I overheard between a worker and an intellectual on this question. The intellectual put the question as I have described it, and the reply of the worker was "Why the hell should Comrade Trotsky have any more privileges than an ordinary member of the Communist International?" ' 'We in Great Britain were willing to listen and discuss with Trotsky,' he added, 'but when Comrade Lenin died and the bourgeoisie thought their chance had come' things had changed. '*On this question we are against Trotsky and for the Comintern.*'[26] Then the 14th session of the plenum on 6th April condemned Trotsky for 'starting a new discussion in the Communist Party'.

Now that the Comintern had provided the personal tone in which attacks on Trotsky were to be made, the British Communist Party moved to correct its earlier assessments. They came out in reviews of Trotsky's *Lenin*, a collection of essays just published in book form. The most personal appeared in *Labour Monthly*, for it had to atone for its previous favourable assessment of him. W.N. Ewer described Trotsky as a 'vain garrulous tattler', a 'sick and neurotic man' who was 'consoling himself by telling himself stories of his own great past'. He struck a note of mock sympathy in the remark that 'it is not good to look upon a strong man in the day of his sickness and mental weakness',[27] though the journal in which he wrote had published one of Trotsky's essays without any such unfavourable comment only eight months earlier. Ewer even abused his position as foreign editor of the *Daily Herald* to attack his fellow Communists in the non-party press in the same terms. Trotsky's work was 'a book which one feels ashamed to read, for one feels one is peeping indecently into a sick room' at 'a big man, babbling of the past like a senile colonel in a club armchair'.[28] Naturally, Ewer got scant sympathy when he broke with the party not long afterwards, and was treated in exactly the same way.

More sympathetic was T.A. Jackson's description of Trotsky's 'fundamental temperamentality' which forced him to feel 'the need for a figure in the centre of the stage', stepping forward into Lenin's shoes.[29] MacManus put it all down to Trotsky's 'intense nervousness' and 'hesitant, uncertain, undecided tone'.[30]

More light was shed by the sudden appearance in London of Max Eastman's book, *Since Lenin Died*. Apart from its description of the struggle from a viewpoint sympathetic to Trotsky's, the book quoted at length from documents, some unavailable in the English language, with a whole chapter devoted to Lenin's will[31] and appendices including Trotsky's letters on party democracy of October 1923, on the 'New Course' of December 1923, and on resignation from the leadership of the army on 15th January 1925.[32] Eastman covered himself and Trotsky by stating that the documents were reproduced from the Berlin Menshevik organ *Sotzialistichesky Vestnik* (from which Reade and Rothstein also took their information), but that leading Bolsheviks had admitted their authenticity.[33]

When the English publishers (the Labour Publishing Association) inserted an advertisement for Eastman's book in the May Day issue of *Workers Weekly*, the party accompanied it with an article describing it as 'a sorry piece of hysterical tittle tattle', its author as 'bourgeois hero worshipper and dilettante', and Lenin's 'Testament' as 'a few disconnected extracts from a letter written some time before his death'.[34] MacManus was more hostile, itemising it as a 'splendid opportunity' presented to 'renegades and counter revolutionists to attack the Russian Communist Party — the very soul and leading spirit of the Russian Revolution', and appealing again to British hostility to theory, saying that the workers would 'stiffen their determination to rely *solely upon themselves*, and leave the intellectuals to their pretentious playfulness — in the interest of "historic truth" — to say nothing of strategy.'[35]

Jackson followed with a review in the *Sunday Worker*. Some attempt was made at a class analysis, describing the conflict as 'that of a group of minor state functionaries (using the slogan "democracy") against the Old Guard', 'neglected geniuses' who set up a 'great wail' to cover up their retreat. Eastman was described as one of 'the idol-making intellectuals of the western world', who 'value all movements by their figure-heads', who had put forward Trotsky as 'Lenin's natural successor' on the 'hero-throne left vacant'.[36] He seemed unaware of the contradiction involved in his own personal attacks on Trotsky and his new argument that Eastman, in replying to such attacks, was personalising matters.

The publication of Eastman's book had come at an inopportune time in the struggle of the Left Opposition in the Soviet Union, and Trotsky's supporters were unwilling to make a fight over such an issue and advised him to disclaim all knowledge of it.

As far as the British Party was concerned, the book was a major embarrassment, and they adopted three different ways of dealing with it. These were to smother it under a wave of unfavourable reviews, to expedite the publication of their own book, *The Errors of Trotskyism*, and to join with the Russian leadership in forcing Trotsky to repudiate it.

Jackson took charge of this, by sending Trotsky a telegram asking him to reject certain views of the book expressed in the bourgeois press, hoping that his reply could be interpreted in such a way as to discredit the book itself:

> Eastman's book widely quoted by bourgeois press. You are represented as the victim of intrigue. The idea is suggested that you are favourable to democracy and freedom of trade. Please send 200 word reply for SUNDAY WORKER — Jackson.[37]

Jackson must have known Trotsky's views (and indeed those of any other Communist) on these questions, and in fact it had been Trotsky himself who had led the struggle against the attempt of Stalin and the others to relax the state monopoly of foreign trade.[38] 'Of course,' Trotsky wrote back, 'I refute in advance and most categorically any commentaries directed against the Russian Communist Party. The assertions of the Press, which you cite, that I am favourably inclined towards bourgeois democracy and free trade, are crude inventions. I, at one with the whole Communist Party, consider that the Soviet system of the Dictatorship of the Proletariat and monopoly of foreign trade are inalienable conditions of our Soviet construction.'[39]

Eastman was quick to show that Trotsky's telegram was 'a refutation and repudiation of nothing whatsoever but the extraordinary statement in your telegram', which had been the very reverse of what was in the book, and asked Jackson 'why did you send a telegram to comrade Trotsky designed to make him believe that the main thesis of my book is exactly opposite to that which it is?'[40] Jackson replied that if Eastman had read the telegram and Trotsky's reply to it carefully enough he would have seen that 'It is not his book which is replied to but the reviews of that book with which the capitalist press was filled.'[41]

This was not going to be enough, for the bourgeois press, Labour circles in general and the left intelligentsia were buzzing with interest.[42] Eastman added that 'the statement in your telegram that my book represents Trotsky as the victim of intrigue is substantially true. And Trotsky in his reply does not deny that he was the victim of intrigue. His silence is eloquent.'[43] He was touching on a raw nerve here, for Jackson had already expressed the opinion that 'Trotsky would be — and when he sees it we are sure he will be — most furious at the use Max Eastman has made of his name and his alleged sufferings.'[44]

Now Albert Inkpin, Secretary of the British Party, wrote to Trotsky enclosing a copy of Eastman's book for his condemnation.

The Politbureau of the Soviet Communist Party dictated the terms of Trotsky's denial of Eastman's book, saying that it contained 'obviously fallacious and mendacious assertions'.[45] Another problem for Trotsky was that Eastman was not a member of any

Communist Party, and that could easily be used against both himself and Trotsky. Maurice Dobb described him as 'one of that small group of intellectuals' who 'joined their sympathies to the cause of the workers', but 'remained largely in a milieu of their own, preserving a distinctive psychology', a milieu further defined in the immediate sense as 'the remote quiet of a Mediterranean bay'.[46] Association with outsiders would not encourage workers within the Russian Communist Party or the Communist International to support the struggle of the Trotskyist Opposition, envisaged up to January 1933 as a purely internal affair.

What was more, Eastman was clearly personally attached to Trotsky as a man and a thinker rather than to the cause he served. This was picked up in left Labour circles. M. Phillips Price described him as 'a keen sympathiser with the lion', striking effective blows at those who are baiting him', making 'no pretence at giving the point of view of the baiters', and 'only concerned with saving the lion's skin'.[47] At the end of 1926 Eastman published his biography of Trotsky as a young man,[48] a preview copy of which Trotsky had himself described as 'making a strange, and to us, unfamiliar impression by its sentimental tone', 'quite unappetising, especially to us Russian Communists', and advising the Russian publisher not to issue it.[49] Apart from its close resemblance to the 'personality cults' of Lenin and Stalin, it could easily be misinterpreted by those who were so ready to talk of Trotsky's 'egoism' and 'Caesarist' and 'Napoleonic' tendencies. Nonetheless, it was due to Eastman, and him alone, that the British Labour movement now knew that:

> For three years an honest Marxian opposition to the bureaucratic course prevailing in the International — an opposition numbering hundreds of thousands and comprising some of the best scientific minds in the movement — had had no opportunity to express its view in *Pravda*, *Die Rote Fahne*, *L'Humanité*, *The Workers Weekly*, *The Daily Worker* or any other Communist Paper. All these papers have meanwhile denounced this opposition without restraint and without scruple or honesty.[50]

The publication of Eastman's book came at a time when the British Party was preparing to publish material of its own, for it had so often been reproached that not a word of Trotsky's had been reproduced on the conflict, whilst the official position was represented at length. The result was *The Errors of Trotskyism*, a book including Trotsky's 'The Lessons of October' and contributions levelled against him by the Central Committee of the C.P.S.U., Zinoviev, Stalin, Kamenev, Sokolnikov and Krupskaya, along with a preface by J.T. Murphy. Stalin, alone of all the contributors, was referred to as 'Comrade'.

The book had been promised as early as January, though it actually appeared late in May (just in time for the condemnations of Trotsky at the party's annual Congress). It turned out to be no more than excerpts translated from the official Russian book *Za Leninizm*, several of which had already appeared in English in the back numbers of *Inprecorr*.[51]

Murphy's introduction struck the lowest note of the whole collection. He explained the reputation of Trotsky in Britain by the low theoretical level of the members which had personalised the politics: 'we saw only leaders, Soviets and masses, and over all the great historical giants, Lenin and Trotsky'. So Trotsky's 'The Lessons of October' was false because it dealt with the revolution 'in a personal sense more than a party sense'. Whilst admitting on the one hand that the Soviet Party was bureaucratised, Murphy argued that the current leaders all agreed with Trotsky about this, and denied that they 'were and are opposed to Party democracy'. Yet factional organisation stood condemned as 'the forming of a party within the party', and 'action from below' was 'Menshevik phrasemongering'. He repeated the old canard that Trotsky had underestimated the importance of the peasantry, because he 'approached the problem from the doctrinaire intellectual angle, and not in relation to the actual social relations developed in the process of struggle'. He wrote:

> We cannot subscribe to Trotskyism on behalf of our party. We want not a 'subscribers' Party, but a 'working' Party. We want not a loose federation of conflicting factions, but a democratically centralised and united Party of the Proletariat. We want no policy of 'leading from below' which sets the rank and file against its leaders, but a living homogeneous party . . . [52]

Now that the Comintern had shown that any and all attacks on Trotsky were welcome, R. Palme Dutt joined in, describing Trotsky's followers as 'elements of the youth appealed to, elements of the Army staffs, elements of the intellectuals ranging themselves, elements of the N.E.P. bourgeoisie ranging themselves [sic!], and then outside Russia the imperialist bourgeoisie, the Mensheviks, the Right-wing Labour organs, the renegades from Communism — all openly staking their hopes on Trotsky.'[53] So far, he did not actually say that Trotsky invited their support, but the implication was clear that his criticism was backed by a broad anti-Soviet alliance, and was in itself a danger, whatever his own intentions.

The others got nowhere near a class analysis. J.R. Campbell implied that it was Trotsky's literary style that had carried him 'away, far, far from the facts', one of which was revealed as 'the long struggle of the Bolsheviks with Trotsky both before and after the Russian

Revolution', which 'will come as a surprise to many who think of Trotsky as being inseparable from Lenin'.[54] Gallacher stuck to Bukharin's personal tone, referring to Trotsky's 'old strain of egotism' through which, 'if he does not keep it in check, if he allows it to drive him against the Party, then he can quite easily undo all that he had done.'[55] Murphy tried the trick of saying that Trotsky's *Lenin* was so self-centred that it had been said that 'Myself and Lenin' would have been a better title — without stating that the person who made the remark in the first place was Maurice Dobb, his own party comrade![56] And they harped on and on that Trotsky was ill; whilst Tom Bell welcomed his 'recuperation' and 'return to activity' when he came back from Sukhum,[57] Ewer went further:

> He will be grateful to those who successfully restrained him. But his scorn for those who tried to exploit him while he was sick, who tried to use the splendour of his reputation as a weapon against the Russian Communist Party, will be devastating.[58]

The appearance of *The Errors of Trotskyism* was in the weekend before the Congress of the British Communist Party, and it was meant to influence the delegates when the condemnation of the Opposition came up. The Communist International was especially anxious to secure this, for it regarded the British Party as a model section, and the enlarged plenum of the E.C.C.I. in February had praised 'the absence of factional struggles in the British Party'. Tom Bell, who had represented the Party at the plenum, had the task of getting the condemnation accepted by the Congress. He described the state of affairs in the Russian Communist Party and the International as 'quite safe', the Left Opposition as 'liquidated' and Trotsky as 'back at work again', justifying the British Communist Party in 'minimising the crisis'. Trotsky's supporters were described as 'petty bourgeois' and 'elements of social-democracy', encouraged by the capitalist press from abroad. A.E. Reade's dismissal (he subsequently went off to Cyprus) was referred to and what little discussion there had been in Britain was summarised:

> As far as our own Party is concerned, we have not had any trouble regarding Trotskyism in our ranks. During the past four years we have been doing much to Bolshevise our Party. Only in one centre of the Party did we find any germs of Trotskyism, and that was in London. This element was merely a tiny fraction, and did not count for very much. Its members declared that they did not have all the facts before them on the question; they protested that they were not well informed. It is

> true that we had not published all the documents that we could have published had we had them at our disposal. Subsequent events showed, however, that this criticism was only a blind. Those who were taking up a pro-Trotsky attitude were really anti-Executive. The Political Bureau dealt with the matter very energetically, and removed from his post the particular comrade who was responsible for raising the matter. Outside of London, our Party has had no difficulty in dealing with this problem. The Political Bureau has thoroughly discussed the question, and adhered to the line of the C.P.G.B. and the Communist International.[59]

The resolution he proposed reaffirmed the resolution passed by the Party Council in November condemning Trotsky. 'Every deviation' from Lenin and the Party was 'a source of inspiration to all the anti-party, anti-Bolshevik and oppositional elements within the Soviet Union', so that 'Trotskyism, without intention, has been a means of strengthening the opposition of the imperialists'. Eastman and the Labour intellectuals who supported him were 'right wing and opportunist' and 'reformist and Menshevik'. The executive of the Comintern were praised for their anti-Trotskyism campaign, and the resolution declared its complete agreement with the Central Committee of the C.P.S.U. It went through unanimously, without any discussion on it at all.[60] That such a condemnation could get through with no opposition justified the faith of the Communist International in its British affiliate — effectively Stalinised long before any other — but it stopped short, as yet, of a description of Trotsky as a conscious agent of the forces he was held to represent. That was to be the next stage, and was only possible after the major defeat for both the working class and the Communist Party in the General Strike.

Murphy now replaced Bell as the main liaison with the Comintern, and in the middle of 1926 he was sent to Moscow to act as the British Section's representative on its Executive Committee. He arrived there whilst the argument was going on over the behaviour of the British Communists in the General Strike. Party patriotism combined with the rancour he had already shown against Trotsky made Murphy unlikely to send back balanced reports of the proceedings there, or to disagree with the official line of the Comintern Executive.

Trotsky's book *Where is Britain Going?* appeared three months before the General Strike. Trotsky had been working on it in the Caucasus through the winter and spring of 1925 and his letter to the *Sunday Worker* had referred to it as 'ready for the press' in May.[61] Although an American version came out before the end of the year, it was not until February 1926 that Allen and Unwin published it in Britain.

Trotsky intended the book as a warning of the dangers before the British Communist Party and the working class in the events leading up to the General Strike. But because it was couched in terms of future eventualities instead of past errors, the leading group in the Soviet Union could see no threat to their politics in it, and it went out to the national sections, in effect with the agreement of the Comintern. As Trotsky recalled,

> In part to avoid unnecessary complications, in part to check up on my opponents, I submitted the manuscript of the book to the Politbureau. Since it was a question of forecasts, rather than criticism after the fact, none of the members of the Politbureau ventured to express himself. The book passed safely by the censor, and was published exactly as it had been written.[62]

The result was a book of great value, extraordinarily prophetic of the conflict shortly to be joined between Labour and Capital. Anyone aware of the role of the General Council of the T.U.C. during the conflict — and of the so-called 'Left' trade union leaders on it — cannot fail to be amazed at statements like:

> The Communist Party can prepare for the rôle of leadership only by a relentless criticism of all the directing personnel of the British Labour movement, only by a day in and day out denunciation of its conservative, anti-proletarian, imperialistic, monarchistic, lackey-like rôle in all spheres of social life and of the class movement.
>
> The left wing of the Labour Party represents an attempt at the resurrection of centrism within the social-imperialist party of MacDonald. It thus reflects the agitation of a part of the labour bureaucracy for a connection with the leftward moving masses. It would be a monstrous illusion to think that these left elements are capable of heading the British proletariat and its struggle for power.[63]

As Trotsky explained later, the book was 'aimed essentially at the official conception of the Politbureau, with its hope of an evolution to the left by the British General Council, and of a gradual and painless penetration of communism into the ranks of the British Labour Party and trade unions.'[64] Something of this got over to the C.P., for their own edition omitted the whole of Trotsky's preface to the American edition, including the words 'the inference to which I am led by my study is that Britain is heading rapidly towards an era of great revolutionary upheavals'. Similarly, when printing the preface to the German edition of May 1926 they missed off the word 'revolutionary' from the phrase 'the revolutionary prediction for the immediate future of British Imperialism', along with an entire paragraph stating that 'the most important task for the truly revolutionary participants in the General Strike will be to fight relentlessly against any sign or act of treachery, and ruthlessly to expose reformist illusions.'[65] All these changes had the effect of blunting the book's message and destroying the urgency of its warnings.

But as far as the leaders of the British Communist Party were concerned, the book represented the views of the Comintern, and its appearance had the effect of polarising the political discussion on entirely different lines. Now the Labour press opposed Trotsky, the Labour intellectuals did the same or equivocated, and the Communist Party sprang to his support. The *Daily Herald* made much of the question of force alone. 'Religion is one of Trotsky's obsessions,' it said: 'Pacifism is another'. But the *Herald* was quick to say that 'in the long run force accomplishes nothing', and in any case Trotsky saw 'all things through Russian spectacles'.[66]

Lansbury's review in his *Labour Weekly* concentrated on the same. Violence was held to be 'the weapon used all through the ages, and we are as we were'; Trotsky's attack upon the church (Lansbury was a Christian pacifist) was put down to 'the fact that he knows only the old Greek Church of the Tzars, which was almost wholly an instrument of repression, and did force its devotees to be anti-Socialist'. The government of Ramsay MacDonald was even described as the working class 'learning the great art of administration', and materialism was condemned because it made Socialists forget their ideals and cross over to the other side.[67] The I.L.P. paper in Glasgow, edited by Tom Johnston, even came out in defence of the monarchy ('in happy China, France and America, they have abolished the monarchy, and a fat lot of good it has done them'), and Trotsky's book was described as 'ruthless, savage, Russian pamphleteering', 'gall and acid' directed to proving that everyone in the British Labour movement was 'either a rogue or a fool'.[68]

Bertrand Russell and Raymond Postgate had more to say, though they disagreed with the book as a whole. Russell supported the republican tone of the book, and considered that Trotsky's assessment of British Labour movement politics was both 'convincing' and 'remarkably well informed'. But Russell drew a false distinction between personal religion ('a private matter') and organised religion ('a reactionary force') and expressed his opinion that a Socialist Revolution in Britain would soon be reduced by economic blockade or the warships of foreign powers. He went so far as to suggest that Trotsky's motive for advocating one was his hatred of Britain, and he was 'not to be trusted when he gives advice'. Indeed, he was an 'enemy', 'a patriot when it comes to the pinch', who was arguing for the change because 'a Communist Revolution in England would be advantageous to Russia'.[69] On the other hand, Postgate, whilst also praising Trotsky's facility with the pen and 'powerful and clear Marxist mind', made the point that Trotsky's knowledge of Britain was not derived from life, but from his 'logical faculty' and the 'assiduous reading of British journals and books'. Although he took Trotsky up on several points of historical inaccuracy, he agreed that he was right in his main theme, but expressed a doubt that he would convince 'any worker whose mind was not already made up'.[70] Even Brailsford's preface to the Allen and Unwin version of the book defended 'the long tradition of open discussion' of the Churches in Britain, put down Trotsky's lack of understanding of the parliamentary tradition to the fact that he was a Russian, described the book as 'a slashing attack upon our whole movement', and deplored its 'ruthless Russian methods'.[71]

But with the British Communists Trotsky began to enjoy a spell of popularity. T.A. Jackson stepped forward to defend him against the attacks of Postgate on his history,[72] and of the *Herald* and *Forward* on his politics.[73] Even his mistake of describing the Labour leaders as a whole as 'Fabian' was defended, and he was billed as 'qualified to speak by years of study, and by an all-but-unique practical experience of economic and social crises'.[74] 'We, for our part,' affirmed Jackson, 'stand by Trotsky, not merely in his main line but in every essential detail.'[75]

R. Palme Dutt, who had continued to maintain a more open attitude to Trotsky and had reproduced his 'Towards Capitalism or Socialism' from *Pravda* in his *Labour Monthly*,[76] produced a particularly favourable review and challenged any of his critics 'to name a single book by a single English author which is as close to the essentials of the English situation as Trotsky's book', expressing the hope that 'he will not stay his hand at this short sketch, but will carry forward his work of interpretation, polemic and eludication, and elaborate his analysis further, which is so much needed in England.'[77] In fact, Dutt had an identical view of the danger represented for the Communist Party of relying on the 'Lefts' in the crisis approaching, and had issued similar warnings himself,[78] such as: 'The Left wing is not for us a goal in itself, but only a means. Our goal consists in revolutionising the working class.'[79] As the General Strike developed he continued to point to the relevance of Trotsky's prognoses. 'Only a couple of weeks before the strike,' he wrote, 'Brailsford in his answer to Trotsky was expressing polite incredulity at Trotsky's statement that the workers in Britain were already in practice far in advance of the I.L.P. leaders and holding it up as a glaring example of Russian "ignorance" of British conditions. After the General Strike the statement appears as the merest commonplace.'[80] Even as late as August 1926, when the British Communist Party had become incensed at Trotsky's criticisms of their mishandling of the affair, Dutt was repeating that 'in a recent article Trotsky has pointed out that the more revolutionary in principle a resolution was at Scarborough,[81] the more easily it was carried: but the closer it came to an even elementary task of action, the stronger was the opposition.'[82]

But in the end the General Strike was a watershed in the relations between Trotsky and the Communists here. Friendly relations had been developing for some time between the rulers of the Soviet Union and precisely those 'Left' trade union leaders who were to sell out the miners. A.A. Purcell had been the chairman of the official trade union delegation that had visited Russia in November and December of 1924, and had returned with a report of conditions so glowing that Friedrich Adler had denounced it for outright dishonesty.[83] It took little time for British bureaucrats to recognise the Russians as kindred spirits sharing (for the moment) identical aims, for not only did they come back with a favourable impression, but saw immediately what the conflict between Trotsky and Stalin was all about and chose their side accordingly. In fact, unlike the British Communist Party, which after all consisted of the finest rank and file workers, they showed no equivocation at all. Whole chunks of official propaganda were reproduced at length in their report:

> Trotsky, who only joined the Party just in time to take a prominent part in the October Revolution, represents liberal non-conformity as against die-hard Communism. He represents the point of view of the more intellectual and independent non-partisan elements and also of the younger and more progressive members of the party. So far the points on which he has come into collision with the conservatives are only significant to those well acquainted with Russian political conditions, and his position on such issues seems generally to have been unsound.[!][84]

As a piece of the official propaganda this report was quite up to date — with its implication that Trotsky only joined the Bolsheviks to get in on the revolution, that he represented non-party and liberal elements — and when it went on to deal with the Red Army there was a laudatory boost for Budyenny, whereas Trotsky was only mentioned in connection with the employment of Czarist officers. An ingenuous view was taken of the organs of propaganda levelled against Trotsky, to the effect that 'the whole Press is against this movement, there is no popular issue at present involved, and the appeal to maintain party unity will for some time be too strong to be resisted';[85] and that 'the authority of the existing government is in all cases strongly upheld. This is evident in the attitudes of the whole Russian press against Trotsky in his most recent criticisms, which latter amounted to an attack on certain phases of the present system of rule.'[86]

Of course, the Russian government's favourable view of the British 'Left' trade union leaders was not only the result of such support. Labour bureaucrats tend to prop each other up through the 'old pals act' as a matter of course. Tomsky had set up a joint trade union committee with the British unions which they hoped would promote unity between the trade unions controlled by the Communists (the Red International of Labour Unions) and those by the Amsterdam centre (the International of Free Trade Unions), and in turn serve as a bulwark of working-class internationalism to protect the Soviet Union from the threat of war from the imperialist powers. It reflected the Russians' desperate search for peace and stability, as well as their fear that the small British Communist Party might be unable to rise to such a task.

In the event the Trade Union 'Lefts' — in particular Purcell, Swales and Hicks — played a crucial role in the betrayal of the General Strike. The General Council of the T.U.C. refused money collected from all over the Soviet Union and offered in solidarity to the miners, Hicks in particular making remarks about 'damned Russian gold'. After the Anglo-Soviet Trade Union Council had served their interests by providing them with a 'left' cover, they pulled out of it some months later.

Trotsky, who had tried his best to warn the Communist Party about these 'Lefts', criticised the Russian leadership and the British Communists for not being able to take more advantage of the situation. He maintained that the position of the 'Lefts' in the Anglo-Russian Trade Union Committee had led to a blunting of the Communists' criticisms of them, leading in turn to a lack of clarity in the propaganda of the party and consequent disarray.[87] 'The thoroughly false policy,' he wrote, 'restricted to the extreme the sweep of the offensive and weakened its revolutionary consequences. With a correct policy the Communist Party could have garnered immeasurably more abundant revolutionary fruits.'[88]

The British Communist Party, whose members had behaved with utmost bravery throughout the strike, was stung to the quick by such criticisms. As early as the beginning of June they had complained of Trotsky's 'hostility' to the Political Bureau of the C.P.S.U.,[89] and the Executive Committee of the Communist International was obliged to record that 'by and large the C.P.G.B. passed the test of its political maturity. The attempt to present it as a "brake on the revolution" is beneath criticism. The E.C.C.I. was completely right when it unanimously approved the attitude of the C.P.G.B.'[90] However, any defeat of the working class on such a scale is bound to set off movements of demoralisation leading in a right wing direction, and this reflected itself in the leadership of the British Communist Party. Trotsky noted that a number of the members of the Central Committee of the British Party had judged the current Comintern theses on war as being too far to the 'Left',[91] and Pollitt and Murphy had both made equivocal statements. The Executive Committee of the Communist International agreed with J.T. Murphy and R. Page Arnot that the aftermath of the General Strike had caused 'vacillations to the right' among the leaders of the C.P.G.B., who had 'refused to criticise sharply the treacherous conduct of the General Council'. Such a position they concluded, 'shielding "generous" endeavours to preserve the Anglo-Russian Committee at any cost, objectively means aid to the opportunists.'[92] There was a certain amount of truth to these criticisms, though we should remember that they were meant to save the face of the Comintern which had given such endorsement to the Anglo-Russian Trade Union Committee in the first place. But it is important to understand that the British Communist Party's evolution towards a final anti-Trotskyist position occurred at this time, and not unnaturally coincided with vacillations towards the right in other areas of their work. Unsurprisingly, they also lost any reservations they may have had about joining the leaders of the Soviet Union in making a final settlement with the Left Opposition. Trotsky foresaw this when he remarked that 'of course these words will supply pathetic functionaries with the pretext to speak of our hostility towards the British Communist Party and so forth.'[93]

On its part, the British Section took violent exception to what they called 'the grotesque picture of an ignorant, non-revolutionary, helpless, British Party drawn by Comrade Trotsky', which they regarded as 'playing into the hands of those elements who stand for the liquidation of the British Party'. Its Political Bureau met on 9th August, 'condemning the suggestion of the Opposition that the Russian Trade Unions should withdraw from the Anglo-Russian Joint Advisory Council' as a course 'dictated either by despair or by an over-estimation of the degree of revolutionisation of the British Workers.' They believed that Trotsky's attitude was 'almost indistinguishable from that of the liquidation of the British Party', and asked the Comintern Executive to convene a meeting 'for the purpose of considering the position of Comrade Zinoviev as Chairman of the E.C.C.I.'[94] The Y.C.L. added its name to this appeal.[95] Already by October 1926 the British Communists were so incensed at Trotsky that they described his views that they had in effect remained passive and waited 'for a sell-out' as 'malignant misrepresentation'[96] and denied that they acted 'as a brake on the British working class'.[97]

There is no evidence of any dissent by the rank and file from this policy, caught up as they were with events at a local level,[98] though Trotsky's views on other topics continued to hold weight with them.[99]

The newly formed 'Joint Opposition' of the followers of Trotsky and of Zinoviev and Kamenev had, in fact, made the British crisis the occasion of their first important intervention against the policies of the Stalin/Bukharin Group on the international plane, and the mortification of the British Communists at their criticism coincided with a counter-attack from Stalin and his followers, whose immediate object was the removal of Zinoviev from his position as Chairman of the Comintern. The British Section, from now on firmly anti-Trotskyist, became a useful platform from which to launch attacks against the oppositionists, and its endorsement of Stalin's politics became automatic. Its enthusiastic approval extended to the wildest excesses of the Comintern, including even its grotesque zigzags over the Second Chinese Revolution of 1926–8. Murphy even ended one of his speeches with the words 'Long Live the Kuomintang!',[100] which was compared favourably with the British Labour Party, described as 'definitely Left Wing',[101] and even granted a fraternal delegate at the Party's annual conference at Battersea.[102] And though Stalin's speech to the 15th Party Congress of the C.P.S.U. was the first full exposition of the theory of 'Socialism in One Country' to appear in the Party's press,[103] it took only a month for the Central Committee of the British Party to declare 'the position of the Russian Party that "Socialism can be built in Russia" ' to be 'correct'.[104] Tom Bell even tried to prove that the Opposition wanted to liquidate the British Party and join the Labour Party instead:

> If it is impossible to build up Socialism in Great Britain then there is no need for a Communist Party in Great Britain, if it is impossible to build up Socialism in Great Britain, then all that we, i.e. those elements who are anxious to work for a transformation of society in Great Britain can do is to follow the *Labour Party*.[105]

From now on there was no doubt about which side the British Party favoured. A telegram was sent from the Party to 'congratulate the Communist Party of the U.S.S.R.' when the Joint Opposition broke up,[106] and Bell spoke in the name of the C.P.G.B. to condemn the dissenters, and to '*approve of the disciplinary measures that had been taken to suppress that Opposition*'.[107]

In fact, a crucial role in the strategy of expulsion now favoured in Moscow was to be played by the British Communist Party. It was J.T. Murphy, on behalf of the British Delegation, who moved the proposal to expel Souvarine from the Communist International.[108] It was Stalin's technique from now on to initiate such expulsions in the foreign parties, and the stage had already been set to move against Trotsky by a resolution from the British, French, Italian, German, Czechoslovak and American parties accepted by the 8th Plenum of the E.C.C.I. in May 1927, which gave the Executive of the Comintern authority to expel him if he persisted in his factional struggle.[109] Despite his disclaimers that he had 'not come prepared to do this', it was none other than Murphy himself who rose to propose the expulsion of Trotsky and Vuyovitch from the E.C.C.I. on 27th September 1927. Trotsky was 'particularly truculent' as Murphy recalls:

> Trotsky arrived about the same time as my secretary and I. We met in the corridor. It was 9 p.m. and the night was cold with thick snow on the ground outside. Everybody had their heavy overcoats and fur hats, and the hat and coat rack in the hall was full. Trotsky was looking around, when Kharhan (my secretary) asked: 'Can I help you, Comrade Trotsky?' Quick as thought he answered smartly: 'I'm afraid not. I'm looking for two things — a good Communist and somewhere to hang my coat. They are not to be found here'.[110]

The meeting was opened by Bukharin, and after Trotsky and Stalin had spoken, they were followed by other Comintern figures, and Murphy's time had come:

> . . . I went to the platform. I expressed the view that the time had come for decision, and that Trotsky himself had made it abundantly clear that the struggle had reached the stage when it was no longer an internal fight concerning differences of opinion among members of one organisation, but a fight against the Communist International itself and all its sections. We had no option but to accept that challenge, and I moved that he be no longer recognised as a member of the Communist International. It was carried with two dissentients. I did not dream when I moved that resolution that some few years later I myself would also be outside the Communist International.
>
> Trotsky marched out with head erect.[111]

Far from taken unawares by the turn of events, Murphy returned almost immediately to report on the expulsions to the Sheffield District Conference of the Communist Party (his own home base), which resolved unanimously to send a telegram to the E.C.C.I. approving of them and 'demanding that speedy organisational measures be taken against the Opposition',[112] which apparently evoked 'great interest' when it was received.[113]

Within a week Murphy was again reporting on the struggle to the 9th Annual Congress of the British Communist Party meeting in Salford. It is clear that he was carrying out a brief from the Comintern to secure the endorsement of their actions from the British Section, and he ranged over a number of wide accusations, such as that the Opposition had attempted to set up another political party inside Russia, and a rival leadership and organisation within the Comintern internationally. He described their support as 'a few university professors, shopkeepers, and middle class elements'. All the speakers from the floor supported him, and the only note of qualification came from Lucy of Exeter, who 'expressed his regret that such old comrades should have to be expelled from the executive'.[114] A stiff resolution was adopted, unanimously and with applause, charging the Left Opposition with playing 'straight into the hands of counter-revolution', adopting an 'anti-Leninist and objectively counter-revolutionary role', and 'acting as propaganda agents of Churchill and Baldwin 'in making irresponsible and slanderous accusations against the leadership of the C.P.S.U.' But this was merely incidental to the resolution, which was no different from those that had been coming out for some time; the nub of the question, buried deep in a snow-storm of Marxist swear-words, was the support offered for the idea that 'Socialism is being steadily built up in the Soviet Union', and 'complete and wholehearted support in every measure necessary to put an end to the disruptive work of the Opposition'.[115]

Among this 'disruptive work' was the last public expression of free opinion in the Soviet Union. On 7th November Trotsky and his followers appeared in the demonstration to commemorate the Tenth Anniversary of the October Revolution. They carried placards calling for an end to bureaucratism and the N.E.P., and for carrying out Lenin's 'Testament'. There they were very roughly handled by Stalin's Security men. Gallacher was a witness to the scene:

> He and his principal associates had to be protected from the angry workers. I was there in the Comintern Square and saw all that happened. He was picked up and sent out of Moscow with only a handful of non-party students protesting, but to the accompaniment of the laughter of the proletarian masses to whom he had made his 'call'.[116]

Again the British Communists in Moscow were the moving spirits in preparing the climate necessary for fresh organisational blows against the Opposition. On the night of 9th November they took the initiative in calling together a meeting of the Congress of 'Friends of the Soviet Union', and they moved a resolution against the Left, 'insisting that it be voted upon immediately as an expression of opinion of all the foreign communists'. Those assembled, some 947 of them including a British and Irish contingent 127 strong, gave their 'entire support' and 'entire' approval to the measures against the Opposition, accused of organising an 'anti-Communist International', and they insisted on 'the severest measures being taken against the enemies of the November Revolution'. One delegate alone — a Frenchman — managed to bring himself to abstain from voting for it.[117]

The vehemence of these denunciations testified eloquently to the crisis and the raising of tension inside the Soviet Union. The only solution that remained to the ruling group in the enormous political and economic upheaval that the Opposition had long foreseen was forced collectivisation in the countryside and a crash industrialisation programme in industry, both of which could only be enforced by the full weight of the repressive organs of state power. The economic policy that the Opposition had advocated gradually over a span of time could by now be carried out at bayonet point, and the Opposition were the first victims of the new methods. On 14th November 1927 the Central Committee and Central Control Commission expelled Trotsky from the Communist Party of the Soviet Union, and on 16th January 1928 he was deported to Alma Ata in Kazakhstan. The following Ninth Plenum of the Comintern in February 1928 signalised the swing towards the policy of the 'Third Period' that was to see the downfall of Bukharin and Stalin's final apotheosis as supreme dictator.

The British Communist Party was expected to promote this change, like all the rest of the Comintern, which of necessity meant identifying any form of dissent with treason. Inside the Comintern, Rust was able to give assurances that the Opposition had no supporters at all in the British Party, and to agree that 'the ideological struggle against Trotskyism must be carried on in a very strong manner and essentially internationally co-ordinated.'[118] Back in Britain it took the form of stepping up the propaganda barrage and calling area meetings to ratify the policies laid down. Trotsky lay accused of attempting 'through the medium of foreigners in Moscow' to send 'false information abroad calculated to endanger the Soviet state'.[119] T.A. Jackson attempted a rebuttal of the charges of the Opposition that the U.S.S.R. was in the grip of a 'Thermidorian Reaction',[120] but by this time the Platform of the Left Opposition had been published abroad in Eastman's *The Real Situation in Russia* and a more extended treatment was required. The British Party did not feel confident enough to attempt an analysis of their own, and issued instead an 114-page booklet made up of material that had already appeared in *Inprecorr*, compiled inside the Soviet Union. It consisted of short quotations from the Opposition statements, generally lifted out of context, was illustrated by cooked-up facts and tables, and spiced with long quotes from official resolutions and condemnations to the effect that the platform of the Left was 'the programme of a new party' of a 'petty-bourgeois Trotskyist character', with 'Menshevik ideology' oozing from 'every pore of the Opposition reasoning and Opposition tactics'.[121] Out of the round-up of local party groups required to condemn the Left, only 22 speakers expressed any criticism of the official line at all, and only 12 of them saw fit to back it with their votes, as against the 241 who spoke in favour and the 921 who voted for it.[122]

In such a way was the British Communist Party prepared for the Sixth Congress of the Communist International, which was to seal the downfall of Stalin's last opponent of stature, and the enthronement of Russian patriotism in place of Socialist Internationalism. It coincided with a lurch to the extreme left in politics and to a rigid authoritarianism in party structure that was to choke off for ever any healthy internal life in the British Section.

What went for Trotsky himself went also for his writings, and other expressions of Opposition opinion. In 1925 T.A. Jackson was describing Trotsky's *Lenin* as 'Bright, vivid, and readable',[123] Charles Ashleigh was praising the 'trenchant and illuminating Marxian viewpoint' and 'muscular but flexible style' of *Literature and Revolution*,[124] and Dobb was still able to refer to 'The Lessons of October' as a 'very brilliant preface' in 1926.[125] But by 1929 Murphy described Trotsky as 'a romantic anarchist who studied Marxism but has never known how to be a Marxist',[126] earning the retort that 'it is a great pity that Trotsky did not take the opportunity, during the visit of Comrade Murphy to Russia, of getting a few lessons in Marxism from him.'[127]

But it is not surprising that the British Communist Party took so long to evolve a coherent picture of what it believed 'Trotskyism' to be. The only attempts at a theoretical analysis were the two books, *The Errors of Trotskyism* and *Where is Trotsky Going?*, two articles by Jackson in *The Communist*, and two series of articles in the *Workers Weekly* during the autumn of 1926[128] and in the *Workers Life* a year later.[129] It cannot be said that any of these were on a remarkably high level. The *Workers Weekly* series tried to deduce from a quotation Zinoviev took from Lenin, about nationalised industry being 'not State Socialism but State Capitalism', an argument for 'the worker, and in particular, the C.P. organising against the state',[130] and then tried to prove from Lenin's formula of the proletarian-peasant alliance that Russia was 'a workers' and peasants' state' — i.e., a state whose rule was actually shared by two classes at the same time.[131] The *Workers Life* series sought to use Trotsky's analogy with the Thermidorian reaction against the French Revolution to prove that he believed the Bolsheviks had been 'carrying out a *purely* bourgeois-democratic revolution and, working all these years, not for their own class — the workers — but for someone else'.[132] Even if we do not accept this as deliberate misrepresentation — it is the very opposite of the theory of Permanent Revolution — it certainly comes from one who was grossly ignorant of the fact that Thermidor was a political shift from one section of the same (bourgeois) class to another, not a complete counter-revolution in property forms. Whatever the reason, it does not restore our confidence in an analysis that had already shown that it did not understand the ABC of the class theory of the state, and identified nationalised industry with Socialism into the bargain.[133] Jackson's articles revealed the same confusion.

Of course, a high level of debate and analysis can only come about through a real clash of opinion involving the free interchange of information. Neither of these happened in the British Communist Party at the time with which we are dealing. The last of Trotsky's major works of analysis to be published by the Party was *Towards Socialism or Capitalism?* which was printed in two parts by *Labour Monthly* at the end of 1925.[134] The other articles that were published were carefully selected from subjects of a literary, journalistic, or purely historical type, such as on Gorki,[135] on Lenin and H.G. Wells,[136] on Chinese anti-colonialism,[137] and on the work of Tolstoy,[138] but certainly not from articles with any bearing on the conflict inside the Soviet Union. But here (again) the censorship exercised over the views of the Opposition was both uneven and gradual. A pamphlet on the 9th Plenum of the Comintern, largely devoted to a denunciation of 'Trotskyism' and issued in June 1928, still bore on its back page an advertisement for *Where is Britain Going?*,[139] and the Tolstoy article appearing three months later was introduced as 'a long and brilliant analysis'.[140]

Nor were signs wanting that the British Communists were reluctant to carry on the campaigns of denunciation, at least to the extent required by the leaders of the Communist International. Time and time again they were pulled back to the question of 'Trotskyism' when they had hoped that it was long over and done with, and were anxious to get on with other things. Tom Bell noted at the time when the Party Council first denounced Trotsky that it was for reopening a controversy that they hoped had been closed;[141] and a series of articles attacking the Opposition that was declared to be closed in October 1926 had to be restarted in the very next issue of the paper.[142]

The fog of ignorance that surrounded the whole subject was no fault of the ordinary rank-and-file member, for he was systematically starved of information, caught off balance by new twists and turns, and fed the most misleading snippets of fact to prevent him from forming a coherent view of either the events of the conflict or the views of the Opposition. A few examples alone are sufficient to establish this. When Trotsky resigned from his office with the army to take up minor positions, it was described as a sort of promotion, 'the best answer to counter-revolutionary penny-a-line hack writers of the Eastman type, who write up pot-boilers about non-existent intrigues',[143] whereas the 'Leningrad Opposition' of Zinoviev and Kamenev at the 14th Congress of the C.P.S.U. in December 1925 was represented as having 'none of the bitterness and critical character of the Trotsky discussion. No one is very excited.'[144]

As far as ideas went, the Opposition was represented as dropping the unconditional defence of the Soviet Union:

> Obviously such a policy makes the Opposition 'conditional defenders' of the Soviet Union. They may pledge their unswerving loyalty in phrases; but their policy encourages the preparations and assists the propaganda of the Imperialists who are planning war.[145]

The suicide of Adolf Joffe was greeted with 'deep regrets'[146] until his support for the Opposition and his last letter were made known, when it had to be dismissed as the 'painful letter of a man half-crazed with suffering'.[147] As far as facts went, the Party press repeatedly assured its readers that there was no grain shortage,[148] then that it was the Opposition who had 'advocated forcible measures against the peasants' which would cause civil war in the countryside,[149] and finally that Trotsky was banished because he tried 'to take advantage of the exceptional economic difficulties caused by the relentless fight against the Kulaks he professed to have so much at heart, and fomented strikes in certain factories and discontent in the army.'[150] Some of the distortions were on such a scale as to be quite ludicrous, as when William Rust assured the readers of *Workers Weekly* that the 700,000 workers and peasants in the Soviet Y.C.L. had 'unanimously' condemned Trotsky's political line,[151] despite the absence in Russia of any building capable of containing such a number, let alone the contrary facts that the majority of the Central Committee of the Communist Youth had declared in Trotsky's favour, and that Zinoviev and Kamenev had violated the Party's statutes in order to disperse it.[152] A last touch by Rothstein to a thoroughly false picture was to deny 'the harrowing story of how "Trotsky and his friends have been arrested, violently dragged out of their houses, shipped into the desert under police guard", and so forth.'[153]

Uncertain of what was at stake, time and again the rank and file protested at the lack of information given them. When Murphy reported Trotsky's expulsion from the E.C.C.I. to the Sheffield District Conference in October 1927, there was 'general agreement when Comrade Hague emphasised the need for more international reports to the membership',[154] and the Stepney Delegation halted the 1928 Congress of the Young Communist League with a demand for a discussion about the reasons for the defeat of the Second Chinese Revolution. Yet, a year later, the London Aggregate was still objecting when it was called upon to approve the removal of Bukharin, on the grounds that 'it presupposes that the Party as a whole has a fair knowledge of the inner party situation of the section. This information the Party has not got and for the Party to understand this statement it must have in its possession more complete information.'[155]

Even if the necessary information were to hand, the chances for the members to be able to discuss and make sense of it were rather thin. The organisation of the local party structure into work groups in 1922 had effectively taken discussion out of the branch and vested it in the leadership of the party locally and nationally. Aggregate meetings and local district congresses were the only opportunity the ordinary rank-and-filer had to listen to and participate in wider-ranging discussions, and these were few and far between.[156]

Sympathy for the views of the Left Opposition grew more markedly among the rank and file of the I.L.P. and the Left intellectuals, grouped around the National Council of Labour Colleges and its magazine *Plebs*, than within the ranks of the Communist Party during this period. Raymond Postgate, an ex-member of the Party, had discussed the question with A.E. Reade as early as January 1925.[157] He reviewed Eastman's book and objected to the tone of the debate: 'There is a good deal to be said for leaving this sort of thing alone,' he went on, 'mere abuse, and dirty controversial methods, in a way answer themselves.'[158] His reply to Bell denied any connection between himself and Brailsford or Eastman, and affirmed his 'loyalty in the class war' despite his recent resignation from the Communist Party.[159] When Trotsky was exiled, he spoke up again for him in the pages of the *New Leader*. 'This is a horror,' he wrote, 'nothing can or should be said to diminish that. At the worst, it may be the beginning of the end.' He correctly identified the evil as bureaucratism, and described Trotsky's criticisms as 'so true that they were admitted by the Central Committee'.[160]

The standpoint of J.F. Horrabin was similar. He was not so much interested in the ideas and struggle of the Left Opposition as in the speed with which the Communist writers could make such a complete turn and write up material from a completely different point of view. Noting that Ewer's attack on Trotsky's *Lenin* appeared in the same magazine as the chapter taken from it on Lenin and H.G. Wells, he reminded those of shorter memories that it 'was before the party ukase against Trotsky had gone forth; so that, presumably, its poor quality was not apparent to faithful Communists at the time.' As for Ewer's parallel of Trotsky and Napoleon, it was brusquely dismissed. 'What comparison can be drawn,' he went on, 'by any fair-minded person, between the tried and proved revolutionist, with years of service to the workers as his record, who took over the army command in Russia and played a magnificent part in saving the Revolution; and the professional soldier who used the events of the French Revolution solely as a stepping-stone in his own personal career?'[161]

The influence of Postgate and Horrabin made it possible for both party members and outside readers to get a clearer view of the issues involved in *Plebs* than in any of the party's publications. Contributions appeared in it from all points of view, both those who attacked as well as those who supported the Left Opposition.[162] The most prominent defence of Trotsky came from M. Phillips Price, *Guardian* correspondent in Russia in 1917, author of well-known books on the Russian Revolution,[163] and afterwards a Labour M.P. for many years. He described Trotsky as 'the founder of the Red Army, a lion of the Russian Revolution, but a wounded one, fighting at bay with his back to the wall against his former comrades in arms', and showed how only garbled versions of the struggle had filtered out, for 'his enemies at home have seen to that, and the enemies of the Russian Revolution have seen to it outside Russia.' He gave in addition a coherent and refreshing analysis of the party bureaucracy and the growth of 'Marxist orthodoxy' as its ideological shield:

> The Bolshevik Old Guard, being merely human, is in this respect no exception to the rule. Stagnation in the body of a bureaucracy and the absence of fresh blood coming from below is, on the Marxian assumption, liable to create stagnation in ideas.

However, in an article otherwise full of insight into the real state of affairs, he ended on the strange note of suggesting that Stalin was not in agreement with the policy of the anti-Trotskyist heresy hunt.[164]

Plebs made up the sum of its contribution to understanding the issues by printing an extract from the American version of *Where is Britain Going?* before it was available here,[165] an article by the French anarcho-syndicalist Louzon on 'The Lessons of October',[166] several of Eastman's letters,[167] and an analysis of what the dictatorship of the proletariat had come to mean in Russia,[168] as well as making Trotsky's *Lenin* available on special offer.[169]

However, this sympathy for the Left Opposition (and Trotsky's own plight) from the left intellectuals brought with it its own problems, and in any case they were not so committed to Bolshevik views as to feel called upon to join a revolutionary organisation. A brief spell in the Communist Party had cured some of them of any further leanings in that direction. There was no real organisational link between them; Horrabin regarded Ewer's label of 'Trotskyist' placed upon him with some amusement.[170] The various views they held had no real cohesion; Phillips Price's background was as much radical as anything else, producing a vague sympathy with the Russian Revolution; whilst the others were Labour and I.L.P. intellectuals of markedly differing ideas and preoccupations. Any support they gave could easily be dismissed by supporters of the party line as being motivated by anti-Communism. Phillips Price was described as 'the central figure of an attempt which is being made at the present time, by a group of intellectuals, to set up the nucleus of an organised left-wing',[171] and Murphy described them as 'hacks of bourgeois politics'.[172] Bell pointed out that 'our differences with Trotsky are a strictly party affair', and he was quite within his rights to remind Postgate that 'unless individuals professing to wage the class war accept such party obligations, we repeat, there is no certainty as to where such individuals will stand in times of trial and struggle.'[173] In fact, their support was more of a hindrance than a help to Trotsky's supporters inside the Communist Party itself. As A.E. Reade was obliged to put it,

> . . . no Trotskyist Communists can regard a deserter's support as flattering: Postgate and his fellows are out to give a kick at the only fighting working-class party: Trotsky and his followers have been advocating a policy to strengthen it. Trotskyists scorn and repudiate the 'encouragement' of the Postgates who are, perhaps, the most treacherous of all the enemies of a Party founded by a Trotskyist greater than Trotsky himself, — Lenin.
>
> . . . however violent the results of discussions in the Communist International may appear to outsiders, and whatever 'splits' may be discovered by those whose wish is father to the thought, Trotskyists and anti-Trotskyists present one united front against the Baldwins, and Rothermeres, the MacDonalds and Postgates and all the traducers of the working class.[174]

But there was obviously no way that the sympathy of the Left Labour thinkers could be turned to the advantage of Trotskyism. Trotsky himself had killed off what potential there might have been by his repudiation of Eastman's book, which had helped to arouse their interest and focus it. He was no more sympathetic to the N.C.L.C. as a body; he refused his sponsorship to the exhibition they held in March 1933 to set forth Marx's ideas,[175] though Brailsford had written the preface to one of the editions of *Where is Britain Going?*, and Brailsford and Horrabin later signed the 'Letter of the Provisional Committee for the Defence of Leon Trotsky' at the time of the Moscow Trials. So whilst their intentions remained friendly, the concrete help they were able to afford was practically nil. Only towards the end of our period do many signs emerge of interest in the views of the Left Opposition among rank-and-file Communists and their sympathisers. By this time the impact of the 'Third Period' line in the isolation of the British Communist Party from the working class was making it obvious that something was drastically wrong with its policies. Whilst unemployment was rising, and the workers were rallying to the Labour Party in enough numbers to vote it into office for a second term, the Communists were making no gains at all.

Interest was aroused when the *Sunday Worker* published Trotsky's article on Tolstoy, the first that they had published by him for many a day. It was less easy to censor out dissenting views from that paper, as it was not technically a party journal at all, but the paper of 'The National Left Wing Movement'. M. Shooter wrote to thank the editor for including something from Trotsky, however old, and asked for something more up-to-date. A correspondent from Ashington took this up in the next issue,[176] and a party member from Lewisham even commented:

> The explanation of his expulsion from the Communist Party has been so one-sided that it would be a pleasure to hear something from Trotsky's side.
>
> We had to take everything for granted when Comrade Murphy reported on his action when he moved Trotsky's expulsion from the Comintern, without hearing a word from the other side.[177]

Of course, letters from those who supported the current line explained that 'all the facts and material have been laid before us', and that 'the whole question has been settled to the satisfaction of the overwhelming majority of C.P. Members in all countries'.[178] But when the comment was passed that 'the unfortunate thing about Trotsky is that he is damned and not dead',[179] an 'ardent admirer of both Lenin and Trotsky' wrote in to complain that 'had this appeared in the plutocratic press what an outcry there would have been!'[180]

Sometimes, it was the violence of the attacks that created the interest. One from Bert Williams[181] made readers complain that it was a 'tirade',[182] 'nothing but a glib and garbled repetition of the propaganda of Stalin and Co. against Trotsky and the Opposition, complete with the same old phrases and with the same lack of any reasoned answer to any of the serious charges made by Trotsky against the Stalin regime.'[183] Once more, an interview with J.T. Murphy, which was meant to stem the criticism,[184] unleashed it again. As a comrade from Birmingham put it, 'if, as the interview accorded to you by Comrade Murphy implies, he is in a position to give an accurate statement of the attitude now taken up by Trotsky, it is a pity he did not do so instead of confining himself to wild generalities.'[185] Another felt annoyed that 'it has become fashionable to denounce Trotsky, Trotskyism and Trotskyists at any and every possible moment.'[186]

Clearly, the attacks on the Left Opposition insisted on by the Comintern were having the opposite effect, and awakening curiosity in their views from party members and outsiders alike. A feeling of unease had arisen, fed by the party's repeated failure to grow and partake in the life of the class in any meaningful sense, as well as by the wild and meaningless zigzags imposed from Moscow. But a vague interest, and a sympathy for an old friend being kicked while he was down, could not be described as informed criticism, or generalised into a coherent political viewpoint on which to build an organisation. Every Communist knew by now that 'Trotskyism' meant expulsion — and workers do not lightly abandon those organisations that have awakened them to political activity. The intellectuals could put out their views freelance, and could always find a congenial home in the Labour Party or the I.L.P., but the only way for the working-class revolutionary was to stay inside and fight to reform the party in a very hostile atmosphere indeed — against friends, family and social milieu. For the Party still held the most courageous and combative sections of the working class, all the more inspired with party pride as their organisation evolved into a sect.

So the debate had a more visible effect upon the intelligentsia than it did upon the working-class rank and file, and a stable organisation was thus out of the question. A few examples will serve to explain why this was so.

Dr. Worrall was an Australian who had visited Russia as correspondent for the daily newspaper of the Australian Labour Party,[187] and was so impressed with what he saw[188] that after a brief spell in the I.L.P. he passed over into the Communist Party, where he became a branch secretary in Portsmouth. He represented his Local at the Tenth (Bermondsey) Congress of the British Communist Party, where he found that he had no principled differences with the new ultra-left Party policy. Along with everyone else he joined in the attack on the 'Old Guard', describing a speech of J.R. Campbell as 'like one made to the Salvation army'.[189] But by the spring of 1929 he had begun to develop differences with the official line. When J.T. Murphy turned down one of his articles on the situation in Germany he sent it to *Inprecorr*, where it was published on the assumption that it represented the viewpoint of the British Party.[190] It was, if anything, even more extreme than the official view, alleging that a revolutionary situation was fast approaching in Germany and calling for solidarity demonstrations from the British Communists. Fritz Heckert replied by pointing out that if this were the case, the German Communists should have been preparing for armed struggle, which was more than they were willing to allow for at the moment.[191] It was a classic case of someone taking the 'Third Period' line too seriously. Along with some over-enthusiastic enquiries about 'armed struggle' to J.R. Campbell, it convinced the British Party that he was either an unstable element or a police provocateur, and a letter was promptly sent out expelling him 'on grounds of political unreliability'.[192]

It was all the more ironic as Heckert was still reporting to the Comintern three months after Hitler had come to power that Germany faced the prospect of rising waves of struggle, and that revolutionary battles were in the offing!

Meanwhile, undeterred, Worrall had sent up a manuscript on 'American Imperialism', and had got into an argument with T.A. Jackson about the meaning of bourgeois and Soviet democracy.[193] Three appeals to the International Control Commission failed to raise an answer, so in October 1929 he sent round a letter on the authority of the Portsmouth Local, appealing to the other branches against his expulsion. It drew a reply from Harry Pollitt to the effect that he had prejudiced his appeal to the Appeals Commission at the next party congress,[194] which confirmed the expulsion by letter on 12th December 1929.[195] But by this time Worrall had discovered for himself just how far Germany was from a proletarian revolution by his attendance as a delegate to the second congress of Willi Muenzenberg's 'League Against Imperialism' at Frankfurt in July, where his observation of police behaviour on working-class demonstrations convinced him that something very different was in the air. He moved on to join the Marxian League then being organised by Frank Ridley, Aggarwalla and Hugo Dewar, came over to a Trotskyist position, and later joined the Communist League.

It was a good example of how the Party had created a Trotskyist by expelling an individual for other reasons, who was then obliged to examine the causes of his rather summary treatment. For all he had done was actually to take the 'Third Period' line seriously, and his only contact with specifically Trotskyist ideas was after he had found himself out on his ear. By that same token, he could play little part in the creation of a Trotskyist movement in this country. For talented as he was — and his many books[196] on dialectics and the philosophy of science drew commendations from Einstein[197] — his 'Trotskyism' was really only a phase in his progress out of active politics,[198] though he long maintained his interest,[199] being one of the pioneers in this country of the application of the theory of state capitalism to the Soviet Union.[200]

The case of M. Shooter of Helston was similar. He described himself as 'a bourgeois by origin'[201] who had studied all the available documents of the controversy in French and English, wrote in Trotsky's defence to the *Sunday Worker* in the autumn of 1928,[202] and a year later was selling the American *Militant* and defending the full position of the Left Opposition.[203] But by this time he had already resigned from the Communist Party because, as he said, 'I have no use for a party that keeps its best brains outside itself. I will never rejoin the C.P. while Trotsky and the other leading intellectuals are in exile.'[204] It had the effect of making his support for Trotskyism quite useless from the point of view of organising a group from among the workers loyal to the Communist Party in Great Britain. As one member put it, whilst agreeing wholeheartedly with his criticisms, 'I certainly do not agree with him in his attitude of remaining outside the C.P. on account of Trotsky & Co.'s exile. Comrade Shooter, your place is inside the C.P., you cannot vent your feelings to any effect outside. Always remember comrades, that the C.P. is not Stalinism, nor is it following Stalinism, but Leninism.'[205]

So the situation at the end of our period was that on the one side some support existed among non- or ex-party intellectuals for Trotsky's struggle, and on the other a trickle of workers were abandoning the Communist Party, but there was still no organisation of the Left Opposition in this country, around which they could form. An editorial in the *Sunday Worker* summarised the situation accurately enough when it carried on in a prophetic way:

> One thing is certain. The Trotskyist International is entirely divorced from the workers. It cannot make contact with them through the Communist Parties. It will do so, therefore, through the Social Democratic Parties, the bitter enemies of

> the revolutionary workers, the sworn foes of the Soviet Union, and the avowed allies of the capitalist 'rationalisers'.[206]

So whilst they could not form a movement, those grouped around *Plebs* magazine did help raise the theoretical questions. A beginning had been made in the analysis of the nature of the Soviet state. One 'Stepan Stepanovitch' described how:

> The 'dictatorship of the proletariat' had by 1921 come to mean not the 'democratic dictatorship of the workers and peasants', but rather that of a small, highly disciplined and centralised section of the workers. While this was the iron necessity of the time, it is not to be regarded as other than a deviation from the original significance of the phrase as either Lenin or Trotsky had defined it.[207]

The formulae here are neither very clear nor well worked out, but they laid the basis at least for understanding an entirely new and unforeseen phenomenon: the degenerated workers' state. This, the most distinctive contribution of Trotskyism to the body of Socialist thought, has practically become an axiom today.

Some insight had also been gained into the behaviour of these institutions on the world stage. M. Phillips Price drew attention to the fact that

> There can be little doubt . . . that many of the unfortunate false steps of the Communist International, which Western Socialists have had experience of in recent years in the realm of international politics, [are] in no small measure due to the crustification of a revolutionary caste in Moscow, which shows itself entirely out of touch not only with its own rank and file at home but with the peculiar problems of the class struggle in Western Europe and America.[208]

When we realise that books such as that of Fernando Claudin have only lately been written around that very theme,[209] it is surely worth the thought that these words were written over fifty years ago.

There was even some awareness that Soviet Marxism had become a religion and not a science. As Horrabin noted,

> If the body of Marxian teaching is not to be freely discussed, if we are to accept, just because it is Marxian, every page of Marx's writing as an unutterable and unquestionable 'Statement of First Principles'; then we had better get ready to accept as deserved our opponents' pet diatribes about 'dogmatic education' . . . if this in the opinion of an I.W.C.er constitutes an 'attack on Marxism', then I, for one, think it's high time we

> ceased calling ourselves an educational movement, and honestly described ourselves as a New Church.[210]

But the most remarkable examples of the ideological impact of Trotskyism on British Socialist ideas at the time came from the I.L.P., then in the process of moving to the left and its final break with the Labour Party. Thus Fenner Brockway, writing to refuse an invitation to attend the 10th Anniversary celebrations of the Russian Revolution put out by the Society for Cultural Relations in Moscow:

> . . . I cannot accept your hospitality. The reason is this: I know that amidst all this triumph, there are hundreds of Socialists lingering in your prisons, and exiled from civilisation, whose devotion to the working class, whose love of social justice and human freedom, has been proved by courage and sacrifice no less than yours.
>
> These men are no less my comrades than you are. Some of them were my heroes in the days before the Revolution, when they faced prison and exile under the Tsar for their Socialist faith. How can I be the guest of those who keep them in prison and exile now?
>
> . . . They are being persecuted, not because of their disloyalty to Socialism, but because of their opposition to dictatorship. *They are a Minority Movement*, and they are therefore suppressed. Their imprisonment is an extreme expression of that intolerance of opposition which is now seeking to silence Trotsky, Zinovieff, Kameneff, Rakovsky, Sosnovsky and Smirnoff.[211]

He followed these remarks with a long list of imprisoned oppositionists, and a fortnight later repeated his description of the Left Opposition as a 'Minority Movement' fighting against bureaucracy for working-class democracy, as its British equivalent was:

> According to the information to hand, Trotsky and Zinovieff are expelled because they have formed 'cells', held opposition meetings, denounced the present day leaders of Russia, etc. *They are in fact, the 'left wing' and 'minority movement' of Russia*. If our Communist friends in this country had any sense of humour they would appreciate that these expulsions are a gratuitous gift to 'the bureaucrats of Eccleston Square'.[212]

As the British Minority and National Left Wing Movements were at that time under attack from the Labour and Trades Union bureaucracies and were led by Communists, the Communist Party was stung to fury at this obvious comparison. 'It was only to be expected,' replied *Workers Life*, 'that the Right Wing and their lackeys in Great Britain would seek to distort this meaning of the expulsion of Trotsky and Zinoviev from the C.P.S.U. by pretending that they were merely pursuing the same tactics in the Russian Communist Party as the C.P. and M.M. in this country pursue in the Labour Movement here.'[213] But the more the Communist Party tried to escape the comparison, the more they helped to reinforce it. 'Are Trotsky and Zinoviev then, leading a kind of "Minority Movement" against a hidebound "Old Guard", and exactly as our own militants, getting expelled for their pains?' asked the *Sunday Worker* of its readers:

> The British Labour Party . . . is but a federation of various bodies, with a bureaucratic centre, but not a controlling body resting on the direct franchise of its members.
>
> The whole composition of the Labour Party, the method of election of its controlling bodies, the methods of representation and of voting at its conferences, places the power in the hands of bureaucrats and official cliques.
>
> *We are forced, therefore, in the British Labour Party, to work by means of 'Minority Movements', to organise opposition to the leaders who will not lead the fight against capitalism.*
>
> *In Russia . . . the workers . . . enjoy a freedom to criticise, and a power to change their leaders unheard of in Britain — or in any other country.*
>
> . . . a full, unrestricted discussion of Trotsky's views and differences [went on to 1925, and even after] there was no let or hindrance upon the discussion of Trotsky's views in the C.P. He might write as many articles and books as he liked, address as many comrades as wanted to listen to him.[214]

On 17th July 1928, the 6th Congress of the Comintern began. The British delegation in Moscow agreed with everything except the tasks of the revolution in India, where Arnot and Rothstein, and in particular Dutt, showed an understanding of the position there in advance of the Russians, and indeed of the Indian delegation.[215] On every other issue they were compliance itself. Murphy was the one who began the criticisms that were to lead to Bukharin's downfall.[216] Arnot defended Bukharin's new draft programme against 'Social Democrats' who described it as 'an instance of Russification' and 'too Russian'.[217] Bell described the 'Trotskyist allegation that the conditions of the working masses are going from bad to worse' as 'a base and lying slander', as well as alleging that the idea 'that Socialism is steadily being built up in the U.S.S.R.' was understood by 'all the class-conscious workers in all countries'.[218]

The Trotskyist Opposition received short shrift at the Congress and the British delegation did not protest. Trotsky's critique of Bukharin's draft was only circulated in part, in numbered copies to selected delegates who had to return them; to begin with, its existence was not even admitted in the British report, which limited itself to allusions to 'purely negative criticism' and 'no constructive policy'.[219] Only after it had been smuggled out of the country by Weston and Cannon[220] and published in the United States early the following year[221] did they feel constrained to mention it, and even then they dealt with none of the contents. Rothstein defended the suppression of the document on the grounds that it was 'a flagrant breach of the constitution of the C.P.S.U.',[222] and Williams complained about the 'illegal means in order to circulate this document, thereby endangering the proletarian dictatorship'.[223]

In spring 1929 Trotsky threatened to become an embarrassment to the British Communist Party in a physical sense. He had been deported from the Soviet Union and was living in exile on the Princes' Isles near Istanbul, where his health was deteriorating. He hoped to gain entry on grounds of political asylum into at least one of the Western European countries, both for medical treatment and to be nearer the European storm-centre of politics, to be able to influence, or at least observe, events more closely, as well as to organise his scattered following. Among the countries where feelers were put out was Britain. The question had already been raised in the House of Commons in February 1929, but a General Election was in the offing, and when the Conservatives were defeated on 30th May, a Labour Government was returned to power with the support of the Liberals. At the end of April 1929 Beatrice and Sidney Webb visited Trotsky, and expressed the opinion that his entry into the country would probably not be allowed, as the future government, being a minority dependent on Liberal Party support, would not be able to fly in the face of Liberal opposition to the request.[224]

This was a cynical evasion on the Webbs' part, as when Trotsky made his formal application early in June it was made plain that the Liberals were in favour of the traditional grant of political asylum, and it was the Labour Party leadership that was against it. The *Manchester Guardian* campaigned for it, and Lloyd George and Sir Herbert Samuel both intervened on Trotsky's behalf,[225] along with a string of other notabilities including H.G. Wells, George Bernard Shaw, J.M. Keynes, C.P. Scott, Harold Laski and Ellen Wilkinson. But Clynes, who was Home Secretary, circulated a memorandum to the cabinet expressing the opinion that 'the admission of Trotsky to this country might be regarded as an unfriendly act by the Soviet Government',[226] and rejected Trotsky's application in an official statement to the House of Commons on 11th July.

Trotsky's appeal raised a good deal of interest and comment at the time, which could hardly be avoided by the British Communist Party. *Punch* printed a cartoon making it all too clear that the Labour Government alone was responsible for keeping Trotsky out, the *Daily Express* printed interviews with him,[227] the *Daily Herald* one of his letters,[228] and a literary magazine even printed a review of one of Churchill's books from his pen.[229]

Of course, the Liberals were not alone in sympathy for Trotsky's predicament, and feeling within the Labour movement was by no means unanimously on the side of the government. The I.L.P. wrote asking him to come and address its Summer School,[230] Maxton did his best to persuade Clynes otherwise, and several I.L.P. branches wrote in support of him to the Home Secretary.[231]

The British Communist Party was out of sympathy with this, and certainly did not feel impelled to protest about the new British policy towards political exiles. When Trotsky had first been deported out of the U.S.S.R., the *Sunday Worker* told its readers that 'the workers of the Soviet Union are strong enough to do without the "great". With a contemptuous gesture they send them where they are appreciated — to capitalist Europe.'[232] Four months later, when the controversy over his entry into Britain had blown up, they expressed the opinion that 'the workers of the Soviet Union don't care tuppence where Trotsky goes so long as he stays away from the U.S.S.R. They are afraid neither of his pen nor his critiques. To suggest that the Soviet Government would have the slightest objection to his presence in London or any other capital is just the usual anti-Soviet lie.'[233]

Strangely, some vestigial feeling for Trotsky's predicament remained, even among the leaders of the British party. Ivor Montague, second cousin to Sir Herbert Samuel, was among those who maintained contact with Trotsky, and kept him informed of the progress of his negotiations with the government, though he appears to have kept a low profile on the affair within the party.[234] He appears to have rendered some concrete assistance, though at this distance in time (and in the face of his own denials) it is difficult to estimate what exactly it involved.[235]

The six short years of this survey cover a profound process of degeneration inside the Communist Parties of both Britain and the Soviet Union. Yet, drastic as it was, it was by no means automatic, being irregular in both course and tempo. It took place, after all, against the background of class struggle on a world scale, set in the context of a human endeavour to control society, and like that struggle itself was in no way preordained, or irreversible. Even within the British Communist Party the fortunes of Trotsky and the Opposition were affected by the ebb and flow of the class conflict, the rise in militancy and expectations, and the bitterness of dashed hopes. It was not surprising that after Trotsky's original condemnation in 1924–5 he should have again become popular among British Communists precisely at the period immediately before and during the General Strike; and it was the defeat of the upsurge, and Trotsky's analysis of the mistaken role of the C.P.G.B. in it, that turned them so bitterly against him. Thus the fortunes of the case put forward by the Left Opposition in this country exactly mirrored the rise in the combativity and self-confidence of the working class, just as their defeat sealed the triumph of the Stalin faction in both Britain and Russia. This link with the grip of Stalinism on the consciousness of the working class is clearly illustrated by remarks made more recently by Bob Edwards:

> Stalin was right about the need to build Socialism in one country. I had a row with Trotsky when he said that the defence of Russia lay in the imminent revolutions in Britain and Germany. I'd just come from the General Strike and I knew it wasn't on.[236]

A neater illustration of the Marxist theory on the relationship between ideas and material conditions could not be made.

For there were materialist reasons why the British Communist Party was so easily able to fit the role prepared for it by the Russian leaders — that of initiator of purges and expulsions in the Comintern. It was not a case of its leadership being 'inept and stupid',[237] but of the party itself being so small that it did not possess enough of a material basis to be able to take an independent line. Since the Second World War we have become accustomed to the fact that the smallest Communist Parties — such as that of the United States — or those existing illegally, or otherwise wholly dependent on Soviet aid — are the most fervent supporters of whatever happens to be the Russian line, whereas those with a mass basis in any country — or wielding state power that does not depend on Russian bayonets — find it easier to express an independent viewpoint. Similarly, British Party representatives in Moscow were always in a position to be able to say that they spoke with the unanimous voice of their comrades back home. The C.P.G.B. was so small, and its general political level was so low, that practically alone among the Communist Parties of the World (not excepting even that of the U.S.A.) there were no factions within it.[238] Parties with large dissident minorities, whether Left or Right, such as in Germany or France, were not in a position to lead the way against the Left in the Comintern, for voices would always be raised against from inside their own ranks.

By the end of this preparatory period we can say that all the ideas for a Marxist critique in Britain of the international policy of the

Communists were already present in some shape or other, however embryonic or vague. But where were the people and the organisation to weld them together and spread them?

Notes

1. 'The Discussions in the Russian Communist Party', in *Labour Monthly*, vol. vi, no. 2, February 1924, pp. 120-123; vol. vi, no. 3, March 1924, pp. 177-181.
2. Ibid. (March) p. 179.
3. Ibid. (February) p. 121.
4. Ibid. (February) p. 123.
5. Tom Bell, 'The Crisis in the Russian C.P.', in *The Communist Review*, February 1924. Many years later Gallacher revealed that in 1923 Zinoviev 'had many talks with me, and the other British comrades. He was most anxious to enlist us in the fight against Trotsky' — *Inprecorr*, vol. vii, no. 68, 1st December 1927, p. 1534. If so, they do not seem to have been unduly influenced by him.
6. Minute of 3rd March 1924, in the Minute Book of Dundee C.P., 11th February 1924 to 30th June 1925. They also heard a talk entitled 'Why Trotsky Was Right'. We would like to extend our thanks to Dr. Martin Durham for this reference, given to us in his letter of 29th October 1981, and in a statement to the Conference of the Group for the Study of Trotsky and the Revolutionary Movement, 10th October 1981.
7. L.J. MacFarlane, *The British Communist Party, Its Origins and Development until 1929*, London, 1966, p. 92.
8. e.g. his essay on Lenin and H.G. Wells in *Labour Monthly*, vol. vi, no. 7, July 1924, which was later included in his collection of essays on Lenin.
9. Harry Wicks, Interview with Al Richardson, 11th March & 1st April 1978.
10. 'Communist Party Council Meeting: The Tasks Before the Movement', in *Workers Weekly*, no. 96, 5th December 1924, p. 6.
11. C.M. Roebuck, 'Trotskyism — A Peril to the Party', in *Workers Weekly*, no. 103, 23rd January 1925, p. 5.
12. i.e. the Russian Communist Party.
13. i.e. the Communist International. Presumably they had in mind M. Phillips Price and Raymond Postgate and others becoming disillusioned with the Communist Party at the time.
14. 'A Splendid Rally of London Members: Keen Discussion on Trotsky', in *Workers Weekly*, no. 103, 23rd January 1925, p. 6. This is a reproduction of the resolution passed at the Party Council — cf. T. Bell, 'The Truth About Trotsky', in *Workers Weekly*, no. 95, 5th December 1924.
15. H. Wicks, 'British Trotskyism in the Thirties', in *International* (theoretical organ of the International Marxist Group), vol. i, no. 4, p. 27.
16. T. Bell, 'The Truth About Trotsky', in the *Workers Weekly*, no. 96, 5th December 1924.
17. 'The Arrest of Trotsky!' in the *Workers Weekly*, no. 101, 9th January 1925, p. 2.
18. Described as 'the simplest and best introduction to the subject' by G.A. Hutt in 'Leninism in Theory and Practice', *The Communist Review*, vol. v, no. 8, December 1924, p. 396.
19. i.e. the District Party Committee (in London).

20. 'Discussion on Trotsky: A Correction', in the *Workers Weekly*, no. 104, 30th January 1925 (the fuller and more correct version of the speech reported in the *Workers Weekly* on 23rd January, 'A Splendid Rally of London Members: Keen Discussion on Trotsky').

21. H. Wicks, Interview with Al Richardson, 11th March and 1st April 1978; *Workers Weekly*, no. 103, 23rd January 1925, p. 6; no. 104, 30th January (the correction).

22. C.M. Roebuck, 'Trotskyism: A Peril to the Party', *Workers Weekly*, 23rd January 1925 (his emphasis).

23. *Communist Papers* Cmd 2682 of 1926, Document 14, pp. 31-35, found at the King Street H.Q. and dated 24th February 1925. There was no secret about this at all, since it is evidently identical to that quoted in 'Our Publications: On the Periodical "The Communist Review" ', in *Inprecorr*, vol. v, no. 29, 9th April 1925, p. 386.

24. T. Bell, 'The "Crisis" in the Russian Communist Party', in *The Communist Review*, vol. iv, no. 10, February 1924, p. 433.

25. *Inprecorr*, vol. v, no. 35, 20th April 1925, p. 470.

26. 'Comrade Bell (Britain)', in *Inprecorr*, vol. v, no. 37, 23rd April 1925, pp. 485-6 (emphasis as in original).

27. W.N.E., 'The Twilight of Trotsky', in *Labour Monthly*, vol. vii, no. 4, April 1925, p. 250.

28. W.N.E., 'Trotsky on Lenin', in the *Daily Herald*, no. 2868 (new series no. 1875), 15th April 1925.

29. T.A. Jackson, 'Lenin the Leader', in the *Sunday Worker*, no. 4, 5th April 1975, p. 5.

30. A. MacManus, 'Trotsky on Lenin', in the *Workers Weekly*, no. 116, 24th April 1925, p. 4. Reprinted in *The Communist Review*, vol. vi, no. 1, May 1925, p. 47.

31. Ch. iii, 'The Testament of Lenin', pp. 28-31.

32. pp. 131-158.

33. pp. 26-7. Some had since been published in *Inprecorr* and *The Communist Review*.

34. 'Since Lenin Died', *Workers Weekly*, no. 117, 1st May 1925, p. 4.

35. A. MacManus, 'Since Lenin Died: Some Facts and Fiction', in the *Communist Review*, vol. vi, no. 1, May 1925, pp. 35-41 (his emphasis).

36. T.A. Jackson, 'Poor Trotsky', in the *Sunday Worker*, no. 9, 18th May 1925, p. 9.

37. Max Eastman, 'Trotsky's Telegram: An Open Letter to the Editor of the "Sunday Worker" ', in the *Sunday Worker*, no. 12, 31st May 1925, p. 8.

38. Cf. M. Lewin, *Lenin's Last Struggle*, London, 1969, pp. 37-40.

39. 'Trotsky's Message to the "Sunday Worker": Inventions Refuted: Trotsky not for Free Trade: At One with the Party', in the *Sunday Worker*, no. 9, 10th May 1925, p. 1.

40. Max Eastman, 'Trotsky's Telegram: An Open Letter to the Editor of the "Sunday Worker" ', in the *Sunday Worker*, no. 12, 31st May 1925, p. 8.

41. T.A. Jackson, *Sunday Worker*, no. 12, 31st May 1928, p. 8.

42. Below, pp. 27-9.

43. Max Eastman, 'Trotsky's Telegram', in the *Sunday Worker*, no. 12, 31st May 1925, p. 8.

44. T.A. Jackson, 'Poor Trotsky', in the *Sunday Worker*, no. 9, 10th May 1925, p. 9.

45. Cf. L. Trotsky, 'Trotsky Trounces Eastman: Lenin's "Will" a Myth. Eastman No Warrant for His Assertions (Special to the "Sunday Worker")' (sic!) in the *Sunday Worker*, no. 19, 19th July 1925, p. 2 (the date of writing was 1st July 1925). Another version, differing on several points from that above, is contained in Comrade Trotsky's Declaration with Regard to Eastman's book "Since Lenin Died" ' in *Inprecorr*, vol. v, no. 60, 30th July 1925, pp. 833-4. Yet another version appears in

Leon Trotsky, *The Challenge of the Left Opposition*, New York, 1975, pp. 310-315. Why the document should have been issued in such diverse forms is a complete mystery to us.

46. M. Dobb, 'Marxism: Mumbo-Jumbo or Science?', in *Plebs*, vol. xix, no. 3, March 1927, pp. 87-8. Cf. Trotsky, Testimony to the Dewey Commission: 'Eastman, I must say, is my friend, but he is not a member of our organisation, he is not a disciplined militant of the Party. He is more or less of a free lance.' — *The Case of Leon Trotsky*, New York, 1937, pp. 429-430.

47. M. Phillips Price, 'A Lion at Bay', in *Plebs*, vol. xvii, no. 6, June 1925, p. 237.

48. Max Eastman, *Leon Trotsky: Portrait of a Youth*, 1926; reprinted, London, 1980.

49. L.D. Trotsky, 'Trotsky Trounces Eastman: Lenin's Will a Myth. Eastman No Warrant for His Assertions', in the *Sunday Worker*, no. 19, 19th July 1925, p. 2.

50. Max Eastman, Letter of 16th November in *Plebs*, vol. xix, no. 1, January 1927, p. 34. The reference to the *Daily Worker* is, of course, to the American paper of that name, the British equivalent not appearing until 1930.

51. e.g. *Inprecorr*, vol. v, no. 8, 23rd January 1925, no. 10, 29th January 1925, and no. 16, 26th February 1925 (whole numbers). *The Errors of Trotskyism* appeared late in May according to an advertisement in the *Workers Weekly*, no. 20, 22nd May 1925, p. 2 ('ready this week-end').

52. J.T. Murphy, Preface to *The Errors of Trotskyism*, C.P.G.B., 1925.

53. R. Palme Dutt, review of Eastman's book in *Labour Monthly*, vol. vii, no. 6, June 1925, pp. 376-381.

54. J.R.C., 'Politics — Not Hero Worship', in the *Workers Weekly*, no. 121, 27th May 1925, p. 2.

55. W. Gallacher, 'How Not to Prepare for Revolution', in *Plebs*, vol. xvii, no. 8, August 1925, pp. 312-316.

56. Compare the preface to *The Errors of Trotskyism* with M. Dobb, 'Lenin and Trotsky', in *Plebs*, vol. xvii, no. 5, May 1925, p. 186.

57. T.B., 'Trotsky', in the *Workers Weekly*, no. 119, 15th May 1925, p. 4.

58. W.N.E., 'Trotsky and his "Friends" ', in the *Labour Monthly*, vol. vii, no. 6, June 1925, pp. 373-375.

59. *Report of the 7th National Congress of the C.P.G.B.*, St. Mungo Halls, Glasgow, 30th May, 1st June 1925, pp. 116-118. A.E. Reade, now expelled, dropped out of political life and went abroad. Later on, he was associated with the debâcle of Mosley's 'New Party'. Long after he had dropped out of active politics his admiration for Trotsky remained, and Wicks remembers calling upon him in his chambers in Lincoln's Inn Fields to enlist his support in the campaign against the Moscow Trials.

60. Cf. note 59 above.

61. 'Trotsky's Message to the "Sunday Worker": Inventions Refuted: Trotsky Not for Free Trade: At One With His Party', in the *Sunday Worker*, no. 9, 10th May 1925, p. 1.

62. L. Trotsky, *My Life*, New York, 1929; new edition, 1960, p. 527.

63. L. Trotsky, *Where is Britain Going?*, New Park edition, 1970, pp. 129-30.

64. Trotsky, *My Life*, p. 527.

65. We owe all these references and the analysis to Brian Pearce, 'The Early Years of the Communist Party of Great Britain', in Woodhouse and Pearce, *Communism in Britain*, London, 1975, pp. 176-7.

66. E.E.H., 'Where is Britain Going? Not Trotsky's Way: Some things the Famous Russian Has Yet to Learn about Us', in the *Daily Herald*, 10th February 1926, p. 9.

67. G. Lansbury, 'Books for the Workers: Trotsky', in *Lansbury's Labour Weekly*,

vol. ii, no. 53, 27th February 1926.

68. T. Johnstone, 'As Trotsky Sees Us: His First Plan — Abolish the Monarchy! Civil War — and Compensation', in *Forward*, vol. xx, no. 11, 13th February 1926, p. 9.

69. B. Russell, 'Trotsky on our Sins', in *The New Leader*, vol. xiii, no. 27, 26th February 1926, pp. 3-4.

70. R.W. Postgate. 'Trotsky's New Book', in *Plebs*, vol. xviii, no. 3, March 1926, pp. 109-11.

71. H.N. Brailsford, preface to *Where is Britain Going?*, George Allen and Unwin, February 1926; now more easily consulted in *Trotsky's Writings on Britain*, vol. II, New Park, 1974, appendix i, pp. 257-259.

72. T.A. Jackson, 'The American Civil War and British Labour', in *Plebs*, vol. xviii, no. 5, May 1926, pp. 171-177.

73. T.A. Jackson, 'The Retreat from Moscow', in *Workers Weekly*, no. 159, 19th February 1926, p. 2. Cf. no. 160, 26th February, and no. 161, 5th March (three-part series).

74. *Workers Weekly*, no. 161, 5th March 1926, p. 2.

75. *Workers Weekly*, no. 159, 19th February 1926, p. 2.

76. L. Trotsky, 'Towards Socialism or Towards Capitalism', in *Labour Monthly*, vol. vii, no. 11, November 1925, pp. 659-66, and vol. vii, no. 12, December 1925, pp. 736-748.

77. R. Palme Dutt, 'Trotsky and his English Critics', in *Labour Monthly*, vol. viii, no. 4, April 1926, pp. 223-4.

78. 'not for the first time', according to E.H. Carr, *Socialism in One Country*, p. 353.

79. *Kommunistcheski International*, vi (43), 1925, pp. 48-64.

80. *Labour Monthly*, vol. viii, no. 7, July 1926, p. 393.

81. i.e. the T.U.C. Conference of September 1925.

82. *Labour Monthly*, vol. viii, no. 8, August 1926, p. 518. Cf. R. Groves, *The Balham Group*, London, 1974, p. 14.

83. *Russia: The Official Report of the British Trades Union Delegation to Russia and Caucasia, November and December 1924*, London, 1925. Cf. *Communist International*, no. 1, 1925, p. 89 ('the first non-Communist Labour book which correctly describes what the delegates saw in Soviet Russia'). Trotsky later revealed that Russian bribery of British trade union leaders began at this time. Cf. L.D. Trotsky, 'Moscow–Amsterdam "Unity" ', 29th November 1937, in *Writings of Leon Trotsky, 1937–8*, New York, 1976, p. 75.

84. *Russia: The Official Report of the British Trades Union Delegation to Russia and Caucasia, November and December 1924*, p. 15.

85. Ibid., p. 16.

86. Ibid., p. 121.

87. Neither space, nor the scope of this work, enable us to investigate the accuracy of Trotsky's contentions. Those who are interested in finding out for themselves should compare Pearce and Woodhouse, *Communism in Britain* (favourable), J. Klugmann, *History of the Communist Party of Great Britain*, vol. ii, London, 1969 (against), or Hinton and Hyman, *Trade Unions and Revolutions*, London, 1975 (against).

88. L. Trotsky, 'What We Gave and What We Got', 23rd September 1927, in *General Strike 1926*, London, 1976, p. 31.

89. I. Deutscher, *The Prophet Unarmed*, London, 1970, p. 223.

90. 'Theses of the E.C.C.I, on the Lessons of the General Strike', 8th June 1926.

91. L. Trotsky, 'What We Gave and What We Got', 23rd September 1926, in *Trotsky's Writings on Britain*, vol. ii, p. 240.

92. J.T. Murphy and R.P. Arnot, 'The British Trades Union Congress at

Bournemouth', in *Communist International*, vol. iii, no. 1, 15th October 1926, p. 1, and opposite p. 10. Cf. the reply of the Executive of the C.P.G.B. in the following issue (vol. iii, no. 2, 30th October 1926, p. 12), and the remarks of Bukharin at the second session of the meeting of the enlarged E.C.C.I., *Inprecorr*, vol. vi, no. 85, 3rd December 1926, pp. 477-8 (speech delivered on 23rd October).

93. L. Trotsky, 'What We Gave and What We Got' (see note 88 above).

94. 'The Facts about Zinoviev: Removed for Breaking Communist Party Discipline: Attitude of British Party', in *Workers Weekly*, no. 182, 13th August 1926, p. 4.

95. 'Resolution of the Executive Committee of the Young Communist League of Great Britain', in *Inprecorr*, vol. vi, no. 65, 7th October 1926, p. 1117.

96. 'Editorial View: Towards a Mass Party', in *The Communist Review*, vol. vii, no. 6, October 1926.

97. 'Thesis on the General Strike' prepared for the 8th Annual Congress of the C.P.G.B., 16th and 17th October 1926.

98. Cf. Reg Groves, Jimmy Lane, Alf Laughton and Harry Wicks, *The General Strike in Battersea 1926*, Battersea Labour Party, 1926, and Harry Wicks, 'The General Strike', *Workers News*, 1926.

99. Among the authors' own treasures is a much-scored edition of Trotsky's *The Lessons of October*, bearing the superscription 'Stewart Purkis, from Reg Groves, first May, 1926'. They were both shortly to join the Communist Party.

100. *Inprecorr*, vol. vi, no. 18, 1st December 1926, p. 1433.

101. 'A Chinese Correspondent', 'What is the Kuo Min Tang? The Party of the Chinese People', in *Workers Weekly*, no. 186, 10th September 1926. Cf. the report of Bukharin's speech in the *Sunday Worker*, no. 128, 21st August 1927, p. 6.

102. *Workers Weekly*, no. 192, 22nd October 1926, p. 4.

103. 'Stalin on Russian Party: Opposition Broken — But May Try Again: No Coalition: Unequal Development of Imperialism' in *Workers Weekly*, no. 195, 12th November 1926, p. 3.

104. 'C.P. Central Committee: Heavy Agenda at Last Week's Meeting: Plenum Report: Future of Miners' Union', in *Workers Weekly*, no. 202, 31st December 1926, p. 1.

105. Meeting of the C.C.C.I. 18th Session, 8th December 1926, in *Inprecorr*, vol. vii, no. 2, 6th January 1927, pp. 16-17.

106. *Inprecorr*, vol. vi, no. 88, 20th December 1926, p. 1511.

107. Tom Bell, Speech to the 18th Session of the Enlarged E.C.C.I., in *Inprecorr*, vol. vii, no. 2, 6th January 1927, pp. 16-17.

108. *Inprecorr*, vol. vii, no. 9, 27th January 1927, p. 185.

109. *Inprecorr*, vol. vii, no. 35, 16th June 1927, pp. 735-6.

110. J.T. Murphy, *New Horizons*, London, 1941, pp. 274-5.

111. Ibid., p. 277. Cf. 'Trotsky's Lament to the Boss Class Press: Why He Was Exiled: Explained by Mover of his Expulsion: Opposed Lenin: Long History of Conflict with Russian Communist Party', in the *Sunday Worker*, no. 208, 3rd March 1929, p. 5.

112. 'The Sheffield District Conference of the C.P.G.B. for the Disciplinary Measures Against the Opposition Leaders', in *Inprecorr*, vol. vii, no. 57, 13th October 1927, p. 1272.

113. 'Executive Action Approved', in *Workers Life*, no. 37, 7th October 1927. Cf. *Party News*, p. 2.

114. 'The Opposition Condemned: Congress Unanimous in Support of the E.C.C.I.', in *Workers Life*, no. 38, 14th October 1927, p. 6.

115. 'The British Communist Party and the Russian Opposition', in *Workers Life*, no. 38, 14th October 1927. Cf. the parallel reproduction of the resolution in *Labour Monthly*.

116. W. Gallacher, *Pensioners of Capitalism: An Exposure of Trotsky and The Social*

Democrats, C.P.G.B. pamphlet, 1934, p. 25.

117. E. Burns, 'Congress of the Friends of the U.S.S.R.', in *The Communist*, vol. ii, no. 11, December 1927, p. 251; 'Foreign Communists Demand: British Resolution Against Opposition Adopted', in *Workers Life* no 43, 18th November 1927, p. 2; 'The Communist Members of the Foreign Delegations Demand Severest Measures Against The Opposition', in *Inprecorr*, vol. vii, no. 66, 24th November 1927, p. 1485 (reproduced from *Pravda*).

118. *Inprecorr*, vol. viii, no. 10, 25th February 1928, p. 222.

119. 'Trotsky & Co. Deported: Official: Illegal Activities After Expulsion from R.C.P.', in the *Sunday Worker*, no. 150, 22nd January 1929, p. 2.

120. *The Communist*, vol. ii, no. 10, November 1927, pp. 191-199, and vol. ii, no. 11, December 1927, pp. 262-269.

121. *Where is Trotsky Going?*, C.P.G.B., February 1928.

122. 'Russian Opposition Discussion: Analysis of Party Meetings in Great Britain', in *Workers Life*, no. 59, 9th March 1928, p. 4.

123. T.A. Jackson, 'Lenin the Leader', in the *Sunday Worker*, no. 4, 5th April 1925, p. 5.

124. C. Ashleigh, 'Pages for the Highbrow', in the *Sunday Worker*, no. 34, 1st November 1925, p. 8.

125. M. Dobb, 'Thoughts on May and October', in *Plebs*, vol. xviii, no. 5, May 1926, p. 166.

126. J.T. Murphy, 'Trotsky's Lament to the Boss Press', in the *Sunday Worker*, no. 208, 3rd March 1929, p. 5.

127. Joseph E. Roche, Letter to the *Sunday Worker*, no. 209, 10th March 1929 ('What Our Readers Think').

128. Russian Party Discussion (5 parts), in *Workers Weekly*, 3rd September–29th October 1926.

129. 'The Russian Opposition' (6 parts), in *Workers Life*, 21st October–23rd December 1927.

130. 'Russian Party Discussion ii — Is It a Socialist State?', in the *Workers Weekly*, no. 188, 24th September 1926, p. 2.

131. 'Russian Party Discussion iii — Is It a Socialist Government?', in *Workers Weekly*, no. 189, 1st October 1926, p. 2.

132. 'The Russian Opposition iv — Thermidor', in *Workers Life*, no. 48, 23rd December 1927, p. 2.

133. The class nature of the property owned by any state depends, of course, on the class character of the state itself — a proposition still not understood by the British Labour movement.

134. *Labour Monthly*, vol. vii, no. 1, November 1925, pp. 659-66 and no. 2, December 1925, pp. 736-748.

135. 'Trotsky on Gorki', in *The Communist Review*, vol. v, no. 8, December 1924.

136. *Labour Monthly*, vol. vi, no. 7, July 1924, pp. 411-420.

137. L. Trotsky, 'The Spirit of Moscow', in *Sunday Worker*, no. 15, 21st June 1925, p. 10 (from *Inprecorr*).

138. L. Trotsky, 'Tolstoy', in the *Sunday Worker*, no. 83, 9th September 1928, p. 6. This piece, already twenty years old by that time, was printed only in extracts, and was followed immediately by a spate of readers' letters demanding articles by Trotsky that were more up-to-date — *Sunday Worker*, 16th September, p. 6, and 23rd September, p. 6, etc. (cf. below).

139. A. Braun, *At the Parting of the Ways*, C.P.G.B., June 1928.

140. Op. cit., note 138 above.

141. T. Bell, 'The Truth About Trotsky', in *Workers Weekly*, 5th December 1924.

142. *Workers Weekly*, no. 192, 22nd October 1926, p. 5, 'the fourth and last article

on the Russian Party discussion appears below'. But cf. *Workers Weekly* no. 193, 29th October 1926, p. 2: 'The Russian Discussion V: The Question of Fractions' (and p. 1, 'Opposition Submits: But Errors Still Maintained').

143. 'Trotsky Falls — Into Three Jobs at Once', in *Sunday Worker*, no. 15, 21st June 1925, p. 5.

144. 'Live Politics in Russia: Big Discussion in the Communist Party', in the *Sunday Worker*, no. 42, 27th December 1925, p. 4. Cf. Deutscher, *The Prophet Unarmed*, p. 253: 'From first to last it was the scene of a political storm, the like of which the party had never witnessed in its long and stormy history.'

145. 'The Russian Opposition and the War Danger', in *Workers Life*, no. 37, 7th October 1927, p. 4.

146. 'Comrade Adolf Joffe: First Ambassador of the Soviet State: A Treaty Builder', in *Workers Life*, no. 44, 25th November 1927, p. 3.

147. A. Rothstein, 'The Real Situation in Russia', in *The Communist Review*, April 1929, p. 212.

148. 'Soviet Grain Outlook', in the *Sunday Worker*, no. 175, 15th July 1928, p. 7; 'No Grain Famine in U.S.S.R.', in the *Sunday Worker*, no. 186, 30th September 1928, p. 3.

149. C. Rappoport, 'Why the Opposition in Russia Was Defeated', in the *Sunday Worker*, no. 152, 5th February 1928, p. 4.

150. 'The Banishment of Trotsky: Declared an Enemy of the Proletarian State', in the *Sunday Worker*, no. 204, 3rd February 1929, p. 4.

151. W. Rust, 'The Truth About Trotsky', in *Workers Weekly*, no. 97, 12th December 1924, p. 6.

152. Deutscher, *The Prophet Unarmed*, pp. 117 & 254.

153. A. Rothstein, 'The Real Situation in Russia', in *The Communist Review*, April 1929, pp. 200-212.

154. 'Party News', in *Workers Life*, no. 37, 7th October 1927, p. 2.

155. *The Communist Review*, November 1929. Cf. H. Wicks, 'British Trotskyism in the Thirties', in *International*, vol. i, no. 4, p. 27. The information on the 1928 Y.C.L. Congress we owe to Dr Martin Durham — Statement to the Conference for the Study of Trotsky and the Revolutionary Movement, 10th October 1981.

156. H. Wicks, op. cit., note 155 above, p. 26. Cf. M. Ferguson, 'Our Inner Party Life', in *The Communist*, vol. iii, no. 1, December 1928, p. 657.

157. 'A.E.E.R.', Letter from Athens dated 8th July, in *Plebs*, vol. xvii, no. 8, August 1925, p. 323.

158. R.W. Postgate, 'Trotsky's Comrades', in *Plebs*, vol. xvii, no. 7, July 1927, p. 1286.

159. R.W. Postgate, Letter to *Workers Weekly*, no. 120, 22nd May 1925, p. 2.

160. R.W. Postgate, 'Trotsky in Exile', in *The New Leader*, vol. xv, new series, no. 66, 27th January 1928, p. 6.

161. J.F. Horrabin, 'The Plebs Bookshelf', in *Plebs*, vol. xvii, no. 5, May 1925, p. 214.

162. Cf. Maurice Dobb, 'Lenin and Trotsky', in *Plebs*, vol. xvii, no. 5, May 1925, pp. 184-191; 'Thoughts on May and October', vol. xviii, no. 5, May 1926, pp. 165-171; 'Whither Russia?', vol. xviii, no. 10, October 1926, pp. 349-356; 'Marxism, Mumbo-Jumbo or Science?', vol. xix, no. 3, March 1927, pp. 87-91; W. Gallacher, 'How Not to Prepare for Revolution', in *Plebs*, vol. xvii, no. 8, August 1925, pp. 312-316.

163. M. Phillips Price, *War and Revolution in Asiatic Russia*, Allen and Unwin, 1918; *My Three Revolutions*, London, 1929. He had probably learned some of the background to the struggle from his encounter with Radek in Berlin in 1922, though the latter's 'Schlageter speech' clearly disgusted him — *My Three Revolutions*, pp. 195-6 and 199.

164. M. Phillips Price, 'A Lion at Bay', in *Plebs*, vol. xvii, no. 6, June 1925,

pp. 236-241, His final remark possibly refers to Stalin's refusal to expel or arrest Trotsky as proposed by Zinoviev, or to the further refusal by Stalin to support Zinoviev and Kamenev in demanding Trotsky's removal from the Political Bureau and the Central Committee — cf. Deutscher, *The Prophet Unarmed*, pp. 138 and 163.

165. *Plebs*, vol. xvii, no. 10, October 1925.

166. R. Louzon, 'How Shall We Prepare for Revolution?' in *Plebs*, vol. xvii, no. 7, July 1925, pp. 269-272.

167. *Plebs*, vol. xix, no. 1, January 1927, p. 34, and no. 2, February 1927, p. 74.

168. 'Stepan Stepanovitch', 'Problems of Dictatorship', in *Plebs*, vol. xix, no. 1, January 1927, pp. 22-23.

169. 'Our New Offer', in *Plebs*, vol. xviii, no. 9, September 1926, p. 331.

170. J.F. Horrabin, 'Trotsky's "Comrades" ', in *Plebs*, vol. xvii, no. 7, July 1925, p. 287.

171. E. Charteris, 'Should the Communist Party be Liquidated? A Reply to M. Phillips Price', in *The Communist Review*, March 1927, pp. 263-279.

172. J.T. Murphy, Preface to *The Errors of Trotskyism*, p. 9.

173. 'T.B.', in *Workers Weekly*, no. 120, 22nd May 1925, p. 2.

174. A.E.E.R. Letter of 8th July in *Plebs*, vol. xvii, no. 8, August 1925, p. 323.

175. L. Trotsky, *The Early Years of the British Left Opposition*, London, 1979, pp. 4 and 7, n. 10.

176. Cf. pp. 24 and 25 above; also notes 138 and 201.

177. Letter to the *Sunday Worker*, no. 185, 23rd September 1928, p. 6. Her conclusion also was not wide off the mark: 'I feel that there is more to his expulsion than we know.'

178. H. Evans, Letter to *Sunday Worker*, no. 186, 30th September 1928, p. 6.

179. P. FitzPatrick, Letter to the *Sunday Worker*, no. 187, 7th October 1928, p. 6.

180. C. McLean, Letter to the *Sunday Worker*, no. 189, 21st October 1928, p. 6.

181. B. Williams, 'Instruments of the Old Order: Trotsky's Opposition and Its Real Significance', in the *Sunday Worker*, no. 203, 27th January 1929, p. 8.

182. F.J. Taylor, Letter to the *Sunday Worker*, no. 208, 3rd March 1929, p. 4.

183. G. Briggar, Letter to the *Sunday Worker*, no. 205, 10th February 1929, p. 4.

184. J.T. Murphy, 'Trotsky's Lament to the Boss Press: Why He was Exiled: Explained by Mover of His Expulsion: Opposed Lenin: Long History of Conflict with Russian Communist Party', in the *Sunday Worker*, no. 208, 3rd March 1929, p. 5.

185. J.E. Roche, Letter to the *Sunday Worker*, no. 209, 10th March 1929.

186. J. Wright, Letter to the *Sunday Worker*, no. 208, 3rd March 1929, p. 4.

187. Letter dated 17th February 1927.

188. R.L. Worrall, 'The Proletariat of Russia', in the *Labour Daily*, 19th January 1928, etc.

189. I.S.Z. London, 'British Communist Party's Tenth Congress', in *International Press Correspondence*, vol. ix, no. 3, 25th January 1929, p. 81.

190. R.L. Worrall, 'The Significance of the May Day Events', in *International Press Correspondence*, vol. ix, no. 26, 31st May 1929, pp. 559-60.

191. Fritz Heckert, 'What Next? May Day and Its Presumable Consequences', in *International Press Correspondence*, vol. ix, no. 27, 7th June 1928, pp. 580-4.

192. Central Organising Department, Letter to Dr. Worrall, 13th July 1929. Cf. 'R.L. Worrall', in *Workers Life*, no. 126, 21st June 1929, p. 4.

193. 'On Sham Democracy', in *Workers Life*, no. 125, 14th June 1929, p. 4.

194. Harry Pollitt, Letter to Dr. Worrall, 9th November 1929, in Dr. Worrall's papers.

195. Secretariat of the C.P.G.B., Letter to Dr. Worrall, 12th December 1929, in Dr. Worrall's papers. Cf. 'R.L. Worrall's papers', and 'R.L. Worrall', in *Workers Life*, no. 152, 20th December 1929, p. 2.

196. Cf. *The Outlook of Science*, 1933, *Footsteps of Warfare*, 1936; *Energy and Matter*, 1948, etc.

197. And, belatedly, from the Communists themselves; cf. A. Pooley, review of *The Outlook of Science*, in the *Daily Worker*, 14th June 1933: 'It is a book to be got into the public library. The writer has done his job in simple and workmanlike style.'

198. Dr. Worrall, Interview with Al Richardson, 26th September 1978.

199. R.L. Worrall, 'The Scientists and Socialism', in *Left*, no. 17, July 1945, pp. 164-5.

200. R.L. Worrall, 'The U.S.S.R.: Proletarian or Capitalist State', in *Left*, no. 9, December 1939, pp. 39-40; and no. 10, January 1940, p. 19; cf. following remarks by Henry Sara, 'Not State Capitalism', p. 20.

201. M. Shooter, Letter to the *Sunday Worker*, no. 184, 16th September 1928, p. 6.

202. M. Shooter, Letter to the *Sunday Worker*, no. 188, 14th October 1928, p. 6.

203. *Militant*, 1st October 1929 and 21st June 1930.

204. Op. cit., n. 202 above.

205. J. Wright, Letter to the *Sunday Worker*, no. 185, 23rd September 1928, p. 6.

206. 'The Banishment of Trotsky: Declared an Enemy of the Proletarian State', in the *Sunday Worker*, no. 204, 3rd February 1929, p. 4.

207. 'Stepan Stepanovitch', 'Problems of Dictatorship', in *Plebs*, vol. xix, no 1, January 1927, pp. 22-23.

208. M. Phillips Price, 'A Lion at Bay', in *Plebs*, vol. xvii, no. 6, June 1925, p. 239.

209. F. Claudin, *The Communist Movement: From Comintern to Cominform*, 1970 (English Edition, 1975).

210. J.F. Horrabin, 'The Plebs Bookshelf', in *Plebs*, vol. xix, no. 4, April 1927, p. 151.

211. Fenner Brockway, 'An Open Letter to Soviet Russia', in *The New Leader*, vol. xv, new series, no. 54, 4th November 1927, p. 4.

212. Editorial, 'What We Think', in *The New Leader*, vol. xv, new series, no. 56, 18th November 1927, p. 4.

213. 'A Democracy that Bureaucrats Dare not Practise', in *Workers Life*, no. 44, 25th November 1927, p. 2. Cf. no. 42, 11th November 1927, p. 3.

214. 'Why Trotsky was Expelled: Not for Leading a "Minority Movement" '. *Sunday Worker*, no. 14, 20th November 1927, p. 4.

215. Cf. *Inprecorr*, vol. viii, no. 72, 17th October 1928, pp. 1323-4 (Rothstein), no. 76, 30th October 1928, pp. 1420-5 (Arnot and Dutt), no. 78, 8th November 1928 (Rothstein) and no. 91, 27th December 1928, pp. 1743-4 (Declaration of the British Delegation).

216. *Inprecorr*, vol. viii, no. 44, 3rd August 1928, p. 777.

217. *Inprecorr*, vol. viii, no. 66, 25th September 1928, p. 1198.

218. *Inprecorr*, vol. viii, no. 63, 17th September 1928, p. 1139.

219. E. Verney, 'The Last Stand of Trotsky's Old Guard', in the *Sunday Worker*, no. 72, 24th June 1928, p. 8. Bukharin at least mentioned it: cf. *Inprecorr*, viii, 70, 9th October 1928, p. 1277.

220. Below, p. 64.

221. It was first serialised in the American *Militant* and then issued as a pamphlet.

222. A. Rothstein, 'The Real Situation in Russia', in the *Communist Review*, April 1929, p. 203.

223. B. Williams, 'Instruments of the Old Order: Trotsky's Opposition and its Real Significance', in the *Sunday Worker*, no. 203, 27th January 1929, p. 8.

224. I. Deutscher, *The Prophet Outcast*, London, 1963, p. 16; cf. Sidney Webb's letter to Clynes of 25th June 1929, quoted in C. Holmes, 'Trotsky and Britain: The Closed File', in *Bulletin of the Society for the Study of Labour History*, no. 39, Autumn 1979, p. 36.

225. Deutscher, *The Prophet Outcast*, p. 17.

226. R. Gott, 'How Trotsky was Kept Out of England', in *The Guardian*, 15th August 1970.

227. *Daily Express*, 18th March 1929, and 29th June 1929; cf. *Writings of Leon Trotsky 1929*, New York, 1975, pp. 65-66 , 151-154.

228. *Daily Herald*, July 22nd 1929; cf. *Writings of Leon Trotsky 1929*, p. 195.

229. *John O'London's Weekly*, 20th April 1929; cf. *Leon Trotsky On Literature and Art*, New York, 1970, pp. 167-173.

230. Trotsky, *My Life*, p. 574.

231. C. Holmes, op. cit., note 224 above, p. 33.

232. 'The Banishment of Trotsky', in the *Sunday Worker*, no. 204, 3rd February 1929, p. 4.

233. 'Spotlight', in the *Sunday Worker*, no. 225, 30th June 1929, p. 7.

234. C. Holmes, op. cit., note 224 above, pp. 36-7; cf. Deutscher, *The Prophet Outcast*, p. 17, n. 2.

235. C. Holmes, ibid. It is difficult to accept Montague's statement that his contact with Trotsky was of short duration. Trotsky was still describing him as a 'very good comrade' in November 1931 (L. Trotsky, 'To Help in Britain', 9th November, in *Writings of Leon Trotsky: Supplement 1929–1933*, New York, 1979, pp. 98-99); and Reg Groves pointed out in conversation with one of the authors that after the Balham Group had come under suspicion with the Party leaders he had received a breakfast invitation to meet Montague in one of the smarter eating spots of London a year later. It is thus not unlikely that he is the figure alluded to by Deutscher in *The Prophet Outcast*, p. 30.

236. Bob Edwards, 'George Orwell "Our Bloody Little Scribbler" ', in *The Guardian*, 12th February 1983.

237. H.M. Wicks, *Eclipse of October*, London, 1958, p. 135.

238. Ibid., pp. 127-8.

Chapter Two

Setting the Scene: The Marxian League, 1929–32

By the end of the twenties various individuals had moved into an oppositional point of view, loosely speaking, and were looking for an organisation and a policy to cater for their needs. Several of them were either members of or associated with the I.L.P., and most of those who had once been in the Communist Party had already left it. This was to place a unique stamp upon the future character of British Trotskyism, which did not appear here until the 'Third Period' sectarian policy of the Comintern had long been under way and did not emerge from the ranks of the Communist Party to begin with as Trotskyism had elsewhere in the world.

A.E. Reade, isolated for so long, had long faded from the scene, and George Weston (Morris) and Harry Wicks were still in Moscow. Those, like Len Potter, who supported Trotsky inside the British Party, did so on the basis of specific issues, such as the defeat of the Second Chinese Revolution of 1926, and not as part of an overall critique.[1] The picture contrasts most starkly with the origins of Trotskyism abroad, where it grew up naturally inside the Communist parties in discussions about the destiny of the Russian Revolution. The contrast with Britain is all the more marked because up to the accession to power of Hitler in January 1933 the International Left Opposition, however separately it may have been organised in practice, still regarded itself as a faction of the Communist International. Its policy was to carry out a struggle within the ranks of the Comintern to reform its suicidal orientation before it was too late. But in Britain Trotskyist ideas were, on the whole, far more developed outside the Communist Party than within it, chiefly among those who floated around the periphery of the I.L.P.

We use the term 'Trotskyist ideas' advisedly in this context instead of 'Trotskyism' as such. For though some of the people involved were properly to be called 'Trotskyists' (Hugo Dewar, Max Nicholls, W. Graham, Gerry Bradley for example), it would be incorrect to describe their organisation, the 'Marxian League', as Trotskyist in any meaningful sense of the word. The most prominent figures in it — Francis Ambrose Ridley[2] and Aggarwalla (more usually known by his pseudonym, 'Chandu Ram') — held views that were too individualistic to be termed Trotskyist, belonging in the category Trotsky would have described as 'ultra-left'.

The organisation was not a stable one, and was bound to disintegrate in the rapidly polarising conditions of 1929–32. Its methods, basically those of open-air agitation and the study circle, were inappropriate for the development of a serious revolutionary movement, and the class origin of its supporters was mainly petit-bourgeois.

Its loose operations on the fringe of the I.L.P. and among overseas student groups reflected the particular and peculiar conditions of the British Labour movement. It was at this very time that the I.L.P. moved towards the left, as the Labour Party, elected to office in 1929, showed itself completely incapable of dealing with the slump, and the numbers of the unemployed rose to nearly three million. Stirrings were already beginning inside the I.L.P. that were to lead to the final split with the Labour Party, in July 1932. The Party was more receptive to revolutionary ideas than ever before.

On the other hand, the Communist Party was in the throes of its vitriolic, acutely insensitive, left sectarian phase. Utterly isolated and down to a mere 2,555 members in November 1930, it treated the rest of the Labour movement with undisguised contempt and hostility, and the development of new ideas through a dialogue with anyone else was simply out of the question.

But this development (or rather gestation stage) of British Trotskyism by means of individuals, on a propagandist basis, could endure only for a while. Only when an authentic working-class opposition emerged inside the Communist Party would it be possible to talk of truly Troyskyist ideas, or the formation of an organisation to defend and propagate them.

In January 1929 Hugo Dewar[3] was taken along to the Lambeth Baths by his friend, Alwyn Wynne, to hear a meeting of the Cook-Maxton Campaign for Socialist Revival. As always, A.J. Cook[4] delivered a passionate speech in support of the miners, of their courage and their sufferings during and since the General Strike, and Maxton[5] denounced the government in a speech full of wit and invective. The hall was packed, enthusiasm ran high, and the audience stamped their feet with such appreciation that clouds of dust rose into the air. Communist hecklers, dotted here and there in the crowd, attempted to expose the 'pseudo-lefts', but with little success.

Shortly afterwards, Dewar joined the Clapham Branch of the I.L.P. In and around the William Morris Hall he met Jack Gribble, a skilled wood-worker whose experience stretched back to the Social Democratic Federation in Britain — the original Marxist group in these islands — and to the 'Wobblies' in America, where he had met Jack London. 'The workers are robbed at the point of production,' he used to say: 'Read Marx, read Jack London!' A spell of unemployment gave Dewar the opportunity to do just that, and later in 1929 he spent a month poring over *Capital* in the National Library at the British Museum.[6]

At Speakers' Corner in Hyde Park he first encountered the remarkable figure of Frank Ridley, then leading a precarious existence as an open-air speaker on British and international topics. Collections were not allowed to be taken in the park itself, so Ridley would accompany the audience to the gate, where they were able to show their appreciation. There Dewar got talking to him, and joined his group of supporters. Others, such as Dr. Worrall, Max Nicholls, W. Graham (Nardell), et al., were recruited to the group in the same way.

Dewar took on the task of acting as internal organiser of the grouping, which sold the American *Militant* and whatever pamphlets by Trotsky were available at the time. Much of the public activity was limited to Hyde Park, but meetings, lectures and social occasions were held in the basement of the Trade Union Club in Little Newport Street in Soho. Dewar kept up his membership of Clapham I.L.P., whilst Gerry and Lee Bradley and others were in the Communist Party, and loosely associated with it also was the group of overseas students.

At that time Ridley's main political collaborator was a law student, Aggarwalla, who was Secretary of the London Branch of the Indian National Congress. The members were basically Indian and Ceylonese students at the University of London or the London School of Economics, and the focal point of their activities was Swaraj House in Percy Street. Other supporters of this group in contact with the Communist Party were D.P.R. Gunawardena ('Phillip') and Colvin R. de Silva, later to become founders and leaders of the Lanka Sama Samaja Party, the mass Trotskyist Party of Ceylon.

Another small grouping had also formed about the same time around Dick Beech in the Communist Party. Along with Jack Tanner, they opposed the official party line and floated plans to print Trotsky's works in this country, though this project never came to anything.[7] Beech was later to become a full-timer for the Chemical Workers' Union, and Tanner, President of the A.E.U. After a further period of alliance with the Communists during the Second World War, involving scabbing and witch-hunts,[8] Tanner finally moved over to an extreme Cold War position.[9]

The Marxian League established contact with Pierre Naville at the Secretariat of the International Left Opposition in Paris, probably in the early summer of 1930.[10] It was imperative that a section be set up in this country, and on 5th September 1931, the Secretariat of the International Left Opposition wrote to their supporters here:

> To Comrade Beech and his friends of the C.P.G.B, Comrade Tanner, Comrade Aggarwalla for the Indian comrades, Comrades Ridley and Nicholls (Marxian League), Comrade Worrall. Copy to Comrade Trotsky.
>
> Dear Comrades
> . . . A meeting must be called of all those elements who are on the side of the Left Opposition, and whom we here address. This conference should immediately constitute itself a committee, which will represent officially the section of the Left Opposition in Britain . . . We propose that you should call this meeting with the least possible delay, say within fifteen days. Comrades Beech and Worrall, for example, could immediately get in touch with one another, and undertake to call together the other comrades, to meet a representative of the International Secretariat. They would be a provisional secretariat of the British Opposition until the suggested meeting . . .[11]

But by this time contact had been established with the Balham Group inside the British Communist Party, and it was quite plain that there were those over here who were much closer to the point of view of the International Left Opposition as well as better placed to carry on the sort of struggle that it envisaged. Though Naville,[12] Shachtman[13] and Cannon[14] all came over to discuss with Ridley and his group, differences between the Marxian League and the International Left Opposition widened rather than narrowed. In August 1931 Arne Swabeck had written a letter to Groves speaking of 'a recent proposal from the Marxian League in London, a group of comrades who are most, if not all, quite sympathetic to the Left Opposition';[15] but when Aggarwalla attended a meeting of the Secretariat in Paris in October, the grounds for agreement were considerably less. Glotzer wrote:

> Dear Comrade Groves,
> About a week and a half ago, while I was in Paris, a meeting of the International Secretariat was held with the presence of an English Comrade (Aggarwalla of the Marxian League) and where the question of the organisation of the Left Opposition in England was discussed . . .
>
> It was the unanimous decision of the International Secretariat, that at present there is not an organisation in England that

> represents the International Left Opposition nor the International Secretariat. The discussion with Aggarwalla disclosed that the Marxian League is still some distance from us, and on several fundamental questions are not in agreement with the views of the International Left, i.e. Trade Unions, the Party, etc. But even the other groups in England show similar tendencies of confusion, and lack of objective. It is our opinion that our task in England today, is the building of an organisation of the Left Opposition . . .[16]

Ridley's group went on to publish three or four issues of their duplicated magazine on current affairs, entitled *The New Man*, which showed even wider differences. By this time the two tendencies were regarding each other with some hostility. As Glotzer wrote to Groves,

> A thousand thanks for 'The New Man' (the title befits the editors). At least it confirms my opinions of this group entirely. I thought at first that perhaps I did misjudge them, but their leaflet, and now this stupid, to put it mildly, organ appears to reinforce my judgement that they are not only not Oppositionists, but far from being Communists.[17]

The discussions between the two organisations had shown deep disagreements on practically all the fundamental issues. As regards the current situation in Britain, the Marxian League was of the opinion that Fascism was on the order of the day:

> . . . while the British ruling class is now more than ever resorting to Fascist methods of rule, it requires time for the Conservative ruling class to make up its mind formally to discard these methods of Democracy with which it has achieved such immense triumphs, and by means of which it has gulled the working class with such triumphant success. The present regime in Britain is a transitional regime between Democracy and Fascism: *and it is the essence of a transitional regime that its acts are the acts of the future while its words are echoes of the past* (it is this phase that in the crucible of Stalinism becomes that monstrous miscarriage, 'Social Fascism').[18]

A further article even envisaged the coming of Fascism via the old Conservative Party rather than Mosley's 'New Party':

> Should this happen the British bourgeoisie may prefer to establish Fascism by means of its old and well-tried servant, the Tory Party, rather than by means of the new-fangled condotierre of the 'New' Party. In that case the Conservative Party would become Fascist in fact but probably not in name.[19]

Ridley's group also wanted to write off completely the need to work in the trade unions, as well as dismissing both the Communist International and its British Section, as being finished and not worth any of the attention being paid to them:

> My two major points were first of all, that by 1931 the Communist International was completely controlled by Stalin, and it was a waste of time trying to permeate it. Trotsky himself was forced to recognise this by the time he formed the Fourth International, but it was too late by then. Hitler had already destroyed the German working class movement.
>
> The second was about the trade union movement. Trades unionism is a necessary product of capitalism. It only flourishes when capitalism flourishes. At that time British capitalism, the city, finance capital and big business, was the senior partner, and now the T.U.C. is the senior partner and finance capital the junior one! Trotsky should have had the foresight to see this. Trotsky was still a Victorian, he took a Victorian analysis of the British Trade Union movement.[20]

Ridley also felt that the struggle against Stalinism should be basically conducted outside the Communist Party, and that all it lacked was a full-timer, to organise it:

> The revolt against the bureaucracy of inefficients which controls the C.P. in this country makes slow progress. The great difficulty with us, lacking a full-time organiser, is to make contacts and discuss the situation — with which thousands of good revolutionaries are disgusted — with Oppositionists in other parts of the country. Our greatest handicap is the lack of anything in the nature of your excellent paper.[21]

Apart from the protests of the other groups in Britain, Trotsky himself replied to Ridley. He wrote:

> Democracy and Fascism are here considered as two abstractions without any social determinants . . . the present government is not an 'antiparliamentary' government; on the contrary, it has received unprecedented parliamentary support from the 'Nation'. Only an upsurge of the revolutionary movement in England can force the government to tread the path of naked, ultra-parliamentary violence . . . Advancing the question of fascism to first place today, is not adequately motivated. Even from the standpoint of a distant perspective one can doubt in what measure it is correct to speak of 'fascism' for England. Marxists must, in our opinion, proceed from the

> idea that fascism represents a different and specific form of the dictatorship as such.[22]

The ideas about the trade unions were, according to Trotsky, 'directed against activity in the trade unions designed to win control of them, which for a Marxist and Bolshevik is obligatory'; and he asked: 'How can the radicalisation of the working class take place outside of the trade unions without reflecting itself inside the trade unions, without changing their character, without calling forth a selection of new leaders?' As for the Comintern, Trotsky asserted: 'the authors stand for the creation of a Fourth International, and, here too, manifest the fundamental quality of their thought: absolute metaphysics.' It was incorrect, he maintained, to write off the Comintern, which contained tens of thousands of revolutionary workers, and even the British Party, which had critical Communists in its ranks who had never been approached by Ridley and his comrades and would only be repelled by their attitude. 'It would be very sad,' he added, 'if the critical members of the official British Communist Party would imagine that the opinions of Ridley and Ram represent the opinions of the Left Opposition.'[23]

The same point was made more directly by 'David Davis' (Reg Groves?) writing in the pages of the American *Militant*:

> 'Spartacus' longs for a 'full-time organiser'. Of what? A new party? This must be made clear before great mistakes are made. *No one has yet been expelled from the C.P.G.B. for oppositional views.*
>
> There has been no fight against the Centrist leaders. Any opposition that has been made has never yet been openly expressed in the party as being based on the International Opposition's fundamental criticisms of the errors of the Comintern and C.P.S.U. leaders.
>
> Despite this, there exists an 'Opposition group' consisting in part of workers who have never been members of the C.P. or who have dropped out, 'fed up'.
>
> This group is, I believe, making contact with workers inside the C.P. — as a group. This work is not being done as normal party work, but as opposition group work, as though no party exists!
>
> This is completely wrong and dangerous. Comrades must realise that Oppositionists who make their opposition in the party and at the same time organise 'Opposition groups' which include non-party members are lacking in the elements of Bolshevism.

> The International Secretariat must at once check this, otherwise those party members who might be won for the fight against the party Centrists, will rightly distrust the Opposition and be thrown into the hands of Pollitt & Co.
>
> The Secretariat must lay down very definite instructions dealing with the following questions:
>
> 1. When may Opposition groups be organised?
> 2. Who may be members of such groups?
> 3. The organisational attitude of the Opposition group to non-C.P. members.
>
> The Secretariat must make absolutely clear that the task of the Opposition is *to organise the opposition to the Centrists within the Party*. Where the Opposition is 'legal' (in a party sense) its *only task* is this. That is, its other tasks are normal tasks of a party member.[24]

In view of the emergence of a real opposition within the Communist Party inside its Balham Group, it was all the more necessary that the position on these questions should be made clear. Arne Swabeck wrote to Groves to say that the Marxian League 'agree with our views without apparently fully understanding them', and 'seem to have an idea that the Left Opposition asks these comrades to split away from the Party'. He was scrupulous to assure Groves that 'the Left Opposition's views are not at all those of splitting the Communist Movement but of unifying it, naturally, expecting every Left Oppositionist to work within the party for our views, endeavouring as much as possible to remain a member of the party without sacrificing these views . . .'[25] A later letter asked Groves not to assume that because *The Militant* printed Ridley's contributions that meant that the Left Opposition took any responsibility for his views.[26]

A split was bound to take place now between those who supported Ridley and Aggarwalla and those who supported Trotsky. Glotzer[27] and Shachtman came over to Britain to assure both Groves and those who supported them in Ridley's group that they were really in favour of serious fractional work inside the Communist Party. In the event, Ridley's group more or less broke up. Max Nicholls, Dr. Worrall, W. Graham, Gerry and Lee Bradley and Hugo Dewar all left. Gerry and Lee Bradley remained in the Chelsea Group of the Communist Party, Graham joined the C.P. in Hackney, and the others simply joined the struggle of the Balham group.[28]

On 7th December 1931 a letter appeared in the *Daily Worker* signed by 'H.D.' (Hugo Dewar) to the effect that he was leaving the I.L.P. and applying to join the Communist Party,[29] whose Tooting

Local he joined shortly afterwards. The case of Dr. Worrall was, of course, considerably more difficult, and two years later he was still applying to join, without any hope of success.[30] Obviously they were all joining the Communist Party to assist the struggle of the Balham Group to form an authentic Left Opposition inside the party along the lines of the policy of the International Left Opposition.

On 19th December Max Shachtman attended a meeting in London at which they were all present, and formally set up a section of the Left Opposition in Britain. The official report written by him proclaimed:

> Every one of the comrades who came together to constitute the group — with perhaps one exception [Worrall?] — is a member of the Party and, without fearing the consequences which the Stalinists now impose upon the struggle for the ideas of Marx and Lenin, they are determined to carry on the fight within the party and, at all events, as a faction of the Communist Party. By this alone, the English Opposition describes a clear line of demarcation between itself and those dilettantes and children of fantasy who have, in England, sometimes taken the name of the Opposition, for a thousand and one reasons, but not for a single one which justified the assumption. On the fringes of the movement in England — as everywhere else — are a number of tiny little sects, stewing hopelessly and in quiet isolation in the stale juice of their own superiority; individuals and individualists; in short, opportunists, do-nothings, sectarians of all kinds have painted themselves up with the colours of the Opposition in the expectation that it would not only obligate them to nothing serious, but that it would relieve them of a slashing criticism and separation from the Left Opposition.[31]

When the *Morning Post* gave an exaggerated report of this assembly, claiming that the Communist Party had suffered a serious split, the *Daily Worker* confidently replied that 'there is no split, and the Trotskyists in this country are a contemptible handful.'[32]

The Indian and Ceylonese group also broke up. Already by the following year Colvin R. de Silva and Vernon Gunasekera had returned to Ceylon, and were beginning the struggle to found the Lanka Sama Samaja Party by leading the strike at the Welawatte Mills.[33] Aggarwalla returned to India, only to be killed some months afterwards in a car accident there.[34]

In that way the Ridley–Aggarwalla Group disintegrated under the harsh condemnation of the leadership of the International Left Opposition. But it had helped to float the idea of an Oppositional Grouping, on however mistaken a basis, had disseminated the ideas of Trotskyism in the pamphlets it sold, had grouped together a good percentage of those who were to lead the movement during the next decade, and had given them their basic training. In a way, the achievement of the Balham Group would have been impossible without their preparatory work.

Yet with the judgement of the international movement it is impossible to quarrel. Ridley's ideas were later set down in full in the book on which he had been working for much of that period, *At the Cross Roads of History*, finally published in 1935. They showed superficiality and an acute hostility towards Trotskyism, sharpened, no doubt, by the factional struggle that had taken place. As far as he was concerned, the theory of the degeneration of the Soviet Union was nonsense, for 'as Trotsky should know, the only alternative left is to turn the ruling party into a ruling bureaucracy which is, in effect, what has been done. Russia, therefore, enjoys today that society for which alone she is fitted.'[35] World Revolution, as such, was a 'Utopia', whose 'romantic protagonist' was Trotsky, 'the Red War-Lord', with a 'vision of the Red Army entering the European capitals with himself at the head', who had fortunately been restrained by the 'realists of the Kremlin' from throwing away 'the life-blood of Russia in a hopeless quest'. Sadly, and uncharacteristically, Ridley permitted polemic to overstep the line between argument and personal abuse:

> To Trotsky, silence is odious, by its very nature. He must have the centre of the stage, with the arc lights shining full upon him. The stage trappings must be set for him to hurl his verbal thunderbolts with the greatest possible effect. And so Trotsky's new movement is organised rigidly upon these lines. Everything centres around Trotsky. He, indeed, is the 'Left Opposition', and it is only tautology for the Trotskyist Press to talk about 'the ideas of Comrade Trotsky *and* the Left Opposition'. The Left Opposition has, in fact, no ideas apart from those of 'Comrade' Trotsky. It is merely an extension of Trotsky's expansive egotism. The ex-war-lord is at once prophet, priest and king: judge, accuser and executioner; and all to his perfect satisfaction. As was once alleged of a particularly eccentric Irish nationalist, Trotsky is 'a party of one', and in such a party there is no room for criticism. While Trotsky makes a special point of denouncing the 'epigones' — courtiers — of Stalin, yet the Trotskyist movement is nothing but a circle of adoring 'epigones'.[36]

Ridley continued on his career as a writer — of nearly thirty books and pamphlets[37] — and later joined the I.L.P., becoming Jimmie Maxton's right-hand man on its National Administrative Council, and for years its chief theorist. An international secularist propagandist in his own right, the last, in a way, in the line of Bradlaugh and McCabe, his path only incidentally crossed that of the Trotskyist movement. Yet, as the first actually to raise the question of the Fourth International, he deserves to be regarded in some way as a pioneer. And when Trotsky was murdered, Ridley knew how to put aside past differences and rise to the occasion:

> We consign such deeds and their apologists to the execration of humanity. For us, Leon Trotsky, far more truly than Abraham Lincoln, 'belongs to the Ages.'[38]

Notes

1. Steve Dowdall, Interview with Al Richardson, 1979.
2. F.A. Ridley (1887–), Secularist, freethinker, Marxist, historian.
3. Hugo Dewar (1908–1980), pioneer Trotskyist, poet, historian, agitator, educationist.
4. A.J. Cook (1883–1931), prominent miners' leader and left-winger.
5. J. Maxton (1885–1946), M.P. and I.L.P. Leader.
6. Hugo Dewar, Interview with Al Richardson, 7th April 1978.
7. L. Trotsky, *The Early Years of the British Left Opposition*, London, 1979, p. 2 and n. 4; *Writings of Leon Trotsky: Supplement, 1929–33*, p. 117 and n. 153, New York, 1979.
8. S. Bornstein and A. Richardson, *Two Steps Back*, London, 1982, pp. 104-5.
9. J. Tanner (1890–1965) was later a director of I.R.I.S. — cf. *The British Road to Stalinism*, London, 1958.
10. L. Trotsky, 'How the I.L.O. is Doing', in *Writings of Leon Trotsky, 1930*, New York, 1973, p. 304; L. Trotsky, 'Personal Sympathies and Political Responsibilities', in *Writings of Leon Trotsky, 1930–31*, New York, 1973, p. 376.
11. 'Willy' Letter of 5th September 1931, from Dr. Worrall's papers.
12. Pierre Naville (1904–), pioneer French Trotskyist, writer and political theorist.
13. Max Shachtman (1903–1972), American Trotskyist leader and later political theorist.
14. James P. Cannon (1890–1974), I.W.W. Organiser, and later Trotskyist leader.
15. Arne Swabeck (1890–) was a prominent American Trotskyist. He was expelled from the S.W.P. (U.S. Trotskyist Party) in 1967 for advocating support for Maoism.
16. Albert Glotzer, Letter to Reg Groves, 8th August 1931.
17. Albert Glotzer, Letter to Reg Groves, 18th February 1932.
18. 'Caius Gracchus' (Frank Ridley), 'England Goes to the Polls', in *The Militant*, vol. iv, no. 29, 31st October 1931.
19. 'Caius Gracchus', 'The Rise of Fascism in Britain', in *The Militant*, 21st November 1931.
20. F.A. Ridley, Interview with Al Richardson, 10th September 1977. Cf. F.A.

Ridley, 'An Old Campaigner Recalls', Interview with Ellis Hillman, in *Socialist Organiser*, no. 126, 7th April 1983.

21. Ridley's original theses could not be found when the editors were compiling *Writings of Leon Trotsky, 1930–31* (p. 426, n. 248), and Ridley's own papers perished in the blitz. His reminiscences have been checked against what Trotsky says about them and also with his own articles appearing in *The Militant*, vol. iv, no. 6, 1st April 1931.

22. L. Trotsky, 'Tasks of the Left Opposition in Britain and India', 7th November 1931, in *Writings of Leon Trotsky, 1930–31*, p. 337.

23. L. Trotsky, 'The Tasks of the Left Opposition in Britain and India', in *Writings of Leon Trotsky, 1930–31*, pp. 339-42.

24. 'David Davis', 'A Criticism of the English Opposition', in *The Militant*, vol. iv, no. 1, 1st June 1931.

25. Arne Swabeck, Letter to Reg Groves, 8th August 1931.

26. Arne Swabeck, Letter to Reg Groves, 6th November 1931.

27. Arne Swabeck, Letter to Reg Groves, 29th September 1931. A. Glotzer (1905–) was a prominent American Trotskyist. He sided with Shachtman in the 1940 split in the American S.W.P.

28. Arne Swabeck, Letter to Reg Groves, 26th October 1931.

29. 'H.D.' (S.W. London), Letter in the *Daily Worker*, 7th December 1931.

30. Reg Groves, Letter to Dr. Worrall, 9th June 1933; cf. Open Letter to the C.P.G.B. in *Red Flag*, August 1933, and W. Gallacher, *Pensioners of Capitalism*, C.P.G.B., 1934, pp. 23-4.

31. 'S' (Shachtman), 'Opposition in England: Party Members Form Nucleus to Fight for Leninism', in *The Militant*, vol. v, no. 2, 9th January 1932.

32. 'Workers Notebook', 'A Dead Party', in the *Daily Worker*, 22nd December 1931.

33. G.J. Lerski, *The Origins of Trotskyism in Ceylon*, Stanford, California, 1968, p. 15.

34. F.A. Ridley, Conversation with Al Richardson, 27th April 1978.

35. F.A. Ridley, *At the Cross Roads of History*, London, 1935, p. 191.

36. Ibid., pp. 210-11.

37. e.g., *Julian the Apostate* (1937), *Spartacus* (1961), *Pope John and the Cold War* (1961), *The Revolutionary Tradition in England: The Cato Street Conspiracy* (1977, with V.S. Anand), *The Jesuits — A Study in Counter-Revolution*, etc.

38. F.A. Ridley, 'Leon Trotsky (1879–1940): The Prophet of World Revolution', in *The New Leader*, 29th August 1940.

Chapter Three

First Steps: The Balham Group, 1930–32

The first British Trotskyist organisation correctly so-called did not originate with the left Labour intellectuals, the I.L.P. or Ridley's group, but inside the British Communist Party itself. Its late appearance, compared with that of the movement in other countries, was a testimony to the low level of political understanding that characterised the British Communist Party within the Communist International, and its emergence during the 'Third Period' of that organisation[1] has probably left its stamp on the British Trotskyists ever since. It came into being after Stalin had in effect achieved his final victory over all the Oppositional tendencies in the Soviet Union, and whilst he was finishing the process of extending his hold over the Communist International.

It was not until the emergence of the Balham Group within the Communist Party that real Trotskyism could organise and take a firm root inside the working-class movement, at least on a local level. It was one thing to hold this or that oppositional point of view, or even the whole Trotskyist programme, in the abstract; it was quite another to be organised and struggling to bring it into the life of the working class.

The British Section of the International Left Opposition owed its existence to two different, if not entirely separated, strands: those who had witnessed, at first hand or otherwise, the struggle of the Trotskyists inside the Russian Party; and those who were groping towards an authentic working-class policy amid the lunacies of the 'Third Period' line as it was being applied in Britain.

In Moscow, a founder member of the British Communist Party, an Irishman who worked under the name of 'George Weston', had become an early supporter of the struggle of the Trotskyists. He had lived there for some time along with his wife and family, and as he was connected with intelligence, he was attached to the staff of

International Red Aid, which often functioned as a cover for such operations during the early years of the Soviet State. In this capacity he appears to have contributed reports of defence work undertaken for prisoners of the class war to the international press.[2]

He was an outspoken man, quite without personal fear. At the height of the anti-Trotskyist hysteria he would pass out the leaflets of the Left Opposition in public and argue their case with groups of workers even inside Red Square.[3]

Also in Moscow at the time was Harry Wicks. As we have seen, he had been convinced of the truth of the Trotskyist case by A.E. Reade when he was still in the Y.C.L.[4] Wicks already had a long history inside the movement which belied his years. Coming from a traditional Labour movement family, he had been a member of the Battersea Herald League that had sent delegates to the founding Conference of the British Communist Party, and had edited a rank-and-file paper among the railwaymen at the time of the General Strike. As a leading light in the Young Communist League, he had been nominated by William Rust for a place at the Lenin School in Moscow.

On the face of it, this was a great honour for a young comrade, since selection was supposed to be rigorous, and only those who had 'done good service to the party — Party work and activity — and who have the character and qualities that would fit them to be real Bolshevik leaders, should be chosen.'[5] Only one place was set aside for the Y.C.L. But it was an open secret that those who went to the Lenin School were recommended by their local branch because they were critical, or in some way a nuisance, both as a way of getting them out of the way and of 'straightening them out'. In Wicks' case, his sympathy for A.E. Reade's views was more than a qualification. Harry Wicks arrived in Moscow in November 1927, a month or so before the 15th Party Congress of the C.P.S.U. voted for the final expulsion of the Left Opposition. Before the School actually began its session, students were subjected to a six-week induction course, conducted by Stewart Smith, a Canadian Communist, dedicated to *The Errors of Trotskyism*. When at the end of it Smith moved a resolution on behalf of the Nucleus Bureau characterising Trotsky and Trotskyism as 'counter revolutionary', Joseph Zack, one of the students, who was a supporter of William Z. Foster's faction in the American Communist Party, moved an amendment deleting the offending words, and Wicks alone supported him.

The course had been an education in more ways than one, for this was the first opportunity Harry had of studying the full documentation of the controversy issued in duplicated form, Trotsky's own articles as well as those levelled at him, some of which he brought back to Britain. A visit later in the course to the backward Soviet

Republic of Daghestan further convinced him of the folly of the theory of 'Socialism in One Country'.[6]

Part of Wicks' education had been to attend the Sixth World Congress of the Comintern, held in the summer of 1928, and Trotsky's critique of the Draft Programme written by Bukharin was circulated in numbered copies among the students, to ensure that they were handed back to the authorities. The same applied to the copy seen at the time by James P. Cannon and Maurice Spector, and in fact the one that was in the end smuggled out of the country to be published by the American Trotskyists was obtained and spirited out of the country by George Weston. He and his family were returning to Britain at the same time as Cannon and Spector were going back to America, and the epoch-making document was taken out of Russia concealed in a teddy bear belonging to Weston's son, and then handed on to Cannon before they parted in Berlin.[7]

Wicks' arrival in Moscow coincided with the final defeat of the Left Opposition, and the rest was more or less a foregone conclusion. He recalls how Yaroslavsky's wife, Kirsanova, who was director of the School, included in her daily reports the unwelcome news of the suicide of Adolf Joffe, and the demonstration at the station when Trotsky went to Alma Ata in exile. He remembers vividly the last public protest of the Trotskyists on May Day, 1929. All the students of the Lenin School had been allocated to different factory groups — in Wicks' case the Avropribor factory — for the ceremonial march past, and as his contingent drew level with where Stalin was receiving the salute from the Mausoleum of Lenin, they were bunched into a narrow group by the police. Suddenly a heap of leaflets were thrown into the air. It was the last defiant gesture of the Trotskyists to be witnessed in Moscow.[8] Later Wicks returned to Britain, and after a short spell in Glasgow was appointed London District Organiser of the Y.C.L., keeping his oppositional views strictly to himself. To begin with, he did not fully understand what lay behind the criticisms levelled by the Balham Group against the Communist Party leadership, and at one party meeting even spoke openly against them.

The suspicions that Wicks had seen confirmed in Moscow were shared back in Britain by another noted surveyor of the international scene, the veteran revolutionary Henry Sara.[9]

Sara was not himself a founder member of the British Communist Party, though his services to the movement stretched back long before it. He first became attracted to revolutionary syndicalism in 1908, when he began publishing a syndicalist magazine and pamphlets on industrial unionism and anti-militarism. He had carried on his anti-war agitation in North London during the First World War, until his arrest under the Conscription Act in 1916 for refusing to join the army. After a spell in the military prison in the Isle of Wight where, like so many other conscientious objectors, he had been very badly treated, he sat out the rest of the war in Canterbury Jail, and was released early in 1919. Immediately he was set at liberty he appeared speaking on platforms on behalf of the Herald Leagues and the Socialist Labour Party.[10]

By this time the attention of the whole revolutionary movement the world over was focused on the Soviet Union, and Sara decided to find out what it was all about at first hand. He smuggled himself on board a ship and travelled to Russia in 1921, journeying as far east as Turkestan, returning by land through a starving and miserable Germany. Back in Britain he joined the Communist Party in 1922 and was sent on a lecture tour of the U.S.A. and Canada, speaking on Bolshevism. In Britain again, he sat on the executive of Hornsey Labour Party from 1924 to 1926, and was expelled for his dual membership of the C.P.G.B. By February 1927 he was off again, this time to Canton as part of the British workers' delegation sent to China with Tom Mann. In the sixteen days they were able to spend there they addressed thirty public meetings, as well as attending the conferences of the Chinese Communist Party and its youth sections held at Hankow.

Again in North London, Sara was the Communist candidate for South Tottenham in the General Election that brought Labour into its second term in office in 1929, where he gained a mere 490 votes against the 14,423 cast for the successful Labour candidate.[11]

In August 1931 Sara was off again, this time to Vienna as a representative of the 'Friends of the Soviet Union'. By this time Austria was on the eve of the Dollfüss dictatorship, and the Government was preparing its weapons against the Austrian Social Democrats and the Schutzbund. Sara was picked up by the police for prohibited Communist activity and unceremoniously bundled out of the country.[12]

Although he was a frequent speaker on party platforms in Finsbury Park and around St. Pancras, Sara was an educator rather than an agitator. Among a bewildering variety of jobs in his youth he had once been a cinema projectionist, and he was quick to realise the propaganda potential of visual presentation. His lantern slide talks were in great demand at party functions, which he addressed on such subjects as conditions inside the Soviet Union,[13] and the life of Lenin.[14] On his return from China he had embarked on a lecture tour that took him to Lancashire, Tyneside and Scotland, on one occasion drawing an audience of 2,000.[15]

Because his own evolution had passed from Anarcho-Syndicalism to Marxism, Sara was wide and tolerant in his personal attitudes, and he had none of the zealot's meanness of spirit. Whilst opposing

Postgate after his exit from the Communist Party, he was not afraid to protest at the peevish tone of many of the official polemics against him,[16] and when the party was in full cry after Bukharin, he wrote in to complain at the misrepresentation of his ideas, some of which concerned those he held in common with Lenin.[17]

Sara had always avoided becoming too closely involved with the top leadership of the British Communist Party. He had not been impressed with the behaviour of some of them before and during the war, and his connections with Sylvia Pankhurst's organisation[18] and the suppression of the Kronstadt uprising[19] maintained his unease and prevented him from taking part in the foundation of the Communist Party. It was not until after his return from Russia that he actually took the step of joining, and almost immediately they had given him the unsavoury task of 'keeping an eye' upon his old friend, the Anarchist bookseller and publisher Charles Lahr, who had himself just resigned from the C.P.G.B.[20]

Never a mechanical follower of party orthodoxy — or indeed, of any other — Sara had already shown that he was well aware that much was wrong both in the Soviet Union and in the British Communist Party. On several occasions he had gone out of his way to refer to Trotsky,[21] and in a review of a collection of Kropotkin's writings he had selected for lengthy quotation a passage in which the great Anarchist had described how careerists and bureaucrats have always pushed aside those heroic spirits who have carried out revolutions[22] — an obvious pointer to the Stalin–Trotsky conflict, for those with eyes to see. However, until he made contact with Groves, Purkis and Williams in 1929, Sara remained quite isolated, and of course, continued to toe the party line in public. His election address of 30th May 1929 called upon voters not to be misled by the words 'Labour Party', explained solemnly that there was 'all the difference in the world' between it and a working-class party, and continued much of the general thrust of Communist propaganda carried on around that election in the rest of the country.[23] He had absorbed some of the atmosphere of the 'Third Period', at least to begin with, and added his own contribution to the ritual denunciations of the time.[24]

Sara was something of a bridge between those who were aware of the direction of the conflict between Stalin and Trotsky — such as Wicks and Weston — and a small group of union militants who had come freshly to the Communist Party and were seeking to transform it into a real instrument of class struggle — Stewart Purkis,[25] E.S. ('Billy') Williams[26] and Reg Groves.[27]

Their route into the Communist Party had been an unusual one, though by no means out of character with the traditions of the British Labour movement. They had been supporters of the

'Catholic Crusade' of Conrad Noel,[28] and had left when the red flag had been hauled down from Thaxted Church when it had been threatened by the church courts.[29] Purkis and Williams were members of the St. Pancras group of the Communist Party, and were active in the Clearing House no. 1 branch of the Railway Clerks' Association. In April 1929 the right-wing leadership of that union expelled Purkis, allegedly for editing a Communist rank-and-file paper, *The Jogger*, but in reality for a record of militancy that went back to the General Strike, when along with Williams and Bert Field he had been instrumental in getting the largest and supposedly most 'reactionary' branch of that union out on strike.[30] But the branch voted to reject Purkis' dismissal by 92 votes to 78,[31] and other branches invited him to address them in deliberate defiance of the executive.[32] It was typical of him that when he got back his contributions to the union's pension scheme, he devoted the entire sum to the needs of the movement.

Purkis was on the London District Committee of the Communist Party and appears to have been the Party's main reporter on railway affairs[33] and the main originator of the strategy by which they intervened inside the railway unions.[34]

Finally, there was Reg Groves, who had been in the Westminster branch of the I.L.P. before coming over to the Lambeth branch of the Communist Party, and then to the Battersea branch, where he met his future wife, Daisy. Daisy was a determined and capable militant already active in the Tailors' and Garment Workers' Union along with her sister, Nell, who was married to Steve Dowdall, a long-serving member of the A.U.B.T.W. and a founder member of the Communist Party.[35] All four of them became attached to a group selling the rank-and-file paper *The Nine Elms Signal* at the railway depot there,[36] which was part of the South-West London area group of the C.P.

Groves' obvious abilities marked him out for a rapid rise in the councils of the Communist Party. Although he refused to go for training in the Lenin School in Moscow,[37] he was already figuring as a star speaker on May Day platforms only a year after his entry into the party, alongside such veteran Communist militants as Ben Elsbury, who was also later to become a Trotskyist.[38] By 1929 Groves was on the London District Committee of the Party, and for a time served as its assistant organiser.[39]

By this time the British Communists were beginning to follow the new 'class against class' line of the Comintern, and this translated itself in British terms into an all-out assault upon the Labour Party. Groves was the writer of the party's main pamphlet for the purpose of the 1929 General Election, a record of the speeches made in parliament by the Labour Opposition on various key issues from

1925 to 1929, to illustrate how far they had fallen from socialism, and indeed, from ordinary working-class attitudes.[40] In March 1930 he had been selected as the party's main speaker for a debate with the Chairman of the Labour League of Youth,[41] and was the first columnist to write for the 'Workers Notebook' in the newly-founded *Daily Worker*.[42] Later in the year he found himself on special assignment in the West Riding, where he spent a week addressing outdoor meetings in a vain attempt to whip up support for the party during the Woollen Dispute.[43]

Public speaking and general agitation formed only a part of Groves' activities. He was a gifted and original historian of the Labour movement, and the Communist theoretical press was filled with his reviews and articles. He soon came to the attention of Riazonov, who wrote from the Marx-Engels Institute in Moscow to ask him to go there to work on the English edition of the Marx/Engels *Collected Works*,[44] though the British party directed him to refuse.

Groves, Purkis and Williams had become established in the Communist Party just before it was due for a shake-up. The Party's numbers had been at a rapid rate of decline since 1926, and the whole of the Communist International was in the middle of a campaign against 'the Right deviation' that was part of Stalin's final break with Bukharin.[45] Scape-goats had to be found among the party's old leadership, and because the British Communist Party was too small to make a habit of the expulsions and witch-hunts that were the norm in others, what resulted was a reshuffle of the old guard — the disappearance of some well-established figures (if only for a while) and the promotion of some up-and-coming ones. The whole process had to be undertaken under the guise of a 'political struggle' against a failed and discredited leadership — with the supposedly guilty scrambling over each other to denounce themselves before anyone else did. Meanwhile, waiting in the wings — or rather, enthusiastically 'leading the struggle' — were the next layer of would-be bureaucrats, figures like William Rust, who, unlike the old leaders (who had actually stood for something in their day), depended merely on a nod from the Kremlin.

The three future Trotskyists took part in this campaign, believing that they were struggling to remove a group whose control of the party had been responsible for its catastrophic decline, and to reorient the party towards a revolutionary and working-class policy. It was some time before Groves and the others were to realise that it was not the application of the Comintern line in Britain that was at fault — the incapacity of the local leaders — but the line itself. In the meantime, they were as much supporters of the new 'Third Period' line as everyone else — possibly even more so.

Thus Purkis interpreted the fall in the numbers belonging to trade unions as 'indicating the swing to the left *out of the unions*',[46] and Groves argued that party members in the G. & M.W.U. should fight against the payment of the political levy (because it was the property of the Labour Party)[47] whilst maintaining that 'the slogan of "A Revolutionary Workers' Government" is only a real, live slogan because the struggle for power is going on now', because '*we are rapidly approaching a revolutionary crisis greater in magnitude than that precipitated by the events of 1926.*'[48]

So it was Purkis who introduced the resolution on the new lines to the Conference of the London District of the Party on 7th April 1929, which shifted emphasis away from work inside the structures of the trade unions to 'concentration on factories, rail depots, docks, etc., with meetings, regular literature sales, and special leaflets, with the object of developing contacts and dealing with matters affecting workers on the job.'[49]

But it was Dutt who was encouraging the new men to attack the old, and he wrote to Groves to encourage him to press home the attack on the old leadership at the annual conference of the Communist Party at the end of the month in Leeds. 'What the International is above all looking for,' he related, 'and is feeling some disappointment (the E.C.C.I. letter on the party discussion) at not yet adequately finding, is *signs* of leadership. This is all-important to bear in mind throughout the Congress.' He ended his note with 'best wishes for a good fight and real advance at the Congress'.[50]

The official report duly described how:

> GROVES (London) insisted that, rightly or wrongly, the question of leadership in the Party was a supreme issue.
>
> Gallacher had said that to represent the Party as being in a bad way led to despair. But the facts made it clear that the Party was losing members and its paper sales decreasing at a time when the Party should be sweeping forward.
>
> In the last six months they had had the woollen, cotton, railway and mining crises.
>
> Six months ago the London Party had pointed to the growing development of the railway crisis. The District started upon a campaign, with the result of seven factory groups under Party leadership and an increase in Party influence increased.
>
> So far as Colonial work is concerned, Gallacher asked if nothing had been done on Meerut. He insisted that so far as the greater part of the Party was concerned nothing had been done.

> They had been told that the Party now accepted the Comintern's line of the present situation. If they read Bell's article in the *Labour Monthly* on the economic situation, could they say there was agreement?
>
> It was easy to repent. But the 'Rights' had not agreed until the Comintern had interfered, and they had been confronted with the Party membership. They realised that repentance was the only way of retaining the party leadership.
>
> They had even had what amounted to an admission by Gallacher that had the leadership repented earlier they would have avoided a revolt of the membership (GALLACHER: 'A lie!').[51]

The supporters of the new line felt that they had won a qualified victory. The new *Daily Worker* came out at the beginning of the new year of 1930, with William Rust as its editor. A leading article by Groves, written for the issue of 23rd January, described how 1929 had been a year of big struggles, in which the Labour Government had been obliged to use the police to break the strike wave, and prophesied greater battles for 1930.[52] Things were all set to go.

Yet within weeks it became apparent to Groves, Purkis and Williams that nothing fundamental had changed. The new line was no more a revolutionary working-class policy than the old had been, the new daily paper had an orthodoxy imposed by Rust even more suffocating than the old, and the decline of the party accelerated further. By this time the C.P.G.B. was reaching its lowest point. An analysis published in July 1931 showed that only a third of the members were employed in the major industries, that only 65% were in trade unions of those who were eligible for membership, and that only 25% of the party supporters were active in the trade union arm of the C.P. (the Minority Movement). Even if we assume that the best militants will be sacked automatically when unemployment is nearly touching three million, out of the 47% of the party who were unemployed, only half were active in the party's National Unemployed Workers' Movement.[53]

Unlike many of the new men brought up in the party, Groves and his friends had never been automatic supporters of the Stalinist point of view in the first place. Groves and Purkis had studied both Trotsky's *Lessons of October*[54] and *Where is Britain Going?* before they had even joined the Party.[55] Shortly after they joined, the sectional meetings were held up and down the country to condemn the Left Opposition.[56] Purkis and Williams failed to support the official resolution on the internal economic situation within Russia at their St. Pancras branch meeting, and Groves abstained on the same issue at his area meeting in South-West London.[57] He had made a careful study of the material in *Inprecorr* dealing with the Second Chinese Revolution, and when one comrade, Len Potter, spoke against the resolution condemning Trotsky's criticisms, Groves gave him his support. Heated arguments went on both during and after the meeting between Potter and Groves on the one side and Claude Healy, South-West London area leader, on the other; but Groves remained unconvinced.[58]

The fate of Groves' pamphlet on *Four Years of Labour Opposition* increased his disquiet. His original draft had dealt with the material in chronological order, but a party editor had altered the text, without consulting him, into a subject classification, and in case the pamphlet might imply criticism of the new policy, he had also added a quotation from the 9th Plenum of the Comintern that 'the Communist Party of Great Britain should come out more boldly, and more clearly as an independent party, change its attitude towards the Labour Party and Labour Government, and consequently replace the slogan of 'Labour Government' by the slogan of 'Revolutionary Workers' Government.'[59]

Nor was the *Daily Worker* much of an improvement on the party's previous papers, *Workers Life* and *The Sunday Worker*. Groves was so disappointed that he wrote to the party Secretariat that 'the political line of the paper is not based on the struggle of the workers. This is, it is true, partly a reflection of the isolation of the Party from the workers' struggles, but much could be done, in spite of our known weaknesses, to remedy this as far as the paper is concerned.'[60] The Editorial Board of the *Daily Worker* replied that 'the first statement is not true. The political line was not, and still to a measure is not sufficiently based on the workers' struggle, but your bold statement cannot be agreed to for a moment.'[61]

In May Groves began his series of contributions to the 'Workers' Notebook' column. By this time he was already groping towards a Trotskyist analysis of the Comintern's policies. On 8th May he had summarised the Indian conflict as being '*at roots*, the issue of the ruling class versus the workers and peasants, capitalism against socialism'. But on the 9th the Editorial Board had reversed this with a statement that 'the issues at this stage are not "capitalism against socialism", as was incorrectly stated, but the driving out of the British Imperialists by the democratic revolution of the working class and peasantry.' The alteration had been made because of the campaign against Trotsky's theory of Permanent Revolution, in which the Communist International had raised the slogan of 'the democratic dictatorship of the proletariat and peasantry' — a bourgeois revolution as a first stage. Groves himself was quite close to the application of the theory of Permanent Revolution to 'Third World' circumstances, for he wrote back, 'do you regard as possible "a democratic revolution of the working classes and peasantry" against the British Imperialists, if the issues are not at root the class issues, the issues of capitalism against socialism? The fight against the British Imperialists, without fighting their allies the Indian bourgeoisie is as difficult to visualise as the fight against the capitalist class without fighting the Social Fascist Labour Government and the T.U.C.'[62]

The letter shows the position Groves was already occupying in his evolution from Stalinism to Trotskyism. He was formulating a statement of the theory of Permanent Revolution in under-developed countries, yet still couched in terms of the phraseology of the 'Third Period'.

In the end, sheer exasperation drove Groves to abandon his contributions to the column, and early in the following year Purkis was also denounced as a 'theoretician of left sectarianism'.[63] It looked as if the struggle to create a party that was both revolutionary and relevant to the working class had come to an end. A worse moment for raising the theoretical and international issues could hardly be imagined, for denunciation of all Oppositions ran parallel with the extremes of adventurism involved in the forced collectivisation and the First Five Year Plan. Stalin was no longer satisfied with recantations, but demanded self-abasement and moral annihilation from all who had ever opposed him.

The worsening of the political climate can be traced in the literature of the British Party. A series of *Outlines* published by the Agit-Prop Department for the use of 'students and party trainers', whilst continuing all the old slanders — that Trotsky believed in simultaneous revolution as the only way to defend Soviet Russia, that he was denying 'the revolutionary role of the peasantry' and planning to despoil them — could still give an intelligible summary of the Opposition's economic proposals,[64] and could still hold back from charging them with being consciously counter-revolutionary:

> The 'Opposition Bloc' of the Trotskyists was an unprincipled alliance of petty-bourgeois elements united to attack the party leadership with a lack of faith and understanding of the proletarian revolution and its tasks . . . The Trotskyist Opposition bloc was anti-party in character (objectively its path was that of the Counter-Revolution).[65]

But now the 16th Congress of the Communist Party of the Soviet Union defined the 'chief danger' as 'Trotskyist, Anarcho-Syndicalist and similar deviation', which wanted all power 'concentrated in the hands of the Trade Unions'.[66] From then on it became obligatory to include a side-swipe at Trotsky, however irrelevant it might be to the topic in hand. Trotsky became one 'who did his best to scotch the Soviet Workers' Five Year Plan',[67] and the tone and level of the attacks dropped lower and lower. A review by Gallacher of Krupskaya's *Memories of Lenin* now included a reference to 'the brilliant Mr. Trotsky, with whom it was impossible to escape the fact that you were in the presence of something of extraordinary importance, something on which the very universe depended for the proper functioning of its many millioned planets',[68] whilst Trotsky's autobiography received fiercely hostile reviews, not only from lightweights like the American Communist leader Earl Browder,[69] but even from the respected Soviet historian M.N. Pokrovsky ('Kerenskies and Trotskies are fashioned by their oratorial talent').[70] Grossly misrepresented and excluded from any right of reply, Trotsky was even blamed for publishing articles in bourgeois newspapers,[71] and his allies and supporters were described as 'flickering phantoms', with 'no role or significance save to create confusion and disintegration among a few of the leftward-moving workers and hinder the advance of Communism'.[71]

In 1932 came the final choking of any expression of dissent, intentional or accidental, past or present.[72] The signal came from Stalin himself in his contribution to the 'Lenin-Liebknecht-Luxemburg Campaign for Theoretical Solidarity', where Rosa Luxemburg was censured for 'leftism' and an inability to follow the lead provided by the Bolsheviks.[73] When the British Communists joined in, T.A. Jackson protested that this was sabotaging the campaign (which after all was partly named after her), and in any case, no one in England could understand the 'mistakes' in question, because the articles in which they appeared had never been translated.[74] He was told to read Stalin's letter,[75] and when his own self-criticism finally appeared he was also forced to make an apology for not recanting sooner.[76]

Although the condemnation of Luxemburg remained,[77] she was, in fact, only the incidental victim of this drastic exercise in rewriting history. The real targets, explained Kaganovich, were 'the counter-revolutionary Trotskyists' who were 'trying to seize on a new flag, the flag of Rosa Luxemburg's mistaken theories',[78] which the *Daily Worker* explained as 'a Utopian and semi-Menshevik scheme of Permanent Revolution'.[79] For Stalin was not so much attacking Luxemburg, who was, after all, long dead — but those who maintained the belief that 'Trotskyism is a faction of Communism', a 'profoundly false and dangerous' conception of 'the advanced troop of the counter-revolutionary bourgeoisie'.[80]

Any criticisms resembling those of Trotsky were sufficient to damn those who raised them from the very beginning. For many years the party had campaigned around the aim of getting the government to extend credits to the Soviet Union, to break the blockades on trade with the U.S.S.R. as well as to provide more jobs for workers here.[81] In the 'Third Period' this policy had been gradually dropped. There was unlimited confidence in both the industrialisation of the Soviet Union and the crisis of capitalism, and the party held that extending trade would be a way of getting the bourgeois economy out of its mess, as well as being a diversion from the defence of the Soviet Union against the threat of war. Naturally the Left Opposition had never dropped the policy, regarding the economic situation as 'a special opportunity to set the British Workers into action' and to 'help to make them real defenders of the Soviet Union and become a source of strength to the Communist Party'.[82] But when J.T. Murphy made the same point in an editorial in *The Communist Review* in April 1932 supporting the first Five Year Plan, and demanding jobs for his home town of Sheffield, he was assailed on all sides. After a condemnation by the Political Bureau he resigned, only to be denounced in the open press.[83] For three weeks afterwards, hardly an issue of the *Daily Worker* appeared without an article attacking him, or without one party branch or another joining in with a resolution.[84] Even though he had prefaced his article with a 'vicious' attack upon the Opposition, he was still accused of 'Trotskyism':

> Murphy has left the line of the Communist International and moved towards the camp of the counter-revolutionary Trotskyites, who have always denied the possibility of building Socialism in one country and continue to assert that the Soviet Union is an integral part of capitalist world economy.[85]

The fact that Trotsky had raised the question of credits did not escape notice, either in the Communist and international press,[86] or among the Trotskyists themselves,[87] but the accusation cannot have been meant seriously. The party changed its line on the issue shortly afterwards,[88] and in view of Murphy's previous role in the Comintern, Trotsky himself was amazed at this 'wonderful story'.[89] It was a curious affair, for Murphy continued to carry out the line of the Communist Party inside the Socialist League,[90] and his autobiography, written at the time of the German invasion of the Soviet Union, shows that his admiration for Stalin and hatred of Trotsky remained unabated.[91] But it did serve as a warning to the Balham comrades of the consequences of raising the political differences on the international plane. The Balham Group evolved towards a Trotskyist position because it continued to support the 'Third Period' line of the Communist Party on the struggle in the trade unions when the Communists themselves were modifying their position on the question. By 1931 the excesses of the sectarian line were becoming evident, even though the policy was not to be changed for another four years, and a 'softening' of the attitude to the official trade unions was coming to be dictated by the increasing isolation of the Communists from the life of the working class. The change was made without a conference, or a full airing of the issues, but was introduced into the pages of the party's literature.

However, the Balham comrades continued to urge the policy after the leadership of the C.P. had backtracked on it. Purkis, after all, had been responsible for getting it adopted by the London District,[92] and he continued to advocate it in the starkest terms:

> ... inside capitalism, all industries will increasingly prove unable to maintain both wages and profits, or indeed, either wages or profits ... That every railwayman may master this basic fact should be the main political concern of the revolutionary who participates in the railway struggle ...
>
> Some may shrink from this argument and urge that to maintain wages and to keep men from the 'sack' is the immediately important thing. These things are, of course, important to every one of us who is immediately affected; but too great a price can be paid for misused or transient victories on minor issues.
>
> And thus it becomes clear that as part of the struggle for international working-class victory the policy of railway workers must be the revolutionary policy of the Communist International.
>
> The railway struggle must not be viewed by revolutionaries as a reformist wage struggle (whole and complete in itself) but as part of the revolutionary struggle.[93]

This policy of trying to bring about immediate politicisation was the natural corollary of an attempt to counterpose agitation 'at the point of production' to work in the official trade unions. Both policies assumed that the Great Depression was indeed 'the final crisis of capitalism', and the Balham comrades shared the view that immediate revolutionary storms lay ahead.[94] Of course, their views were no different from those previously held by the Communist Party leaders — including Palme Dutt for one, in the previous issue of the same journal. But stark isolation was beginning to have an impact on the party. A report by Dick Beech to the American *Militant* described how, during several strikes in London, 'The workers were solid and prepared to fight, but the offer of assistance or help from the Minority Movement or the Communist Party was point blank refused.'[95] Even Moscow was insisting that some alteration should be made. In January 1931 the Political Bureau issued a statement directed against Purkis and Freda Utley, who had analysed the textile industry in the same fashion:

> This pouring of cold water on local struggles which result in victory and not a 'revolutionary' defeat is typical of the Left sectarian, who cannot understand that local victories encourage the masses to join in the larger struggles, and who is afraid that such victories will create illusions and weaken the fight against capitalism. 'Only those who are convinced that capitalism cannot pay will fight to end capitalism,' writes Purkis in the same article — obviously meaning that a fight for defending wage standards had nothing to do with ending capitalism unless the strikers are convinced beforehand that there is no hope for them under capitalism.[96]

Thus the first criticisms made by Groves and Purkis of the Communist Party were from a leftward direction at a time when the Party itself was in a 'left' phase. They described the party as 'shot through with social democratic tendencies',[97] and its trade union policy as the 'hiding of the revolutionary implications of the struggle'.[98] Even its electoral policy, where Pollitt was advertised as 'the only workers' candidate' in Whitechapel, was 'an ultra-right line'.[99]

Contact with the international Trotskyist movement only modified this outlook very gradually, and by the time wider issues came up, the Balham comrades had already been isolated on the trade union question.

Though Groves was an avid reader of *Inprecorr* and by no means a mechanical follower of the Comintern line,[100] and Ridley had been disseminating Trotskyist pamphlets for some time, the link between the struggle in Britain and the wider movement was only gradually made. The only visible tendency espousing 'Trotskyism' was the Marxian League, not only outside the Communist Party, but even for the most part peripheral to the Labour movement as well — and it had a more extreme view of the trade unions than their own. Their attraction to Trotskyism came from elsewhere.

Though they lived in neighbouring areas of London, Groves first met Wicks when they both got jobs in the company that handled the sales of Soviet oil products in London.[101] The Russians on the staff of the same company were for the most part old revolutionaries, who were either in Britain to work, or had links from before the First World War. As Wicks recalls:

> . . . I did work, on party instructions, in the economic department of Russian Oil Products. I was one of five people in the economic department, but in that economic department

> the Russians used to assemble. (It was at the time that Sokolnikov was ambassador here.) And they used to assemble for talks about the Russian party situation, and I gathered, as a result of listening to their discussions, and so on (as a result of my friendship with two of the girls, Russian girls), I sensed the feeling of the Russian situation and economy. I sensed their feelings towards the Opposition, and I knew their sympathies, and they used to buy the Russian Opposition Bulletin, not from me, but from Leicester Square, at the shop. And they would talk about it, and one of the people who was more outspoken on that was a chap who was the son of an Old Bolshevik, Tsiurupa, who was on the Central Committee in Lenin's time. And so I was interested in his views and comments during the discussion. So I knew that they were sympathetic to the Left Opposition's criticism of Stalinism in the Russian Party.[102]

Soon Stalin's regime began to round up and destroy the revolutionary generation of 1917, and they began to be recalled, one by one. When a group of them refused, the *Daily Worker* made a point of mentioning that Soviet law demanded the death penalty in cases of refusal to return, should they ever be caught again on Russian territory.[103] Groves remembers meeting some of them in the rooms and corridors, ashen-faced and trembling, but unable to explain why.[104]

Early in 1931 Groves visited Henderson's left-wing bookshop in the Charing Cross Road and brought back copies of the American *Militant* to study for the first time.[105] By the summer of 1931 he had got in touch,[106] and by August had written to Trotsky himself.[107] First Albert Glotzer[108] had come from Trotsky in Kadiköy, and then Max Shachtman came over from New York[109] to begin the task of setting up a viable grouping of the International Left Opposition in Britain.

Shachtman met Groves, Sara, Purkis, Williams, Wicks and Weston[110] in South London, and tried to persuade them to establish an open presence behind which other oppositionists inside the party could rally, even though immediate expulsion would be the result. Though the group were unwilling to invite ejection in this way, they did agree to bring out a duplicated magazine on an open and regular basis to publish material from the International Opposition. The low wages, the high unemployment, and the relatively high cost of American material because of the exchange rates had prevented the Trotskyist case from being aired properly up to that time, despite the efforts of Ridley's group. But the main result of contact with the international movement was the setting up of a proper organisation, and a break with the casual attitude to organisation and activity of Ridley's group. Trotsky's reply to Groves emphasised that 'The British Left Opposition must begin systematic work. You must establish a central staff, even if a small one. You must establish your own publications, even if on a modest scale. It is necessary to carry out sustained activity, analysis, criticism, and propaganda.'[111]

Since the struggle had already begun over the trade union issue, they hoped to gather support by linking it with the wider international questions, such as Germany, so that they could not be isolated and expelled before they had time to get their views known and rally people around them. They knew that directly criticising the Comintern would immediately court expulsion, identifying them as Trotskyists, so they hoped to stay on the concrete and day-to-day issues, to be able to carry on work as a group, at least for a time. In the event, it was their trade union perspectives which enabled the C.P. leaders to isolate them anyway, concentrating attacks on these and avoiding the wider issues.

Events, and the International Trotskyist movement, were pushing them along faster than they would have liked. When Ridley's group broke up, the Balham comrades held a conference with those who had left on 19th December 1932, to set up a British Section of the International Left Opposition. A report of this by Shachtman in the American *Militant* described them as members of the Communist Party, with one exception:[112] some of them had been 'active in it for years', 'determined to carry on the fight within the party and, at all events, as a faction of the Communist Party' for 'the ideas of Marx and Lenin'. But, describing their struggle as 'a continuation on a higher plane and in an organised manner of a struggle against bureaucratism and opportunism which they have conducted, under other forms, in the recent past of the party'.[113] Shachtman was clearly identifying them to the C.P. leadership, who could not fail to recognise the Balham Group here, inviting their expulsion along the lines of his theory of the 'sacrificial lamb'.[114] For when the *Morning Post* relayed the report as a 'serious split' in the Communist Party, and the *Daily Worker* retorted by describing the British Oppositionists as 'a contemptible handful', the party leadership was warned in advance.[115]

Groves knew, of course, that to have any chance of success their policy would have to take on a theoretical aspect. 'The work of the proletarian group,' he had written (on the Chartist Left), 'who were precisely the group that had some scientific theory to guide them, deserves special study today; the failure of this group ruthlessly to expose and uproot "centrism" and take an independent line should be burnt into the consciousness of the contemporary revolutionary movement.'[116] But he preferred to begin in a way that would be intelligible to the ordinary party member, as to how socialist agitation was to be carried on in the work situation. He knew all too well the deep prejudices that have always existed in England against the discussion of purely theoretical questions, not only in the wider movement, but in the Party itself. His own preference for grassroots activity led him to hope that the group could gradually develop a dialogue in the direction of the wider political issues.

However, before this could be done international affairs intruded themselves. The Communist International was gradually developing a hysteria over the threat of imminent war, and the Japanese invasion of Manchuria was raising this to fever pitch. On 19th March 1932, the *Daily Worker* went out with a heading 'War Menaces You', and announced that 'World War Has Begun'. Next day Henry Sara, speaking on a party platform at St. Pancras, made open criticism of this alarmism and irresponsibility. Pollitt's reply was not only a rebuke, but a plain threat of expulsion: 'this opportunist poison must be plucked out of the Party, and all who disseminate it ruthlessly fought, as objectively helping the war preparation of the imperialists by the doubts and confusion they create in the party.'[117]

In fact, if the Balham comrades had limited their main criticisms of the party to international policy, or to the question of ultra-leftism in general, there can be little doubt that they would have scored off Pollitt and the others in a most damaging way. Germany was now in acute crisis, with each emergency regime on presidential decree moving further to the right. As Hitler's power was looming up, the Comintern was continuing the German party's role in a most irresponsible manner.[118] But Balham made the main thrust of their criticism against the changes made in the party's trade union policy since the Leeds Congress, which placed them, in effect, not on the right of the party (which was itself in an ultra-left position), but on its left. The references to Germany and the war situation, tacked on as an afterthought at the end, meant that they were attacking the Party from the left and the right at the same time, making it extremely difficult for the ordinary member to understand their point of view. It gave the party an opportunity to dismiss them as 'left sectarians', as well as being oppositionists for the sake of it.

On 18th March, after a preliminary exchange of letters with the Secretariat,[119] the group delegated Groves to prepare their statement, which appeared in the *Daily Worker* a month later:

> The group recognised that the experiences of the last two years and the present position of the party make imperative a critical examination of our political line and our methods of work.
>
> Insofar as the C.C. resolution is a step in this direction we

> welcome it. We raise two points of criticism:
>
> (1) The question of the trades unions and our work inside the branches. The formulation on Page 9 of the resolution is incorrect. We refer to:- 'every member and all workers who sympathise must be members of the reformist trade unions in order to carry on the struggle against the reformists and for the transformation of the trade union branches from organs of class collaboration into organs of class struggle.'
>
> It is implied here that it is possible to 'transform' the unions into organs of class struggle.
>
> The whole line of the party at the Leeds Congress had been that job organisation can alone be the unit of an 'organ of class struggle', that the structure, scope, organisation, constitution and leadership make them unsuitable as organs of class struggle, that their capture is unlikely because of the bureaucracy, and that our principal work lies in building up the workers' weapons of struggle in the pits, factories and workshops.
>
> We do not deny the importance of work within the trade unions, or that the branches can be of great value in building the job organisations, but the emphasis in the resolution is upon the union.
>
> The dangers of such an emphasis are too well known by experience to need repetition here.
>
> (2) The International Situation. The resolution is to guide us in our work; it cannot set down our work and policy without first estimating the chief factors in the international situation.
>
> In this resolution the two dominating features — the War in the Far East, and the approach of political crisis in Germany — are omitted!
>
> Such an omission is extremely serious and must be remedied at once.
>
> In view of the present unsatisfactory state of the Party, as depicted in the resolution, we suggest:-
>
> A full open discussion in the Party and Party Press as a preliminary to the Party Congress.[120]

The reply of the Secretariat was naturally focused on the trade union issue, completely avoiding discussion on the international questions, where they were on much shakier ground. It claimed that the Balham comrades had not understood the Central Committee Resolution, for the new trade union orientation was not a change 'in policy or line', but in 'methods of work and approach and organisation, whereby the policy laid down at Leeds can be carried through and a mass C.P. built'. It lectured the Balham group that 'work in unions and factories is not different work in different places', and side-stepped the international points by claiming that 'the resolution was not intended to be a political and economic analysis and therefore did not deal with the international situation.'[121]

On 14th May the group got together a reply, complaining of the evasion of the international issue, but still standing by their union policy. 'The suggestion that we are against, or underestimate work in the unions is unjustified,' they wrote, 'our objection was, and is, that trade union branches must be transformed from "organs of class collaboration to organs of class struggle". This we deny. The history of unions, their past and present makes them unsuited to be effective organs of class struggle.' Their main criticism continued to be levelled against 'changes in the methods and forms of work' made 'without having before us the basis of such changes'.[122]

The Secretariat was thus able to write them off as 'a well known sectarian group within the party', whose 'fundamental opposition to the line of mass revolutionary work in the trade unions' was 'a barrier to mass work and a hindrance to the development of the Minority Movement into a mass organisation of the revolutionary trade union opposition.' The further statement that 'international events should find their reflection in our work and organisation' was so general that it was easily dismissed as 'high sounding phrases' which 'will not get us very far'.[123]

As Groves and Purkis had been his protégés in the past, and continued to quote him to embarrassing effect, Dutt was now on the spot and the Secretariat had to get him off it by saying that when the Balham Group had quoted him, they had distorted his views by omitting a crucial paragraph,[124] though it was obvious to others that he 'objectively comes out on the side of the Balham Group'.[125]

The consequences of concentrating on the trade union question were catastrophic. An example of how easily feeling could be mobilised against the Balham comrades was provided by letters from F.C. Vint and C.H. of the Stratford Rail Cell which appeared a week later in the *Daily Worker*, supporting the Secretariat and explaining how 'union branches can be won for the class fight'.[126] In vain did Sentinella and Steve Dowdall write in to say that Balham Group members *were* active in their trade unions (Dowdall was a long-standing member of the A.U.B.T.W.). The damage was done and the group was isolated. An attempt was made to isolate Groves and Purkis with the claim that 'the reference to sectarianism was meant to apply not to the entire group, but to several of its leading members', whose 'wrong views' were preventing the Party from making 'the sharp turns to work in the unions, which is so absolutely essential'.[127]

In fact, there was only limited political capital to be made out of defending the previous trade union policy, even if the change had been decided without real discussion, for such point-scoring had little to do with the struggle of the International Left Opposition. Even if the Balham comrades had been associated with Dutt in the past, they must have known that they could not rely on any support from him in a direct challenge to a policy imposed from Moscow.

Moreover, their attempt to defend a 'Third Period' trade union line in no way represented the views of the International Trotskyist movement. As Shachtman noted later:

> I do not believe the section on the trade unions is quite correct. If the dispute rests upon a poor formulation or a shading of differences, then it is a small matter, comparatively. If there is something more profound involved, then the utmost caution should be exercised by our English comrades against falling into an ultra-leftist split on the trade union question. How serious the dispute is, I do not pretend to appreciate from this distance, but I get the impression that the 'Balham Group' is on the wrong tack.[128]

So the battle had already been lost over the trade union issue before the Balham comrades managed to raise the international questions that identified their position as a Trotskyist one.

The situation in Germany was the burning concern of the day. Whilst fratricidal polemics were splitting the German working class, Hitler was poised to take power. Socialists blamed the growth of a right-wing backlash on the extremism of the Communists, who in turn explained the advance of Hitler by the preparation of the 'Social Fascists'. The Comintern continued to press these 'Third Period' policies, and all the sections were assured that the German Communist Party was going from strength to strength, preparing itself for the revolutionary battles that lay ahead. And the British Communist Party differed not an iota. Pollitt continued to maintain that 'Social Fascism has reached its highest stage in Germany, and yet it has been unable to prevent the sharpening crisis from taking place', and to rejoice over 'how rapidly the [Communist] Party is forging ahead'.[129] When Trotsky was sounding the alarm, and proposing the United Front of Socialists and Communists against Hitler, Dutt could only remark that 'it is significant that Trotsky has come out in defence of a united front between the Communist and Social Democratic parties. No more disruptive and counter-revolutionary lead could possibly have been given.'[130]

It was more necessary than ever that Trotsky's views on this crisis should be made known in Britain, and Purkis was urging that they should be published by the group. But Groves was still against raising the international issues in this way, and fought for a policy of 'British material, not Trotsky documents' with 'great bitterness and vehemence'.[131] Finally it was decided to bring out the first issue of their duplicated magazine, *The Communist*, wholly devoted to Trotsky's *Germany: The Key to the International Situation*, which appeared in May 1932. It appeared without an address and was sold from hand to hand to limit the chances of premature expulsion,[132] though they well knew that this would follow shortly. Wicks took up copies to distribute to the summer camp held near Leeds by the Y.C.L., in July,[133] and incidentally to the I.L.P. Conference nearby, while preparations were made for the future. Arne Swabeck wrote from the international movement:

> Should your group in England propose to organise a new party? It is our opinion that that would be decidedly wrong. Despite the false and wrong means of the leadership, the present party still remains the Communist Party. Moreover, it still remains a true reflection of the Comintern, which, despite all of the criminal revisionism of the Stalin regime still remains the World Party.
>
> . . . The Left Opposition will endeavour to regenerate the party ideological concepts, endeavour to fight for correct views, correct practices, to fight to replace the bureaucratic leadership and to lay the base for unity of the Communist ranks. We believe the object at this moment should be to build the nucleus of the future cadres of the party leadership, in other words, to build a fraction which will function as a fraction of the Communist movement and not as a new or separate party. That would mean that your group would not take over the full responsibilities and duties of a party but would endeavour to carry on the fight to have the party accept correctly these duties and responsibilities. When your group clearly and precisely states its position in support of the International Left Opposition, there will likely be some expulsions from the party to follow, but it is our firm opinion that this would not in the least change your perspective or your position. You should remain an organised fraction and work together in that manner with all Communist workers accepting your platform. The mere mechanical separation by taking away membership cards in the official party from members of your group would not in the least in reality separate you from the Party.[134]

The next step was to introduce the German question into their public work. For some time they had been co-operating with Clapham I.L.P. and other local bodies in the South-West London Anti-War Committee, and in July 1932 they proposed that it should hold a series of open-air meetings in various parks and commons from 17th July onwards on the theme of 'Solidarity with German workers'.[135] At the time the Comintern sections in Western Europe were placing all their emphasis upon the 'Anti-War Congress' that Romain Rolland and Henri Barbusse were preparing to convene in Amsterdam on 27th August, so they passed a resolution describing it as 'pacifist trickery' and explaining that 'the only guarantee of victory for the workers of Russia lies in the development of world revolution.' At first the party appears to have missed the reference to the theory of the Permanent Revolution, and printed the resolution in full.[136] But three days later the *Daily Worker* carried an article by J.R. Campbell describing it as 'mischievous' and containing 'phrases which conceal Trotskyist meaning'.[137]

The question of the incredible strategy carried out by the German Communist Party had already been raised inside the Party at a London aggregate,[138] where Pollitt had pointedly asked how far the Balham comrades went with *The Communist* which had been passed on to him. Purkis replied by open letter, making a full critique of the stagnant state of the party, defending Trotsky to the full, and launched into an attack upon the handling of the German situation:

> In 1930 Trotsky warned the Party that their forecasts of the early collapse of Fascism were not justified. Twelve months ago, Trotsky pointed to the United Front of the Communist and Social Democratic organisations as the only policy which could ensure the defeat of Fascism, the break-up of Social Democracy, and success in the struggle for proletarian power. Today events tardily compel the Party towards Trotsky's line. But time in this struggle is the life and death factor. The line which Trotsky pointed out two years ago, the Party begins to shuffle towards today. These delays and weaknesses of both the Communist International and the German leadership threaten disaster to the U.S.S.R. and to the whole working-class movement.[139]

The fat was in the fire now, and the struggle moved from arguments about trade union questions on to the international plane. For that reason Purkis' letter in fact meant a whole new orientation and activity for the group. As Max Shachtman wrote from New York:

> We have just received the open letter from Comrade Purkis

> and I take it that it means the commencement of an open break. Difficult as this will be from many angles it will at least enable the group to function publicly under its own banner and without suffering the gag and fetter of the King Street High Priests. The group will not be the loser thereby. The bureaucracy has been able to maintain itself for so long a period only because the ideas of the Opposition have been kept concealed in their underground safety vaults.[140]

Trotsky also wrote approving of the way things had been brought into the open, sketching out the form and content of the future work, whilst disagreeing about Purkis' estimate of Harry Pollitt, whose reputation in the Comintern for being a lightweight was proverbial.[141]

Leaving Purkis to make the full statement of the group's open views, Groves continued to press the views of the Opposition inside the Communist Party. On 9th August he wrote to the Party Secretariat on behalf of the Balham Group to express their 'dissatisfaction with the measures already taken by the Party to bring the German situation before the workers', and to demand 'a widespread campaign without further delay' of district meetings, pamphlet literature, etc., leading up to a national demonstration.[142]

His reply was an invitation from R.W. Robson for Groves, Sara and Wicks to meet him in the District Party Headquarters. When they got there on 16th August, Robson was nowhere to be seen and, taking the hint, Sara walked out. Waiting for them was a delegation of Gallacher, Pollitt and Beauchamp, who had constituted themselves as 'a special meeting of the Working Bureau of the District Party Committee'. Groves gives a vivid description of Gallacher's tirade and Pollitt's inquisition, an attempt to make them disavow their ideas, disown *The Communist* and renounce their struggle inside the Party.[143] Beauchamp's memory is less vivid, about branch activity in Battersea being 'brought to a standstill by internal wrangling' organised by a 'Trotskyist group meeting secretly at the Reform Club in Furnival Street, Holborn, with the aim of taking over the leadership of the Battersea branches'.[141]

Next day Robson wrote informing Groves and Wicks of the unanimous decision of the Working Bureau to expel them for their 'absolute refusal' to state that they would accept party policy 'and abide by its discipline'.[145] A further circular from the District Party Committee went out to inform all Balham members that the group was 'liquidated' as 'clearly and self avowedly a centre for anti-Communist agitation' disseminating a policy of 'defeatist petit-bourgeois distrust of the working class, thinly veiled in high-sounding revolutionary phrases, and opposition to the line of the Comintern and the C.P.G.B.'[146]

An invitation was extended to all group members to meet local and district party representatives, but this only turned out to be another purge session. As Steve Dowdall recalls,

> . . . when it was leading up to the expulsion, David Springhall — he was the Big White Chief in the District, and Comintern man — said to me, 'I'm surprised at you, Steve . . . I'd sooner be shot than expelled from the Party'. 'You would maybe,' I said, 'but I wouldn't!'[147]

Springhall put on a similar performance at Hugo Dewar's expulsion from the Tooting local. 'I can still see the sweat streaming off his face,' Dewar remembered. 'It seems extraordinary, but he had worked himself into a bit of a frenzy.'[148] In such a way the British Communist Party rid itself of its first real internationalist opposition — the thirteen members of the Balham Group,[149] Dewar from the Tooting Group, and Wicks from the Church Road Group — and into the bargain both Groves and Wicks were then immediately sacked from their jobs in Russian Oil Products, the start of long years of unemployment. A week later the Party opened the period of its 'pre-Congress' discussion.

The statement produced to justify the expulsions to the party was careful to avoid the German problem and concentrated instead upon the trade union issue and their anti-war agitation. Their views were described as forming 'a barrier against the party making a sharp turn in the trade union work' with 'a harmful and disintegrative effect upon the party work locally', whilst 'mistakes of a right-opportunist character' had been committed by agreeing to hold a joint May Day march to Hyde Park with the I.L.P., which had dropped 'differences of tactics' and 'completely blurred over the differences in principle' between the C.P. and the I.L.P.[150]

Since they had been prevented from taking part in the pre-Congress discussion, the Balham comrades replied in a cyclostyled leaflet, contrasting the claim of 'full, free and open discussions' with the expulsions. After charging the party with replacing Leninist norms of internal debate with 'orders from above, phrase-mouthing and bureaucratic stifling of criticism', they repeated their opposition to the Barbusse World Anti-War Congress, and again raised the alarm over Germany:

> The growth of Fascism in Germany menaces the existence of the party and the workers' organisations and brings Germany near to the anti-Soviet bloc. What happens in Germany will decide for years ahead the fate of the European Workers. Our

> group discussed the German situation, organised, through the local anti-war committee, solidarity meetings; demanded a discussion throughout the party, and a wide campaign amongst British workers. But the party remained silent on the German events.[151]

There was no longer any possibility of avoiding the uncomfortable problem of Germany, and a reply appeared over Gallacher's name in an issue of the *Daily Worker* devoted to the pre-conference discussions, mixed up with a good deal of personal abuse. Groves and Purkis were described as 'the erstwhile Catholic Crusaders' who had 'apparently dropped Christ and adopted Trotsky', whose talk of 'comradely discussion' really amounted to 'trickeries'. As far as Gallacher was concerned, Trotsky's German policy 'proposed liquidation of the struggle, liquidation of the party, by proposing an organisational compact with the Social Democrats', whereas the German Communist Party:

> vigorously carrying out the line of the Communist International, the line of the united fighting front of the working class, has exposed the rottenness of Trotsky's arguments. They have made a mighty advance in the development of the fighting front and erected a powerful wall against the advance of the Fascists.[152]

The only way left to intervene in the discussion was to get out a second issue of *The Communist*, the group's duplicated magazine. Gallacher's claim that 'an organisational compact with the Social Democrats would have weakened the whole front, and would have made the advent of Hitler almost a certainty' was effectively demolished by printing Trotsky's 'Letter to a German Worker', whilst a wealth of statistics illuminated the disaster course of the German Communists, whose support in the form of poll ratings was demonstrated in graphic form. A significant editorial statement also defined the group's relationship with the Communist movement and the main thrust of its policy:

> The expelled party members, who are members of the Left Opposition, will strive to retain their membership of the party. We joined the C.P. because it is the party of revolution. We are not joining any other party. We — expelled and unexpelled party members — shall work as a party fraction. We shall not only endeavour to win party members, but also our fellow workers to Leninist policy, and then recruit them into the party to fight for that policy.[153]

The final attempt of the Balham Group to intervene in the discussion and to appeal for reinstatement took place at the 12th Congress of the Communist Party held at the Latchmere Baths, Battersea, from 12th to 15th November. The tone of that gathering was set by the announcement that appeared beforehand in the *Daily Worker* that Zinoviev and Kamenev had been expelled from the Communist Party of the Soviet Union, having 'degenerated into enemies of the party and the Soviet power' and 'worked illegally to set up a bourgeois organisation for the restoration of capitalism'. *Pravda* was quoted to the effect that 'the party has rid itself of a score of traitors',[154] and not long afterwards the news came through that the Spanish Communist Party at the demand of Moscow had thrown out its leadership for the second time running. When the delegates gathered, outside the hall stood Reg Groves and Harry Wicks, handing out statements appealing for free discussion and reinstatement, whilst the walls behind them bore such slogans as 'Reinstate the Expelled Left' and 'Not National Socialism, but World Revolution'. One leaflet protested at the exclusion of Zinoviev and Kamenev, defended the record of Christian Rakovsky, and contained two letters by Trotsky, one being an account of his present position, and the other the famous proclamation of the October Revolution by the Military Revolutionary Committee.[155] Their own appeal defended their record in the party, as seeking to establish a real United Front of workers' organisations, not a bloc of the Communist Party with its own satellite groups, and as being more active in the trade unions than several members of the Central Committee. Yet again they returned to the urgent question of the day:

> Do the party leaders attach importance to the German revolution? Have we any part to play in that struggle now? Or are they silent in the interests of Socialism in One Country? Events are showing that our demands were justified. We ask the delegates to the Party Congress to demand that an effective campaign be begun at once.

'A leadership that suppresses the point of view of its critics is afraid of open discussion,' they explained: 'A leadership that refuses to explain measures taken against its critics has a weak case. Our group has nothing to fear from open discussion. We have fought all along for the thrashing out of differences before the whole party.'[156] At the door stood William Rust, snatching the words out of the hands of the delegates as they filed into the hall.

Inside, the discussion was muted, for 'scores of contributions' had already been refused circulation 'for the one good reason that the party leadership disagreed with them'. The party statutes were changed, instructing the District Congress to select future delegates on the basis of support for 'the line of the party'.[157] The expulsion of the Political Bureau of the Spanish Communist Party went through without a challenge, even though none of the delegates had the faintest knowledge of the facts of the case, and the ejection of Lenin's old comrades Zinoviev and Kamenev received 'wholehearted support'.[158] As to the Balham Group itself, its policy was described in Pollitt's own speech as 'the full Trotskyist line, the line that Socialism cannot possibly be established in one country on the one hand, while you make united fronts from the top with the Social Democrats on the other; the line that you must build factory committees and factory councils and do nothing at all in the unions; that the way to fight war is to make alliances with those people whose only objective is to help in the actual carrying through of the war preparations.' The group had, according to him, 'resorted to the most despicable practices' to circulate 'poisonous Trotskyist literature', 'lied and slandered' and 'been in constant communication with the Trotskyist emissaries from France and America'. 'If we sense this Congress aright,' he went on, 'it will give no opportunity to this Group of putting its poisonous views across . . . It is the party's duty to mercilessly crush whatever little influence and poison is left'; and then, he added, it was up to the Economic League 'to take the Murphys, the Saras, the Purkises and the Groves to their bosom'.[159]

He returned to the topic of his closing speech to Conference:

> I ask the Congress delegates to go away from this Congress full of contempt, hatred and loathing for the miserable gang of counter-revolutionaries who, on the walls outside the Congress, have written the slogan 'NOT NATIONAL SOCIALISM BUT WORLD REVOLUTION'. We ask you to remember this, and to warn any in the Congress who may support them, but who have not the courage to express that support, that if they dare to raise their heads inside our movement with any of this counter-revolutionary propaganda, that we will smash and destroy them (Cheers). The scoundrels who can write that thing: 'Not National Socialism, But World Revolution' in face of the numberless sacrifices that have been and are being made ceaselessly by millions of our Russian comrades to build world socialism; why language fails to express the contempt and loathing which all genuine revolutionaries should feel for this gang.[160]

For the Balham Group there was now no turning back. The Congress delegates had been immunised against their appeal, and their friends passed them with faces turned away, some making hostile gestures. It was a whole way of life, a whole circle of friends, workmates and acquaintances that was now closed to them. 'We had become so well known in the Communist Party,' recalls Daisy Groves, 'we had helped to run bazaars, and collected money, and all that sort of thing for the Party — and we had a lot of good friends in the Party — when suddenly, they'd pass you in the street, and call you a "Social-Fascist", or something like that.' 'Personally, I was very upset at being expelled,' Steve Dowdall remembers, having spent eleven years of his life in the party:

> It came as a great shock to me, because I had worked very hard. I had never been what you would call 'a good political entity', as Reg is, and others had related to me how I used the expression 'a Jimmy Higgins', and that's all I ever considered myself to be. I wasn't in any way an intellectual, but, I can only presume, joined from my own experience during the First World War, plus the political happenings concerning the Soviet Union, or Russia, as it was in those days. To a large extent it was emotional on my part.[161]

They were all, in fact, to experience in small scale the isolation of the Trotskyists during that 'midnight of the century' that was the thirties, the age of Hitler and Stalin. Soon, all but two of the group were unemployed, whilst others survived on casual jobs as gravediggers, and so on. Political life had dwindled from the wider horizon of a party into the suffocating confines of a small group.

Notes

1. Cf. S. Bornstein and A. Richardson, *Two Steps Back*, London, 1982, pp. 2-3.
2. 'G.W.', 'English Imperialism and the Chinese Counter-Revolution', in *Inprecorr*, vol. v, no. 73, 8th October 1925, p. 1083; 'G' (Berlin), 'The Chinese Relief Work of the Workers' International Relief and the Shame of the Amsterdamers', in *Inprecorr*, vol. v, no. 74, 15th October 1925.
3. Harry Wicks, Telephone conversation with Al Richardson, 31st October 1966.
4. See above, p. 2.
5. A. Inkpin, Letter to Districts and Locals, 9th May 1925; *Communist Papers*, cmd. 2682, document no. 8.
6. Harry Wicks, Interview with Al Richardson, 11th March and 1st April 1978.
7. Sam Gordon in *James P. Cannon as We Knew Him*, New York, 1976, p. 56.
8. Cf. footnote 6, above.
9. Henry Sara (1886–1953).
10. Most of the material in this and the following paragraphs has been obtained in conversations over the years with Reg Groves, and from the following

sources: David Chalkley, Interview with Al Richardson, 14th November 1978; 'Henry Sara Stands in Tottenham: Long Record of Anti-War Agitation: For Industrial Unionism', in *Workers Life*, no. 117, April 1929, p. 3; Guy Aldred, *A Call to Manhood: Letters to the Editor*, Glasgow, 1940, pp. 10-11; A.J.P. Taylor, *A Personal History*, London, 1983, p. 64 (Sara in Germany) and p. 76 (Sara in Russia). This last source, Taylor's autobiography, is highly subjective, and should be checked with all the others, particularly Alex Murie, Interview with Sam Bornstein, 17th August 1984: 'Sara was a big man, both physically and mentally.'

11. 'The Communist Figures', in *Workers Life*, no. 124, 7th June 1929, p. 4.

12. *Daily Worker*, 1st and 3rd August 1931.

13. *Workers Weekly*, 2nd October 1925, p. 3.

14. *Workers Life*, no. 52, 20th January 1928.

15. *Workers Life*, no. 56, 17th February 1928.

16. 'Further Jottings on R.W. Postgate', in *The Communist*, vol. iii, no. 5, May 1928, pp. 290-6.

17. 'Organised Capitalism' — an exchange between Henry Sara and H.P. Rathbone in *The Communist Review*, vol. ii, no. 9, September 1930, pp. 373-9 (a polemical exchange that took place in the *Daily Worker* between 28th March and 28th April 1930).

18. Sara was one of the two men present at the meeting at which the Bow Branch of the Workers' Socialist Federation considered the resolution it was going to send to the W.S.F. annual conference on 2nd April 1919, one of them being 'opposition to conscription and to all militarism'. As men are not recorded as being present at any other of the Bow Branch's meetings, this was obviously an unusual event — Minute Book for the Bow Branch of the W.S.F., file no. 20, Pankhurst Archive, Amsterdam.

19. R. Groves, *The Balham Group*, London, 1974, p. 20.

20. Sara naturally informed him of it — Sheila Leslie (Lahr), Conversation with Al Richardson and Sam Bornstein, 1978.

21. *The Communist Review*, vol. vi, no. 11, March 1926, pp. 492 and 495; vol. vi, no. 12, April 1926, p. 538.

22. 'An Anarchist with a Temper', in the *Sunday Worker*, 14th October 1928.

23. Election Address: 'Parliamentary Election, Thursday, 30th May 1929, South Tottenham Division. Henry Sara, The Communist Candidate'.

24. *Daily Worker*, 9th April 1930 (on E.E. Hunter, a former S.L.P. member who had just got a job as parliamentary correspondent of the *Daily Herald*).

25. Stewart Purkis (1885–1969).

26. E.S. Williams (?–1963).

27. Reg Groves (1908-).

28. W. Gallacher, 'We Have no Room for Trotskyists', in the *Daily Worker*, 23rd August 1932.

29. 'Obstacles to Unity', Letter from Stewart Purkis, James Desormeaux and E.S. Williams, in the *Sunday Worker*, no. 165, 6th May 1928, p. 10.

30. Groves, *The Balham Group*, p. 12.

31. S. Purkis, 'A Sidelight on Mondism', in *Labour Monthly*, vol. xi, no. 4, April 1929, pp. 229-232.

32. 'Railway Clerks in Revolt', in the *Daily Worker*, 25th June 1930.

33. S. Purkis, 'Will Rail Clerks Discuss Issues that Matter?', in the *Daily Worker*, 30th May 1932.

34. S. Purkis, 'Temporary Crisis or Steady Decline of the Railways', in *Labour Monthly*, vol. x, no. 11, November 1928, pp. 653-662; 'Railworkers and the Coming Struggle', vol. xi, no. 2, February 1929, pp. 85-9; 'A Sidelight on Mondism', vol. xi, no. 4, April 1929, pp. 229-232; 'Railworkers and Revolutionary Struggle', vol. xi, no. 10, October 1929, pp. 592-602; 'Danger Ahead', vol. xii, no. 11, November 1930,

pp. 663-669.

35. Steve Dowdall and Daisy Groves, Interview with Al Richardson, summer 1982; cf. Reg Groves, 'Sixty Years of Struggle', in *Socialist Review*, March 1983. Dowdall died in December 1982, aged 86.

36. Groves, *The Balham Group*, p. 34.

37. Ibid., p. 19.

38. *Workers Life*, no. 67, 4th May 1928, p. 3.

39. Groves, *The Balham Group*, p. 20.

40. Reg Groves, *Four Years of Labour Opposition: A Communist Examination of the Labour Party's Record in the House of Commons from 1925 to 1929*, C.P.G.B. pamphlet, 1929.

41. *Daily Worker*, 21st March 1930.

42. R. Groves, Letter to the Secretariat, C.P.G.B., 26th February 1930; *Daily Worker*, Editorial Board, Letter to R. Groves, 24th March 1930; R. Groves, Letter of 14th May 1930, etc.; cf. Groves, *The Balham Group*, p. 29 and references.

43. Groves, *The Balham Group*, pp. 31-33; cf. *Daily Worker*, 9th June 1930.

44. Riazonov, Letter to Reg Groves, 30th March 1930. In the following year, Stalin implicated Riazonov in the so-called 'Menshevik Trial'. He was dismissed from the Institute, and exiled to Saratov. Trotsky places the year of his death as 1933; others set it in 1935 and 1938. Cf. *Writings of Leon Trotsky, 1932*, New York, 1973, n. 311, p. 403.

45. Cf. Bornstein and Richardson, *Two Steps Back*, pp. 1-2.

46. S. Purkis, 'Railworkers and Revolutionary Struggle', in *Labour Monthly*, vol. xi, no. 10, October 1929, p. 1598 (his emphasis).

47. R. Groves, 'Mondism and Our Industrial Policy', in *The Communist Review*, vol. i, no. 7, July 1929, p. 413.

48. R. Groves, 'Our Party and the New Period', in *The Communist Review*, vol. i, no. 9, November 1929, pp. 604-609 (his emphasis).

49. 'London Communists in Conference: Keen Debates on the New Line and Its Application', in *Workers Life*, no. 116, 12th April 1929, p. 4.

50. R. Palme Dutt, Letter to Reg Groves, 27th November 1929; cf. R. Groves, *The Balham Group*, p. 23 and reference.

51. *Workers Life*, no. 150, 6th December 1929, p. 6.

52. R. Groves, 'A Year of Struggles in Britain', in the *Daily Worker*, 23rd January 1930.

53. 'Party Life', in *The Communist Review*, vol. iii, no. 7, July 1931, pp. 292-296.

54. See p. 20 above, and note 99, p. 44.

55. Groves, *The Balham Group*, pp. 13-14.

56. See p. 24 above, and note 122 (March 1928).

57. Groves, *The Balham Group*, p. 16.

58. Steve Dowdall and Daisy Groves, Interview with Al Richardson, summer 1982.

59. Reg Groves, Conversation with Al Richardson, 23rd September 1978; *Four Years of Labour Opposition*, especially p. 15, 'Our Attitude to the Labour Party'.

60. Reg Groves, Letter to the Secretariat of the C.P.G.B., 26th February 1930.

61. Editorial Board of the *Daily Worker*, Letter to Reg Groves, 24th March 1930.

62. Reg Groves, Correspondence with the *Daily Worker* Editorial Board.

63. Groves, *The Balham Group*, p. 31, and n. 29.

64. *Outline*, nos. 3 and 6: 'For Marxist-Leninist District School Material' and 'The Tactics of the Proletariat After Conquest of Power' (undated, but references in no. 3 to Ramsay MacDonald's membership of the Labour Party show that they predate the formation of the National Government in 1931).

65. *Outline*, no. 6, pp. 17-18.

66. 'T.U. Right Wing Condemned', in the *Daily Worker*, 5th July 1930.

67. 'Workers Notebook', *Daily Worker*, 22nd April 1931.

68. W. Gallacher, 'An Intimate Appreciation of Lenin', in *Labour Monthly*, vol. xii, no. 8, August 1930, p. 508.

69. E. Browder, 'Trotsky Admires Trotsky', in the *Daily Worker*, 27th January 1930.

70. M.N. Pokrovsky, 'About a Certain "Experiment" in Autobiography', in *Labour Monthly*, vol. xii, no. 9, September 1930, p. 572.

71. W. Joss, 'The Expulsion of J.T. Murphy and Its Lessons', in *The Communist Review*, vol. iv, no. 6, June 1932, p. 298.

72. R. Palme Dutt, 'Notes of the Month', in *Labour Monthly*, vol. xvi, no. 3, March 1932, p. 141 (on the Declaration of the Four).

73. 'Epoch Making Letter of Stalin Calls to Battle in Defence of Leninism', in the *Daily Worker*, 5th January 1932 (reprinted from *The Communist*).

74. T.A. Jackson, 'Rosa Luxemburg and Her Mistakes', in the *Daily Worker*, 12th February 1932.

75. Ibid., editorial comment.

76. T.A. Jackson, 'Lenin and Rosa Luxemburg', in the *Daily Worker*, 4th May 1932 (and editorial comment).

77. Cf. the refusal of the Left Book Club to publish Paul Froelich's classic biography of her (until after Gollancz had broken with the Communists over the Molotov/Ribbentrop Pact), and the acid review by 'P.F.' in *Labour Monthly*, vol. xxii, no. 7, July 1940.

78. *Daily Worker*, 6th January 1937.

79. 'Rosa Luxemburg and Her Mistakes', in the *Daily Worker*, 12th February 1932; cf. Trotsky, 'Hands Off Rosa Luxemburg', 28th June 1932, in *Writings of Leon Trotsky, 1932*, pp. 131-142.

80. *Daily Worker*, 5th January 1932.

81. e.g. Editorial, 'Credits for Russia Means Less Unemployment', in the *Sunday Worker*, no. 33, 25th October 1925, p. 4.

82. A. Swabeck, 'MacDonald and Rationalisation', in the American *Militant*, vol. iv, no. 15, 18th July 1931; cf. Trotsky, 'World Unemployment and the Soviet Five-Year Plan', 21st August 1930, in *Writings of Leon Trotsky, 1930*, New York, 1975, pp. 353-362.

83. Statement by H. Pollitt on behalf of the Political Bureau, *Daily Worker*, 10th May 1932, and *Communist Review*, vol. iv, no. 6, June 1932, p. 303.

84. e.g. May 13th, 14th, 18th, 20th — practically every issue up to 2nd June.

85. 'Murphy Expelled from the C.P.' (Pollitt's statement, see note 83 above).

86. J. Shields, 'J.T. Murphy's Desertion to the Class Enemy', in *Communist International*, vol. ix, no. 13, 15th July 1932, p. 430 (quoting from the *Sozialistische Arbeiterzeitung*).

87. Cf. note 1 above, and 'Anglicus', 'A Letter from England', in the American *Militant*, 11th June 1932.

88. Cf. W. Rust, 'Murphy — The Man Who Would Not Be Put Down — Clumsy Stunt on Soviet Credits to Cover Cowardly Desertion', in the *Daily Worker*, 1st June 1932.

89. L. Trotsky, Letter to Reg Groves, 27th May 1932, in *The Early Years of the British Left Opposition*, London, 1979, p. 2; cf. *Writings of Leon Trotsky: Supplement, 1929-1933*, New York, 1979.

90. Bornstein and Richardson, *Two Steps Back*, pp. 27-8, 46. His chief theoretical work, *Preparing for Power* (London, 1934; 2nd edition, London, 1972), explains how the original break between the Labour and Communist Parties was an unfortunate one. He was thus already anticipating the 'Popular Front' turn of the Communist Party for which he was to become the keenest advocate inside the Labour Party.

91. J.T. Murphy, *New Horizons*, London, 1941, pp. 142, 250, 262-4, etc.

92. Above, p. 67.

93. S. Purkis, 'Danger Ahead', in *Labour Monthly*, vol. xii, no. 11, November 1930, pp. 668-9.

94. Cf. Groves, *The Balham Group*, pp. 31, 43, 51, etc.; and 'Anglicus', 'England at the Crossroads', in *The Militant*, vol. iv, no. 35, 12th December 1931.

95. 'Black Diamond', 'Stalinist Decay in England', in *The Militant*, vol. iv, no. 6, 15th March 1931.

96. P.B., 'The Theoreticians of "Left Sectarianism and Spontaneity" ', in *The Communist Review*, vol. iii, no. 1, January 1931, p. 11.

97. 'A British Worker', 'Party and C.I. in England', in *The Militant*, vol. v, no. 11, 12th March 1932.

98. 'Anglicus', 'Growing Revolt Against National Government Marks British Scene' (Letter dated October 3rd), in *The Militant*, vol. iv, no. 28, 24th October 1931.

99. David Davis, in 'What the London "Worker" Won't Print', in *The Militant*, vol. iv, no. 5, 1st March 1931.

100. Above, pp. 70-1.

101. R. Protz, 'Harry Wicks', in *Socialist Worker*, 6th January 1973.

102. Harry Wicks, Interview with Al Richardson, 11th March and 1st April 1978. Sokolnikov was recalled to the U.S.S.R. in autumn 1932. He died in a labour camp in 1939.

103. 'Refusal to Go Back to Russia: Case of Soviet Employees in London', in the *Daily Worker*, 10th April 1930.

104. Conversation with Reg Groves, 29th May 1981.

105. Groves, *The Balham Group*, p. 45.

106. Arne Swabeck, Letter to Reg Groves, 8th August 1931. Thanking Groves for a letter he had received the day before, he goes on to say: 'we are glad to notice your statement that you are a member of the British Party but wholeheartedly in agreement with the viewpoint of the Opposition . . .'

107. Albert Glotzer, Letter to Reg Groves, 27th October 1931. 'P.S. Comrade Trotsky asks me to transmit the following to you: That he has your letter sent about two months ago . . .' Groves' own letters back have not survived, so far as we are aware.

108. Albert Glotzer visited Kadiköy for a few weeks at the end of 1931 to help maintain the contact between Trotsky and the American Trotskyists. In 1940, after playing a prominent part in the international movement, he split from it along with Max Shachtman to form the Workers' Party.

109. Max Shachtman (1903–1972) — see last note. In later years he became anti-Communist.

110. George Weston's name is inexplicably omitted from the thumb-nail sketch in Groves' *The Balham Group*, p. 49. We owe this information to Harry Wicks, Interview given to Al Richardson, 11th March and 1st April 1978.

111. L. Trotsky, 'The British Elections and the Communists', 10th November 1931 (Letter to Reg Groves), in *Writings of Leon Trotsky, 1930-1*, New York, 1973, p. 348 — printed in an abbreviated form in the American *Militant*, 5th December 1931.

112. Presumably Dr. Worrall: cf. above, p. 58 and below, p. 115. A letter dated 9th February 1932 from Pierre Frank representing the *Ligue Communiste* (Opposition) welcomed the group as a section of the Left Opposition.

113. 'S' (Shachtman), 'Opposition in England: Party Members Form Nucleus to Fight for Leninism', in *The Militant*, vol. v, no. 2, 9th January 1932.

114. Cf. Groves, *The Balham Group*, p. 49; Harry Wicks, 'British Trotskyism in the Thirties', in *International*, vol. i, no. 4, p. 29.

115. 'Workers Notebook', 'A Dead Party', in the *Daily Worker*, 22nd December 1931.

116. Reg Groves, 'Class Leadership in the Chartist Movement', in *Labour Monthly*, vol. xi, no. 4, p. 244.

117. Henry Sara, 'Pollitt and the Party Line', in *The Call*, no. 1, November 1939, p. 4.

118. Cf. Bornstein and Richardson, *Two Steps Back*, p. 1.

119. Groves, *The Balham Group*, p. 54.

120. 'The Vital Importance of Our Work in the Trades Unions', Resolution received from the Balham Group of the London S.W. Local', in the *Daily Worker*, 14th April 1932, p. 6; cf. Groves, *The Balham Group*, p. 54.

121. 'The Secretariat Writes', in the *Daily Worker*, 14th April 1932, p. 6.

122. 'The Burning Question of Communist Work in the Trades Unions: Balham Group's Sectarian Fight Against Correct Party Line', in the *Daily Worker*, 27th May 1932.

123. Ibid.

124. Ibid.

125. J. Shields, 'Discussion Page', in the *Daily Worker*, 30th September 1938.

126. 'Union Branches Can Be Won For Class Fight', in the *Daily Worker*, 7th June 1932.

127. 'Balham Group Working in the Trade Unions: Resolution Should Be Discussed Again', in the *Daily Worker*, 19th June 1932.

128. M. Shachtman, Letter to Reg Groves, 14th August 1932.

129. H. Pollitt, 'The Revolutionary Tide in Germany: Capitalism Resorts to Open Fascism', in the *Daily Worker*, 8th April 1930.

130. R. Palme Dutt, in the *Daily Worker*, 26th May 1932.

131. 'Statement from Members of the Committee of the British Group of the Left Opposition', 9th April 1933, p. 1.

132. Groves, *The Balham Group*, pp. 10-11, gives the date as May, and that is the date on most of the surviving copies. But the Maitland/Sara/Wicks Collection in the Modern Records Centre at Warwick University has another copy, also bearing the number '1' and containing the same material, but dated March. It may be that this was a trial run, produced for group discussion before it was circulated to outsiders.

133. H. Wicks, Interview with Al Richardson, 11th March and 1st April 1978.

134. Arne Swabeck, Letter to Reg Groves (no date).

135. Groves, *The Balham Group*, pp. 64-5. Cf. the Advertisement in the *Daily Worker*, 16th July 1932 (for the following Sunday).

136. Groves, *The Balham Group*, p. 67 (full text).

137. Ibid. Campbell was not far off the mark: Trotsky had described the conference as 'a booster campaign for the worst in the gallery of reformist traitors' — L.D. Trotsky, 'The Coming Congress Against War', 13th June 1932, in *Writings of Leon Trotsky, 1932*, p. 115. The six Trotskyists at the conference alone voted against Barbusse's thesis — op. cit., note 201, pp. 388-9.

138. Groves, *The Balham Group*, p. 65.

139. S. Purkis, 'An Open Letter to Harry Pollitt', 27th July 1932, in Groves, *The Balham Group*, pp. 86-90.

140. Max Shachtman, Letter to Reg Groves, 14th August 1932.

141. L.D. Trotsky, 'After the British Expulsions', in *Writings of Leon Trotsky: Supplement, 1929-1933*, p. 149 (6th September 1932). Cf. J. Valtin, *Out of the Night*, New York, 1941, p. 321; and on the quality of the leadership as a whole, from a Comintern official, H.M. Wicks, *Eclipse of October*, Chicago, 1957, p. 135.

142. R. Groves, Letter to the C.C. of the C.P.G.B., 9th August 1932. Cf. Groves, *The Balham Group*, p. 66.

143. Groves, ibid., pp. 67-9.

144. Kay Beauchamp, Letter to *Tribune*, 21st August 1981. Her memory, or her politics, appear to play her false here, as she appears to think that the Balham Group

was agitating against an anti-fascist alliance of Britain, France and the U.S.S.R. — a turn in Russian policy that was still three years away.

145. R.W. Robson, Letter to Groves, 17th August 1932.

146. Circular of the London District Party Committee 'To All Members of the Balham Group', 17th August 1932.

147. Steve Dowdall (and Daisy Groves), Interview with Al Richardson, summer 1982.

148. Hugo Dewar, Interview with Al Richardson, 7th April 1978.

149. Listed in Groves, *The Balham Group*, p. 94.

150. 'Resolution on the Standpoint and Activities of the Balham Group' (no date).

151. 'To Our Comrades in the Communist Party from the "Liquidated" Balham Group', in Groves, *The Balham Group*, pp. 81-5.

152. W. Gallacher, 'We Have No Room for Trotskyists', in the *Daily Worker*, 23rd August 1932.

153. 'Bureaucratic Discipline or Communist Policy', in *The Communist*, no. 2, September 1932, p. 2.

154. 'Zinoviev and Kamenev Expelled', in the *Daily Worker*, 12th October 1932.

155. 'To the Delegates of the Party Congress, Battersea, November 1932, From the British Group of the Left Opposition of the C.I.', 7th November 1932, in Groves, *The Balham Group*, pp. 95-9.

156. 'An Appeal to Congress Delegates from the Balham Group', in Groves, ibid., pp. 91-4.

157. 'The Battersea Congress', in *The Communist*, no. 3, January 1933, pp. 1-2.

158. 'Expulsions from the C.P. of the Soviet Union — Resolution Passed by the Battersea Congress', in the *Daily Worker*, 17th November 1932; *The Revolutionary Way Out*, C.P.G.B., 1932, p. 26.

159. H. Pollitt, *The Road to Victory* (opening and closing speeches at the 12th Congress of the C.P.G.B., Latchmere Baths, Battersea, November 1932), pp. 55-6; cf. the *Daily Worker*, 14th November 1932 (where the last remark becomes 'held up for admiration' by the Economic League) and Groves, *The Balham Group*, p. 72.

160. Pollitt, *The Road to Victory*, p 92.

161. Steve Dowdall and Daisy Groves, Interview with Al Richardson, summer 1982.

Chapter Four

The Communist League, British Section of the International Left Opposition, 1932–34

The change in the circumstances of the Balham Group had been very sudden — the Communist Party leadership had seen to that — and whilst not all the Trotskyists had been removed, those that remained had not been able to assist the Balham comrades without incurring the risk of instant expulsion themselves. But the immediate effect had been to transfer the core group, consisting not only of the most experienced comrades, but also of those who functioned together as a unit, outside the party, leaving the younger and less well-established to carry on without their immediate guidance. Even the most experienced comrades had nothing in their past to prepare them for the task of posing as a 'Left Opposition' aiming to democratise and educate in Marxism a party which had just expelled them, whilst functioning as an outside body in an atmosphere of bitter sectarianism. For the Communist Party itself was no exception to the rule that the smaller a group becomes, the greater is its hostility towards everybody else.

The general orientation nonetheless remained towards the Communist Party, as this was still the strategic line of the International movement. 'We are a faction of the Party,' wrote Trotsky to Groves, 'but we are a very peculiar faction, which has been expelled from the Party and is acting outside of the Party.'[1] Accordingly, the next issue of *The Communist* bore the following policy statement:

> The expelled party members, who are members of the Left Opposition, will strive to retain their membership of the Party. We joined the C.P. because it is the Party of revolution. We are not joining any other party. We — expelled and unexpelled Party members — shall work as a Party faction. We shall not only endeavour to win Party members, but also our fellow

> workers to Leninist policy, and then recruit them to the Party to fight for that policy[2]

But this bald statement could not resolve the large number of problems that arose from it, such as whether they should confine their attentions wholly or largely to the C.P. (which refused to speak to them), or broaden their approach to take in those sympathetic in the I.L.P. branches locally; whether they should accept that the minute sect left behind after the antics of the 'Third Period' amounted to a real Communist Party in any case; if so, whether they could claim to be of it whilst outside, or for it whilst making the most trenchant criticisms: in a nutshell, how does a body function as a faction of another one, when it is to all intents and purposes completely separate?

Moreover, as a section of the International Left Opposition, they now assumed the responsibility of becoming its public face in this country, of assimilating its traditions, of drawing upon its collective experience, and of themselves contributing to its development. Internationalism was no longer just a question of reprinting the movement's statements in *The Communist*, but one of taking an active part in the formation of the policy itself and interpreting it in the conditions appropriate to this country. The need was now urgent to extend international links; and on its part the International movement required a firmer, more centralised and more effective apparatus, amid the rapidly worsening European situation in which Hitler's star was rising, to prevent its sections from degenerating into a string of disparate sects in an atmosphere of heightened national tension.

An opportunity arose for this when the Social Democratic Students of Denmark invited Trotsky from Turkey to address them on the Fifteenth Anniversary of the October Revolution. It was a good moment to bring together Trotsky, his secretarial staff, and as many representatives of the European sections as possible, to discuss the international situation, particularly in Germany, and to lay some of the groundwork for the pre-Conference of the Opposition that was shortly to meet in Paris.

Trotsky arrived on 23rd November, and two days later the British delegate, Harry Wicks, landed at Esbjerg *en route* to Copenhagen. Conducted to the Dalgas Boulevard on the outskirts of the city, he was admitted into the villa of the 'danseuse', where Trotsky and thirty others began to make reports, compare notes, and draw up plans for intervention. Wicks went up to give his report:

> I went into this box room and Trotsky, in his Russian way, greets you warmly, embraces you, as if you are an old soldier in

> the movement instead of a youth. We got talking about the English situation, and what work we were doing . . . I can remember my discussion with Trotsky about working in the Party, which was our main orientation at that time, that all of our propaganda and our talks were addressed to the Party members. The Party members were very thin on the ground, and those who were in South West London were unemployed — long-term unemployed, that is. So we discussed, and I can remember his advice, that you chose your time, your own ground. He wasn't critical on our orientation to the C.P., and the way we were not seeking 'demonstrative expulsions', which we didn't take kindly to. So we had a discussion then on the English movement, the possibilities that existed in the trade union movement, and the need for work in the trade union field. But the overall influence of Trotsky at that time was [directed] to the Party, addressing oneself to the Party. Although we had got a line-up in the I.L.P., and we had got our contacts in the South West London Anti-War Front, yet the orientation, as I say, was overwhelmingly to the Party.[3]

Wicks next raised the question of attempting to use his contacts in the economic department of Russian Oil Products to make contact with the Russian Left Opposition, and of the understandable reticence of the staff as to his being a reliable channel of communication. Trotsky accordingly wrote out a pencilled letter to be sent through Wicks giving the Russians a means of making indirect contact with him via his son in Berlin.[4] Unfortunately, within weeks of Wicks' return to London this avenue was closed off by Hitler's accession to power in Germany.

Then they moved on to Wicks' experiences in Moscow, including his study of insurrectionary tactics at the Lenin School, whose thesis on the Irish Uprising of 1916 so interested Trotsky that Wicks later sent it on from London by the hand of George Weston.

Their discussions were interrupted on the 27th by Trotsky's engagement to speak to the Danish students, the famous 'Copenhagen Speech', during which Wicks shared the platform with Trotsky, Natalia, and Raymond Molinier. The English text was already in Wicks' hands before the lecture, and he brought it back for the I.L.P. to publish in Britain.

When they were able to resume discussion, attention now switched to the concrete method by which they could breach the wall of silence erected against them by the British Communist Party leadership:

> The important thing was that from Trotsky one had the idea of

> encouraging the small beginning, the necessity for a paper, and of the necessity to use 'Red Aid' for raising the question of persecuted Oppositionists — persecuted in Russia, persecuted in India (Roy in India was incarcerated), and 1932 was the year that Ch'en Tu-Hsiu in China was jailed. So Trotsky's line was ... 'We were in the Party, we were orientated towards the Communist Party. We try to embarrass the Stalinists by these class war prisoners, whom the Stalinists didn't recognise.[5]

On the very difficult point then troubling the British section, as to whether to confine their attention to the Communist Party, or to start responding to the positive overtures coming to them from outside (especially the I.L.P.), Trotsky was most illuminating:

> In the British Section the question under discussion is whether one ought to limit oneself to internal work within the Communist Party or create independent ties with workers outside the party. This question, which at various times has arisen before all the sections, is not one of principle. The attempt to derive the scope and character of our activity from the concept of 'faction' would be purely doctrinaire. The transition from 'propaganda', i.e. the education of cadres, has always provoked difficulties and differences of opinion within young revolutionary organisations, without their being faced by the dilemma 'faction or party?'. The decision of the question must depend upon the real forces and situation. But since all our sections, including the youngest, the British, have taken over very valuable cadres from the Party, we must endeavour as quickly as possible to find our own points of support in the workers' organisations, naturally without giving up even for a minute the struggle for the unification of the Communist ranks.
>
> The inclination of certain comrades (as in France) to interpret the rôle of the faction in such a sense that the Opposition must not take a single step outside of Party limits is completely false. Our actual relation to the Comintern finds its expression not in abstaining from independent action, but in the content and direction of such action. It would be ridiculous to behave as if we belonged, in fact, to the official organisation of the Comintern. We must carry out such policies as will open the gates of the Comintern to us. For this, we must become stronger, which cannot be achieved if we tie our hands as against the Stalinist bureaucracy by artificial and false discipline. We must turn to the workers where they are, we must go to the youth, teach them the ABC of Communism,

> build cells in factories and trade unions. But this work must be carried out in such a manner that ordinary Communists can see that for us it is a question not of building a new party, but of reviving the Communist International.[6]

The question posed itself more sharply in Britain than anywhere else, for the Communist Party was nearly at the point of self-extinction. As Trotsky himself noted, their numbers had dropped 'in ten months from fifteen thousand to three thousand dues-paying members', and a narrow concentration on the rump that remained could only be a dead-end policy:

> We all agree that to counterpose the adventuristic slogan of a second party to the existing party, as the Stalinists accuse us, would mean to block our way to the Communist workers themselves. But to blur our difference with Centrism in the name of facilitating 'unity' would mean not only to commit political suicide, but also to cover up, strengthen, and nourish all the negative features of bureaucratic centrism, and by that fact alone help the reactionary currents within it against the revolutionary tendencies.[7]

The main question of the day was clearly the German crisis, and the divisive policy of the Comintern in face of Hitler's rise to power. Some of the comrades, for example Dr. Worrall, had first-hand experience:

> It was very menacing. I caught it, even in words. The attitude of the German Communists! First of all, 'Why stage a civil war? Let Hitler take power! He will collapse! And then we'll march in.' This literally was the attitude, and even in those days I knew enough politics to know it was crazy. I remember hearing a big, burly, German Communist worker describing how he saw a fascist crowd of many thousands, and folding his arms across his chest he was laughing, joking. They just didn't believe what was in front of their eyes . . . I remember a march of workers. I don't know who organised it because I just came across it by chance. It was a long procession, and very quiet, and I was following it, certainly at the side. There were open trucks with police, back to back, with guns, not enclosed at all, open vans. I had never seen them before, but I will never forget the expressions on the faces of the police. They were like caricatures of Pincher dogs, just waiting to leap at the throat of someone. You couldn't mistake the look in their eyes — the drawn mouth, the pale faces, killers, just waiting to be let loose! That was memorable, never to be forgotten![8]

As Papen, and then Schleicher lost power, and by stages the political spectrum moved further to the right, the bragging tone of the German Communist Party increased, and its hostility towards the Social Democracy remained unabated. Frantically, the Balham comrades attempted to alert the movement here to the dangers involved, and to put pressure upon the Communist Party to change course before it was too late. Issue after issue of their duplicated magazine was taken up with the German affair, often to the exclusion of everything else.[9] A special leaflet directed to Communist workers warned that:

> We are faced with a disaster as great as that of 1914. But it can be averted. There is still time: the revolution can and must beat fascism. The forces of a united working class in Germany will be irresistible, would defeat Hitler, and open a new epoch in History. The Stalinist leadership is too deeply compromised to be able to turn quickly and decisively.
>
> Call local and district party conferences to discuss the policy followed in Germany, and to plan a serious solidarity campaign in this country. Make the Communist International break its craven silence with which it has met the new crisis. Return to the policy of Lenin. For the United Front of the Communist Party and the Social Democratic Party against Fascism![10]

But the British Communists would accept no criticism. As Wicks explains, until Hitler assumed power they had 'looked at the German Communist Party in the same way as they looked to Russia as an example. They looked to Germany as the land where there was going to be the classical proletarian revolution. The English Communists, all through the twenties, were fed with the news of the powerful "Red Fighters' League", and the powerful German Communist Party with its millions of votes. And then, when the question of Hitler [arose], and the electoral graph started rising in mid '32, came the sensational victories of the National Socialists.'[11]

As the British Communists turned a deaf ear to their appeals, they went out into the broader movement. 'At the time of 1932, before Hitler came to power,' recalls Dewar, 'I was on the streets every night of the week, putting across the view that the advent of the Nazis to power inevitably meant war unless the entire working-class movement took a united stand in a struggle for Socialism.'[12] The one body open to their influence was the South-West London Anti-War Committee, the only such still active, according to the grudging tribute of R.W. Robson.[13] Again they appealed to the wider movement in a leaflet advertising their frequent meetings on Clapham Common:

> Demand that the Labour and Socialist International and the Communist International meet together for united working-class action. Urge that Social Democrats and Communists join forces in Germany to defeat Hitler. The shameful treachery of 1914 must not be repeated! Deeds not words! Demand proletarian unity against Fascism and War.[14]

Limited though its appeal inevitably was, the Communists would not even allow this small voice to challenge the wretchedness of their capitulation. They sent along as many delegates as they could to cram the committee and remove the Trotskyists from it. At a joint I.L.P./C.P. meeting on 22nd February they poured scorn upon the idea that 'we approach Arthur Henderson and Herbert Morrison for a United Front',[15] and at the following monthly delegate meeting of the S.A.W.C. on the 27th ridiculed the suggestion of a United Front with 'the vile Social Democrats'.[16] Finally, in their inimitable style, they crammed the committee, reversed its line, and secured the removal of the Trotskyists — Groves himself, Sid Kemp of the I.L.P., Steve Dowdall of the A.U.B.T.W. and Isabel Mussey of the Balham Women's Guild.[17] But before a fortnight was out the new line had arrived from Moscow, and the Communist Party was writing to the Labour Party, I.L.P., T.U.C. and Co-op with the suggestion of joint activity.[18]

But it was a bit late by then. As one of the Opposition's leaflets stated so pointedly, 'Now that Hitler is in power, has made serious attacks upon the German working class, has control over the state forces, the Comintern begins to shuffle over from the fatal policy of the "Red United Front", to a halfway house between that policy and the line of Lenin.' 'To gloss over this failure,' they explained, 'and steal over to a new policy (or an alleged new policy) is the action of bureaucrats, not revolutionary leaders.'[19]

The message of the Opposition was totally lost on the C.P. Andrew Rothstein continued to hold that the German workers were not 'demoralised', but 'fighting the Fascists in more and more organised fashion, under the leadership of the Communist Party, whose rapid reorganisation on an illegal basis has shown the vigorous life and will to resist which exists in the heart of the working class', all the more combative because it was, by Hitler's good offices, 'freed more and more from the subtle Social-Democratic poison which paralysed its energies and broke its ranks in January 1933.'[20] And whilst the Comintern was instructing its sections to offer a 'United Front' to the Second International organisations on the basis of a suspension of all criticism, Gallacher could still say that

Trotsky's policy was 'the voluntary surrender of the revolutionary struggle in order to maintain bourgeois democracy and actually represents the grossest betrayal of the revolutionary movement.' For, he added, 'if the party had made a voluntary surrender of the revolutionary struggle and united with Social-Democracy "to save bourgeois democracy", the proletarian movement would have been destroyed.'[21]

But every defeat of the working class produces a crisis, not only for the organisations directly responsible for defeat, but also for the revolutionaries who try to avoid it. Gloom, despondency and disorientation spread equally among the Trotskyists, especially those who had struggled so manfully. A resolution protesting about the 'inactivity of the leading Committee of the British Section' alleged that it had failed to 'respond to the critical developments in Germany', demanded the election of a new committee of seven, and called for a 'campaign for a printed paper to be issued on May 1st'.[22]

It was as well that the pre-Conference of the International Left Opposition was about to meet in Paris, which it duly did between 4th and 8th February 1933. This time Groves travelled as delegate, rather reluctantly, 'and sat through complex, heavily-jargonised discussions in French and German, with someone whispering occasional explanations in English'.[23] The main document still defined the International Left Opposition as 'a faction of the Comintern', and its separate national sections as 'factions of the national Communist parties',[24] but the truth was that the voting of Hitler's emergency powers, and the subsequent collapse of the workers' organisations without a fight, had already altered the whole picture as regards the greatest of the Comintern's sections outside Russia. In this sense the pre-Conference, deliberating on the basis of documents circulated long before, was already behind the times.

A month later Trotsky drew out the conclusions of the German débâcle for the sections of the international left:

> But it would be criminal to tie oneself to a corpse. The K.P.D. today represents a corpse.
>
> The scorn of the vanguard of the German workers for the bureaucracy which has deceived them will be so great that the slogan of reform will seem false and ridiculous to them. They will be right. The hour has struck! The question of preparing for the creation of a new party must be posed openly . . .
>
> Here it is natural to ask how we act toward the other sections of the Comintern and the Third International as a whole. Do we break with them immediately? In my opinion, it would be incorrect to give a rigid answer — yes, we break with them. The

> collapse of the K.P.D. diminishes the chances of the regeneration of the Comintern. But on the other hand the catastrophe itself could provoke a healthy reaction in some of the sections. We must be ready to help this process.[25]

This was a most abrupt turn at short notice, invalidating almost immediately the main policy of the first International Opposition conference, though no one could deny that the speed of the German events, and the utter collapse of Europe's strongest Labour movement, merited a strategic reassessment. But Trotsky knew all too well that 'this sharp turn in our policy, provoked by the turn in the situation,' would give rise to difficulties within the Trotskyists' own ranks, and would not be 'absorbed all at once by all our comrades'.[26] 'In fact,' noted a Belgian comrade, 'the turn did arouse a stir especially among the members and sections who up until that time had been working strictly in a faction. There was confusion more or less everywhere and many comrades and sections were opposed to this radical political change.'[27]

The particular conditions of the British group meant that the new turn hit them with redoubled force. To begin with, several of its members had been recruited from Ridley's organisation, which had deliberately cast its net wider than the Communist Party and its periphery. They had left in agreement with the thesis that the C.P. was not dead, and that the correct policy was to work as a faction inside it. Then, when Wicks returned from Copenhagen, they had been told not to interpret this policy in too narrow an organisational sense, but to build up support at the same time in other areas of the Labour movement. Finally, they were now meant to write off completely the Comintern's second largest section, and to place a question-mark over the usefulness of the others.

Stuart Purkis was among the first to express unease. 'I want more German material, and considerable discussion,' he wrote, 'before I can support the proposed change of line.'[28] Dewar went further, believing that the new policy implied calling for another party in Britain as well, and demanded a reaffirmation of the policy laid down by Trotsky at Copenhagen. 'In spite of its profound errors and the criminal policy of its bureaucracy,' he claimed, 'the Communist Party remains the one revolutionary party differing fundamentally from all other parties. Because of this we reject any talk of creating a Second Party, considering that our task is to assist in the defeat of the present leadership of the Party, to bring the Party back to the teachings of Marx and Lenin, and make it the instrument for the emancipation of the working class.'[29] However, in addition to propaganda material directed at the party, he did believe that they should 'participate as an organised group, with its own policy and programme of action, in all phases of the class struggle.'[30]

The new turn only added to some deep-going problems that had been troubling the internal life and external functioning of the group for a considerable period. The enormous demands made on a group of some thirty members,[31] of being active in local work, of carrying out internal fractional activity, and of being the mouthpiece of the policy of the International movement during that six months of international crisis, would have produced rifts in even the most tightly-knit body. And the Communist League was far from that. Its members were drawn from ex-and present I.L.P.ers, ex- and present Communists, ex-members of Ridley's group, scattered all over London and active in a variety of organisations. The only functioning effective unit was the Balham Group itself, and it tended not to be closely integrated into the wider body, but worked more or less as a separate unit. The wider organisation, represented by the Executive Committee of the group, wanted to place all the weight of the group on the crisis in Germany, to focus on international issues, and to function essentially as the International Left Opposition's public face in this country. The Balham Group, on the other hand, wanted to concentrate on the day-to-day issues, and fight the struggle against the Communist Party's practice within the Labour movement at the level on which they encountered it locally. In effect, the Executive had taken second place, and the tone and public pronouncements of the organisation had been set by the Balham comrades — inevitably so, in the circumstances that had surrounded their expulsion.

Groves had less confidence in the guidance of the International movement than the rest of the executive, whom he believed were not interested in activity as such, but only in issuing documents and discussing them, and it was upon his proposal that the old committee had been accused of passivity at the time of the German crisis, a general meeting of the Group had been called, and the old committee had been replaced by a new committee amenable to his opinions.[32] On the other hand, Harry Wicks and George Weston (supported by Billy Williams and Stuart Purkis) wanted the main priority of the group to be the production of the documents of the International Left Opposition in this country. They pointed to the 'almost complete ignorance of the substance and history of the Trotskyist controversy'[33] in the British Communist Party and the prohibitive price of the American Trotskyist publications (due to the unfavourable relations between the pound and the dollar and the relative poverty of the unemployed in Britain). Secondly, they urged the full training of the group members in the theory and practice of the movement. They placed third the organisation of fraction work inside the Party. And finally came general propaganda outside.

They also had grave misgivings about Groves' conduct of the struggle of the Balham Group, and his policy of 'British Material, not Trotsky documents'. They disagreed fundamentally with his policy on the trade unions, and attacked the tone of his statements addressed to the C.P. during the struggle as 'bitterly anti-Party', expressing 'a desire to snatch any opportunity to attack the Party leadership [rather] than to think out and prepare material which would build up amongst the workers respect for the Opposition policy.'

Groves and Dewar saw this as a policy of passive propagandism; the Balham Group called a general meeting at short notice, removed the old committee, and replaced some of its personnel, whilst retaining Purkis on it. In this way they gained 'the hegemony of their viewpoint in the Committee'.[34]

The first effect of the change in leadership was the implementation of Trotsky's policy on the production of a paper of their own, *Red Flag*. A preliminary attempt had already been made to bring out such a production as an agitational paper by the Balham Group when it issued two duplicated runs of *Red Flag*, 'A Paper for South-West London Workers', in October 1932. But in April 1933 their duplicated theoretical magazine announced that 'we are determined to begin, next month, the publication of our first printed paper',[35] and on May Day a full printed issue of *Red Flag* appeared, almost wholly given over to international Trotskyist matter, including a letter from Germany and Trotsky's 'The Tragedy of the German Proletariat', following more or less the view of the old group executive. The introductory statement described its policy:

> We do not, at this stage, seek to form a new party or a new International. We are a group of revolutionaries who have been expelled from the Communist Party for advocating the policy and principles upon which the Communist International was founded. Our object is to win the Communists back to that policy, and such an object concerns all working-men and women since without a functioning, effective, Leninist International we cannot hope to overthrow capitalist rule.[36]

For the first time the Trotskyists had a proper public presence, and were able to reach out for more support. Dewar, who was a salesman, ran the business side, and his address was on the back. He recalls the first subscriptions coming from an official organisation in Moscow and from Patrick Gordon Walker in Oxford, through which they were able to make contact with Hilary Sumner-Boyd (Charles Sumner). But 'the bulk of the sales went in street corner meetings and through contacts. Most of the contacts we had lived in South London. We had some in Hackney. There wasn't a wild outbreak of enthusiasm right, left and centre . . . then eventually we got outlets in Glasgow and in Edinburgh, Liverpool and Manchester, but pretty small. It was a matter of pennies really, and sometimes difficult to get even then — you know, street corner meetings, trade unions, that sort of thing.'[37] 'I would say we seldom sold more than 2,000 copies,' Groves recalled. 'That is a lot to sell for a small group — except on demonstrations, when we exceeded that.'[38]

A letter arrived from Trotsky to congratulate them on their 'modest step forward', and to urge the continued thrust of their propaganda towards the Communist Party:

> We can say without the least exaggeration that the British Communist Party has become a political thoroughfare and retains its influence only in that section of the working class which has been forcibly driven to its side by the decomposition of both capitalism and reformism.

It was, in effect, an endorsement of the line of the old executive, for it also recommended a deep study of the past of the C.P.G.B. in their 'excellently hectographed' bulletin *The Communist*, as well as its use for a full debate of those questions at issue within the group.[39]

The group was now in a position to follow up another of Trotsky's suggestions, to raise the cases of the Trotskyist class-war prisoners as a way of breaking down the wall of silence imposed by the Communist Party leadership.

Foremost among these was the founder of the Chinese Communist Party, the veteran revolutionary Ch'en Tu-Hsiu, who had broken with the Stalinist policies that had caused the defeat of the Second (proletarian) Revolution of 1926–7, and had come over to the Trotskyists. Recruiting over half the Communist Party members in Shanghai, they had led important strikes there, and spread their support to other cities. But in a mopping-up operation to prepare for a drive against Mao's 'Kiangsi-Hunan Soviet', Chiang smashed the illegal city organisations, and on 15th October 1932 the police arrested Ch'en Tu-Hsiu, Peng Shu-Tse, and eight others. Press reports that they were to be transferred to a military court in the capital raised a storm of protest, including that of Sun Yat-Sen's widow, so in the end they were given a civilian trial in open court. Their heroic conduct did not prevent sentences of thirteen years being passed on them, later reduced to eight on an appeal to higher authorities; and they were released only when the jail was bombed by the Japanese in 1937.

The Chinese revolution was a cause dear to the hearts of the British Trotskyists. Henry Sara had visited China with Tom Mann whilst Ch'en Tu Hsiu was still Party Secretary, and Mann at least would find it difficult to refuse his support.[40] Harry Wicks had been in Moscow 'when seasoned revolutionaries in the Comintern Eastern apparatus were being grilled for non-acceptance of the fatal Stalin line in China', and 'Chiang Kai-Shek's butchery of countless Chinese comrades was then too fresh in the minds of these men for them to conform.'[41]

So *Red Flag* drew attention to the Nanking trial, pointing out that 'it is typical of the present leaders of the Communist Party of Great Britain and of the International Labour Defence that not one word of protest had been raised on behalf of our comrade', that 'the Communist press is silent when the worker arrested does not accept the present policy of Stalin.' It called upon the working-class organisations, and in particular International Labour Defence, to 'see that this question is taken up with a view to a national campaign for the release of Chen'.[42] No response was forthcoming, not even when they repeated their appeal in the following issue:

> The silence of the Stalinists, their refusal to protest against the imprisonment of our comrade, renders aid to the executioners and is a stab in the back for the Chinese revolutionary movement. The C.I. leaders by such an action stain the pages of the revolutionary movement with another infamous crime.[43]

The only way left now was to address themselves to Tom Mann direct. An 'open letter' reminded him of his attendance at the opening session of the Congress of the Chinese Communist Party presided over by Ch'en in 1927, and of Ch'en's record in the movement in general. They attributed the silence of the I.L.D. to 'fraction considerations' rooted in a fear of admitting that one whom they had falsely denounced as a 'counter-revolutionary' was now in the prison of a real one. 'You have never before failed a class war prisoner,' they reminded him: 'we are confident that you will not fail Chen Du Siu.'[44] Within a week came back Tom Mann's letter of support, describing Ch'en and his associates as 'a capable and courageous body of comrades', whom he had defended during their previous imprisonments and, as a duty, would do so still.[45] It was the first real breakthrough for the British Trotskyists. It enabled them to get the signatures of Maxton, Brockway, Alex Gossip, Jack Tanner, Dick Beech and many other Labour movement notables on an appeal for protests to the Chinese Embassy, copies of which went to the T.U.C. General Council and Harry Pollitt.[46]

That did not prevent the C.P. leaders from brazening out the whole episode, though their reaction showed that they had suffered considerable embarrassment:

> It may be worth while noting that Chiang Kai-Shek has said that he has nothing against the Communists, if they would follow Trotsky's line; it was the Stalin elements he was against.
>
> But, ignoring all this, a small group of ignoramuses in London who, anxious to get out of the party when the struggle commenced to get serious, and who seized on Trotskyism as a pretext, are now presenting themselves as authorities on China. The great and growing Chinese Communist Party, the splendid leaders of the Soviet government, the heroic leaders and fighters of the Red Army, all of whom support the C.I.: what do these know of China compared to the oracle of Balham?[47]

While he yet wrote, the army of Chiang was poised to annihilate the Soviet base, and the Chinese Red Army was about to lose four-fifths of its men on 'The Long March'; but a party that had evaded the obvious lessons of Germany was not likely to be shaken at all by any news from the Far East.

However, this protest was not without its results. A young Japanese, Eiichi Yamanishi, who was studying in Britain at the time, was attracted to the group by its defence of the Asian revolutionaries, and entered it using a pseudonym to protect his identity (the Japanese Army, having already seized Manchuria, was beginning its campaign of 'government by assassination' to take over the state from the civilian authorities). Groves recalls going out on to Clapham Common to help him with his English, and Worrall keenly remembers his political duels with an American in the Organisation.[48] When Yamanishi returned to Japan, later to become one of its foremost translators of English literature, he also translated Trotsky's works, and became the originator of the large and thriving Trotskyist movement in that country.[49]

With British Communists there was less success. The political atmosphere in Britain was saturated with 'Third Period' Stalinism, for Russia had just gone through the turmoil of the forced collectivisation and the First Five-Year Plan, and the crisis had produced a more pronounced intolerance that was displaying itself in new administrative measures against those in opposition. In J.R. Campbell's words, it was 'necessary therefore to take up the cudgels in a sharper fashion against counter-revolutionary Trotskyism',[50] which was otherwise described as 'a current of counter-revolution',[51] 'the advance-guard of the counter-revolutionary bourgeoisie in its struggle against Leninism',[52] and 'the plundered, the hyaena of the battlefields of a class struggle',[53] whose defenders in this country were 'poor, feeble-minded misfits'.[54] Trotsky himself was a 'venomous lackey of the bourgeoisie',[55] the 'commander of the advanced guard of counter-revolution',[56] whose journalistic work made him 'dependent on the income received from the anti-working class, bourgeois press of Europe and America'.[57] 'Well may the renegade Trotsky join with Krupp, Thyssen and Co., in a fervent "Heil Hitler",' concluded Willie Gallacher from a study of his writings on Germany.[58]

On the other hand, 'the confidence of the working class of the Soviet Union in their Party and its leader, Comrade Stalin,' according to Ralph Fox, 'has never stood as high as at the present time.'[59]

The publication of the first volume of Trotsky's magisterial *History of the Russian Revolution* in June 1932, followed by the other two volumes in January 1933, should have lifted the debate on to a higher level. Henry Sara, who lectured for the N.C.L.C., took the opportunity to raise some of the broader issues in the form of reviews. 'Those who at one time were hostile to Trotsky's point of view, after acquainting themselves with his position, have to admit that there is far more behind all the controversies than just a personal issue,' he wrote. He discussed 'the enormous amount of prejudice which has been accumulated against him', and noted that those responsible for his expulsion from the C.P.S.U. 'today have themselves been expelled from the Comintern'. He was able to rebut the charges that Trotsky had Caesarist ambitions to replace Lenin on his death, and that he had opposed the industrial development of Russia after it. 'Over and over again,' he affirmed, 'it was Leon Trotsky who put forward proposals which were opposed by his colleagues, who afterwards accepted the very proposals which they had previously turned down, giving Trotsky no credit for his farsightedness, but charging him with obstruction.'[60] The value of the book was clear: 'Trotsky, like Moses, has made history, and, like Marx, he can write it.'[61]

But whilst Trotsky was revealing the revolutionary implications of the Russian Revolution, the Communist Party writers were engaged in an extensive exercise in rewriting it to conform to the latest requirements of the Russian machine. In 1933 R. Palme Dutt published his study, *Lenin*, described in the Comintern press as 'welcome', 'particularly in England, where there is much misunderstanding and confusion deliberately created by the Trotskyists and the I.L.P. leaders.'[62] This was because, whereas Maxton's book on the same subject published a year earlier[63] mentions Trotsky on several occasions, and recommends some of his books in its bibliography, Dutt nowhere mentions Trotsky, Zinoviev or Kamenev, whilst referring to Plekhanov, Axelrod and Vera Zasulich, and quoting directly from Theodore Dan!

The contrast between Dutt's book and those of Maxton and

Trotsky was evidently to the disadvantage of the former, so Ralph Fox made another attempt. His presentation went so far as to tamper with the report of Lenin's speech to the Soviet Congress in 1917, to fit it in with Stalin's theory of 'Socialism in One Country';[64] he accused Trotsky of sacrificing the Finnish Revolution,[65] of shooting Bolsheviks in the Civil War to shift the blame for his defeats,[66] and even of being absent from the Eighth Party Congress when he was preventing the collapse of the Far Eastern Front against Admiral Kolchak![67] In sum, it was, as Wicks explained, 'the most outrageous of all the efforts to distort the history of Bolshevism by means of a biography of Lenin.'[68]

But in playing about with history in this way, Fox had at least to mention Trotsky, and this alone cast doubt upon the method used in Dutt's book, leading some party members to wonder whether Fox was influenced by 'Trotskyism'. 'The general charge of "Trotskyism",' wrote Dutt to Pollitt, 'does not seem to me to be proved. The author gives a rather long and, in my opinion, unnecessary amount of space and attention to Trotsky, mixing praise and blame, but clearly intending the blame to predominate; both praise and blame bear a too narrow personal character, and this may have the opposite effect on many readers to the author's intentions.'[69] On the other hand, Trotsky's book was 'a bulky, three-volume pamphlet against Leninism', presenting 'an apologia of his past — and his present',[70] in which Rothstein read a 'contempt for the rank and file of the proletariat'.[71] 'The Lordly Trotsky, as ever,' he explained, 'knows only leaders: all the rest and the party organisation as a whole may pass their resolutions if they please — they remain mere cyphers, "the dung of factional differences".'[72] 'Trotsky's own carefully selected quotations nowhere suggest the Soviets taking power,' he added, and 'he now denies that the dictatorship of the proletariat exists in the Soviet Union'.[73] Descending from generalisations to facts, he explained how 'Trotsky exaggerates the wavering of many party leaders (including Stalin) during the first two or three months after their return from Siberian exile.'[74] Nonetheless, the barrage of hostile criticism appears to have had some effect, particularly on the C.P. membership, as Trotsky described sales of his *History* as 'quite pitiable'.[75]

In the meantime, the numbers, and effectiveness, of the British Communists were plunging to zero. The members in good standing with their dues amounted to 3,000, and those not paid up, to 2,000; 3,000 of the members were not organised in party units; half of the membership was in London, and 61% were unemployed, only half of whom were in the National Unemployed Workers' Movement. The number of factory newspapers had sunk from over 50 to 33, for only a tenth of the members were in factory cells anyway.[76] In an atmosphere of unemployment, bitterness, and impotence, sectarianism had a field day among the membership. 'Between the Social-Democrat and the Fascist there is only the "irreconcilability" as between the sly, slow, cunning poisoner and the open, brutal, garrotter and the cut-throat,' explained William Gallacher.[77] Doublethink reached appalling depths. Whilst he was writing that 'in no other organisation is there the freedom of discussion that exists in the Communist International and the parties of the Communist International,'[78] Dutt was writing to a correspondent in Bradford to explain that the fear of expressing free opinion within the party was 'a dangerous thing, when we have the counter-revolutionary propaganda of the Trotskyites, with their suggestions of the "servility" of our party, the "assimilation" of the Communist "functionary" and so on.'[79]

Although they shared this treatment along with the I.L.P. and the Labour Party, extraordinary lengths were resorted to in order to create an atmosphere of suspicion towards the Trotskyists among the membership. For example, when Kreuger the Swedish 'match king' went bankrupt and committed suicide, it was found among his papers that he had given £7,100 to Karl Kilbom, leader of the Brandlerite Independent Communist Party of Sweden. When this was reported in the *Daily Worker*, Kilbom was described as 'leader of the Trotskyist group in Sweden', even though Trotsky was in opposition to the Brandlerites as much as the Stalinists, and had no compunction in describing Kreuger as a swindler and a hypocrite.[80] Suspicion even permeated the ranks of the Trotskyists themselves, for the group was still hesitant about admitting Dr. Worrall to full membership rights, in view of the slander spread around by the Stalinists that he was a police agent. In the end, it was decided to send a letter to the Communist Party on 7th April 1933, asking them to substantiate the charges against him by placing what material they had at the disposal of the group.[81] Even this request was turned into a smear:

> . . . the Trotsky groups in this and other countries attract around them 'stool pigeons' of all kinds. These know that all the slanders that can be gathered will be found in these groups. They also know that if there is anything done of particular interest to the police, that these renegades will only too gladly spill it if they get to know about it. Not long ago this group had the cheek to write to us and ask us if we could tell them if one of their members was a Yard agent. This was a crude attempt to cover up the fact that their group was an actual centre for supplying information to the enemies of the party.[82]

The atmosphere created by this sort of propaganda was deadly to any attempt to discuss the issues on their own merits, and to suggest some other policy. 'People who knew you personally,' recalls Groves, 'would stand up and shout "Fascist!" and you would say "What is this doctrine that makes people do things like that?" They don't do it now — they are after other people, I dare say — and yet afterwards they'd cut you in the street. They wouldn't talk to you, they'd interrupt your meetings (with the) shout "Fascist".' [83]

The six members that the group still had inside the Communist Party had a daunting task.[84] 'We shall clear our feet of the counter-revolutionary rubbish some of the fellows have tried to throw across the discussions,' threatened Gallacher. 'We have got rid of most of them. Others (there are not many) will be weeded out as the struggle develops.'[85] The first to be dealt with was Wally Graham (Nardell) in Hackney. He had managed to become better established than some of the others, and had been sent by his Local to the Battersea Congress of the Communist Party at which the Balham comrades had made their appeal for reinstatement; though of course the atmosphere had prevented him from doing more than observe what was going on.[86] Vainly protesting against the suicidal German policy, he was suspended from membership on 5th March for calling for a united front of Socialists and Communists, only to learn that the day after that the Communist International had now called for the same thing! On 23rd May he was called before the District Party Committee, accused of 'Anti-Party Activities' and of being a member of an 'Anti-Party' group, and expelled. He did not deny his support for the Trotskyists, but defended it on the grounds that:

> . . . inside the Party democracy has disappeared, criticism is not allowed. Questions are decided not by discussions but by commands from above. This is bad for the Party, since creation of a Bolshevik leadership demands full discussion within the Party. A Bolshevik Party is created by the testing of every policy in the fire of the struggle and by the membership understanding every new turn of the policy. Apply this to the united front policy: were the members allowed to discuss in a proper manner the turn in the policy of the C.I.? Those who do are expelled.[87]

Next it was the turn of Gerry Bradley in Chelsea. Bradley had been a soldier in the First World War, and the slaughter he had seen made him a founder member of the Communist Party, and one of the early full-time organisers of the Unemployed Workers' Movement. When he had left Ridley's group he was under a cloud, and the Balham comrades were reluctant to admit him because of his flamboyant personality. 'You should understand that Gerry Bradley had run into quite a lot of trouble in the Communist Party,' explains

Groves, 'and his methods of propaganda were not always approved of. He went into Madame Tussauds, demonstrated, was arrested, and imprisoned ... We were very chary about bringing him in, actually, because we didn't want the reputation. The party would have been delighted to attack us on whatever they had against Bradley.'[88] However, he was well established in his area, which had one of the more active of the West London groups, and was able to make a wider impact than the others.

At that time the Communist International had instructed its sections to open negotiations with the Social Democratic organisations for a front against Fascism, whilst the Labour Party had been strengthening its support among the working class in a series of by-elections and local elections.[89] The 'for the record' unity overtures had not altered the sectarianism of the Communists, for during the East Fulham by-election on 25th October they had called upon the electorate to refuse to support any party, and to scrawl 'Communist' on their papers. This was the opposite of the United Front policy, which was not opposed in principle to electoral pacts, or to supporting other working-class parties. Accordingly, the three Chelsea cells sent off the following resolution to the Sub-District Party Committee:

> That these cells, in view of their experience in the East Fulham By-Election, consider the policy of advising the workers of East Fulham to spoil their ballot papers by writing 'Communist' across them or to refrain from voting, to be incorrect.
>
> This in practice isolates us from the majority of workers organised under the Labour Party who accept its policy and believe in its leaders. It gives valuable assistance to the Tory candidate inasmuch as the abstention from recording its vote by a section of the working class increases the possibility of the Tory securing a majority. The workers see this and resent it.
>
> It may be argued that it is immaterial whether a Tory or Labour man comes into power, for they are both capitalist — going towards Fascism. These cells disagree entirely with this attitude for the following reasons.
>
> If the Tory and Labour parties are the same, then we must argue that their actions when in power have the same effect upon the minds of the working class. This can be easily disproven by a simple analysis. The workers expect Tory legislation from a Tory and their reaction to this is normal. From a Socialist they expect Socialist legislation and getting Toryism they react away from the Labour Party. In this way

> they learn, as Lenin says, from their own practical political experience. Similarly this unreasonable attitude adversely affects our approach to the United Front.
>
> In view of this disagreement we feel that it is urgently necessary that a full discussion on the subject be opened in the Party press immediately, owing to the serious and extensive implications of this line.[90]

The Chelsea comrades tried to press for a discussion of the full implications of the Leninist United Front policy in the current circumstances. They criticised the 'ultimatist policy of the United Front from below, which isolated the C.P. from the mass of the workers, and made an important contribution to the defeat of the German working-class movement', unconvinced by the Comintern's explanation 'which merely touches the surface, putting the blame for failure on methods of work, slackness, etc., and not on points of basic policy.'[91]

The Sub-District Party Committee met, refused their demand for an open discussion, and vetoed the raising of the issue at the West London Sub-District Conference. But when the Conference met, the Political Committee failed to dissuade the Chelsea delegates from bringing forward their amendments to the official resolution, or from raising their own. But they did make sure that the resolution itself was not circulated, and only allowed three of the six proposed speakers to address the congress at the end, so that no one else could intervene in the discussion. Springhall, the Comintern man, interrupted and cross-examined the last speaker, presumed to be the weakest, 'because he was making his first public speech', and then the platform replied, Haselden being given ten minutes and Mahon no less than thirty-five. 'The main argument used against us,' they complained, 'was to the effect that the antagonism with which we were met by the workers of East Fulham during the election was the result, not of our policy, but of the fact that we had done no work in the locality for the past two years.'[92] The truth was the opposite: before they had become active, the party had only three members in the area, and now they had twelve organised in three cells, with their own paper, had fought two evictions and had been approached by the power workers to run a paper for their plant.

A barrage of abuse greeted them, accusations of being 'petty bourgeois liquidators',[93] 'anti-working class elements'[94] who were 'running away from the struggle',[95] and the official spokesman stuck to the 'Third Period' line with great vehemence:

> This movement in the Labour Party gives the greatest importance to the sharp struggle waged in the Congress

> against the viewpoint of the Chelsea cells which amounts to a denial of any differentiation within the Labour Party and to directing the Party back into the situation of 'critical support' of the Labour Party.

The final resolution passed by these none-too-scrupulous methods described the Chelsea objections as a challenge to the policy of ' "class against class" and the independent leadership of the Party', 'petty-bourgeois defeatist sentiments in face of certain difficulties of the Party in overcoming its isolation, and in their general character are of a Trotskyist nature.'[96]

Now that the magic word 'Trotskyism' had been pronounced, administrative measures followed rapidly, when the London District Committee moved in to expel Gerry and Lee Bradley, and to impose a new local leadership against the majority views of the Chelsea members. Even then, the report of the incident, whilst noting that eight of the Chelsea comrades repudiated the resolution, failed to point out that the other ten supported it.[97] 'We have a position,' they complained, 'where all critics are persecuted and expelled, all discussion suppressed, the will of the majority disregarded, and a leadership imposed whose only recommendation is uncritical acceptance of the "official" line. Under these conditions it becomes impossible to alter the policy or tactics of the Communist Parties.'[98] They added: 'The label "Trotskyism" applied to our policy is irrelevant, but it is noteworthy that the policy of qualified "support" for the Labour Party which we advanced was also the policy put forward by Lenin.'[99] Ten other members, the majority of the Chelsea group, continued to support their case for reinstatement and a full and proper discussion. It was typical of Bradley that he should have put up a terrific struggle before they were able to get him out, and he took great delight in embarrassing them in his oratorical displays in Hyde Park, where he could collect crowds of several hundred by using the classic platform style. But his appeal for a return to Leninism failed to draw any other party support, whilst the Communist League was rapidly exhausting its remaining support inside the C.P.G.B.

By this time Labour was rising from the circumstances of the defeat of 1931. During the local elections Labour doubled its number of London County Council seats, and gained another 137,000 working-class votes, whilst the Communist vote dropped in the nine areas contested by their candidates.[100] Lack of support had not deterred them from standing against Labour in the Hammersmith by-election, where their candidate, Ted Bramley, despite the support of the I.L.P., lost 80 votes on his previous showing in the constituency.[101] The poor character of these results was thrown into relief by the fact that the party was now supposed to be following a 'United Front' tactic towards the Labour Party, which could hardly find the offer attractive in the circumstances. 'The Communist Party takes part in all elections, on the basis of its party programme, no matter what other parties and candidates are contesting,' maintained Harry Pollitt: 'The present United Front Campaign makes no difference to this vital political principle. There is no contradiction between being associated with other parties in united front activity against the capitalist attack, and opposing the same parties in elections.'[102]

The Communist League, however, defended the Leninist position on the question. 'We must place the Labour and Trade Union leaders in the position where they must fight or reveal their impotence to their followers,' their leaflet ran. 'We have no hesitation in saying publicly that the Communist Party candidate does not provide a satisfactory alternative to the Labour candidate', for 'the next stage in the development of the working-class struggle must be the overthrow of the national government and its replacement by a Labour government, which will immediately open up possibilities for an advance to the establishment of workers' rule . . . We urge all working men and women to vote Labour on Tuesday.'[103]

The same problem of the United Front came up at a National Conference of Action called in Bermondsey by the Communist Party and the I.L.P. to coincide with the arrival of the Hunger Marchers on 24th February. On this occasion the Trotskyists called for an abandonment of the Communist split unions,[104] support to the unemployed associations set up by the T.U.C. and for a vote for the Labour Party in elections.[105] The Communist Party's reply was to suggest that they were calling for an 'abandonment of "independent leadership" (i.e. London busmen's strike, Fords strike, etc.)', 'action in the unions only through pressure on the leaders' and the 'dissolution of the National Unemployed Workers' Movement'.[106] Even their willingness to discuss with their readers the policy of supporting the Labour Party in elections was distorted to make it sound as if they did not know what to do:

> They're all at sea as to what should be done here. In the latest issue of their paper, the *Red Flag*, they say: 'We know that we're against the National Government, but should we support the Labour Party? Some of us think we should. Please write and say what you think.' Now they are waiting for their readers to tell them what to do.[107]

What they actually said was, of course, rather different from this:

> No one will suggest that we have reached the stage where we can call for the dictatorship of the proletariat. Since this is so it seems to many that only the slogan of 'The Labour Government', on the basis of militant demands, can bring the movement together, bridge the present gulf that lies between the reformist workers and the small revolutionary section and carry the whole movement forward to a higher stage . . . We believe that the policy advocated by Lenin and the Communist International in its revolutionary days is the one most likely to aid our advance. We refer our readers to *Left Wing Communism* by Lenin . . . We invite the opinions of our readers on this question to which we will return in future issues.[108]

The Communist leaders, of course, must have found it remarkable that revolutionaries should invite discussion of their views from the rest of the movement, as their own practice was to talk, and not to listen, not only to those outside their ranks, but even to their own membership, whose attempts at discussion were choked off by administrative measures.

The last expulsion was that from the Peckham High Street Cell of the Communist Party, in which the chief victim was Arthur Cooper. A member of Camberwell Trades Council and later the representative of the Clerical Workers' Union on the London Trades Council, Cooper always moved with political circumspection. 'Everybody was very secretive, and we were anxious that anybody who came to us from the Party should remain there, if possible, in order to recruit some members, before getting thrown out.' recalls Groves. 'Cooper I met at some meetings that we held, and he came often, but we never met privately or separately, as far as I remember.'[109] Through the summer of 1934 Cooper and the High Street Cell kept up a criticism of the mistaken policy of the C.P.G.B.:

> Hitler's coming to power in Germany, the Brighton T.U.C. march, and the conduct of the Anti-War and Anti-Fascist campaign have made us uneasy as to where the Party is going. In fraction meetings we have raised our objections only to be met with furious personal attacks leaving our points unanswered. We have made continual efforts to get some explanation of points in the C.P. policy which seems to us to be dangerously wrong ... Of course we were attacked as 'Trotskyists' . . .[110]

When the Party leadership moved in to expel Cooper and McCool, the Peckham High Street Cell refused to accept it, and broke up, with five people joining the Trotskyists. At the same time criticism of the role played by Stalinism in the German defeat produced a string of expulsions in Tottenham, from which three others moved over to Trotskyism.[111]

Cooper remained a loyal Trotskyist up until his death in 1982. At about the same time as he first became associated with the group in secret, it was also joined by an even more remarkable figure. Denzil Dean Harber was already a member of the Communist Party whilst a student at the London School of Economics. He had learned to speak Russian fluently, and when he had finished his degree in the summer of 1932 he got a job as an intepreter for a Canadian journalist visiting the Soviet Union:

> This was in the period when the authorities had not realised how dangerous it was for all foreigners to travel as they wished, and they travelled very extensively — not just in places like Moscow, but in the Ukraine, and the great wheat-growing areas of Russia. The policy apparently was to go to a market town, find a peasant who had come in with his cart, and go back to his village and spend the night with him. So obviously, they got a very good picture of the effects of collectivisation, and Harber came back absolutely shattered. He believed in the wonders of the Five Year Plan . . . He went out with a lot of illusions and came back badly shattered . . . In the meantime, Harber had been poking about in a shop in Charing Cross Road, and came across a copy of the *Bulletin of the Opposition* in Russian. Having read that, he said that 'This is the answer, this is what it is all about', and he began to start getting politically active again.[112]

At the same time he set about recruiting his former L.S.E. friends, and shortly before the group split, Margaret Johns and Stewart Kirby also joined the Trotskyists.

A man of immense intellectual ability, Harber was to play a leading role in the Trotskyist movement right up until the 1950s, and although 'in no way a man who could attract solid working class support', 'he had good ideas, he was a theoretician and could muster his arguments and could develop them well'.[113]

Other talent accrued to the group at the same period. Hilary Sumner-Boyd ('Charles Sumner') was contacted as a student at Christ Church in Oxford. He had joint American-English nationality, and was to be active in the British Trotskyist movement for some years. Shortly after he attended the founding conference of the Fourth International, where he represented the British Section and took the minutes, he departed to Turkey, where he pursued a distinguished academic career as an expert on its history and literature.[114]

By this time most of the Ceylonese students at the L.S.E. had gone back, though 'Phillip' Gunawardena was able to get an article published by the Communist Party before he went.[115] The 'T' circle, as they came to be called in Ceylon, could not of course openly break with the Communists, until they were able to show that Stalinism meant collaborating with Imperialism, on the eve of the Second World War.

In line with Trotsky's instructions, the group did not neglect agitation in the broader Labour movement:

> Wet, fine, snow, any weather if it was practicable, we had a meeting on Clapham Common every Sunday morning. (It was earlier in the morning, there were a lot of meetings in the afternoon.) . . . We built up a regular crowd of two or three hundred, and when anything happened — like Hitler made a speech — the crowd swelled up, because people knew of the meeting. We had some influence among the tram workers, who sometimes carried our platforms in front to the meeting spots. We had some support among the busmen at Merton, and we had a group in Wimbledon.[116]

Nor was basic education work neglected. Nine issues of *The Communist* came out before the end of the year, including articles by Trotsky and Shachtman,[117] and in all twelve printed issues of *Red Flag* between May 1933 and November 1934, with over a dozen articles either by Trotsky or from other members of the International Left Opposition. Cadre schools were organised with some success,[118] though on occasion a valuable opportunity for wider influence was missed, such as when Trotsky refused his endorsement to an N.C.L.C. exhibition on Karl Marx held at Transport House on 11th and 12th March 1933, because its prospectus began with a statement from Henri de Man, author of the notorious De Man Plan in Belgium as well as of books attacking Marxism.[119]

The organisation moved towards a tighter and more disciplined structure. The National Conference of 18th June split up the membership into groups of between three and 20, depending upon workplace or residence, each with delegate rights.[120] *Red Flag* became the main organ, and *The Communist* their discussion journal, to be issued 'as the occasion arises'.[121] They took the title of 'The British Section, International Left Opposition' with the name of 'The Communist League'.[122] By the end of the year 1933 they had accumulated fifty-two members.[123]

A report made for the International Secretariat about this time shows quite a healthy picture:

> . . . a large part of the members are in the official party and work secretly for the Opposition . . . The impression that I got

> was that these groups carry on quite a remarkable activity among workers' organisations, in the trade union movement of their districts, and in other movements of united front (against war, Fascism, unemployment, etc.). It seems that their influence among workers in general and within various political organisations (Communist Party, I.L.P., Labour Party) is very wide and far surpasses their numerical forces. It often happens that their proposals are adopted by meetings of workers belonging to the Labour Party, Trade Unions, and other organisations.[124]

The only sour notes he had to report were that the old Executive Minority (Wicks, Purkis and Weston) maintained their opposition to declaring the German Communist Party a write-off and complained of the lack of democracy within the group, and that only Wicks was taking part in the work of his group. 'It is to be feared that with their point of view,' he went on, 'and their isolation from the daily work they may become discouraged and indifferent.'[125] In Purkis's case this prophecy was soon to be realised, for the following year he dropped out, and went back to his old religious beliefs as a follower of Conrad Noel.

It was a creditable balance-sheet for a year's struggle by a handful of comrades against very heavy odds, but the particular perspective of the Communist Party work was almost exhausted, and the basis for it was fast disappearing. As the Communist Party's swing to the 'Popular Front' policy gathered momentum, even the opportunity for discussing a perspective for revolution dropped away, for the slogan of the Comintern was the defence of democracy against Fascism, and its thrust was directed away from the workers and towards the middle classes and the Establishment.[126] Already much of the propaganda of the group on the United Front as applied to elections had raised far more of an echo among Labour Party Workers than it had among the Communists, and this was a pointer to the future. On a more immediate question, developments within the I.L.P. could not be ignored.

Notes

1. L.D. Trotsky, 'After the British Expulsions', 6th September 1932, in *Writings of Leon Trotsky: Supplement, 1929–33*, New York, 1979, p. 149.
2. 'Bureaucratic Discipline or Communist Policy?', in *The Communist*, no. 2, September 1932, p. 2.
3. H. Wicks, Interview with Al Richardson, 11th March and 1st April 1978.

4. L.D. Trotsky, 'To an Unknown Comrade', November 1932, in *Writings of Leon Trotsky, 1932*, New York, 1973, p. 328. Cf. *The Case of Leon Trotsky*, New York, 1968, pp. 274-5.

5. H. Wicks, Interview with Al Richardson, 11th March and 1st April 1978.

6. L.D. Trotsky, 'On the State of the Left Opposition', 16th December 1932, in *Writings of Leon Trotsky, 1932-3*, New York, 1972, p. 30.

7. Ibid., p. 36. Cf. p. 55 ('The International Left Opposition, Its Tasks and Methods', December 1932).

8. Dr. Worrall, Interview with Al Richardson, 26th November 1978.

9. E.g. 'Why Has Schleicher Replaced Papen?', in *The Communist*, no. 3; L.D. Trotsky, 'Letter to a Social Democratic Worker', in *The Communist*, nos. 4 (April) and 5 (May); L.D. Trotsky, 'Maria Reese and the Comintern'; M. Reese, 'Letter to the C.C. of the C.P.G.B. and the C.I.'; and K. Freidberg, 'Letter to Piatnitsky', in *The Communist*, no. 7.

10. 'Germany! To All Communists and Militant Workers', in R. Groves, *The Balham Group*, London, 1974, p. 104.

11. H. Wicks, Interview with Al Richardson, 11th March and 1st April 1978.

12. H. Dewar, Interview with Al Richardson, 7th April 1978.

13. *The Communist*, no. 3, January 1933, p. 2.

14. 'Unite! To Working Men and Women in S.W. London', in Groves, *The Balham Group*, p. 107.

15. British Section of the Left Opposition, *Even Now They Blunder!* (leaflet).

16. Groves, *The Balham Group*, p. 75.

17. Letter to the South-West London Anti-War Committee.

18. S. Bornstein and A. Richardson, *Two Steps Back*, London, 1982, p. 11.

19. *Even Now They Blunder* (see note 15 above).

20. R.F. Andrews, 'Trotsky on Germany', in *The Communist Review*, vol. v, no. 5, May 1933, pp. 227-8.

21. W. Gallacher, *Pensioners of Capitalism: An Exposure of Trotsky and the Social Democrats*, C.P.G.B. pamphlet, 1934, p. 15.

22. Resolution to the Communist League (undated).

23. Groves, *The Balham Group*, p. 74. The 'someone' was apparently Pierre Naville, who tried to help Groves out between his own contributions — R. Groves, Interview with Al Richardson, 2nd April 1978.

24. 'The International Left Opposition, Its Tasks and Methods', in *Documents of the IVth International*, New York, 1973, p. 25.

25. L.D. Trotsky, 'K.P.D. or New Party?', March 12th 1933, in *Writings of Leon Trotsky, 1932-3*, pp. 137-8.

26. Ibid.

27. G. Vereeken, *The G.P.U. in the Trotskyist Movement*, London, 1976, p. 51.

28. Communist League, *Internal Bulletin*, no. 5, 24th May 1933.

29. 'Pre-Conference (1933) Statement of Comrade Dewar'.

30. Ibid.

31. R. Groves, Letter to A. Graham (Albert Glotzer), 7th January 1933.

32. See above, p. 104 and note 22.

33. 'Statement from Members of the Committee of the British Group of the Left Opposition', 9th April 1933.

34. Ibid. Cf. H. Davis (George Weston), S. Purkis, H. Wicks, E.S. Williams, 'Statement from Members of the 1931–1933 Committee of the British Group of the Left Opposition', 18th April 1933.

35. Preface, *The Communist*, no. 4, April 1933.

36. 'For Lenin and Trotsky: Why the Red Flag Appears: To Regenerate Revolutionary Movement', in *Red Flag*, vol. 1, no. 1, May 1933, p. 1.

37. H. Dewar, Interview with Al Richardson, 7th April 1978.

38. R. Groves, Interview with Al Richardson, 2nd April 1978. An estimate of

'nearly 1,000' is given in the 'Report of the Situation of the English Section' by 'Vitte' (Demetrious Giotopoulos) to the I.S. on 22nd September 1933.

39. L.D. Trotsky, 'Greetings to the "Red Flag" ', 19th May 1933, in *Writings of Leon Trotsky, 1932-3*, p. 237. Cf. *Trotsky's Writings on Britain*, London, 1974, vol. iii, p. 65.

40. See above, p. 64, and below, p. 265.

41. H. Wicks, 'He was Shot by the Nazis', in *The New Leader*, vol. xxxiv, no. 15, 20th June 1942.

42. 'Communist Opposition Leader Sentenced', in *Red Flag*, vol. i, no. 3, July 1933, p. 1.

43. 'Save the Life of Chen Du Siu', in *Red Flag*, vol. i, no. 4, August 1933, p. 3.

44. 'The Case of Chen Du Siu: An Open Letter to Tom Mann', in *Red Flag*, vol. i, no. 5, September 1933, p. 4.

45. 'Tom Mann's Reply: I Count It My Duty', in *Red Flag*, vol. i, no. 6, October–November 1933, p. 4.

46. 'Save the Life of Chen Du Siu', in *Red Flag*, vol. i, no. 7, January 1934, p. 4.

47. Gallacher, *Pensioners of Capitalism*, p. 13 (his emphasis).

48. Dr. Worrall, Interview with Al Richardson, 26th November 1978.

49. L. Moyes, *Origins of Japanese Anti-Stalinism*, Gakushu Series, no. 1, California, 1971, chapter 3.

50. J.R. Campbell, 'Mr. Trotsky and the I.L.P.', in *The Communist Review*, vol. vi, no. 12, December/January 1933–4, p. 435.

51. L. Magyar, 'The Bankruptcy of Trotskyism', in *Labour Monthly*, vol. xvi, no. 6, June 1934, p. 370.

52. Ibid., pp. 371-2.

53. Ibid., p. 365.

54. Gallacher, *Pensioners of Capitalism*, p. 13.

55. Ibid., p. 22.

56. R.F. Andrews (Andrew Rothstein), 'Trotsky on Germany', in *The Communist Review*, vol. v, no. 5, May 1933, p. 228.

57. Op. cit., note 50 above.

58. Gallacher, *Pensioners of Capitalism*, p. 11.

59. R. Fox, 'Fifteen Years of the Russian Revolution and the British Working Class', in *The Communist Review*, vol. iv, no. 11, November 1932, p. 529.

60. H. Sara, 'Trotsky and the Russian Revolution', in *Plebs*, vol. xxiv, no. 9, September 1932, pp. 196-8.

61. H. Sara, 'Trotsky on the Russian Revolution', in *Plebs*, vol. xxv, no. 5, May 1933, p. 117.

62. 'B.B.', 'Lenin', in *Inprecorr*, vol. xiii, no. 56, 22nd December 1933, p. 1288.

63. J. Maxton, *Lenin*, London, 1932.

64. R. Fox, *Lenin*, 1934; contrast 'We are starting on the construction of Socialism' with the version in J. Reed, *Ten Days that Shook the World*, reprint, London, 1970, p. 129.

65. 'It was the price of Trotsky's policy' — cf. H. Wicks, *Notes on the History of Bolshevism*, Marxist League pamphlet, n.d. (1936), p. 3.

66. Cf. Wicks, ibid., p. 5.

67. Ibid., p. 6.

68. Ibid., p. 2.

69. R. Palme Dutt, Letter to Harry Pollitt, 4th October 1933.

70. A. Rothstein, 'Trotsky on the Russian Revolution', in *Labour Monthly*, vol. xv, no. 12, December 1933, pp. 761-7.

71. R.F. Andrews (Andrew Rothstein), *The Truth about Trotsky*, C.P.G.B. pamphlet,

February 1934, p. 31.

72. Rothstein, 'Trotsky on the Russian Revolution', in *Labour Monthly*, vol. xv, no. 12, December 1933, p. 766.

73. Andrews, *The Truth about Trotsky*, pp. 28 and 37.

74. Ibid., p. 34.

75. I. Deutscher, *The Prophet Outcast*, London, 1970 ed., p. 216.

76. Report in *The Communist*, no. 6, June 1933.

77. Gallacher, *Pensioners of Capitalism*, 1934, p. 26.

78. Ibid., pp. 20-1.

79. R. Palme Dutt, Letter to D. Wilson, 20th November 1932.

80. 'Workers' Notebook', 'Kreuger and Trotskyists', in the *Daily Worker*, 12th September 1932; cf. L.D. Trotsky, 'Questions on Soviet Life and Morality', 17th September 1932, in *Writings of Leon Trotsky, 1932*, New York, 1973, p. 186, and 'Another Lie Nailed', in *Red Flag*, vol. i, no. 4, August 1933, p. 1.

81. *Red Flag*, vol. 1, no. 4, August 1933, p. 4. Cf. above, p. 58.

82. W. Gallacher, *Pensioners of Capitalism*, pp. 23-4.

83. R. Groves, Interview with Al Richardson, 2nd April 1978.

84. R. Groves, Letter to A. Graham (Albert Glotzer), 7th January 1933.

85. W. Gallacher, 'We have no Room for Trotskyists', in the *Daily Worker*, 23rd August 1932.

86. 'W. Graham Expelled from Communist Party', in *Red Flag*, vol. i, no. 3, July 1933; cf. Groves, *The Balham Group*, p. 72.

87. W. Graham, 'To the Members of the Hackney Local and the Communist Party' (leaflet), June 1933.

88. R. Groves, Interview with Al Richardson, 2nd April 1978.

89. Cf. Bornstein and Richardson, *Two Steps Back*, pp. 7 and 11.

90. 'An Open Letter to C.P. Members' (leaflet signed by 13 initials).

91. 'Communists Resign', in *The New Leader*, 16th February 1934.

92. 'An Open Letter to C.P. Members'.

93. Ibid.

94. 'Communists Resign', in *The New Leader*, 16th February 1934.

95. 'An Open Letter to C.P. Members'.

96. K. Haselden, 'The First Congress of the West London Sub-District', in *The Communist Review*, vol. vi, no. 12, December–January 1933–4, pp. 437-440.

97. *Daily Worker*, 6th January 1934. Cf. 'Why Need They Lie?', Statement issued by the Chelsea Group of the C.P.G.B.

98. 'Communists Resign', in *The New Leader*, 16th February 1934.

99. 'Why Need They Lie?' (see note 97 above).

100. 'R.G.' (Groves), 'Vienna and the London Elections', in *Red Flag*, vol. 1, no. 8, March–April 1934, p. 1.

101. 'Crazier Month in the I.L.P.', in *Red Flag*, vol. i, no. 9, May–June 1934, p. 4. Cf. Bornstein and Richardson, *Two Steps Back*, p. 7.

102. H. Pollitt in the *Daily Worker*, 17th March 1934.

103. Communist League, *Five Communist Reasons for Voting Labour* (leaflet).

104. i.e. the United Clothing Workers and the United Mineworkers of Scotland — cf. Bornstein and Richardson, *Two Steps Back*, pp. 2 and 12.

105. 'The National Conference of Action', in *Red Flag*, vol. i, no. 7, January 1934, p. 4.

106. Andrews, *The Truth About Trotsky*, p. 69.

107. Gallacher, *Pensioners of Capitalism*, 1934, p. 13.

108. 'The National Conference of Action: A Discussion Article', in *Red Flag*, vol. 1, no. 7, January 1934, p. 4.

109. R. Groves, Interview with Al Richardson, 2nd April 1978.

110. Statement signed by seven members of High Street Cell quoted in 'More Expulsions', in *Red Flag*, vol. i, no. 11, October 1934. Cf. the American *Militant*, 27th

October 1934.

111. 'More Expulsions', in *Red Flag*, vol. i, no. 11, October 1934.

112. Margaret Johns, Interview with Al Richardson, 4th February 1978.

113. John Goffe, Interview with Al Richardson, 18th May 1978.

114. Obituary: Professor H. Sumner-Boyd, in *The Times*, 18th September 1976. It describes him as 'an intellectual Marxist but he was totally liberal at heart and was a counsellor and refuge for many students in times of political turmoil.'

115. D.P.R. Gunawardena, 'The Indian Masses Move Forward', in *Labour Monthly*, vol. xiv, no. 2, February 1932, pp. 87-92.

116. R. Groves, Interview with Al Richardson, 2nd April 1978.

117. E.g. no. 6 (Trotsky on the Second Five-Year Plan), no. 8 (Shachtman on 'The Price of American Recognition'), no. 9 (Trotsky's 'Letter to an I.L.P. member').

118. R. Groves, Letter to A. Graham (A. Glotzer), 7th January 1933.

119. London Division N.C.L.C., 'The Karl Marx Exhibition', in *Plebs*, vol. xxv, no. 2, February 1933. Cf. *The Early Years of the Left Opposition: Five Previously Unpublished Letters by Leon Trotsky and Two Articles by Frank Ridley and James Maxton*, London, 1979, pp. 4 and 10, n. 7; *Documents of the Fourth International*, New York, 1973, p. 67 ('the vainglorious critic of Karl Marx').

120. 'Draft Constitution of the British Section, International Left Opposition (Bolshevik–Leninists)' to be put before National Conference, 18th June 1933. Secretary: Hugo Dewar.

121. 'Resolution on Future Tasks', in *Discussion Bulletin*, no. 7, 22nd June 1933.

122. In consequence of its decision that the Comintern was now moribund, the Trotskyist movement internationally changed its label, from the above to 'International Communist League', in August 1933.

123. 'The Present Situation and Our Tasks', Internal Bulletin of the R.S.L., 27th February 1943. These are Harber's figures from a decade later, but unlikely to be far out.

124. 'Witte' (Demetrious Giotopoulos), 'Report on the Situation of the English Section to the International Secretariat', Paris, 22nd September 1933.

125. Ibid.

126. Cf. Bornstein and Richardson, *Two Steps Back*, pp. 20-52.

Chapter Five

The I.L.P. and the Split, 1933–34

Although the British Communist Party did its utmost to rally demonstrations of the unemployed, its isolation prevented it from being more than a spectator in the crisis that threw the Labour movement into confusion when the Second Labour Government fell in 1931. It was otherwise with the I.L.P., which was heavily involved. Apart from the fact that Ramsay MacDonald himself had been one of its members until fairly recently, we should not forget that until after the First World War the I.L.P. made up what direct membership the Labour Party had, and even after that date, when individual membership was allowed for local parties, the I.L.P. remained the focus of the Labour Party's Socialist aspirations, and held a majority of its activists. Unlike the Labour Party as a whole, the I.L.P. *had* produced a policy to deal with unemployment, only to see it utterly disregarded by large numbers of M.P.s who still claimed to be members whilst refusing to be guided by that policy. During the election of 1931, relations with the Labour Party worsened when the I.L.P.'s candidates were refused endorsement by National Headquarters, the sticking point being over whether I.L.P. M.P.s should abide by the Labour whip in the House of Commons or follow the policy laid down by their own organisation. After prolonged negotiations a special conference of the I.L.P. resolved the problem by a decision to disaffiliate from the Labour Party in July 1932.[1]

Apart from Wise, Kirkwood and Dollan, the majority of the old leadership and of the Party's remaining M.P.s were in favour of the split, as there was a general feeling that the Labour Party — and reformism itself — were utterly discredited. The I.L.P. now moved rapidly towards the left. Following the vote on disaffiliation, Maxton himself made a short speech calling for 'the unity of revolutionary socialist forces',[2] and sympathy for left Socialist and Communist ideas began to grow.

Prominent among the membership in London was the 'Revolutionary Policy Committee' led by Dr. C.K. Cullen, Medical Officer of Health for Poplar, and Jack Gaster, a lawyer, who became convinced that the way forward was for the I.L.P. to associate with the Communist International and to absorb the British Communist Party into a united Communist Party in this country. But the I.L.P.'s working-class roots were in the North of England and on Clydeside, and they remained loyal to the old leaders, who wanted to keep the I.L.P.'s independence and room for manoeuvre. The London membership of the I.L.P. being its most middle-class section, it is not surprising that it should have come first under the influence, and then under the control, of the apparatus of the Communist Party.

The I.L.P. leadership, to counter the demands of this increasingly Stalinist faction, decided to cast around for other, non-Moscow, left Socialist and Communist trends, to provide itself with the information and the theory to be able to criticise the policies and organisational methods of the Comintern. It also felt the need for international allies and links, and indeed at the same time in Europe there was a whole layer of such parties developing, either splitting from Social Democracy towards the left, or from the Communist International in various directions. A growth in internationalist sentiment meant a break with the provincial horizons of British Socialism, and an encounter with European Socialism and Communism — not only the ideas of Trotsky and the Left Opposition, but also those of Brandler and Thalheimer in Europe, Lovestone in America, and dissident Socialists in France, Poland, Norway, Holland, and many other places. 'In the course of this struggle,' noted Brockway, 'the I.L.P. experimented in many directions, at one time approaching the Communist International, at another moving towards the Trotskyist position.'[3]

Maxton had already shown in his biography of Lenin that he did not accept the Comintern's propaganda on Trotskyism,[4] and *The New Leader* commissioned Josef Kruk of the Polish Independent Labour Party, who 'was a personal friend of both Lenin and Trotsky', to write a review of Trotsky's *History*, which he described in glowing terms as 'written with that mastery and brilliance characteristic of the greatest political author in Europe', 'a master of interpreting dialectical materialism and Marxism'.[5] Maxton recommended the book for its 'wide knowledge of social affairs, a deeper understanding of the real working of history, and a clearer view of the tasks of a working-class movement', written by one 'recognised throughout the world as the greatest individual menace to the capitalist order' and feared also by the rulers of Soviet Russia.[6] The use the I.L.P. leaders were able to make of Trotsky's book to counter the influence of the Communist Party was, so Andrew Rothstein thought, 'of great value to those reformist leaders, particularly in the I.L.P., who are now moving heaven and earth to restrain the revolutionary rank and file from joining forces with the Communist Party in this country'; and it was 'no wonder these leaders advertise Trotsky's books and use his language at every convenient opportunity.'[7] The I.L.P. also contributed to disseminating Trotsky's current writings in Britain by publishing the Copenhagen speech in a pamphlet with a preface by Maxton in which he described Trotsky's part in the Russian Revolution as 'secondary only to Lenin himself',[8] and by printing smaller articles in the party's press.[9] A representative of the international Trotskyist movement came to London to report on the situation of the Communist League and of the movement in general, and recorded Brockway's response as follows:

> 'I wanted you to know that in our organisation there is shown a great sympathy for the ideas of comrade Trotsky', he told us. To the question posed, whether this sympathy shows itself in the entire base of the organisation, he replied: 'I can assure you that what I think, also Maxton, Paton, Smith, think, and the same is proved by the organisation in London, to the measure that it can be proved.'[10]

In Smith's case it was probably true. He had been associated with the work of the Balham Group in the South-West London Anti-War Committee before the 'Revolutionary Policy Committee' had even existed, through Clapham I.L.P.,[11] where he was in a good position to be able to judge the differences between Trotskyism and Stalinism, especially over the German affair. The interview he had with Trotsky after the Paris Conference shows that he retained his favourable opinions.[12] But there can equally be little doubt that some of the others encouraged the ideas of Trotskyism only in order to counteract the influence of the Revolutionary Policy Committee, which was attempting to recruit the I.L.P. to Stalinism.

But propaganda alone could not accomplish this, so the I.L.P. leaders decided to demonstrate in a concrete manner the divergences between Russian policy and Socialist Internationalism. One of the first actions of Stalin's government after Hitler had come to power was to renew the Treaty of Berlin, one of the economic agreements of the Rapallo alliance of Germany and Russia, and to expand trade agreements between the two states. Whilst abroad Communist organisers were trying to get dockers to refuse to handle ships flying the swastika flag,[13] German trade with the Soviet Union was actually expanding. As Jock Haston, then an active Party worker in the seamen's union, remembers:

> I was shipping into Antwerp on a Dutch ship, flying the Panama flag, in 1933 after Hitler first came to power, and we were in Hamburg every six weeks. I was shipped originally out of Nieuport, and one of our functions was to take literature into Hamburg in the early stages. There were three of us on that ship, and every time we went into Hamburg there were Russian ships, laden to the gunwales with all the raw materials geared up to nourish the war machine. Because the line of the Comintern at that time was to blockade trade with Nazi Germany. And whilst we were actually battling physically all over the world to prevent ships carrying out trade with Germany, the Russians in practice had no restraints, in any shape or form, and that really worried me, but it didn't really make any impression on me until I was injured and recovering in hospital at home, and began to think the problem over and began to draw away from any form of active party work.[14]

Here was an ideal opportunity for the I.L.P. to show the divergences between the policy of the Soviet Union and the needs of the international working-class movement. On the other hand, when C.A. Smith asked Trotsky whether he supported 'an industrial and transport boycott of Fascist Germany' he could only agree that he did.[15] All the Communist Party could use to reply was that 'in reality, Trotsky and the I.L.P. leaders only use the "extremely left" criticism of the U.S.S.R. to cover up the provocative character of their boycott proposal, which would not have assisted the German working class, but would have played excellently into the hands of the war-mongers not to mention the capitalist competition of German industry!'[16]

Another way of heading off the attraction of the Comintern for the ranks of the I.L.P. was to strengthen its own international links. In February 1933 the I.L.P. added its signature to the appeal of the number of left wing parties for an alliance of the Second and Third Internationals in a common front against Nazism, and on 27th–28th August most of the parties and groups involved came together to discuss their common strategies at a conference in Paris, with John Paton of the I.L.P. as its Secretary. The International Trotskyist movement also intervened to use the conference to promote the idea of a new International, which was, of course, rejected. But at the same time some of the I.L.P. leaders took the opportunity to make direct contact with Trotsky, then in exile in France. Paton remembers Trotsky 'seated in his study, behind a huge table on which were arranged several neat piles of papers (it was the desk of a thoroughly methodical man)', discussing 'for several hours the Socialist questions in which we were interested'. 'He revealed a surprising knowledge of even the by-paths of the English political situation and was obviously a keen student of our journals,' he went on. 'His judgements on men and events were extraordinarily shrewd and often barbed with keen wit. The recent union of the I.L.P. with the Communist Party he described as 'miscegenation: the child will be a dark despair'. The purpose of the visit, however, to enlist his support for the I.L.P. and its sister parties in their committee, was an utter failure:

> He was well served by his intelligence service, and was perfectly informed on the internal difficulties of our International Committee. The failure of our conference he'd foreseen, and he said he proposed almost immediately to launch a new International based on the large number of his groups throughout the world. But here Schmidt and I had much to say. We made it clear to him that we believed he'd be heading for a disastrous failure. This was one of the matters on which we'd been anxious to see him. We wanted the co-operation of his groups in the work of our own committee.[17]

Another encounter took place between Trotsky and C.A. Smith. He asked Trotsky to explain why he rejected the I.L.P. view that his criticism of the Comintern was unbalanced and over-exaggerated, and wanted a new International to be created. He was given a thumb-nail sketch of the internal bankruptcy of the Communist International, and its criminal errors over Germany in particular. His advice to the I.L.P. was 'to remain independent at all costs until it has completed its evolution from reformism to revolution, from an empirical to a theoretical basis. You require a firm grasp of the revolutionary theory of the capitalist state, a correct evaluation of social and economic forces, adequate information of the movement of revolution and reaction outside Great Britain, and a definite plan of the revolutionary course within Britain — a plan flexible in detail but rigid in principle.'[18]

Some of this good advice was bound to rub off, and Smith in particular used it to good effect in his clashes with the Communists and the Revolutionary Policy Committee. Gallacher noted the argument that 'as the Russian delegates "dominate" the Communist International then it follows that the Communist International concerns itself with Russia to the disadvantage of the revolution in other countries' as being 'an argument worthy of the good doctor', and one for which he must thank Trotsky.[19] J.R. Campbell considered that 'all the arguments against closer association of the

I.L.P. with the C.I. and the ultimate creation of one revolutionary party in Great Britain' were a combination of 'Right Wing slanders with Trotskyist counter-revolutionary calumny', and that 'the association of some local I.L.P. leaders who are attacking the C.I. with a small group of expelled Trotskyists is now patent to everyone.'[20]

Armed with what they had drawn from the international movement, the I.L.P. leaders were able to pass over to the offensive with some effect. In one exchange Brockway point blank accused the Third International of betraying the workers, and Pollitt retorted by calling him 'worse than any Trotskyist',[21] whilst Maxton punctured all the bluster about the German Communists going from strength to strength[22] at a meeting in Edinburgh by showing that he had accurate knowledge that the German Communist Party 'no longer existed'.[23] Whereas at the Conference of 1933 Gaster and Cullen had been able to get through a resolution by a narrow majority, instructing the N.A.C. to explore ways in which the I.L.P. could 'assist in the work of the Communist International', at the following Easter Conference the suggestion for conditional and sympathetic affiliation was heavily defeated.[24] Gallacher had realised the source of their defeat when addressing a *Labour Monthly* Conference in the East End of London, when he admitted that the gulf between the Communist Party and the I.L.P. did not have its origins in 'historical objections, nor in the last few months' differences, but in a series of new objections not rooted in the rank and file experiences of the I.L.P., but in the Trotskyist sewer.'[25] Rothstein, in noting their 'feverish popularisation of Trotsky', believed that the I.L.P. leaders had 'sought the aid of Trotsky in stemming the tide' of the 'growing sympathy with Communism among the rank-and-file of the Independent Labour Party'.[26]

Defeated at a national level, the Communists had much greater success with the supporters of the Revolutionary Policy Committee in London. These were sincere militants attempting to rid themselves of the I.L.P.'s reformist legacy and grope towards an authentic revolutionary position, and were by no means the hardened Stalinists that some of them later became. For example, in January 1932 the Communist International had criticised the British C.P. for not showing up the differences they had with the I.L.P. They had then lumped together the Labour and I.L.P. leaders, and the supporters of the R.P.C. as 'Social Fascists', and had even on occasion accused them of being influenced by Trotskyism![27] As J.R. Campbell tried to prove:

> The little group of Trotskyists expelled from the Communist Party began to make contact with the members of the

> Revolutionary Policy Committee above referred to. They were welcomed with open arms. Here was a ready-made theoretical basis which enabled the revolutionary pose to be maintained, whilst providing arguments against the early establishment of a United Communist Party in Great Britain.[28]

Neither, to begin with, were the R.P.C. members attracted to the British Communist Party as such, as opposed to the Communist International. 'The tactic of the united front is likely to achieve more success in the present situation than a slightly enlarged membership of the Communist Party', they affirmed in their bulletin,[29] and Gaster was even more critical of the British C.P.:

> It calls itself the party of Marx and Lenin, but, quite frankly, must not a revolutionary party be a party of convinced revolutionary socialists who can form the spearhead of the wider working class movement and not consist largely of people who are vaguely militant and desirous of smashing the Capitalist system, who have acquired a parrot-like knowledge of some phrases of Marx and Lenin, and who interpret the very necessary discipline which a revolutionary party must exert upon its members, as a blind faith in its leadership? One of the results of the confusion as to whether or not the C.P.G.B. should be a mass party makes it appear to some I.L.P.ers as largely a party of jargon and phrases with a rank-and-file prepared to substitute blind faith in those phrases for a reasoned understanding. Blind faith whether in a mystical god-head, or dead economist, or working-class leader is an impossible basis for reasoned action.[30]

For a while, indeed, relations between the Revolutionary Policy Committee and the Communist Party were so poor that when they met to discuss their attitude to I.L.P. disaffiliation from the Labour Party, they refused entrance to the *Daily Worker* reporter sent to cover the meeting.[31]

But the day-to-day collaboration of the two parties in London — in which the R.P.C. supporters were the strongest supporters from the I.L.P. side — was bound to have an effect in the long run. Where two political organisations run on parallel courses, the one with the stronger structure always recruits from the weaker. Where the I.L.P. was unsure of its ideas and still working them out, the C.P. was strongly convinced of its own, and the London membership of the I.L.P. was not so stable as in the provinces.

The R.P.C. supporters were naturally prominent in the joint meetings called by the I.L.P. and the C.P. as long as their collaboration lasted. Jack Gaster, Karl Westwood, Jock Dunbar,

Warbey and Bronson all went along to a conference called by the Communists to debate the appeal to the Internationals with 'a large group of I.L.P.ers',[32] and soon direct Communist influence began to show. Cullen was already in close correspondence with Pollitt in the summer of 1933,[33] and the I.L.P.'s National Secretary began to suspect that 'some of the members of this group maintained close relations with, if they were not actually members of, the Communist Party and were engaged in the well-known Communist tactic of "boring from within".'[34]

Here, clearly, was an important field for the intervention of the International Left Opposition, in which the British Section was in a position to play an important part. 'The I.L.P. occupies a rather important position in the British working class movement,' ran an early notice, 'not because it has a formidable following, but because the impotence of the [Communist] Party has fortified the idea among the workers that it is becoming a real centre of opposition against the Labour Party. On the other hand it has a large number of individual adherents, and especially of late, it is attracting those young workers who are entering the movement for the first time.'[35] But the evolution of the I.L.P. was even more significant on the International plane, where it was a key part of a developing centrist current that opened up the possibility of recreating a real workers' International. As Trotsky explained:

> At the present time the Social Democracy is everywhere experiencing an acute crisis. In a number of countries more or less important left wings have already separated themselves from the Social Democratic parties. This process flows from the whole situation. That it has not yet taken on a more developed character is due to the mistakes of the Stalinist bureaucracy, which puts a brake on the internal differentiation in the ranks of reformism and closes the door of communism to the revolutionary wing. The appearance of independent socialist parties, as well as autonomous organisations, is a vote of direct and deserved defiance directed against the Comintern.[36]

Such an evolution opened up great possibilities for the Trotskyists, not only of breaking out of isolation or of providing a new way of influencing Communist workers, but of being able to re-forge the workers' International shattered by Stalinism. 'For us to seriously approach these organisations on a clear principled basis,' explained Trotsky, 'will signify a new chapter in the development of the Left Opposition and thereby of the rebirth of revolutionary Marxism in the world workers' movement. A great international revolutionary organisation inspired by the ideas of the Left Opposition would become a centre of attraction for the proletarian elements of the official Communist parties.'[37]

One way of doing this was to address directly the Conference of Left Socialist and Communist Parties then meeting in Paris, and the Left Opposition intervened, pointing out that 'if these organisations come together today for the first time at a common conference to try to find bases for joint work, all of them have by this very fact openly admitted the necessity of welding together the proletarian vanguard on new foundations,'[38] and declaring that 'the orientation towards a new International is dictated by the whole course of development.' At the end of the Conference they signed the 'Declaration of Four' along with the German S.A.P. and the Dutch O.S.P. and R.S.P., undertaking to 'direct all their forces to the formation of this International in the shortest possible time on the firm foundation of the theoretical and strategic principles laid down by Marx and Lenin.'[39]

It was precisely upon this question of the need for a new workers' International that the I.L.P. equivocated most. 'We wish to unite as effectively as possible the revolutionary socialist movements of the world,' explained Brockway. 'Many of them are within the Communist International, but many of them find the organisational control and tactics of the Communist International intolerable.' 'I hope the I.L.P. will maintain its objective of revolutionary unity whatever its international associations may be,' he went on. 'Within such a party all revolutionary Socialists should find a basis of common action — all revolutionary Socialists except those content to accept the present organisational basis and tactics of the Communist International. I express this opinion now because it will be a disaster if the useful discussions which are proceeding within the party on Trotskyism led to a cleavage.'[40] As he later explained, 'the establishment of a revolutionary Socialist party can be attempted in one of two ways: a few theoreticians can lay down a watertight programme and invite those who agree with it to join; this is the method of the Trotskyists, and the Fourth International has remained in a vacuum.'[41] His way was a loose international alliance, but at the same time as keeping its committee of left socialist allies, Brockway reaffirmed that 'the I.L.P. maintains its desire to find a basis of co-operation with the Communist International.'[42]

This was trying to keep options open in all directions, hedging of the purest Brockway type. As Trotsky put it, 'having entered into an alliance with the Communist Party, the I.L.P. has not determined its international position. It broke with the Second International and made an alliance with the Third, but it also enters into a working alliance with left Socialist parties.' He asked point blank: 'Is it willing to share the fate of the historically doomed Comintern, does it want to try to remain in an intermediate position (which means to return by roundabout ways to reformism), or is it ready to participate in the building of a new International on the foundations laid by Marx and Lenin?'[43] The I.L.P.'s equivocation at the Paris Conference took the form of giving the Comintern another chance, before considering another International. Its statement ran that 'if the Third International proves unprepared to change its tactics and organisation, the time will have come to consider the formation of a new International.' 'This section contains the very essence of the present policy of the I.L.P.,' Trotsky noted. 'Having shifted decisively to the left, to Communism, the members of this party refuse to believe that the Communist International, which has numerous cadres and material and technical means at its disposal, is lost for the revolutionary movement.'[44]

It was, in fact, this flirting with Stalinism that threatened to hasten the disintegration of the I.L.P. A census of branch opinion showed that two-thirds of the party were only going along with it unwillingly, and a string of major resignations including Paton and the entire Lancashire area showed that it was becoming a disaster for the party.[45] The theoretical weaknesses of the I.L.P. played a major role in aggravating the situation. Maxton's remarks in his preface to Trotsky's Copenhagen speech, that the Stalin/Trotsky conflict was 'a matter on which only Russian Socialists are competent to decide'[46] showed that he accepted implicitly the theory of 'Socialism in One Country', rejecting the whole basis of Socialist Internationalism. 'Our struggle with it concerns precisely the question as to whether Socialism is a national or an international matter,' wrote Trotsky in reply. 'Admitting the possibility of the theoretical and practical solution of the problems of Socialism within national limits, Maxton admits the correctness of the Stalinist faction, which bases itself on the theory of "Socialism in One Country".' It was this insularity that prevented the I.L.P. approaching the problem of the International with any clarity. 'By these few words,' Trotsky noted, 'the international character of Socialism as a scientific doctrine and as a revolutionary movement is completely refuted. If Socialists (Communists) of one country are incapable, incompetent, and consequently have no right to decide the vital questions of the struggle of Socialists (Communists) in other countries, the proletarian International loses all rights and possibilities of existence.'[47]

Political clarity on the question of Stalinism was a life or death question for the I.L.P., and time was fast running out (as was much of their support). 'In the realm of ready-made revolutionary formulas, the bureaucracy of the British Communist Party is immeasurably better equipped. Precisely in this lies its present advantage over the leadership of the I.L.P.,' Trotsky warned. 'And it must be said openly this superficial, purely formal advantage may, under the present circumstances, lead to the liquidation of the I.L.P. without any gains accruing to the Communist Party and to the revolution. The objective conditions have more than once pushed tens and even hundreds of thousands of workers towards the British Section of the Comintern, but the leadership of the Comintern was only capable of disillusioning them and throwing them back.' He ended with a grim warning, all too true in the long run:

> We see too clearly that if this party should ingloriously disappear from the scene Socialism would suffer a new blow. And this danger exists; and it is not far removed. In our epoch it is impossible to remain long in intermediary positions. Only political clarity can save the I.L.P. for the proletarian revolution.[48]

An article addressed to Trotsky's British supporters urgently made the same point:

> In its present composition, it is clear, the I.L.P. is not viable. It is getting weaker and it is losing members not only on the right but also on the left, because its leadership has no clear policy and is not capable of imbuing the party with confidence of its strength. It is possible to stop this further disintegration of the I.L.P. only by imparting to it Marxist views on the problems of our epoch, and in particular a Marxist analysis of the Stalinist bureaucracy.[49]

Trotsky's advice for the salvation of the I.L.P. was to move towards Marxist theory in a serious manner, 'by freeing itself from all unclarity and laziness with regard to the ways and methods of the socialist revolution and by becoming a truly revolutionary party of the proletariat',[50] through the study of the First Four Congresses of the Comintern, by assimilating the lessons of the struggle of the Left Opposition both with regard to Russia and the Chinese Revolution, the German débâcle, etc., and finally, 'to establish correct relations with the class'. 'This presupposes a policy of revolutionary realism,' he wrote, 'equally removed from opportunistic vagueness and sectarian aloofness. From the point of view of both these closely connected criteria, the I.L.P. should review its relations to the Comintern as well as to all other organisations and tendencies within the working class. This concerns first of all the fate of the I.L.P. itself.'[51]

Obviously, though he wrote article after article in their direction, Trotsky had no illusions that the I.L.P. leadership were capable of this necessary task of education and organisation. In the end, if

Marxism were to be brought to the I.L.P., it would have to be taken there by Marxists themselves. That was a task reserved for the British Section, the Communist League. The guidelines for such a strategy were laid down by Trotsky in a document he wrote in June 1933:

> The International Left Opposition faces a new task: to accelerate the evolution of the left Socialist organisations towards Communism by injecting its ideas and its experience into this process. There is no time to lose. If the independent Socialist organisations remain in their present amorphous state for a long period of time, they will disintegrate. The political tasks of our epoch are so acute, the pressure of hostile forces so powerful — to this it is necessary to add the intrigues of the reformist bureaucracy on the one hand and the Stalinist bureaucracy on the other — that only a powerful ideological bond on the firm basis of Marxism can assure a revolutionary organisation the ability to maintain itself against the hostile currents and to lead the proletarian vanguard to a new revolutionary epoch.[52]

It followed that 'the Bolshevik-Leninists must enter into open discussions with the revolutionary Socialist organisations', and that it was necessary to 'demonstrate that principled irreconcilability has nothing in common with sectarian snobbishness.'[53] The International Secretariat suggested to the British Trotskyists that the best way that these tasks could be undertaken was by the entry of their group as a faction into the I.L.P. as a whole.

The British Trotskyists had not, of course, neglected the extraordinary ferment then going on in the ranks of the I.L.P. Apart from those who had passed over into the movement from Ridley's Marxian League, others, such as Groves, had spent part of their formative years in the Labour movement in the I.L.P., and contact with its large Clapham branch in the South London Anti-War Committee had never been interrupted. When Wicks visited a Y.C.L. summer camp outside Leeds in July 1932, in order to distribute copies of *The Communist*, he also took the opportunity to visit the special conference of the I.L.P. that was meeting in nearby Bradford at the same time, to discuss disaffiliation from the Labour Party and to sell copies there.[54] A leaflet put out over Dewar's name, addressed to the I.L.P., pointed out:

> It is necessary that you make clear your position, especially on the basic problems of the revolution. The lack of this formulation makes it possible, in the I.L.P. today, to find those who stand for immediate adhesion to the C.P.G.B. rubbing

> shoulders with those whose rightful place is in the Labour Party. Your conference decisions, your party organ, the articles and speeches of your leaders all reflect the confusion and lack of clarity which at present exists within the I.L.P. On very few of the main issues has the I.L.P. taken a clear and unambiguous stand. This we believe to be because the I.L.P. is a 'Centrist' organisation. This is not a matter of abuse, but a political definition: *the I.L.P. stands midway between reformism and Communism*. Such a position cannot be tolerated by revolutionaries, because 'Centrism' smears over the vital distinctions between reformism and communism, and tries to bridge the gulf between the two. The revolutionary seeks, not to hide, but to emphasise disagreements, to sharpen distinctions, to clarify always and to conduct an open and ruthless struggle against reformism and *against centrism*.[55]

In July 1933 the National Committee of the group established a committee to develop and co-ordinate its I.L.P. work, to draw together its contacts to set up an organised fraction, and to issue leaflets.[56] Advertisements for *Red Flag* began to be placed with *The New Leader*,[57] and notices for meetings addressed by Trotskyists began to appear in it.[58] A balance sheet drawn up stated that ten I.L.P. branches had been so addressed, that the group had seven members in the I.L.P., and that the paper was being sold by branches in Liverpool itself, Kirkdale, Huddersfield, Glasgow Govan, and Hampstead, Clapham and Wimbledon in London.[59]

But the type of work that had been done had already placed serious obstacles in the way of future entry into the I.L.P. In the context of the group's understanding of their task as a fraction of the Communist Party and the Communist International, they had been recruiting out of the I.L.P. and orientating the people they influenced towards the Communist Party. For example, when David Chalkley had been sent by Tooting I.L.P. as a delegate to the South-West London Anti-War Committee, and had become convinced of the correctness of the politics of the Trotskyists on it, he had been recruited out of the I.L.P. and into the group.[60] Those who had left the I.L.P. when Ridley's group broke up might well ask themselves why they had bothered in the first place. What was worse, at the time the Easter Conference of the I.L.P. in 1933 had carried the motion to seek ways to assist in the work of the Communist International, a statement had been put out by four I.L.P. group members advising I.L.P.ers to leave their party and join the Communist Party. Whilst criticising the Communist Party on such issues as 'Socialism in One Country', the 'United Front from Below', the Amsterdam Congress and bureaucratism, it stated that

> The British Section of the C.I. is the only existing revolutionary party in this country. The undersigned members of the I.L.P. believe that the place of revolutionary workers is inside the Communist Party. Recognising that the present policy of the C.P. requires drastic changes, and appreciating fully the weaknesses of its tactics, we maintain that criticism of the C.P. is no legitimate excuse for staying outside. The I.L.P. is a Social-Democratic Body, product of a past era, has its very economic basis torn from it. Therefore, correctly to criticise the I.L.P. is to leave it . . . the R.P.C. (Revolutionary Policy Committee) accepts the fundamental basis of the C.I. (Communist International), and since new parties are the product of major political events, and cannot be created at the will of individuals, to pose the question of a new party outside both the C.P. and the I.L.P. is a waste of precious time. The R.P.C. cannot build a substitute for the C.I. . . . realising that it [i.e. the C.P.] is the only revolutionary party, we intend to enter it, to work as Communists, at the same time seeking, by every legitimate means, to change those points in its policy which we consider wrong. We appeal to all revolutionary workers in the I.L.P. to adopt the same position.[61]

Whilst this statement was fully in line with the policy of the International movement,[62] it was a most unfortunate one in view of the subsequent change of policy in Britain, especially when two of the names appended to it on Groves' initiative were added without consultation with the individuals involved.[63]

Then, on 21st August, the Administrative Secretary of the International Left Opposition, Bauer (Erwin Ackerknecht), wrote to the British Section under I.S. instructions urging entry into the I.L.P.:

> . . . all the information that we receive on the internal situation in the I.L.P. makes us pose the question whether your organisation ought not to concentrate nine tenths, if not ninety-nine hundredths, of its forces on the work within the I.L.P.? It seems to us, moreover, that there are no obstacles whatsoever for the entrance of the members of your section — all of them or of their majority — into the I.L.P. At the Brussels Conference Paton said that the I.L.P. now consists of six or seven factions. Under these circumstances there is every reason to believe that you could become the strongest of the factions . . . You could and should enter into the I.L.P. so as to lead it to the path of Bolshevism as well as to guard it from Stalinist machinations: these two tasks coincide with each other. Your work can be successful only under one condition:

that you enter the I.L.P. not only to split this or that part from it but to help the party *as a whole* to become strengthened revolutionarily by cleaning itself from opportunist tendencies and foreign elements . . .[64]

The National Committee of the group met to consider its attitude to these proposals. It rejected them as resting 'upon an exaggerated idea of the importance of the I.L.P.' which, despite a few hundred youth, was 'predominantly petty-bourgeois, not proletarian, and within it the right wing is as strong, if not stronger, than the left and centrist wings combined.' 'The past and present of the I.L.P. makes it difficult to see it developing into a revolutionary party as it is at present,' they added. 'It is soaked with the heritage of its past — in fact it is difficult to distinguish the past from the present I.L.P. at times — and is very seriously compromised in the eyes of the militant workers, so much so that few of the I.L.P. even believe in its transformation into a revolutionary party.' They objected that they would not be allowed to enter publicly as a fraction, but as individuals, and that 'this would be an announcement to those militant workers who follow our press, etc., that we had forsaken the platform of the Bolshevik/Leninists for that of the I.L.P.'[65]

The problem was further complicated by some remarks added in French to the bottom of Bauer's letter, to the effect that entry into the I.L.P. implied that they kept their press and group as independent entities, and that one or two comrades should remain outside the I.L.P. to take responsibility for their press and public activity. The group objected to this as showing 'an intellectual approach to the question', and asked: 'A paper issued in this way would be maintained, run and sold by whom, and would be read by whom?' 'Anyone with money can publish a paper but unless it was connected with the activities and situation of the advanced workers it would count for nothing.'[66]

Trotsky intervened to correct the misunderstanding:

On the question of the I.L.P. the Secretariat has altered so much of my proposition that it suggests to our English Section — if my information is correct — that some comrades should not enter the I.L.P. so that they can continue publishing the paper. This plan, after a long conversation with Smith, who makes the best impression personally, seems to me of no use. The I.L.P., and this is to its credit, has expelled two members because they were also members of the Communist Party. The I.L.P. will also distrust us for the same reason. This distrust can only be overcome if our people get into the I.L.P. with the desire to influence the party as a whole and to become powerful there but not to work toward breaking away a small

> part from the whole party. The publication of a small, monthly paper under the circumstances is senseless because the same articles are published at the same time or earlier in *The Militant*.[67]

The International Secretariat did its utmost to bring the British Trotskyists round to its view. It despatched Demetrious Giotopoulos, leader of the Greek ArcheoMarxists, to Britain; and he arrived whilst the discussions were in full swing.

> I made contact with the leadership precisely on the evening when it approved the declaration-response to the letter of the I.S. proposing the entrance of the British Opposition into the I.L.P. The decision containing the contents of this declaration had been taken in the preceding meeting. In this declaration, which the I.S. should have received already, the leadership pronounced against the proposal of the I.S. . . . The attitude of the leadership and its arguments was as follows:
>
> They took into consideration the past of the I.L.P. and the repercussions of that past among the more advanced workers of the country. By its past, the I.L.P. is, among the advanced workers, a compromised party . . . actually the I.L.P. is not a proletarian organisation . . . a very small fraction, perhaps 10%, are workers . . . Also, they fear being discredited among the Communist workers by the fact that they, the Communist Left Opposition, enter into a party like the I.L.P. compromised in these circles by its past and its policies.[68]

Groves, Sara and Purkis discussed at length with Giotopoulos in cafés, etc., but were 'unable to make him understand the peculiarities of the British Labour movement, or to see what we really wanted to do'.[69] For, here again, the differences of the British Trotskyists lay rooted in their evolution from the Communist Party at the height of its 'Third Period', and their local horizons in South London. Their activity was directed towards the people with whom they made direct contact in the organisations where they worked. Naturally, they saw the I.L.P. in its most middle-class form — its London membership. They had no contact with its supporters in Yorkshire or on Clydeside, where it was completely proletarian. Similarly, their attitude towards the I.L.P. as a whole was conditioned by their own past. 'In *The New Leader*,' one of their statements ran, 'it is constantly emphasised that both the 2nd and 3rd Internationals are bankrupt, both have betrayed the working class and that both are useless to the I.L.P. But actually there is a very big question covered by the terms "bankrupt", etc. The Communist Party is a proletarian party: the Labour Party is a bourgeois Party. Instead of standing in the middle and condemning in general, it is necessary to state our attitude to each. It is impossible to condemn impartially reformism and Communism: the one we are out to destroy, the other to change.'[70] As Wicks put it in a nutshell:

> Now here were people that had been steeled in the English movement. The difference between a Communist and an I.L.P.er is the difference between a proletarian and a middle-class person. This was how one looked at the I.L.P. The I.L.P. was a middle-class organisation. Now this business of the political perspectives of going in and influencing a very experienced set of parliamentarians like Maxton and McGovern wasn't on — on their own ground — in the period we're talking of, in 1934. There was Campbell Stephen, there was Fenner Brockway, there was a whole group of very experienced politicians. It was projected that we, as a small group, rooted by and large in South-West London, could influence this organisation. It wasn't feasible, and what's more, from the point of view of the people, the personnel, Communist essentially, they felt unable to do it. The only people it appealed to were the intellectuals. Now in this respect Denzil Harber had no roots. He had no roots in the Labour movement. In fact, when you change parties, it is not a question of you changing personally, you have to account to the people you are known to. Harber had no roots anywhere. He didn't have to account to anybody. He didn't know of the antipathy between the proletarian and the middle-class I.L.P.er.[71]

Trotsky, however, believed this reluctance sprang from 'fear of malicious criticism of the Stalinists', 'the fear of public opinion of the bureaucracy only because we were connected with it in the past',[72] even though the National Committee comrades denied this.[73]

The real reasons for this resistance to such a radical change in their functioning lay deeper, as Trotsky foresaw when he first analysed the movement of the Socialist organisations to the left; and they were to recur in the International movement every time a change in policy or orientation was effected:

> The transition from one stage of struggle to a higher one has never been accomplished without internal friction. Some comrades, homesick for the mass organisations, exhibit a desire to gather fruits that are still unripe. Others, anxious about the purity of the principles of the Left Opposition, regard all attempts to approach the larger mass organisations with distrust. 'What good can be expected from Nazareth?

> How can one approach organisations at the head of which are centrists? We are quite ready,' they say, 'to unite with the rank-and-file workers, but we do not see any sense in approaching the centrist leaders,' etc., etc. Such a purely formal manner of posing the question is erroneous. They are greatly affected by propagandist sectarianism.[74]

Feeling on the International Secretariat continued to harden in favour of the entry perspective. Even Naville, who came to Britain an opponent of the idea of going into the I.L.P., came back a convinced supporter.[75] Trotsky returned again to the general analysis, and how the question of entry flowed naturally from it. He outlined how the I.L.P. was a left-centrist party, how it contained a number of factions and opinions marking different positions in evolution from reform to revolution of the most varied character, and that 'in front of each centrist grouping it is necessary to place an arrow indicating the direction of its development, from right to left or from left to right.' In the case of the Left Socialist parties, it was the destructive policy of the Communist International that had accumulated 'a mass of explosive material' in their ranks, which 'is one of the most important prerequisites for the creation of new parties and a new International'. 'A Marxist party should, of course, strive to full independence and to the higher homogeneity,' he explained, 'but in the process of its formation, a Marxist party often has to act as a faction of a centrist and even a reformist party.' The I.L.P.'s theoretical helplessness gave the advantage to the Communist Party as things stood, but it also opened up opportunities for the British Trotskyists. Time was fast slipping away:

> It is not sufficient to have correct ideas. In a decisive moment one must know how to show one's strength to the advanced workers. As far as I can judge from here, the possibility for influencing the I.L.P. as a whole is not yet missed. But in another couple of months, the I.L.P. will have completely fallen between the gear wheels of the Stalinist bureaucracy and will be lost, leaving thousands of disappointed workers. It is necessary to act, and to act immediately.
>
> It is worth entering the I.L.P. only if we make it our purpose to help this party, that is, its *revolutionary majority*, to transform it into a truly Marxist party . . .
>
> Only the Bolshevik-Leninists can do this work. But to do this they must courageously destroy the wall that divides them today from the revolutionary workers of the I.L.P.[76]

The National Committee's reply, written a month later, disagreed with the sense of urgency. 'Actually we do not regard the situation as one that will be resolved within such a short time,' they wrote. 'The date of the decisive struggle is likely to be fought out at the end of March next year at the annual [Conference] of the I.L.P.' But their main proposals, to continue with faction work from outside, rested upon an analysis of the I.L.P. entirely different from Trotsky's:

> This party broke with the Labour Party through the widespread effects of the world economic crisis, and as a result of the general reaction from the disastrous failure of the second Labour Government. The feeling of the rank and file compelled the leaders of the I.L.P. to make a show of outraged virtue and support the break. From then on the I.L.P. was occupied in justifying its separate existence and its chief, and almost only way of doing this during the past twelve months has been its propaganda and sentimental appeals for 'unity'. In other words, the general policy of the I.L.P. has reflected its 'centrist' position. Today its leadership is that of reformists and centrists, in the main, its structure is still that of a party organised to capture seats in parliament, its programme still leaves unanswered the vital questions confronting the revolutionary workers. The bulk of its leading members are hopelessly saturated with reformist and centrist conceptions; its rank and file is lacking in basic revolutionary principles . . .
>
> At present there can be discerned roughly three groupings within the I.L.P. These groupings are by no means sharply defined and tend on many issues to merge into each other. Within each grouping there are several shadings, but for the purposes of brief political description we can speak of three groups. There is that of the Right, which has five or six members on the N.A.C. and finds its chief support at present in the proletarian districts, e.g. Lancashire, Yorkshire, Wales, etc. There is the Left which is badly led, and which finds its chief support in the London area, which is overwhelmingly petty-bourgeois in composition. There is the Centre, which holds the I.L.P. together with its vagueness and blurring of the revolutionary and reformist conceptions. The Right is naturally working to return to the Labour Party, as is the Centre, only in a more roundabout way, whilst the Left is in such theoretical chaos that it has been unable to make any serious inroads into the following of the Right wing, or to make any effective changes in the structure of the party.

On this basis they proposed to continue as before, working to influence the I.L.P. from outside, co-ordinating their faction work, building up groups of sympathisers around *Red Flag*, using leaflets, outside speakers, etc. Otherwise, they pointed out, *Red Flag* would cease to exist, C.P. fraction work would effectively cease, along with all other phases of work, and 'we should become a fraction, a very crippled fraction, we suggest, in the I.L.P.' But what weighed with them in particular was their setting within the London area, and their lack of confidence in being able to challenge the I.L.P. leaders at a national level:

> Our entry at present would mean, at the most, influence and possible control in three or four branches in the London area. Compared with our present position this seems to us to be less advantageous. At present we are able to reach these self-same branches through the joint discussion between them and our own group, and also to reach many other London branches by sending speakers and by the distribution of literature. Through our paper, which is not only bought by members of the I.L.P., but which is on sale at a number of branches all over the country, we are able to influence members in the discussions taking place. As a fraction we could not reach these people, at least for a considerable period of time after entering.

They thus had no confidence in their ability to reach out to wider layers than they had already contacted, objecting to Trotsky's perspective of touching 'the revolutionary majority', or being able to leap from forty to a thousand. 'The proposal of Comrade Trotsky,' they concluded, 'is based upon an exaggerated idea of the size and present state of the I.L.P., and upon a decision being reached in the I.L.P. at a speed not in our opinion justified by the actual circumstances.'[77]

Trotsky took up their arguments again, returning to the points he had made. 'In comparison with your small group, the I.L.P. was a big organisation,' he agreed, but 'your small lever is insufficient to move the Labour Party but can have a big effect on the I.L.P.' He concluded that their analysis of the I.L.P. resulted from their being 'inclined to look at the I.L.P. through the eyes of the Stalinist party, that is, to exaggerate the number of petty-bourgeois elements and minimise the Proletarian elements.' He advised them to give up *Red Flag* and use the American *Militant* and the International press of the Left Opposition as well as the I.L.P.'s *The New Leader* and its internal discussion bulletin, *Controversy*. On their perspective of open work from outside, again he tried to demonstrate that a small group can become a mass party if it first becomes a fraction of a mass organisation; but that it cannot in any way expect the workers to leave their mass organisations and join it:

> You speak of the advantages of influencing the I.L.P. from the outside . . . Taken on a wide historical scale your arguments are irrefutable, but there are unique, exceptional circumstances that we must know how to make use of by exceptional means.
>
> Today the revolutionary workers of the I.L.P. still hold on to their party. The perspective of joining a group of forty, the principles of which are little known to them, can by no means appeal to them. If within the next year they should grow disappointed with the I.L.P., they will go not to you but to the Stalinists, who will break these workers' necks.
>
> If you enter the I.L.P. to work for the Bolshevik transformation of the party (that is, of its revolutionary kernel), the workers will look upon you as upon fellow workers, comrades, and not upon adversaries who want to split the party from the outside . . .
>
> Remaining as an independent group, you represent, in the eyes of the workers, only small competition to the Stalinists. Inside the party you can much more successfully insulate the workers against Stalinism.[78]

But the reluctance remained. A further discussion of the question at a National Committee meeting on 5th October produced the further objections that 'whilst it is true that our being outside the I.L.P. might tend to create the impression that our work represented recruiting efforts for our own organisation, the very fact that our entry into the I.L.P. would of necessity have to be preceded by a public statement of our reasons for so doing would in itself keep alive these very suspicions', and that 'some of our members left the I.L.P. not so long ago and would experience some difficulty in rejoining.'[79]

Although Trotsky made clear that his view and the resolutions of the I.S. were not intended to force the British Comrades 'by a bare order to enter the I.L.P.',[80] or 'to submit to it silently',[81] but were offered as help and advice, the inevitable appearance of a faction inside the British section which wished to follow the policy of entry was bound to raise wider issues of international discipline in the long run.

A dozen of the group's younger members adopted this position.[82] Drawn from the L.S.E. group and the teachers, they tended to be the less experienced and more middle-class section of the membership — Denzil Harber, Stewart Kirby, Wally Graham, Dr. Worrall, Max Nicholls, Margaret Johns (who had only just joined), and Roma Dewar (who supported I.L.P. entry but became active in the Labour

League of Youth); while outside the group and already in the I.L.P., waiting for them to join, were Sid Kemp and Bert Matlow.

Their views appeared in the Internal Bulletin on 12th October, over the signatures of Allen, Graham and Chalmers.[83] They began by pointing out that revolutionaries cannot expect to be guaranteed success when they undertake a new policy, and analysed carefully the dilemma of the I.L.P., especially in the field of its international links. Since the Conference of the Left Socialist Parties in Paris was not going to be successful in forming an international, and return to the Second was not acceptable to the I.L.P.'s rank and file, the only two options left were within the Third, or to join the Bolshevik/Leninists in setting up a Fourth. 'In the final analysis,' they concluded, 'the real struggle is neither between Leninism and Left Centrism, nor between Bureaucratic Centrism and Left Centrism, but between Stalinism (Bureaucratic Centrism) and *Leninism*'. Posing the problem in this way, three possible results were projected for the I.L.P.: that it would split into fragments, to the recruiting advantage of the C.P.G.B., that it would suffer a merger with it, or that it would keep its independence — and the time necessary to be able to sort out its ideas. Obviously, the Stalinists were angling for the first and second alternatives, or a combination of them, since it gave decisive advantage to the weight of their bureaucratic apparatus. It followed equally that the third alternative was the most desirable for the revolutionaries, and that each side should choose the appropriate weapons and strategy:

> Where we are strong, the Stalinists are weak; and vice versa. We have an overwhelming superiority in relation to principles and ideas, while the Stalinists have at the given moment the advantage in the organisational field. But this fact, important as it is, does not pre-determine who is to be the victor. It does, however, clearly indicate that one should expect significant differences in the strategy and tactics used by the two sides . . .
>
> The basic strategy of the Stalinists is to rob the I.L.P. of its independence as a party in one way or another and to accomplish this task at the earliest possible moment, i.e. before these 'Trotskyist' objections have time to become more deeply rooted in the rank-and-file. We submit to the membership of the British Section of the International Left Opposition that for us to fail to throw our entire effort into the defence now of the *independence* of the I.L.P. would play into the hands of the Stalinists, permitting them to select the time and weapons of battle — and all to their advantage as against ours. An early splitting up of the I.L.P. would enable the Stalinists,

1. F.A. Ridley at the I.L.P. Conference — cartoon by Jack Anderson.

2. Hugo Dewar at work.

4. Harry Wicks in 1973.

3. Henry Sara (*left*) on the platform with A.J. Cook.

THE MILITANT

"UNITY" MONGERS SURRENDER!

Now For A Real Left Wing!

Y.C.L. WANTS—
"BROAD" YOUTH LEAGUE

LEON TROTSKY
"THE REVOLUTION BETRAYED"

The RED FLAG

Monthly Organ of the British Section, International Left Opposition.

Number One. Vol. 1.

One Penny

FOR LENIN AND TROTSKY!

On The Anti-Fascist Front.

A LETTER FROM GERMANY.

Why The RED FLAG Appears.

TO REGENERATE REVOLUTIONARY MOVEMENT.

5. The Trotskyist press — open and entrist.

YOUTH IN RED RUSSIA 2d.

Official Report of First British Young Workers' Delegation to Soviet Russia

Published by

NATIONAL CAMPAIGN COMMITTEE

First Young Workers' Delegation to Soviet Russia

SECRETARY:

MISS D. ROBERTS, c/o 67 Camden Road, N.W

6. Starkey Jackson (*centre*) with the Young Workers' Delegation to Russia, 1926.

7. Margaret Johns in 1978.

8. Reg Groves canvassing at Aylesbury, 1938.

9. Denzil Dean Harber in 1938.

> with their organisational advantage (numbers, press, etc., etc.) to enlist hundreds of I.L.P. workers to our tens — and worse still, allow thousands to sink more or less immediately into the swamp of political indifference.

It followed that it was up to the Trotskyists to choose a strategy of total entry, to make use of their organisational flexibility and the strength of their Leninist ideas. 'Once we have broken down the organisational wall between ourselves and our fellow Leninists in the I.L.P,' they explained, 'we shall be able effectively to combine our forces and stave off the collapse of the I.L.P.', and by defending the independence of the I.L.P. 'make it possible to use our strongest force — our Leninist principles; and compel the Stalinists to make use of, not their strongest weapon (organisational numbers, daily press, money etc.) but their weakest, Stalinist principles.'

But by trying to intervene from outside as a separate group all they could accomplish was to assist the Stalinists in splitting up the I.L.P., picking up a few members of the C.P.G.B.'s hundreds in the 'ghoulish task in the scavenging of what remains on the battlefield', thrusting thousands more into political apathy. The group strategy, they maintained, of trying to act as an independent party by picking up members 'building from the ground up', smacked of Lenin's infantile disorder, 'Left-wing Communism'. Moreover, their small size prevented them from establishing an alliance with the I.L.P. in the United Front. 'Can a party of forty or fifty (or double that, or even ten times that) expect to establish, or even if established accomplish much by, a united front with a party that can count its members in thousands?' they asked. 'What example in revolutionary history can be pointed to?' They concluded: '. . . every week, every day, of delay in applying the proper tactic presents that much more of advantage to the Stalinists.'[84]

In linking the concept of entry to that of the United Front the Minority comrades were, in fact, posing an entirely different mode of operation within the Labour movement from that of the Majority. Apart from holding out the possibility of winning over the I.L.P. 'as a party', they were demonstrating the Marxist concept of party-building, a process of uniting with the working class in its classwide organisations by providing them with a strategy for building mass revolutionary parties. The two views counterposed here, in fact, remain with the Trotskyists still: of trying to build a party by individual accretion to a small group, or directing Marxist ideas at the institutions of the whole working class.[85]

A further paper presented by them went over the alternatives available to the group yet again: of total entry, with its perspective of producing a new Marxist Party of thousands in a matter of months, of sending most of the group inside but keeping a few out to produce *Red Flag* (which corresponded to their position *vis-à-vis* the Communist Party in 1932) and to 'act increasingly as an independent party' recruiting very gradually in small units, holding out the possibility of a membership amounting to a few hundred at best over a long period of time. The first tactic, they considered, would provide greater numbers, an organisational framework, a press, meeting-places, and other essential equipment: and taking a look at the group's past, they added that 'practically every reason that justified our trying to win over the C.P.G.B. from bureaucratic centrism applies with almost equal force (some with even greater force) to our NOW trying to win over the I.L.P. from other brands of centrism.'[86] In this sense, by in effect trying to form a party by recruitment to a group, and keeping small factions in other working-class institutions, it was the group Majority who were projecting a totally new strategy (and in that sense the W.R.P. and the S.W.P. are its direct descendants).

The group came together in the New Morris Hall at Clapham on 17th December and almost all the members spoke, with Groves prominent in defending the Majority's case, and Denzil Harber and Stewart Kirby that of the Minority.[87] When the vote was taken, 26 members supported the National Committee Majority, and eleven Harber and Kirby. At the end of the meeting the Minority representatives announced that they could not accept the decision, and intended to enter the I.L.P., elect their own leadership, and become directly responsible to the International Secretariat.[88] The split was now complete.

The Majority reacted angrily by addressing a statement to the International Secretariat on the violation of Bolshevik norms of discipline, which this action involved, and on the Secretariat's encouragement of it. 'An organised group can only work effectively on the basis of majority decisions,' they reminded them, and 'provided that all the necessary conditions are observed which make for adequate discussion, adequate expression of points of view, the majority decision must be regarded as the way upon which the organised group can reach a decision and operate that decision.' To operate in any other way, they added prophetically, 'is to pave the way for continual breakaways, frequent fractional disturbances, and to destroy the possibility of establishing an effective centralised leadership.'[89]

The International Secretariat replied that posing the problem in general terms about discipline was an empty concept, since the British Section was only a recent addition to the international movement, whose work 'consists essentially of individual propaganda activity', and that 'discipline is only possible under a leadership enjoying authority, and which has demonstrated, through various important phases of development, its capacity to weigh up situations and draw the necessary practical conclusions.' Moreover, it reminded the Majority comrades that 'discipline is not confined to the national framework', that the International Secretariat could have dealt with the whole entry question 'on the ground of formal discipline', but had not done so because, 'having appreciated in advance the limits of the political experience of the British Section', they wished to give it 'a chance to carry out a transition with the least possible shocks from a period of group study and propaganda to a period of a much larger political activity.' They accused the Majority of having 'provoked a split' to avoid a fractional struggle out of 'sectarian conservativism'. Finally, they ratified the split and laid down the future status of the two groups:

> In any case, the split is a fact. And it means that there will be no organisational link at all between the two groups. There can be no question of the national committee controlling the work of the minority, since that control would render its work impossible. From now on, the two groups will have equal rights, one and the other, in their affiliation to the International Left Opposition.[90]

Majority and Minority were bitter at being thus reduced to equal terms. On 5th January the Minority wrote to the International Secretariat and asked what their relationship was now expected to be with the Majority. Trotsky wrote back that 'no organisational relationship at all is envisaged', but that, as they had not yet entered the I.L.P., they were wasting time 'for purely fictitious reasons', that 'you are not responsible for the Majority', and that 'the split can only be justified by practical success within the I.L.P.' He urged them to put out a statement, making clear what had happened, as a preliminary step to entering the I.L.P.:

> We were all agreed on the fact that after its entry into the I.L.P. the British Section would have to put an end to its existence as an independent organisation. But you have split. It is not now a question of a section, but of its task. The existence of an organisation of Bolshevik-Leninists can in no way hamper you if you declare openly that you are splitting with that organisation, that you no longer accept its discipline, and are broadly speaking no longer bound to it. Such a declaration, totally in conformity with the actual situation, must demonstrate to all the members of the I.L.P. all the more clearly the honesty of your intentions.[91]

On 16th February *The New Leader* published the Minority's letter to the National Council requesting membership in the I.L.P. 'We enter with the sincere intention of participating in all possible Party activities,' they wrote. 'While doing so, we wish to retain the right, as other members of the I.L.P., of comradely criticism and the right to fight and to propagate (within the limits of the Party Constitution and discipline) our opinions, in particular the necessity for the I.L.P. helping to build up the Fourth International.' The National Council replied by stating that they were 'entitled to apply for branch membership as individuals', but that 'an organised group cannot be admitted to the Party to advocate a particular policy.'[92] By their hesitations they were losing precious time, and it was not until 23rd March that they published the statement asked for by Trotsky and the International Secretariat:

> The building of a new Party would be painfully slow. The possibility of a speedier way of establishing an effective revolutionary Party is provided by the I.L.P., which, despite its past mistakes, represents a potential revolutionary force. Provided that it avoids the false policy that has strangled the C.I. [Communist International] it will become the future revolutionary party of this country.
>
> The British Section of the I.C.L. [International Communist League] has been liquidated by the International Secretariat. Many former members disagree with us on this matter, but we are convinced that developments in the I.L.P. will lead most of them shortly to join us . . .
>
> In entering the I.L.P. we state unreservedly that we do not give up any of the principles of Bolshevik-Leninism. While observing the Constitution of the I.L.P., we shall fight for their theoretical development and practical application in the work of the I.L.P.

To it was appended a note by the I.L.P. repeating their conditions of entry, explaining that the Trotskyists would be 'expected loyally to carry out the decisions of the Party', and stating that the issue of the Fourth International, to be debated at the Easter Conference, had been 'consistently opposed' by the I.L.P.[93]

The Majority naturally objected to the terms of this statement, especially to the remarks that the section had been 'liquidated'. They described the progress of the factional dispute up to Christmas, and how they had rejected the policy of total entry. Then they went on, in a way not calculated to assist the work of the Minority:

> Our International Secretariat then suggested that the minority who favoured their tactic should be allowed to enter the I.L.P. to try the proposed tactic. This they did not think likely to be effective unless there ceased to be, officially, a Section of the International Communist League. If such a Section existed the

> approach of the minority comrades to the I.L.P. on the lines of a willingness to disband in order to work within the I.L.P. would be impossible. In view of this the International Secretariat decided that, for the time being the Communist League should be regarded as a 'sympathetic' organisation, not as the official section. This measure was part of the effort to win the I.L.P. Our Communist League members do not agree with this approach and the statements of the minority and the work of the minority should not therefore be regarded as in any way the responsibility of the Communist League.
>
> The statement that we are 'liquidated' in the sense of [having] ceased to exist as an organisation or as meaning that we are no longer connected with the International Communist League is therefore false.[94]

The split left a legacy of factional bitterness that never really healed. As Dewar recalled, 'in judging our attitude at that time towards those who had broken discipline over a purely tactical matter, it must be borne in mind that this was a serious blow, coming right out of the blue. This was purely disruptive, explicable only as the action of one or two "leaders" who wanted to set up their own little organisation.'[95] What was worse, the way it had been handled at the international level had left an unfortunate legacy of suspicion between the British Trotskyists and the International Secretariat, reinforcing national prejudices and obstructing chances of future co-operation. 'We didn't think very much of the International organisationally as having much authority,' recalls Dewar. 'The tendency was not to indulge, really. This may have been not immediately at the beginning, but at a later stage it was particularly true with the I.L.P. discussions, which really put us off.'[96] At one point Demetrious Giotopoulos had let the Majority comrades know that Trotsky's proposal to enter the I.L.P. was one to which he was opposed, giving them the impression — which puzzled Trotsky as to its origin — that the decision had not been unanimously reached on the International Secretariat, where in fact it had received his vote as well.[97] On the other side, not all the correspondence from the International on the matter had been put before the membership. As Wicks remarked:

> Henry Sara and myself, and others of that calibre, were not privy to the arguments that went on for the motivation of this turn of the Communist League into the I.L.P., and as a matter of fact — it doesn't seem possible — but thirty odd years later that letter from Trotsky to Groves discussing this change of line is the first I've heard of it! That doesn't seem credible, does it?

> But that correspondence was never available to the membership, and what internal bulletins there were it was not published in. I read that in astonishment in the correspondence that has been published by Pathfinder.[98]

And their feelings were returned by the I.S. 'The tone in which the national committee refers to the other sections and to our international organisation is particularly surprising and disagreeable,' they wrote. 'It sees everywhere an alleged lack of understanding of the principles of Bolshevism as the cause of fractional clashes, etc., while moreover, the national committee of the British Section alone pursues a correct organisational policy.'[99]

But beneath all the disagreement over tactical and organisational issues, the main conflict was, in fact, over two entirely different concepts as to how to build the revolutionary party — by winning over mass organisations of the class by entry and fractional work, or by general recruitment and propaganda work. As Dewar describes the Majority's attitude to their work:

> You see, I don't recall that there was ever any entrist tactic, because we were in everything we could be in. We didn't leave the I.L.P., we didn't leave the trade unions, we didn't leave the Labour Party. We naturally had connections, you see. I, for example, was on the management committee of the Balham Labour Party through the unions, and on the Wandsworth Trades Council. Everybody was in that position that you had these connections with. We had close connections with the Balham Labour Party through the Youth Group, and from that we drew people out into the organisation (or we didn't, they just remained there). So there weren't really any entrists, the organisation wasn't dissolved in favour of going into the Labour Party. We naturally worked in any sphere that we could find, to put across ideas.[100]

Here was an entirely different concept from that of the Minority, with its strategy of winning over the I.L.P. as a whole to Bolshevik principles by organised fraction work.

Not that the Minority group were much more firm in strategy, or in principles. They were now deprived of the experience of the older comrades, those rooted in the working-class movement with experience of the functioning of a larger Communist organisation. They had none of the prestige of Sara, or the experience of Groves and Wicks. They were also affected by the spirit of propagandism, and had little idea of how to set about their task. They wasted precious time before they really got to work in the I.L.P. — time that greatly assisted the Stalinists in their task of destroying the party, and most of the year was wasted before they had worked out an organisational structure. Their two-stage conception of organisation was unworkable — both then and when they later tried it out in the Labour Party in the shape of 'the Militant Labour League'. Low in morale, and utterly lacking in any working-class support, with a determined enemy already entrenched, they had a very difficult prospect ahead of them.

Notes

1. Cf. S. Bornstein and A. Richardson, *Two Steps Back*, London, 1982, p. 14.
2. J. McNair, *James Maxton — the Beloved Rebel*, London, 1955, p. 213.
3. F. Brockway, *Inside the Left*, London, 1942, p. 237.
4. Cf. above, p. 000.
5. J. Kruk, 'Tactics of Revolution', in *The New Leader*, vol. xxii, new series, no. 55, Friday 20th January 1933, p. 9. Cf. also *The New Leader*, vol. viii, 1932, and vol. xxii, new series, no. 56, 27th January 1933.
6. J. Maxton, 'The Most Honoured Man', in *The New Leader*, 17th February 1933.
7. A. Rothstein, 'Trotsky on the Russian Revolution', in *Labour Monthly*, vol. xv, no. 12, December 1933, p. 761.
8. 'L. Trotsky, *The Russian Revolution*, with a foreword by James Maxton, M.P.', Labour Literature Department (undated, but described as 'just issued' in *The New Leader*, 16th June 1933, p. 9). Cf. *The Early Years of the British Left Opposition*, London, 1979, p. 5 (letter to Reg Groves) and p. 10 (Maxton's Preface).
9. E.g. in *The New Leader*, vol. xxiv, new series, no. 93, 13th October 1933 ('Can the Comintern be Reformed?', pp. 6-7, and 'The I.L.P. and the New International', p. 13), in *Controversy*, no. 1 ('Whither the I.L.P.?') and 'Trotsky on Maxton' in *The New Leader*, vol. xxiii, new series, no. 86, 25th August 1933, p. 2.
10. Witte (Demetrious Giotopoulos), 'Interview with Brockway', in 'Report on the Situation of the English Section' (to the International Secretariat), Paris, 22nd September 1933. Cf. Bornstein and Richardson, *Two Steps Back*, p. 18, n. 18.
11. R. Groves, *The Balham Group*, London, 1974, p. 64; Harry Wicks, Statement to the Conference of the Group for the Study of Leon Trotsky and the Revolutionary Movement, 20th September 1980.
12. Cf. below, p. 131.
13. Cf. J. Valtin, *Out of the Night*, London, 1941, pp. 402-3.
14. Jock Haston, Interview with Al Richardson, 30th April 1978.
15. 'An Interview by C.A. Smith', *The New Leader*, 13th October 1933 — *Writings of Leon Trotsky, 1933-4*, New York, 1972, p. 61.
16. R.F. Andrews (Andrew Rothstein), *The Truth About Trotsky*, C.P.G.B. pamphlet, February 1934, p. 50.
17. J. Paton, *Left Turn!*, London, 1936, pp. 420-422. Schmidt, Leader of the Dutch O.S.P., later merged his group with the Dutch Trotskyists.
18. 'An Interview by C.A. Smith', 29th August 1933, in *Writings of Leon Trotsky, 1933-4*, pp. 58-62.
19. W. Gallacher, *Pensioners of Capitalism*, C.P.G.B. pamphlet, 1934, pp. 34-5.
20. J.R. Campbell, 'New Opportunist Arguments against the Communist International', in *Inprecorr*, vol. xiii, no. 33, 28th July 1933, pp. 730-1.
21. 'T.C.', 'The Growth of Fascism in Britain', in *The Militant* (U.S.A.), vol. vi, no.

41, 2nd September 1933 (article dated 14th August).

22. Cf. above, p. 103.

23. Gallacher, *Pensioners of Capitalism*, p. 18.

24. Cf. Bornstein and Richardson, *Two Steps Back*, pp. 14-15.

25. Allen, Chalmers (Harber?) and Graham (Nardell), 'Statement on the I.L.P.', Internal document of the Communist League, p. 3.

26. Andrews, *The Truth about Trotsky*, p. 5.

27. 'Anglicus', 'The I.L.P. and British Communism', in *The Militant* (U.S.A.), vol. iv, no. 23, 4th June 1932. Cf. Bornstein and Richardson, *Two Steps Back*, pp. 16-7.

28. J.R. Campbell, 'Mr. Trotsky and the I.L.P.', in *The Communist Review*, vol. vi, no. 12, December/January 1933–4, p. 435.

29. R.P.C. Bulletin, May 1933 issue, quoted in W. Rust, 'Towards a United Revolutionary Party', in *Labour Monthly*, vol. xv, no. 7, July 1933, p. 427.

30. J. Gaster, 'The Present Position of the I.L.P.', in *Labour Monthly*, vol. xv, no. 1, January 1933, p. 34.

31. 'I.L.P. Meeting Excludes Representative of Daily Worker', in *The Daily Worker*, 25th July 1932.

32. 'The United Front', in *The New Leader*, vol. xxii, new series, no. 61, 3rd March 1933. Cf. the *Daily Worker*, 29th July 1932 (advertisement for joint meeting).

33. R. Palme Dutt, Letter to Harry Pollitt, 24th July 1933.

34. Paton, *Left Turn!*, p. 391. Cf. McNair, *James Maxton — the Beloved Rebel*, p. 233.

35. 'Anglicus' (Reg Groves), 'The I.L.P. and British Communism', in *The Militant* (U.S.A.), vol. iv, no. 23, 4th June 1932.

36. L.D. Trotsky, 'The Left Socialist Organisations and Our Tasks', 15th June 1933, in *Writings of Leon Trotsky, 1932–3*, New York, 1972 , p. 274.

37. Ibid., p. 275.

38. 'Declaration of the Bolshevik-Leninist Delegation at the Conference of Left Socialist and Communist Organisations', 17th August 1933, in *Writings of Leon Trotsky, 1933–4*, p. 38.

39. 'Declaration of Four on the Necessity and Principles of a New International', 26th August 1933, ibid., p. 51.

40. F. Brockway, 'The Editor Returns', in *The New Leader*, vol. xxiv, new series, no. 104, 29th December 1933.

41. Brockway, *Inside the Left*, p. 237.

42. Op. cit., note 40 above.

43. L.D. Trotsky, 'Whither the I.L.P.?' (24th August 1933), in *Writings of Leon Trotsky, 1933–4*, p. 57.

44. L.D. Trotsky, 'The I.L.P. and the New International', 4th September 1933, in *Writings of Leon Trotsky, 1933–4*, p. 72.

45. Brockway, *Inside the Left*, pp. 252-3.

46. Quoted in Trotsky, *The Russian Revolution*, p. 5.

47. L.D. Trotsky, 'Is Soviet Policy a Matter on Which only Russian Socialists are Competent to Decide?', 9th August 1933, in *Writings of Leon Trotsky, 1933–4*, p. 33.

48. Op. cit., note 43 above, p. 57.

49. L.D. Trotsky, 'Principled Considerations on Entry', 16th September 1933, in *Writings of Leon Trotsky, 1933–4*, p. 86.

50. Op. cit., note 43 above, p. 56.

51. Op. cit., note 44 above, p. 78.

52. L.D. Trotsky, 'The Left Socialist Organisations and Our Tasks', 15th June 1933, in *Writings of Leon Trotsky, 1932–3*, pp. 274-5.

53. L.D. Trotsky, 'It is Necessary to Build Communist Parties and an International Anew', 15th July 1933, in *Writings of Leon Trotsky, 1932–3*, pp. 307-8.

54. Harry Wicks, Interview with Al Richardson, 11th March and 1st April 1978.

55. British Section of the International Left Opposition, 'To Our Comrades of the Independent Labour Party' (undated leaflet, but after March 1933).

56. Sara, Groves, Dewar and Dowdall, 'Our Work in, and Relation to, the Independent Labour Party', Statement of the N.C. Majority, p. 3; Statement of the N.C., British Section, 5th September 1933; 'Our Relations with the I.L.P.'

57. *The New Leader*, vol. xxiii, no. 94, 20th October 1933. Cf. articles in *Red Flag*, vol. i, no. 3, July 1933 ('Soviet Foreign Policy') and no. 4, August 1933 ('A United Communist Party?' and 'Towards New Revolutionary Advance').

58. E.g. 13th October 1933 (Groves speaking to Clapham I.L.P. on 'A New International?'), and 3rd November 1933 (Sara speaking to Wimbledon I.L.P. on 'International Socialism').

59. 'Report on Work Done in Relation to the I.L.P.' (internal document).

60. David Chalkley, Interview with Al Richardson, 14th November 1978.

61. T. Kernot, P. Solomons, J. Sainsbury, M. Gibbs, 'To All Comrades of the I.L.P.', 19th March 1933 (leaflet).

62. Cf. J. Carter, 'The British I.L.P. Turns Leftward', in *The Militant* (U.S.A.), vol. vi, no. 30, 10th June 1933, and 'British Group Leaves I.L.P., Statement Supports Left Opposition', in *The Militant* (U.S.A.), vol. vi, no. 34, 8th July 1933.

63. 'When challenged on this matter by the I.L.P. Headquarters two of the four signatories have repudiated the statement' — H. Davis (Weston), S. Purkis, H. Wicks, E.S. Williams, 'Statement from Members of the 1931–3 Committee of the British Group of the Left Opposition', 18th April 1933.

64. E. Bauer, Letter of 21st August 1933, to the British Section of the I.L.O.

65. 'Our Relations with the I.L.P.', Statement of the N.C. British Section, in reply to the letter of the International Secretariat, 5th September 1933.

66. Ibid.

67. L.D. Trotsky, 'How to Influence the I.L.P.', 3rd September 1933, in *Writings of Leon Trotsky, 1933–4*, p. 71. It is impossible to discover at this interval who on the I.S. was responsible for this modification. Witte (Giotopoulos) at the time was wholly in favour of entry, though later he was to split from the Left Opposition along with the Greek ArcheoMarxists on the grounds that it was capitulating to Social Democracy; and although Bauer (Ackerknecht) also supported entry, he too later left the Trotskyists to join the German S.A.P. when a similar policy was proposed for the French Section. See below, p. 169. Bauer had previously opposed the change of policy towards the Comintern after the German collapse, arguing that it had not shown its complete bankruptcy.

68. 'Witte', 'Report on the Situation of the English Section' to the I.S., Paris, 22nd September 1933.

69. Reg Groves, Interview with Al Richardson, 2nd April 1978.

70. 'To our Comrades of the Independent Labour Party', leaflet published by H. Dewar for the British Section of the International Left Opposition.

71. Harry Wicks, Interview with Al Richardson, 11th March and 1st April 1978.

72. L.D. Trotsky, 'Principled Considerations on Entry', 16th September 1933, in *Writings of Leon Trotsky, 1933–4*, p. 87.

73. 'Notes for Discussion of the I.L.P. Question at the National Committee Meetings', 5th October 1933.

74. L.D. Trotsky, 'The Left Socialist Organisations and Our Tasks', 15th June 1933, in *Writings of Leon Trotsky, 1932–3*, p. 276.

75. L.D. Trotsky, 'Summary of the Discussion', 6th August 1934, in *Writings of Leon Trotsky, 1934–5*, New York, 1971, pp. 63-4.

76. L.D. Trotsky, 'Principled Considerations on Entry', 16th September 1933, in *Writings of Leon Trotsky, 1933–4*, pp. 84-6.

77. H. Sara, R. Groves, H. Dewar, S. Dowdall, 'Our Work in, and Relation to, the Independent Labour Party: Statement of the National Committee Majority'.

78. L.D. Trotsky, 'The Lever of a Small Group', 2nd October 1933, in *Writings of Leon Trotsky, 1933-4*, pp. 125-6.

79. 'Notes for Discussion of I.L.P. Question at National Committee Meeting', 5th October 1933.

80. L.D. Trotsky, 'The Lever of a Small Group', 2nd October 1933, in *Writings of Leon Trotsky, 1933-4*, p. 126.

81. L.D. Trotsky, 'The Fate of the British Section', 25th September 1933, ibid., p. 100.

82. D. Harber, 'The Present Situation and Our Tasks', 27th February 1943, Internal Bulletin of the R.S.L.

83. Allen, Chalmers and Graham, 'Statement on the I.L.P.', 12th October 1933. At the end of the document 'Chalmers' is replaced by 'W. Chalcroft', but as Harry Wicks assures us he never supported the documents, we presume it must be a misprint. 'Chalmers', in fact, was D.D. Harber, 'W. Graham' was Nardell, and 'Allen' was an American active in the group at the time.

84. Ibid.

85. Cf. the remarks in our own book, Bornstein and Richardson, *Two Steps Back*, pp. v-vii.

86. 'On the I.L.P.' (unsigned one-page document).

87. Harry Wicks, Interview with Al Richardson, 11th March and 1st April 1978.

88. 'Draft Statement of the Present Position of the Majority and Minority', 19th December 1933.

89. Ibid.

90. 'On the Declaration of the 17th December of the Majority of the National Committee of the British Section', 23rd January 1934. (International Secretariat.) The above version, translated independently from the French, departs in a few inessentials from that in 'The I.S. Reply to the British Majority', in L.D. Trotsky, *Writings of Leon Trotsky: Supplement, 1934-40*, New York, 1979, pp. 440-1, which represents Trotsky's first draft for the letter submitted to the I.S.

91. L.D. Trotsky, 'Problems for the British Minority', 23rd January 1934, James P. Cannon Archives. Cf. the slightly different version in *Writings of Leon Trotsky: Supplement, 1934-40* , pp. 442-3.

92. 'Trotskyists and the I.L.P.', in *The New Leader*, vol. xxv, new series, no. 5, 16th February 1934, p. 4.

93. 'A Trotskyist Declaration', in *The New Leader*, vol. xxv, new series, no. 10, 23rd March 1934.

94. 'Our Alleged "Liquidation" ', in *Red Flag*, vol. 1, no. 9, May/June 1934.

95. H. Dewar, Notes sent to Al Richardson on Entry into the I.L.P. *re* the notes in *Writings of Leon Trotsky, 1935-6*.

96. H. Dewar, Interview with Al Richardson, 7th April 1978.

97. Note to Trotsky's Letter of 23rd January 1934; cf. L.D. Trotsky, 'The Fate of the British Section', 25th September 1933, in *Writings of Leon Trotsky, 1933-4*, p. 100.

98. Harry Wicks, Interview with Al Richardson, 11th March and 1st April 1978.

99. International Secretariat, 'On the Declaration of the 17th December of the Majority of the National Committee of the British Section', 23rd January 1933.

100. Hugo Dewar, Interview with Al Richardson, 7th April 1978.

Chapter Six

Inside The I.L.P., 1934–36

Quite apart from the internal difficulties about their own entry into the I.L.P., the group of a dozen Trotskyists were moving into what was already a complex situation, where the I.L.P. leaders were themselves carrying out a complicated balancing act. Whilst being obliged to break with the Labour Party and the Second International due to the feelings of the rank and file, they were unwilling to be drawn into the net of the C.P.G.B. and the Comintern. Apart from indulging in left rhetoric (feigned or genuine) from time to time, they sought to innoculate their membership against Stalinism by appealing to dissident Communists and Socialists abroad, by playing on sympathy for Trotsky, and by borrowing some of his arguments on the bankruptcy of the Communist International over what had been happening in Germany. In the meantime, they were bound by Conference decisions to joint activity with the British Communist Party, and to seeking ways by which they could 'assist' the work of the Communist International. They had to go through the motions of corresponding with Moscow whilst trying to show up the bureaucratic ultimatism of the Comintern leaders, to gain enough time to demonstrate to their supporters the opportunist and sectarian character of the Stalinist line, in the hope of reversing the policy at the next annual conference. Meanwhile, the Revolutionary Policy Committee was opposing Brockway and Maxton from inside the London Division of the I.L.P., attempting to reinforce the links with Moscow whilst keeping a wary eye on its British representatives, trying to pull the I.L.P. to what they considered to be militant and revolutionary politics, but falling gradually and inexorably under the spell of Stalinism itself. The attraction of Moscow was all the stronger as they saw the use made by Maxton and Brockway of Trotsky's name and ideas in covering their own left flank. At the same time the party as a whole was in a most unstable condition, having half broken with reformism without yet becoming revolutionary. In the circumstances of the thirties, time was not going to be generous with the I.L.P., caught vacillating in the middle of events: Maxton might be perfectly comfortable 'on the horns of a dilemma'[1] but most of the rank-and-file were under more urgent pressures: to return to the mass movement, whose institutions were at least large enough to afford some protection; to move towards Stalinism, another possible bulwark in the Soviet Union; or to support the Socialist Revolution, a way out of the deadlock that seemed less feasible. The one solution proposed by the I.L.P. leaders — staying exactly where they were, 'in the Middle of the Road' — was in fact the least viable, and its victory in the short term led to the party's ultimate stagnation and disintegration.

Maxton expressed the party's problem clearly enough, as well as the weakness of his own position:

> The arguments which have been advanced are that we have either to identify ourselves with the Labour Party or the Communist Party. I think that this is quite a wrong view and that the attitude which the I.L.P. has taken hitherto is right, which is, that both these parties are wrong. The I.L.P. has its separate policy distinct from either and this is its justification for its existence as an independent party. If I could accept the policies of one or the other of these two parties I would go into it and work in it wholeheartedly. But I am against both and the I.L.P. is distinctive from both. I am as definitely opposed to mass terrorism as the result of revolution under Communism as I am against mass misery under gradualism.[2]

Brockway's position outside parliament and in the party had to be more radical than this, and in many respects he formed a bridge between Maxton and the parliamentary group and the Revolutionary Policy Committee. 'Our policy must become revolutionary instead of reformist,' he proclaimed: 'adopt the revolutionary attitude of mind, live in the revolutionary spirit, brace yourselves for the revolutionary struggle that is before us.'[3] He regarded the co-operation of the I.L.P with the C.P.G.B. as a step towards 'the creation of joint councils, the new instruments of the workers',[4] and much to Paton's dismay, 'with his usual susceptibility to an attractive phrase had incorporated "Workers' Councils" in the speeches he was making all over the country (without, of course, attempting to define them), and was unwittingly doing much to make the path of the R.P.C. easy.'[5]

Brockway was to admit later his 'share of responsibility for the adoption of these impractical schemes', a 'permanent warning against theoretical elaboration of revolutionary structure unrelated to the actual conditions of the class struggle.'[6]

In this he was, of course, only following the point of view of the R.P.C., which in turn was in the process of evolution towards the policy of the Communist Party. It should be remembered that the C.P.G.B.'s hostility towards the Labour Party at this time went hand in hand with the most pronounced ultra-leftism, and that for them the question of workers' councils was linked to the rejection of reformism and Labourism in general. At the disaffiliation conference Gaster had proposed the reorganisation of the I.L.P. as a revolutionary movement 'comprised solely of active workers organised, as far as possible, on an industrial basis', which would use parliament 'merely as a propaganda field' and 'definitely reject it as a method of achieving Socialism'.[7] At the same time the I.L.P. had accepted an R.P.C. resolution to instruct I.L.P. members in the unions to suspend payment of the political levy to the Labour Party, or else divert it to the I.L.P., a policy that was not only an utter fiasco, but cost the Party most of its industrial influence, led to a catastrophic drop in numbers, and had to be abandoned a year later at the instigation of Cullen himself.[8] All this was the very stuff of 'Third Period Stalinism' and, as Paton observed, 'must had fed the delusion of the Communist leaders that, before long, it [the I.L.P.] would be swallowed by the Communist Party.'[9]

Communist influence on the I.L.P. was not in the first instance based on ideological considerations, but was mainly imparted through organisational links. Co-operation at a local level — obviously strongest where the R.P.C. was well represented[10] — threatened to weaken branch activity and dissipate the energies of the I.L.P. activists into the 'innumerable "committees" for this and auxiliary organisations for that, which the Communist Party spawns with something of the fecundity of a herring.'[11] At a national level a small controlling body of I.L.P. representatives met with their opposite numbers of the Communist Party, fully aware of 'the innumerable opportunities such a contact would open up for Communist propaganda in the I.L.P.' When Paton proved obstructive, the C.P. proposed further co-operation and the issuing of the Committee's joint statement over the signatures of Pollitt and Brockway alone.[12] On the international plane the I.L.P. opened up a long correspondence with the Executive of the Comintern. Kuusinen in Moscow looked forward to further collaboration and the formation of a 'single, strong, and mass Communist Party' on the basis of the acceptance of the programme of the Comintern, in which the latter reserved to itself the 'right of comradely criticism', whilst objecting to Brockway's use of the same right from the side of the I.L.P.[13] Paton replied that such criticism was 'essential on both sides',[14] whilst Brockway objected to the organisational practices of the Third International in reversing policies, dismissing leaderships, expelling dissidents from above, and at the same time sacrificing the revolution in the interests of Soviet diplomacy with the great powers.[15] In the end this sparring produced an acceptable result for the I.L.P.: the final letter of the E.C.C.I. took six weeks to arrive, was issued 'through a news agency',[16] and was addressed, not to the N.A.C., but to the I.L.P. members at large. In the meantime both the British Communist Party and the Comintern had been indiscreet enough to subject Brockway in particular to a good deal of personal abuse, as going over 'to the counter-revolutionaries', 'a hound of Fascism and War', etc., all of which was certainly the wrong tack to take with the I.L.P., with its strongly anti-sectarian traditions and its instinctive dislike for the sharper forms of polemic and denunciation.[17] Relations with the Comintern were finally broken off at the Easter Conference of 1934, but at a terrible cost: such long-established figures as Paton had resigned over the issue, along with the whole Lancashire area, and there had been a considerable haemorrhage of members from branches across the country.

Brockway drew heavily upon the analyses of Trotsky in his polemic with the Communist International. When Pollitt reported to the Thirteenth Plenum of the Comintern he drew attention to the fact that when the I.L.P. opened the pages of *The New Leader* to discussion on the international questions, 'it is noteworthy that Trotsky was called upon to open this series of discussion articles',[18] whereas Kuusinen described Brockway as 'in full conformity with the anti-Soviet slanders of the counter-revolutionary traitor, Trotsky', 'old scrap' taken 'from the arsenal of the Second International' to 'create a contradiction between the peace policy of the Soviet Union and the interests of the workers' movement in other countries'.[19] On his part Brockway was obliged to defend Trotsky and other dissidents from abuse as 'corrupt renegades' and 'international riff-raff',[20] while trying to claim that his assessment of the Comintern had been independently arrived at. 'I have often been called a "Trotskyist",' he admitted later: 'much of my criticism of Russia's policy was similar to Trotsky's but my conclusions were reached quite independently.'[21] Whatever the origin of his criticisms, they had a salutory effect upon those who were breaking with Stalinism or Social Democracy, especially by publicising Moscow's responsibility for the dreadful defeat in Germany on a scale that was not open to the Trotskyist groups, with their slim material means. 'I had letters from all over the world,' he added, 'many of them from prominent figures in the international movement, thanking the I.L.P. for having raised so clearly the fundamental issues regarding the Communist International.'[22]

The truth was, however, that what the I.L.P. leaders wanted to safeguard was their own independence from the Comintern apparatus, their control over their own organisation in Britain, and the freedom in the future to make their own adjustments on a purely national level. They were quite willing to make vast concessions to Stalinism elsewhere, if it would only leave them alone in the British Isles. Paton reminded Kuusinen of the I.L.P.'s policy at the Paris Conference against the New International, and its 'solitary struggle for the amendment of the Conference declarations which it believed to be unfair to the Communist International';[23] and Brockway was even prepared to concede the main ideological prop of the Russian Bureaucracy, the theory of 'Socialism in One Country'. 'The I.L.P. wishes [it] to be clearly understood,' he wrote, 'that no criticism is made, or implied, of the C.P.S.U.'s conduct of its own affairs within the U.S.S.R.';[24] for if there were limits to internationalism in one direction, the I.L.P. could always claim the same sort of immunity in the other. Thus, separate and national roads to Socialism are no fresh discovery of 'EuroCommunism', but were a necessary conclusion from Stalin's rise to power in the first place. What the I.L.P. leaders unfortunately lacked was state control of a national base from which to challenge Russian domination of 'Communism', something Stalinism has been obliged to concede since 1945.

All these factors created an exceptionally difficult environment for the operation of the Trotskyists. Obviously in the short run the main danger was that the I.L.P. as a whole, or in significant part, would fall victim to Stalinism. The evolution of the party, and of the R.P.C., in this direction had to be halted without delay. On the other hand, as Brockway and Maxton were using Trotskyist ideas to defend themselves against Moscow, the difficulty arose of distinguishing a genuine revolutionary position from a temporary flirtation with it in the eyes of the rank-and-file. And when the Stalinist danger was over, how could they avoid the bureaucracy turning on them after it had got what it wanted? Finally, how exactly was a group of a dozen inexperienced comrades to operate as a faction inside a totally alien institution? What relations, if any, were they to establish with the R.P.C.? How were they to get their view circulated amongst the membership?

In fact, the greatest success of the Trotskyists came at the beginning of their struggle, before they had been properly organised as a group within the I.L.P., and in the period up to the following Easter Conference. They got the London I.L.P. at its Divisional Conference to defend Trotsky against the slanders of the Stalinists, and brought forth a bitter denunciation from the Communist Party as to why it had defended the 'reactionaries' on the N.A.C. and Trotsky, 'the paid man of the bourgeoisie', along with a demand to know whether it supported the Second, Third or the formation of a Fourth International.[25] Although the London Divisional Council and Marylebone got through a resolution, instructing the N.A.C. not to associate with 'the proposed Fourth International', by 24 votes to 15, and the motion from Islington for the Fourth International itself only picked up nine votes, Sid Kemp and Ernie Patterson from Clapham managed to get through another motion, by 21 votes to 19, recommending that the I.L.P. should not affiliate to the Third International.[26] A similar picture emerged from the Scottish Division where, although the motion for the Fourth International was lost, an amendment was carried to delay a decision until the Annual Conference;[27] whilst the Tyneside and Yorkshire Conferences rejected the Third International, and the Lancashire District passed an amendment to reaffiliate to the Second.[28] It was 'a good indication that the efforts of the Stalinists to win over the I.L.P. are meeting with a definite and well-informed opposition.'[29] Even the Revolutionary Policy Committee itself began to be influenced: William Rust reported to the Comintern that they 'were breaking off the united front, fighting the Communist International, and concluding an unprincipled alliance with the Trotskyists for the setting up of a 2½ or a Fourth International', that they had 'now disintegrated, and to a certain extent come under the influence of Trotskyist elements'.[30]

The main battle over the international future of the I.L.P. came up at its 42nd Annual Easter Conference, held in the Co-op Hall in York on 31st March and 1st April 1934. The official resolution supported the status quo of associating with the left Socialist Parties of the London Bureau, and was faced with three amendments: one, from Dumfries in Scotland, on a completely Stalinist line for immediate sympathetic affiliation to the Comintern; one put up by the R.P.C. from Poplar, calling for conditional sympathetic affiliation by sending a delegation to Moscow to discuss the members' doubts; and one from Clapham, sent in by the Trotskyists, for the Fourth International. Both the R.P.C. and the fully Stalinist resolution fell by substantial margins (51 for, 98 against; 34 for, 126 against), so the immediate danger of I.L.P. absorption by the Communists now passed, and the day-to-day co-operation that was drawing such opposition from the members also ceased.

Ernie Patterson argued the case for the Fourth International, seconded by Lechstein from Cardiff. He showed that the last year's experience of the I.L.P. with the Comintern did not warrant placing any confidence in it, any more than in the Second International—an argument the Communist Party described as 'a rehash of Paton's equal blame', and as being 'stonily received'; and his resolution was defeated by 137 votes to 20. The Conference then went on to accept by 102 votes to 64 McGovern's motion for the N.A.C. of continued support to the London Bureau.

Patterson did manage to mount a good case against the I.L.P. policy of withdrawing support for the political levy, which he wanted to make compulsory upon I.L.P. members, but his proposal was changed to a permissive payment by another London amendment. However, in another speech he showed that the Trotskyists had still not got the feel of how to approach the I.L.P. members, when he proposed that the party's policy of a general strike in the event of a war should be converted into an opportunity for 'overthrowing the capitalist government threatening war'. Other delegates in the provinces described this 'leftism' as 'a London disease', and the motion fell by 79 votes to 63.

Although the arguments of the Trotskyists had not been carried on any substantial point, they had assisted in polarising the Conference against the Comintern, as well as helping to divide the Stalinist vote itself. Considering that it was an almost single-handed performance from one London branch, the Trotskyist intervention had not been without success, leading pro-C.P.ers present to object to 'Trotsky propaganda among the I.L.P.'[31] Defeat certainly did not affect Trotsky's own personal popularity with the I.L.P. rank-and-file, or with the leadership. When *The New Leader* published the news of Trotsky's expulsion from France,[32] Maxton attempted to persuade the Home Secretary to give him political asylum in the Channel Isles;[33] and when this failed, McGovern attempted to get Eamonn de Valera to offer the same in Ireland [34] — sadly without success.

Trotsky was less satisfied with the position of the I.L.P. While he approved of the organisational break with the Labour Party, and advised that 'complete and unconditional political and organisational independence of a revolutionary party is the first prerequisite for its success', nonetheless, the instincts of the working class towards unity made it necessary for the I.L.P. 'immediately to turn to it'. He was disappointed that the I.L.P. 'turned not towards the trade unions and the Labour Party, but towards the Communist Party, which had during a number of years conclusively proven its bureaucratic dullness and absolute inability to approach the class.' Now that it had halted this process half-way, it was 'simply hanging in mid-air'. Its flirtation with the Comintern, its attachment to the London Bureau, its position of appealing for unity to the Second International led him to ask 'are there not somewhat too many Internationals for one party? Can the English worker make head or tail out of all this confusion?'[35]

At the same time the movement of the working class was rapidly bearing out the correctness of his views on the Labour Party. At a time that the I.L.P. was trying to extricate itself from its damaging policy of withdrawing from the political levy, the Labour vote began to mount dramatically in a series of by-elections and local council contests,[36] whereas the I.L.P. only made itself ridiculous by supporting a Communist parliamentary candidate whose vote actually fell.[37] The International Secretariat wrote to the British Trotskyists noting that 'the municipal elections in England have an extremely important symptomatic significance', and that it was 'the direct duty of the Bolshevik–Leninists to make the I.L.P. turn its back on the Comintern and to make it face the Labour Party.'[38]

The Trotskyists in the I.L.P., however, were experiencing grave difficulties in organising their work. The original nucleus of Margaret Johns, Denzil Harber, Stewart Kirby and the others had largely joined the Holborn and Finsbury branch of the I.L.P., where they soon recruited others from the same L.S.E. milieu —John Archer, who had just got a job attached to the wheat commission of the Ministry of Agriculture, and Tony Doncaster, who was later to become a successful bookseller in Essex. To this group later on were added Doncaster's friend John Goffe and the Canadian student Earle Birney, who worked under the pseudonym of E.M. Robertson whilst over here and later returned to become Canada's poet laureate.

Their greatest success, however, was the rapid recruitment of well-established I.L.P. activists, with whom it was possible to forge a working relationship now that artificial organisational barriers had been removed with the entry of the group into the I.L.P. The most useful to begin with was Sid Kemp, who had been Clapham's delegate to the I.L.P. conference since 1931, and had been a supporter of the revolutionary position in the party. At the Bradford disaffiliation conference he had supported an unsuccessful resolution by Gaster on parliamentarism, showing that 'they could not put their policy into power through the parliamentary method', and that 'capitalism would not go until it was pushed over'.[39] Associated with him in the Clapham group was Ernie Patterson, then caretaker of the New Morris Hall and later to become General Secretary of the Construction Workers' Union, a capable and influential speaker. Equally effective as an orator was Karl Westwood in West London, afterwards Labour parliamentary candidate for Richmond. Down in Norwood was Joe Pawsey, already well established as a delegate to the I.L.P. Conference of 1932, who was to give long service to the Trotskyist movement. Into the Islington Branch of the I.L.P. came the Scottish Marxist Bill Duncan, a Post Office employee, and from Devon Hilda Lane, who after serving on the South-West Divisional Council became secretary of Islington I.L.P. and its candidate for the L.C.C. elections.[40]

Perhaps their greatest original asset was the experience and organisational ability of Albert Matlow. Springing from an East End family of small shopkeepers, he was already active in Poplar I.L.P. in 1926, though his influence had waned for a while in the I.L.P., when he resigned for a short time in protest at the policy of disaffiliation from the Labour Party.[41] He was not only 'the strongest, clearest political personality, who knew what he wanted and argued very firmly for it', but what the group lacked even more — 'an effective organiser'.[42] By November 1934 he was speaking in public for the group on 'Trades Councils as Workers' Soviets'. It was around him that a proper functioning group came to be organised.

It was much needed. Apart from interventions at divisional and national conferences, lack of organisation and their own paper had led to a propaganda form of activity outside, and internal turmoil and paralysis. The American *Militant* was sold, and a few pamphlets were issued. The Islington Branch of the I.L.P. put out the appeal of the International Secretariat that 'France is now the Key',[43] and the Acton Branch got out Trotsky's 'Centrism and the Fourth International'[44] and 'Once More on Centrism',[45] whilst promising their readers that they would 'continue with extracts from the works of Marx, Engels, Lenin and Trotsky, as well as with news of international events of special importance to the working class',[46] none of which actually materialised. For, as the International Secretariat described it,

> The entry into the I.L.P. naturally did not cure the weakness of the group. Long months were devoted to internal discussion of all strategic and tactical questions; to identifying the questions which underlay practical work, adapted to the specific situation of Britain. It was not easy to advance. Naturally, it was necessary to carry out conscientiously the political work of a militant of the I.L.P. to gain the confidence of the comrades. The principal difficulty consisted in the necessity to test out the ground in order to find out how to defend in action and propaganda the correct political line without breaking discipline.[47]

At the same time, this period of discussion was in stark contrast with the note of urgency in Trotsky's advice to enter the I.L.P. in the first place, and valuable time and energy were wasted on obscure factional conflicts and personal disputes that always come to the fore when a political grouping lacks organisation and focus in its activity. Dr. Worrall was expelled on one occasion,[48] and on another even Harber had resigned from both the group and the I.L.P.[49] Much time slipped by. As Trotsky admitted ruefully, 'The I.L.P. would be a different thing today if our British Section had entered it a year ago to defend within it the policy we had developed in a series of articles and letters.'[50]

It was not until 3rd November that a conference was called of the Trotskyists within the I.L.P., which brought together 40 members from sixteen I.L.P. branches, with the possibility of another 20 to be picked up. There was a group leader for discussion proposed in each federation, and the first issue of its *Bulletin* was devoted to the conference itself.[51] Sid Kemp was its first chairman. Some idea of the quality of the new recruits to Trotskyism gained at this time can be gauged from those who rapidly began to play an important role in the I.L.P. — and in the future — figures like John L. Robinson, Frederick Marzillier, Arthur Ballard, Ted Grant and Sid Frost, and foremost of all, C.L.R. James. The group was able to make a much more sustained impact at the next I.L.P. conference, to dominate several of the branches in London and Liverpool, and to spread its influence into Wales, Glasgow and Yorkshire. With the adherence of C.L.R. James it became nationally known, so that the Stalinists could no longer afford to ignore it as they had in the past.

Robinson came into the I.L.P. from a middle-class background as a result of a rationalist critique of his Christian upbringing. He was encouraged to develop by Jock Dunbar, and first made contact with the Trotskyists through Max Nicholls and Cynthia Walker, whom he urged to join the I.L.P. because 'it seemed to me that there was a good field for Socialist work there', and after that became acquainted with Harber and the L.S.E. group.[52] Marzillier had witnessed the destruction of the German labour movement when employed over there, and when he got back to Britain in the middle of 1933 joined the Islington branch of the I.L.P. and also became influenced by Jock Dunbar and Bill Duncan. 'I believed I should take part in some movement which would be instrumental in fighting fascism,' he explained. 'I considered joining the Communist Party, but as it was in the Stalinist period I blamed the Stalinist leadership for a large part of the collapse of the German working-class movement, I decided not to. I also believed in those days that reformist socialism as exemplified by the British Labour Party was not the right field for me to operate in, so I joined the I.L.P.'[53] Soon he was speaking on Trotskyist platforms on such subjects as 'Germany After the War'.[54] C.L.R. James, cricket correspondent of the *Manchester Guardian* and later to mark out a distinguished career as an author, poet, philosopher and political theorist, also came into the group at this time, recruited from the circle that used to meet in the house of the leading cancer research scientist Israel Heiger in Hampstead Garden Suburb.[55] Arthur Cooper and George Weston came over to the I.L.P. group from the Marxist League of Groves and Dewar, and other useful recruits included Cund, Don James and Doug Orton in

Liverpool, and Arthur Ballard and the Indian journalist Raj Hansa in London.[56] Even more significant from the standpoint of the future evolution of British Trotskyism was the arrival of Max Bosch (Sid Frost) and Ted Grant from South Africa after a brief stopover in France in December 1934:

> I came across to Britain along with Ted in the autumn of 1934, arriving in England in December. We sailed from South Africa in a ship that was German-owned, which the comrades thought a bit risky at the time, in view of Hitler's recent accession to power, but we docked safely in France and made our way to Paris in an eight-hour night train journey. We had been given details on how to make contact with the comrades there before we left South Africa. We were to walk along a famous boulevard (Montparnasse, I think) opposite a certain café, and after about an hour someone came out and made contact. The Trotskyists used to meet in the café there, and soon we met Lev Sedov, his wife, Erwin Wolff, Pierre Frank, Bauer and Raymond Molinier.
>
> We met Bauer first of all, and it was he who introduced us to Sedov and the rest of the French comrades. He was an interesting fellow, open-minded and willing to talk . . . At that time he had just broken with Trotsky, and he was keen to win people over to his view as much as possible. It was at that time that the Trotskyist movement first began 'the French Turn', and at that time I supported his view against that of Trotsky! Bauer had a friend in England, of dual nationality, British and German, an engineer working in London and married to a British girl . . . When we came over, Ted and I went to his address, and we used to visit him regularly in the evenings. At that time Bauer (an emigré from Germany) was trying to get a British or a South African passport. I tried to organise it, so I wrote to our comrades in South Africa to send me on some forms. At that time it was not difficult, but it didn't work out.
>
> Frank and the others were against entry as well. Molinier later became a gangster, so I understand. We had a talk lasting two or three hours with Sedov, about the situation in France. He could not speak English, so we talked in German, and I interpreted what was being said to Ted, who was sitting with us. We went over a lot of things, and particularly the new 'turn' to entry in the Social Democratic parties.
>
> We stayed in Paris altogether about a fortnight, meeting among others Erwin Wolff, who was later killed. Then we got

> ready to go across to England. The comrades in France used to make jokes about the disorganised and split circumstances of the British Trotskyists — Bauer especially. For some reason he didn't like Wicks, in particular, at all. When we made contact with them, we joined the Marxist Group in the I.L.P. in Bloomsbury. There were Harber, Earle Birney, Margaret Johns and Stewart Kirby.[57]

Grant, in turn, was soon speaking for the group on 'Workers' Movements in South Africa' in the spring of the following year.[58]

In this way the group began to extend its influence in I.L.P. circles and become more effective in its interventions. Issue no. 3 of their *Marxist Bulletin* was advertised in *The New Leader*[59] and the first public advertisement of the group's existence appeared not long after.[60] Another propaganda outlet came with the launching of the I.L.P.'s own internal discussion bulletin, *Controversy*, in November 1934. Trotsky wrote for the first issue, and group articles appeared with more or less regularity afterwards — even if Trotsky occasionally had to disguise his identity under the label of 'Statistician'.[61] To these outlets were added more regular duplicated pamphlets, such as the texts of the appeal of 'the Four' for the Fourth International and Trotsky's articles on 'Stalin's Treachery and the World Revolution',[62] Trotsky's interview with Earle Birney in November 1935,[63] his article on 'Dictators and the Heights of Oslo'[64] and his 'Letter to an I.L.P. Member'.[65]

As the main immediate problem for the new organisation remained the threat to the I.L.P. from Stalinism, the group was slow to realise that, with the rejection by the Conference of 1934 of sympathetic affiliation to the Communist International, the high point of Stalinist influence in the I.L.P. was now past. They were less well prepared for the next stage of the struggle, with the I.L.P.'s own bureaucracy, which sought to dispense with their services now that the danger of absorption into the Comintern had passed over.

This new balance of forces showed itself in the first public intervention of the Marxist Group in the London Divisional Conference of the weekend of 16th and 17th February 1935. Here the Divisional Council was firmly in the hands of the Revolutionary Policy Committee, now more strongly than ever committed to Stalinism. The National Administrative Council of the I.L.P. confronted them from above, and the Marxist Group from below. 'The Conference resolved itself into three camps,' ran the official report '— the Revolutionary Policy Committee, the Trotskyists and the others' (by the latter it meant the official line). Matlow led a vigorous attack upon the Divisional Council's policy of breaking with the London Bureau in order to associate with the Communist International, describing its proposals as 'loose phrases strung together; the stock-in-trade of pseudo-revolutionaries', and sought to 'convince the Conference on the need for a Fourth International'. In the event the R.P.C. policy was decisively defeated, but so was the Trotskyist one defended by the Clapham, Islington, and Holborn and Finsbury branches; and it was the N.A.C. proposal of continued support for the London Bureau (defended by the St. Pancras branch) that prevailed. A significant change of climate was reflected in the *New Leader* reports of both this and the following Easter Annual Conference,[66] where the views of the three branches were consistently described as 'Trotskyist', though no reference at all was made to the Stalinism of Gaster, Cullen and their friends. This coincided with the attempts of Gaster and Cullen to use organisational discipline against the London comrades, through their control of the Divisional Council. Their names were removed from the list of the Party's outside speakers, and they were even deprived of the right to speak in the name of the branches whose majority supported them. Gaster called for the exclusion of the whole of the Marxist Group from the I.L.P. When they protested against the Kirov frame-up at a meeting of the 'Friends of the Soviet Union', the London Division suspended them from membership and threatened them with a 'disciplinary Court', a threat which was withdrawn only after a campaign.[67]

The Annual Conference of the I.L.P. at Derby in April 1935 turned into a three-sided battle, with the Stalinists continuing to register a decline, and the slim forces of the Trotskyists getting the worst of it. On general perspectives, Matlow proposed the amendments of the Clapham, Holborn and Finsbury, and Finchley and Hendon branches, seeking to replace the usual haze and confusion of I.L.P. orthodoxy with clarity and precision. On the question of the capitalist crisis and the menace of Fascism, he opposed the idea that Fascism was advanced by capitalism as an antidote to working-class militancy, but asserted that capitalism used it 'as a definite manoeuvre to secure a temporary way out of their own difficulties'. He ridiculed the idea that 'the existence of the U.S.S.R. increased the capitalist crisis',[68] but made the mistake of maintaining that there were fewer strikes in 1933–4 than at any other time since the War — a slip that Cullen immediately pounced upon. Cullen's own contribution, of course, took the form of an advertisement for the Soviet Union, to which Robinson, speaking on behalf of Finchley and Hendon, rejoined that the progress of the U.S.S.R. had been considerable, but would have been so much the better without the mistakes of the bureaucracy.[69] On the domestic questions of the movement, Arthur Ballard speaking for Norwood attacked the 'Social Fascist' theory that lay behind the N.A.C.'s proposals, and more particularly 'the destructive and inaccurate analysis of the Labour Party, a party in which the rank and file workers still have faith.' He objected to the weak criticism of the Communist Party, pointed out the obvious truth that it was not the I.L.P.'s job to reform the Comintern, and showed how the latter was already changing its line so fast that in France the C.P. now stood to the right of the Socialist Party.[70] Cund from East Liverpool followed him with the remark that the N.A.C. statement was as 'clear as mud', and Matlow returned again to the urgent necessity for the I.L.P. to turn itself to the mass institutions. He 'stressed the need for the Party to work inside the Trade Unions, to urge the rank and file to put pressure on their leaders to force their leadership to carry through their demands.' The point was reinforced by Marzillier as regards the Labour Party as well, that if the I.L.P. wanted to prepare the workers for Soviets and remove their illusions in 'boss-class democracy', then they should 'assist the workers to fulfil their immediate electoral desire for a Third Labour Government and give critical support to Labour Party Candidates.'[71]

When the debate shifted to the problems of the coming war and the diplomacy of the Soviet Union, Earle Birney reaffirmed the necessity to defend the Soviet Union as a workers' state, despite the negative features of its bureaucracy. He showed that the N.A.C.'s policy of a General Strike throughout the world in the event of war was not possible without a revolutionary International, to which they were themselves opposed. Robinson then spoke to contrast the Soviet policy of balancing between power blocs to achieve peace as opposed to building up the workers' movement until the capitalists could not call upon them to fight. Matlow again raised the question of the Fourth International — to the effect that the policy of bringing together the Second and Third Internationals was hopeless, and that the I.L.P. should rather assist the fight for a new one.[72]

In the event, the Revolutionary Policy Committee gained between 20 and 30 delegate votes throughout the Conference, and the Trotskyists eight or nine, with the N.A.C. winning hands down. But crucial questions had been raised that in the long run were to be decisive for the I.L.P. Not the least of these was the question of the Labour Party. The arguments of Southall of Birmingham and Alec Smillie for the N.A.C. against critical support for the Labour Party, that 'the I.L.P. would have to take its share of responsibility for the failure of the next Labour Government and the consequent disillusion of the workers', had not been very convincing ones. The November election results were about to rub this in, with the return of only four M.P.s for the I.L.P., one for the Communists, and 154 for the Labour Party. It continued to trouble Brockway, for in his summary of the Conference he devoted a long piece to it:

> We cannot follow the 'Trotsky' line of a United Front with the Labour Party and the Trades Union Congress at all costs . . . It may be true that the mood of the workers is to try out a Third Labour Government and that only when they have had experience of it will they turn to a revolutionary Socialist policy. But that does not mean that we must co-operate in bringing about a Third Labour Government. One might as well say that as Mosley realises the failure of a Third Labour Government will give him his chance, that the British Union of Fascists would support the Labour Party, at the next election![73]

This continued attention to the Communist Party and studied neglect and hostility towards the mass institutions was, in the end, to prove the utter ruin of the I.L.P., as it dwindled almost to vanishing point before re-entering the Labour Party. 'There is also a great deal to be learned from the experience of the I.L.P. in England,' noted Trotsky. 'This party wanted to turn its back not only on the Labour Party but also on the trade unions and the Co-op Party. In doing so, they had no programme of their own. The last Conference proved, however, that you can't get very far with pure negativism and conservativism. The I.L.P. finds itself in continual retreat and in internal disarray.'[74] In this sense Matlow was being in no way 'melodramatic' when he stated that 'we are bringing revolutionary life to the I.L.P., while the Revolutionary Policy Committee, wanting to merge it with the Communist Party, are bringing it death.'[75]

By this time the atmosphere within the I.L.P. was infinitely more sharp and factional than a year before. The Stalinists had set the tone by their attempts to use their control of the London Divisional Council for purges of the classic type, and by the venom and personal abuse of their polemics. Andrew Rothstein, not one to worry about matters of tone, described the Marxist Group as 'renegade Communists and political adventurers who are the mouthpiece through which Trotskyism focuses counter-revolutionary confusion and disorganisation into the ranks of the revolutionaries',[76] whilst the Communist Party prepared to pull out its followers, doing the maximum damage in the process. Feeling among the rank-and-file of the I.L.P. was growing against unprincipled factionalism, illustrated by the carrying of a motion by a majority of 63 to 60, against the recommendation of the N.A.C., that unofficial groups were 'bad in principle'.[77] This could not affect Communist sympathisers, who were preparing to go shortly in any case, but it left a bitter inheritance for the Marxist Group, who would inevitably become identified with the Revolutionary Policy Committee in the eyes of the ordinary member. It certainly would not, as Pollitt affected to believe, result in 'every latitude and facility given inside the I.L.P. to the poisonous vapourings of a few nondescript Trotskyists',[78] or as Rust would have it, enable 'parasitic Trotskyists' to continue to be 'fostered by the I.L.P. leaders who use them in the struggle against the Comintern.'[79]

Opinion was certainly turning against the Stalinists inside the I.L.P. McGovern had made a particularly crude attack on them at conference, calling the Comintern 'a joke' and the C.P.G.B. 'a commercial traveller touting for custom for its Soviet paymasters'; and when Pollitt himself addressed the conference he was given the bird, with shouts of 'Moscow gold' and 'Soviet bureaucracy'.[80] But what angered the I.L.P. members was the patent disloyalty of the Revolutionary Policy Committee itself towards the party shown on every hand — their employment of Communist Party lecturers, their sneers at the party leaders and near adulation of those of the C.P., their refusal to sell *The New Leader* when it took a line against them, the breakdown of party democracy by fastening on R.P.C.-controlled branch resolutions taken previously at unofficial group meetings, and their obvious preparations, 'dishonestly denied', to split the party. They forfeited what sympathy they could have gained when they made use of any bureaucratic machinery there was to hand, such as when they tried to use their control of the London Divisional Council to purge the Trotskyists and, when they lost control of it, brought charges of 'anti-party conduct' against the new London Organiser.[81]

The first to be pulled out were the youth. The Guild of Youth Conference had passed a resolution of sympathetic affiliation to the Young Communist International as early as May 1934,[82] only to reverse the position with some difficulty at a special conference on 18th November.[83] After the Derby Conference many of them resigned from the I.L.P. Guild of Youth, announcing their adherence to the Young Communist League in the Moscow press.[84] The turning point for the adult supporters of the R.P.C. came with their loss of control of the London Division at its Conference later in the year. Whilst the Marxist Group were able to rally only seven votes behind the call for the Fourth International, the Stalinists received only eight votes for their own resolution of support for the new policy of the Soviet Union, and of reliance on the League of Nations and pacts with Britain and France: the condemnation of this policy by the N.A.C. was overwhelmingly carried.[85] A further resolution condemning the social patriotism of the Labour and Communist parties went through by 21 votes to 15, and a Trotskyist one from Clapham, denouncing the Communist International and the League of Nations by seventeen votes to fifteen. The final humiliation was the election of John Aplin, a noted opponent of Stalinism, to the position of London Organiser, from which he promptly laid charges against them of 'disruption'.[86] On 31st October the Revolutionary Policy Committee resigned from the I.L.P. en bloc, denouncing the propaganda of *The New Leader* against the foreign policy of the Soviet Union as 'treachery to the working-class movement',[87] and announcing that 'there is one revolutionary party — that is the C.P.'[88] A string of branch resignations in Harrow, Poplar and Stepney followed, with the final total of recruits to the C.P.G.B. put at 100[89] by the Communists and 50 by the I.L.P.[90] Those left concluded that 'the party will be healthier now that those who have long advocated the Communist policy have gone to the Communist Party.'[91]

The circumstances in which the Stalinist faction split from the I.L.P. were not, in fact, a result of the struggle inside the I.L.P. and its internal logic, but were rooted in deep-going basic changes on the international plane. The Soviet Union had now come into the League of Nations, had signed a one-sided pact with France, and was hoping to complete the new alliance structure by a similar one with Great Britain. The 'Third Period' policy of extreme sectarianism had now given way to the 'Popular Front', of alliances with Socialists and bourgeois politicians, all on the nationalist basis of opposition to Nazi Germany. The conclusion of such an alliance in France, along with Russia's approval of its defence measures, was turned into a directive binding on all the parties in the world at the Seventh World Congress of the Comintern. The task of Communists in such 'democratic' countries was now to support a military pact with the Soviet Union against Germany 'to preserve peace', along with support for League of Nations actions, and the necessary measures of rearmament. Such a rapid evolution of the Communist policy now placed the Revolutionary Policy Committee in an unenviable position within the I.L.P., committed as it traditionally was to pacifism and opposition to imperialist war. Now the I.L.P. was squarely to the left of the Communist Party, and this leftwards evolution was confirmed by other indications — the adoption of support for workers' councils, for a general strike, and even for a revolution ('if the capitalists threatened war').

This meant a deep-going shift in the I.L.P., and the consequent withdrawal of the R.P.C. altered the whole position as far as the Trotskyists were concerned. As Harber pointed out:

> Since, however, the Stalinists have shown themselves to be so weak inside the I.L.P., and since the Right Oppositionists can have no desire to help them in splitting the party, it is probable that the centrist leadership, supported by the Right Wing, will be able to resist this attack. We should in future consider our

> main enemy to be, not so much the Stalinists, but the hopeless centrists and right wingers who form the present leadership of the party. While there was still a chance of the Stalinists or Right Oppositionists getting control, we had to direct our main attack against them and avoid criticising the leadership too strongly. Under the existing circumstances, however, we must now turn our attack upon the supporters of a 2½ International.[92]

From now on, it was a question of challenging the flat pacifism of the N.A.C. and the residue of impractical ultra-leftism it had imbibed from its association with the Communists, rather than Stalinist ideas at first hand. There was the additional complication of the I.L.P.'s own move to the left, and the opposition they shared (from different premises) to League of Nations' Sanctions and Imperialist War. For the I.L.P. leaders had also foreseen the evolution of the Comintern to patriotism: as soon as Maxton had heard of the Franco-Soviet Pact he prophesied that Russia could not 'seek an alliance with the British government without moderating the class struggle carried on by the Communist Party here.'[93]

A basis for continued co-operation was provided by the Abyssinian crisis of the autumn of 1935. On 3rd October the Italian army invaded the poor country of Abyssinia, in alleged retaliation for the attack on their frontier post at Wal-Wal a year earlier. Embarrassed at this challenge to British and French control of Africa, the 'democracies' induced the League of Nations to impose sanctions on Italy, whilst (on the side) negotiating the Hoare-Laval Pact with Mussolini by offering him part of Abyssinia (instead of the whole). On the one hand British and French relations with the dictators worsened, and on the other there was great indignation from the public when the news of the proposed pact leaked out, and Hoare was obliged to resign from the foreign office. Even though all the powers broke the sanctions on the quiet — including the Soviet Union, which took the opportunity to sell oil to Italy — here was a golden opportunity for the Communist Party to renew their drive for an alliance with Russia against the dictators, for support to the League sanctions policy, and for 'collective security' through imperialist alliance systems.

The response of the I.L.P. and its Trotskyists was a very positive one. C.L.R. James was allowed to write some splendid articles in *The New Leader* defending the Marxist attitude to the War, and a speaking tour was mounted by the I.L.P. all across the country. 'Let us fight against not only Italian Imperialism, but the other robbers and oppressors, French and British Imperialism,' he wrote. 'Workers of Britain, peasants and workers of Africa, get closer for this and for other fights. But keep far from the Imperialists and their Leagues and covenants and sanctions!'[94] He accused Britain of mobilising world and domestic opinion in order to keep Abyssinia under neo-colonialist control, 'as tight as anything Italian Imperialism ever intended', but to exclude Italy from the spoils. Further articles defined the League's 'collective security' as 'their pre-war alliances and war preparations, dressed up for the masses'.[95] A damaging polemic against the Stalinist attitude hit directly home:

> Had the present crisis developed late in 1934, or even early in 1935, the C.P. and the I.L.P. would have been side by side. But in May, 1935, Stalin and Laval concluded a military alliance, and together issued the notorious communiqué in which Stalin repudiated the Leninist doctrine of 'the enemy is in your own country', and gave his blessing to the doctrine of national defence.
>
> The Soviet Union wants to use the League to preserve peace for as long as it can. It objects to the imperialist proposals of the Council of Five, but it supports sanctions. If it wants France and Czechoslovakia to help it against Germany through the League it must show itself a good League member now. The whole situation is deplorable, but there is no help for it and we have to face it.
>
> But what cannot be condoned is that the C.P. everywhere, instead of following its own class policy, is doing exactly what Litvinov is doing at Geneva. That is the beginning and end of the whole business.[96]

Andrew Rothstein, in reply, could only pretend that the allegation of Stalin blessing national defence was 'bosh', the charge of the C.P. making an 'about turn' similarly so, and the military alliance of Stalin and Laval as 'sheer bosh for which James has nothing but the authority of the Nazi press and the *Daily Herald*'.[97] Trotsky, on the other hand, was delighted with the I.L.P.'s 'serious evolution to the left' and the publication by *The New Leader* of 'the best articles in the Labour Press'.[98] Relations with the I.L.P. became much more friendly, with the visit of Harold Isaacs to Fenner Brockway, and the opening up of correspondence between Brockway and Trotsky.[99] Even more positive were the meetings staged all over the country to protest at the danger of war involved in the League sanctions policy, in which James shared the platform with other I.L.P. leaders at Shoreditch, Barking, West London, Glasgow, South Wales and Southampton, where he angered the Stalinists by showing that the Popular Front 'had not stemmed Fascism in France'.[100]

On his part, Trotsky redoubled his efforts to win over the I.L.P.

He began by showing that the I.L.P.'s previous association with Stalinism had left its mark on its ideas and practice, that 'it did not pay sufficient attention to mass work, which cannot be carried on outside of the trade unions and the Labour Party', that it 'turned into a sort of appendage to the Communist International' and 'appeared to the workers to be a Communist Party of the second order'. 'It is a secret to nobody,' he stated bluntly, 'that Stalinism long overawed the leaders of the I.L.P. with those rubber-stamp formulas which comprise the miserable bureaucratic falsification of Leninism.' And whilst the I.L.P. had evolved 'from pacifism toward proletarian revolution', it had still 'halted in the middle of the road'.

By way of illustration he picked out the resolution on the war and the general strike passed at the Derby Conference. There, they had agreed to urge a general strike to stop war and a social revolution should war occur, or if Britain were involved in a war against the U.S.S.R. He went through an analysis of types of General Strike, showing that a general strike without a proletarian insurrection cannot stop war, that even if the revolutionary forces were strong enough to launch one the government would have been too weak to go to war in the first place, and in any case 'a general strike as a punishment for a given capital crime of the government' was 'revolutionary phrasemongering'.

Having here put his finger on the weakness of the I.L.P.'s position — its leanings towards abstract propaganda in place of concrete action — he showed how this reflected itself in the main problems confronting it in the Labour movement:

> . . . it remains a fact about every revolutionary organisation in Britain that its attitude to the masses and to the class is almost coincident with its attitude toward the Labour Party, which bases itself upon the trade unions. At *this time*, the question of whether to function inside the Labour Party or outside it is not a principled question, but a question of actual opportunities.
>
> In any case, without a strong fraction in the trade unions, and consequently in the Labour Party itself, the I.L.P. is doomed to impotence, to the 'united front' with the insignificant Communist Party than to work inside mass organisations.

Then he went on to the most important point, its international links. 'A struggle against war and for revolution is unthinkable without the International,' he noted, and showed how the I.L.P. was still bent on friendly collaboration with the Comintern, that it had not yet made up its mind as to whether the latter could still be reformed, and that it had halted midway between the Third International and the struggle for the Fourth. Finally, he showed in an appended note how, by its policy of the 'refusal' of military service, the leadership maintained its 'pacifist illusions'.[101]

Nonetheless, Trotsky evidently had high hopes of the evolution of the I.L.P. at this period. 'There is a crisis in the British Independent Labour Party,' he wrote to Georges Vereecken; 'the Stalinists have left the party; the Leninists have been very much strengthened; and one can anticipate with certainty that the rupture of the I.L.P. with the Comintern will force it (not without a new crisis) toward the Fourth International.'[102]

Perhaps more could have been made of the possibilities, but the Marxist Group itself was divided by factional dispute over the proper attitude to be adopted to the Labour Party in the General Election of November 1935. The group was split over whether the I.L.P. should field as many candidates as possible, whilst campaigning for a boycott of all Labour candidates who supported the League of Nations' sanctions, or whether the I.L.P. should support all Labour candidates where there was no I.L.P. candidate in the field. In November 1935 Earle Birney and Ken Johnson travelled to Norway to get Trotsky's advice on the problem. He told them that the I.L.P.'s parliamentary group should be opposed for urging the workers not to bear arms if war came ('defeatism against the workers, not revolutionary defeatism against capitalism'), described the I.L.P.'s decision to run as many of its own candidates as possible as correct, but opposed the refusal of the I.L.P. to support Labour candidates who endorsed the sanctions of the League of Nations in seats they were not themselves contesting. 'The Labour Party should have been critically supported not because it was for or against sanctions but because it represented the working-class masses,' he remarked. 'In war, as in peace, the I.L.P. must say to the workers: "The Labour Party will deceive you and betray you, but you do not believe us. Very well, we will go through your experiences with you, but in no case do we identify ourselves with the Labour Party programme".' Whilst stating that the question of I.L.P. entry into the Labour Party was not as yet posed, Trotsky had different advice for the youth section. 'Since the I.L.P. youth seem to be few and scattered, while the Labour Youth is the mass youth organisation, I would say: "Do not build fractions — seek to enter." For here the danger of Stalinist devastation is extreme.'

Another disturbing question to which Trotsky turned his attention was that of unofficial groups inside the I.L.P. Although the resolution condemning them at the Derby Conference had gone through without the blessing of Brockway and Maxton, a number of indications were surfacing that the example of the Revolutionary Policy Committee was having a bad effect upon the membership of the Party. In the first weekend in January 1936, the London Division took a decision to 'instruct the N.A.C. to dissolve all unofficial groups within the party', and an N.A.C. resolution to the same effect was only defeated in the Yorkshire conference by an amendment from Sheffield (where John Goffe was active) to the effect that groups were not in themselves harmful, and that the N.A.C. would remove the causes of their existence 'by laying down clear and principled lines of policy'.[103] 'Can we trust the Trotskyists any more than we could trust the R.P.C.?' asked one member. 'Are they not doing exactly the same things? Are they not transferring group decisions to branches just as mechanically and uncritically, and with as little regard for the arguments of minorities?'[104] Against this, Trotsky pointed out that factional organisation was the norm in the Bolshevik Party, and that the I.L.P. leadership in any case was such a group — 'a centrist group, protected by the Party machinery' — and 'organisational measures should be resorted to only in extreme cases'.[105]

But as the Abyssinian crisis progressed, the difference between the pacifism of the I.L.P.'s leaders and the revolutionary stance of the Trotskyists became more marked, and widened the gaps between them. Especially was this the case with the struggle for the Fourth International. When Maxton addressed the Divisional Conference in Glasgow, he pointed out that whilst he had 'the utmost respect' for Trotsky's 'work and views', and opposed the Comintern's 'driving the workers of Europe behind the policies of their capitalist governments', he was 'still opposed to the formation of the Fourth International.[106] Brockway later revealed the real source of their hesitations in his autobiography:

> Trotsky's dealings with his followers convinced me that, despite his advocacy of 'proletarian democracy', he had the same instinct for personal power as Stalin and that were he head of the Russian state he would treat dissentients from his policy with a ruthlessness similar to Stalin's. The personal authority which Trotsky imposed on the little groupings of the 'Fourth International' was that of an absolute dictator; unless his word were obeyed in every respect, expulsions followed on the pattern of the Communist International, irrespective of majorities and minorities.[107]

This was the old fear, of international authority preventing the I.L.P. leadership from making national accommodations, with the amusing twist of comparing Trotsky's moral authority with the real dictatorship of Stalin, to which Brockway had paid court for so many years. Even the Marxist Group itself was less firm on its attitude to this international challenge. Its majority had disagreed with Trotsky's policy in the General Election of support for Labour Party candidates who supported sanctions,[108] and now held back from appending their signature to the 'Open Letter to All Revolutionary Proletarian Organisations and Groupings' for the formation of the Fourth International.[109] In the climate now hardening in the I.L.P., they were afraid that such outright association with outside and international groups would feed the drive to ban official groups, and threaten them with premature expulsion. So instead, Trotsky advised writing a letter of their own to the I.L.P. leaders, pointing to the treachery of the Third International, and saying that the struggle against war and sanctions was possible 'only under the banner of the Fourth International'.[110]

All the signs showed that a showdown was imminent between the Trotskyists and the I.L.P. leadership, and that it would centre upon the questions of Marxism and pacifism, the need for the New International, and the attitude to the Labour movement here, involving also a drive to throttle the revolutionary minority within the I.L.P.'s own ranks.

The chief question, setting the limits of all the others, was that of the International. In March 1936 Brockway replied to Trotsky's criticism of the London Bureau, that it 'had no common policy':

> Trotsky states that the parties attached to the London Bureau are going 'in all directions'. This is quite untrue. They are moving increasingly in one direction . . .
>
> Trotsky is the last person to sneer about the size of the affiliated parties in Bulgaria, Romania and Poland. They work under illegal or semi-legal conditions, whilst even where they work under legal conditions most of his own groups are the merest cliques.
>
> One regrets having to retort sharply to Trotsky in this way, because a Socialist with his revolutionary record should be using his influence to bring all Revolutionary Socialists together internationally. Instead of that he is exaggerating differences from the sectarian angle of his own collection of groups.[111]

Trotsky's reply welcomed the new sharp tone that had crept into the I.L.P.'s polemics, pointed out that in the only international initiative of the London Bureau it split three ways (the number of people on its committee!), that small groups with clear ideas and programmes may be of value, but those without were the merest zero, and that, whereas the Trotskyist sections were 'selective bodies which came into existence on the basis of quite definite ideas and methods', the London Bureau was a temporary association of 'different, hybrid organisations with quite a different past, different ideas, and a different future.'[112]

The decisive clash between the two tendencies took place at the Fourth Annual Conference of the I.L.P., held in Keighley on 11th and 12th April. The question of the United Front and the Labour Party was dealt with first. 'It is impossible for revolutionary Socialists to function effectively through the Labour Party,' ran the basic resolution. 'Membership of the Labour Party means the denial of revolutionary policy and purpose.' On the other hand, it stated that 'the I.L.P. cannot form a united front with the Communist Party on a broad basis "without an agreement in principle".' This was confronted by a resolution on 'electoral policy' proposed by Clapham and Islington, to the effect that 'the I.L.P. must in future elections make the United Front proposals to other working class parties with the objective of eliminating the danger of a split vote and lessening the chances of the ruling class candidate, and that 'the sooner a Labour Government with a working majority is returned, the sooner will the workers lose faith in Reformism.' It condemned the Communist Party's new policy of uncritical support for Labour, and affirmed the Leninist position that 'the workers, when they become disillusioned, will accept the revolutionary leadership of the I.L.P. and form their own democratic machinery of struggle and government–workers' councils.'[113] On this issue the 'Trotskyist line of "critical support" ' was defeated by a combination of those who would not support Labour because of the war danger and its support for sanctions, and those who would not support any other than I.L.P. candidates.[114]

On the question of the International, the leadership, whilst condemning both the Second and Third Internationals, continued to support its utopia of a 'united revolutionary organisation' somehow springing out of the 'increased activity' of the London Bureau:

> . . . he did not believe it to be possible or desirable to create a united revolutionary International out of the small groups accepting the Trotskyist viewpoint; and then 'from the height of Oslo, form a new International'.
>
> The real basis for a new International must come from the development of Socialist movements and groups working their way to a revolutionary position, together with such sections, now affiliated to the Third International, which were tending away from present policies.
>
> The contacts which the I.L.P. had with parties affiliated to the International Bureau for Revolutionary Socialist Unity would form the beginning of the new International built up on certain fundamental guiding principles which were already in existence on the basis of the bureau.[115]

In Brockway's view, the Trotskyist attempt to form a Fourth International was 'the artificial method of imposing a rigid programme and then inviting parties to associate with it', whereas a common programme 'must grow historically and naturally from experience, co-operation, the development of a common mind and method.'[116]

Matlow, speaking for Clapham branch, and C.L.R. James, for Finchley, put the case for the Fourth International 'based upon the principles of the first four Congresses of the Third International', pointing out that the London bureau had neither policy nor programme, and was sure to fail without them.[117]

Not only was the National Administrative Council's view overwhelmingly carried, but to it was appended a paragraph from the London Division, that the I.L.P. 'resolutely opposes the formation of the "Fourth International" (added: "as proposed by the International Communist League") as being not only inopportune, but also opposed to the interests of international unity and lacking any contacts with the mass workers' movement.'[118]

Conference also reverted to the I.L.P.'s pacifism on the question of revolution itself. Matlow's attempt to amend the party statutes by inserting a mention of 'the revolutionary overthrow of the capitalist system' produced the counter-argument that if it were introduced into pamphlets for public sale it would drive the party 'into illegality',[119] and conference had also been unimpressed by what Reg Bishop called his 'superior and academic discourse on civil war'.[120]

The high point of the conference, however, came over the Abyssinian debate. To begin with, *The New Leader* had taken up a position in support of Abyssinia, and advised the workers to refuse to handle munitions, oil and war materials going to Italy. But on 13th September 1935, the Inner Executive, followed then by the N.A.C., had changed the line to no support for either side, referring to it as a conflict between 'rival dictators'. The battle began by a motion to refer back the report, led by C.L.R. James in 'a typically torrential speech'.[121]

> . . . he showed that the I.L.P., in its obligation to the colonial peoples must assist them in their struggle against Italian Fascism.
>
> He drew attention to the resolution of the International Bureau for Revolutionary Socialist Unity, which had been accepted by the I.L.P. The statement declared that:
>
>> 'It is necessary to support the anti-Imperialist mass movements arising among "coloured" peoples in all countries in connection with the Abyssinian crisis, and to

> create a firm alliance between the International working-class movement and suppressed peoples.'
>
> And as practical measures to be taken the statement laid down:
>
> (1) International working-class boycott of Imperialist Italy and its allies.
> (2) The prevention of transport of troops to Africa.
>
> James maintained that if the workers here had taken such independent action they would immediately have come into conflict with the government here, and the situation of 'fighting your own government' would become a real issue.[122]

He appealed 'as a black worker for help for the black population of Abyssinia,' recalled McNair. 'This appeal moved conference deeply, but it was later used against him in the discussion to prove that he was nationalist, not socialist.'[123] John Aplin, London Divisional organiser, and Jones, representing Lancashire Division, spoke to support him, along with Jack Huntz, C.A. Smith, and even Fenner Brockway. Maxton did not speak himself, but Buchanan did, refusing to accept 'the verdict of the League of Nations' that Italy was the aggressor, ridiculing the idea that the workers could override the reformists in the trade unions, while McGovern added that 'it was the job of the I.L.P. to stand aside from quarrels between dictators'. In the end, James' resolution to refer back was carried by one vote, and a resolution from Sheffield and Lancashire affirming revolutionary defeatism and charging the decision to change party policy with being 'in direct conflict with declared party policy and a contradiction of party discipline' went through with an even wider margin, 70 votes to 57.[124]

Now the fat was in the fire, for the parliamentary group, which had initiated this change from socialism to pacifism, was now exposed before the party as being a minority group forcing their own policy upon it, as well as behaving in exactly the same way as the parliamentary Labour Party when the I.L.P. had split from it. Next day, Maxton read a statement on behalf of the parliamentary group, the Inner Executive and the N.A.C., that they were 'unable conscientiously to operate the decision reached yesterday', that 'having regard to the narrowness of the majority' conference should 'express its confidence in the National Council and allow liberty for the expression of differing views within the party.'[125] They proposed to throw the question back to a referendum of the membership at large.

Then Brockway got up and supported the proposal, for 'he felt it would be a bad blow for the Party if the decision taken before involved the loss, particularly, of the chairman.'[126] 'Although many of my supporters thought I had "ratted",' he explained, 'I had no doubt I had done the right thing from a long view', for 'faced with the prospect of losing Maxton and the parliamentary group, the Majority would rally to them.'[127] So not only did he sacrifice the colonial struggle to the pacifism of the M.P.s, but he also condemned the I.L.P. as a party to being an appendage of Maxton, and doomed it forever. 'This "bombshell" from the Party National Council left the delegates stunned,' he remarked,[128] and conference carried the suggestion in a downcast mood by 93 votes to 39. 'The pacifist-parliamentary clique of Maxton and Company,' commented Trotsky, 'which regards the party merely as a handy tool, forced it by means of a rude and brutal ultimatum back into a pacifist prostration.'[129]

Before the referendum was to take place, the I.L.P. devoted a special printed issue of its discussion bulletin, *Controversy*, to dealing with the matter. Maxton, McGovern and Southall defended the view of the parliamentary group, and writing in favour of conference policy were Brockway, Bob Edwards and C.L.R. James. Maxton argued, among other things, that 'to take a pro-Abyssinian line was to aid British Imperialism', that the Italians were 'for the most part decent working men and women like ourselves', and the Abyssinians were 'decent workers on the land, living in primitive conditions, tyrannised over by a barbaric feudal monarch, and urged to fight to defend him in his feudal splendour and his right to exploit them.' McGovern was even cruder in this 'equal blame' argument. 'You urge on the ignorant African natives to their doom and back the brutal Emperor at the same time,' he wrote. 'If Mussolini succeeds in capturing the whole of Abyssinia, will the natives be worse under his rule than that of the Negus?'

C.L.R. James attempted to sketch out the lines of a Socialist attitude on the problem. He outlined the theory of imperialism as the export of capital, pointed out that Abyssinia, being feudal, was not waging war in pursuit of markets and blasted the argument that this was merely a conflict between rival imperialisms. He attacked the parliamentarians fiercely for their 'single perversion of party policy, and disregard of every accepted principle of socialism', and concluded with exceptional foresight: 'if the Party allows the Inner Executive to get away with this, then the Party, after four years of struggle and sacrifice to reach where it is today, will have started on the backward road.'[130]

It did just that. Obviously, more weight was bound to be given to the views of the parliamentary group, which represented the traditions of the party and had all the prestige. McGovern wrote in to protest that James' remarks went 'beyond the bounds of common decency', including 'lies about Maxton and myself'.[131] On his part, James tried to take up one of his taunts, that 'you support war by the use of Abyssinian lives and refuse to use your own bodies for the war which you back', by volunteering to take service under Haile Selassie.[132] But despite the fact that the debate aroused considerable interest (the pamphlet ran into two editions),[133] the Inner Executive won their point by a vote of three to two in the referendum.[134]

Apart from abandoning the Abyssinian people to their fate, this decision showed that no conference control over the M.P.s of the I.L.P. was going to be effective in the future, and marked a new stage in the evolution away from any of the norms of working-class democracy. For after this most arrogant treatment of the delegates came a motion from the N.A.C., proposed by John Aplin, which declared that 'the present system of organised groups be brought to an end'.[135] An amendment written by Goffe and seconded by Matlow failed to be carried to the effect that 'organised groups in themselves are not harmful to the Party', proving as they did that 'active discussions of policy are going on', and that the N.A.C. could easily remove the causes for such groups' existence by 'laying down clear and principled lines of policy'.[136] So, after having given generous latitude to a Stalinist faction to break all the norms of party loyalty and discipline, the N.A.C. had decided to use this to strike at the revolutionaries, none of whom had been proved to have done anything of the sort. Bowing to the inevitable, in May the group placed an article in *Controversy* over the name of May Matlow entitled 'The Marxist Group disbands'.

All in all, it was a shabby affair. Commenting on the voting, Trotsky remarked that 'we see that there are dictators not only in Rome and in Addis Ababa, but also in London', and that 'of the three dictators, I consider the most harmful the one who grabs his own party by the throat in the name of his parliamentary prestige and his pacifist confusion.' As for Brockway, he wrote, 'he believes it is better for the British workers to have Maxton as chairman with a false point of view than to have a correct point of view without Maxton', having 'turned over to Maxton that oh so paltry parcel of principles.' He concluded: 'The cause of the I.L.P. seems to me to be hopeless.'[137]

But by this time in any case the world had quite outgrown the pacifism of the I.L.P. With I.L.P. numbers down below five thousand, the Labour Party was clearly the main arena of class conflict in Britain, whilst elsewhere loomed up the Moscow Trials and the Spanish Civil War. Where people were busy making their own choices, and preparing to fight and die for them, nobody really cared any more whether Maxton and McGovern took sides or not.

Notes

1. J. McNair, *James Maxton — The Beloved Rebel*, London, 1955, p. 325.
2. Statement to the N.A.C., 7th November 1931, quoted in McNair, ibid., p. 233.
3. F. Brockway, *The Coming Revolution* (Chairman's Address to the I.L.P. Conference, Blackpool, Easter 1932), I.L.P. Pamphlet, pp. 10, 15–16.
4. F. Brockway, *The Next Step* (Chairman's Speech to the I.L.P. Conference, Derby, Easter 1933), I.L.P. Pamphlet, p. 15.
5. J. Paton, *Left Turn*, London, 1936, p. 400.
6. F. Brockway, *Inside the Left*, London, 1941, p. 244.
7. I.L.P., *Report of the Special Conference, Bradford, 30th–31st July, 1932*, I.L.P. pamphlet, p. 32.
8. Cf. Paton, *Left Turn*, pp. 398-9; Brockway, *Inside the Left*, p. 243.
9. Paton, ibid., p. 425.
10. C.K. Cullen, Speech at I.L.P. Annual Conference, Blackpool, March 1932 — official report, p. 42.
11. Paton, *Left Turn*, p. 428.
12. Ibid.
13. Letter from Kuusinen to the N.A.C. of the I.L.P., 21st June 1933 in *The I.L.P. and the Communist International: Full Text of the Correspondence*, I.L.P. pamphlet, 1934.
14. Letter from Paton to the E.C.C.I., 7th July 1933, ibid.
15. Letter from Brockway to the E.C.C.I., 8th January 1934, ibid.
16. Paton, *Left Turn*, p. 426.
17. McNair, *James Maxton — The Beloved Rebel*, p. 236; Brockway, *Inside the Left*, p. 251.
18. H. Pollitt, Report to the XIIIth Plenum of the E.C.C.I. in *Inprecorr*, vol. xiv, no. 5, 30th January 1934, p. 136.
19. Kuusinen, Letter to the N.A.C. of the I.L.P., 20th February 1934, in *Inprecorr*, vol. xiv, no. 14, 2nd March 1934, pp. 399-40. Cf. *Supplementary Letters*, I.L.P. pamphlet (giving a text with a slightly modified wording).
20. F. Brockway, 'The I.L.P. and Moscow', in *The New Leader*, vol. xxiv, new series, no. 106, 12th January 1934, p. 4.
21. Brockway, *Inside the Left*, p. 263.
22. Ibid., p. 252.
23. J. Paton, Letter to the E.C.C.I., 6th October 1933.
24. F. Brockway, Letter to the E.C.C.I., 8th January 1934.
25. 'Communist Reply to London I.L.P.', in *The New Leader*, vol. xxv, new series, no. 2, 26th January 1934, p. 5.
26. 'More I.L.P. Policy Debates', in *The New Leader*, vol. xxv, new series, no. 3, 2nd February 1934, p. 4.
27. 'T.C.', 'The I.L.P. and the Comintern', 17th January 1934, in *The Militant* (U.S.A.), vol. vii, no. 4, 29th January 1934.
28. 'T.C.', 'The British Hunger March', in *The Militant* (U.S.A.), vol. vii, no. 12, 24th March 1924; and see note 26 above.
29. See note 27 above.
30. W. Rust, in Discussion on the Reports of Kuusinen, Pieck and Pollitt to the XIIIth Plenum of the Comintern, in *Inprecorr*, vol. xiv, no. 15, 5th March 1934, pp. 381-2.
31. 'The I.L.P. Conference' (Report), in *The New Leader*, vol. xxv, new series, no. 12, 6th April 1934, pp. 4-5; Eric Whalley, 'The Conference of the I.L.P. and After', in *Labour Monthly*, vol. xvi, no. 5, May 1934, pp. 273-9.
32. 'Trotsky Goes', in *The New Leader*, vol. xxv, new series, no. 14, 20th April 1934, p. 3.

33. 'Where is Trotsky to Go?', in *The New Leader*, vol. xxv, new series, no. 15, 27th April 1934, p. 3.

34. 'They Fear Trotsky', in *The New Leader*, vol. xxv, new series, no. 16, 4th May, p. 5.

35. L.D. Trotsky, 'Cardinal Questions Facing the I.L.P.', in *Writings of Leon Trotsky, 1933-4*, New York, 1972, pp. 187-9.

36. Cf. S. Bornstein and A. Richardson, *Two Steps Back*, London, 1982, p. 7, and above, p. 117.

37. Cf. 'Crazier Month in the I.L.P.', in *Red Flag*, vol. i, no. 9, May–June 1934, p. 4.

38. International Secretariat, Letter to the British Section, Bolshevik–Leninists (undated).

39. Conference Report, I.L.P. Special Conference, Bradford, 30th–31st July 1932, p. 40.

40. *The New Leader*, 9th February 1934, 27th April 1934.

41. C.K. Cullen, Speech at I.L.P. Conference, in 'Communism — Live Issue at I.L.P. Conference', in the *Daily Worker*, 22nd April 1935. Cf. Chappell and Clinton (eds.), *Trotsky's Writings on Britain*, vol. iii, London, 1974, p. 245; *The New Leader*, 9th November 1934.

42. John Goffe, Interview with Al Richardson, 18th May 1978.

43. I.L.P. Islington Branch, *The Bolshevik-Leninists to the World Proletariat! France's Turn Next! For the Fourth International* (duplicated pamphlet). Cf. L.D. Trotsky, 'France is Now the Key to the Situation', March 1934, in *Writings of Leon Trotsky, 1933-4*, pp. 238-244.

44. Acton Branch of the I.L.P., 'Leon Trotsky on Centrism' (duplicated pamphlet); cf. L.D. Trotsky, 'Centrism and the Fourth International', 22nd February 1934, in *Writings of Leon Trotsky, 1933-4*, pp. 232-7.

45. Cf. L.D. Trotsky, 'Once More on Centrism', 23rd March 1934, ibid., pp. 265-8.

46. See note 44 above.

47. 'On the Activity and Progress of the English Bolshevik–Leninists', in the *Bulletin of the League of Communist-Internationalists*, Amsterdam, no. 1, 1st May 1935.

48. Margaret Johns, Secretary, Central London Group, Letter to Dr. Worrall (undated).

49. Albert Matlow, Letter to Dr. Worrall, 3rd November 1934.

50. L.D. Trotsky, 'The Stalinists and Organic Unity', 19th July 1934, in *Writings of Leon Trotsky: Supplement, 1934-40*, New York, 1979, p. 505.

51. Cf. note 49 above; Frederick Marzillier, 'Reply to Comrade Theodorson', in *Controversy*, March 1936, p. 4.

52. John Robinson, Interview with Al Richardson, 3rd June 1978.

53. Frederick Marzillier, Interview with Al Richardson, 2nd December 1978; 'A Reply to Comrade Theodorson', in *Controversy*, March 1936, pp. 3-5.

54. Advertisement in *The New Leader*, vol. xxvii, new series, no. 58, 22nd February 1935, p. 6 (Clapham Branch, 22nd February).

55. John Robinson, Interview with Al Richardson, 3rd June 1978. A good example of C.L.R. James' impact on middle-class I.L.P. opinion is to be found in Ethel Mannin, *Comrade O Comrade*, London, 1945, pp. 133-5.

56. Hansa's real name was A. Deva Angadi — *Socialist Outlook*, 11th December 1953, p. 4. Under the name of 'Jaya Deva' he wrote *Japan's Kampf*, London, 1942. For the influence of the Liverpool branch, see W. Rust in the *Daily Worker*, 28th April 1936.

57. Max Bosch (Sid Frost), Interview with Sam Bornstein and Al Richardson, 4th June 1983.

58. Advertisement for a meeting of Clapham I.L.P., in *The New Leader*, vol. xxvii, new series, no. 60, 8th March 1935.

59. *The New Leader*, 18th January 1935.

60. Ibid., 8th February 1935.

61. Cf. ch. iv. p. 155, note 9 above; and p. 289, note 43 below. Why Trotsky's name is disguised in this article but elsewhere appears openly is inexplicable.

62. W.C. Burrow (ed.), *Stalin's Treason and the World Revolution*, 'printed and published by the I.L.P. Marxist Group'. Cf. L.D. Trotsky, 'An Open Letter to the Workers of France', 10th June 1935, in *Writings of Leon Trotsky, 1934–5*, New York, 1971, pp. 305-14.

63. 'Conversations with Trotsky', 'published by E. Robertson of Holborn and Finsbury I.L.P.'. Cf. L.D. Trotsky, 'Once Again the I.L.P.', November 1935, in *Writings of Leon Trotsky, 1935–6*, New York, 1970, pp. 197-208.

64. Marxist Group, 'On Dictators and the Heights of Oslo', full text of the article sent to *Controversy*; cf. L.D. Trotsky, 22nd April 1936, in *Writings of Leon Trotsky, 1935–6*, pp. 317-320.

65. 'Letter to an I.L.P. Member', 'published by J. Pawsey'; cf. L.D. Trotsky, 'Cardinal Questions Facing the I.L.P.', 5th January 1934, in *Writings of Leon Trotsky, 1933–4*, pp. 186-190. Trotsky's 'Europe and America' was also published by the group at this time.

66. 'London Branches Debate Policy', and 'Letter to the Editor', in *The New Leader*, vol. xxvii, new series, no. 58, 22nd February 1935, p. 4; 'The I.L.P. Conference', subsection, 'The Trotskyist Case', in *The New Leader*, vol. xxvii, new series, no. 67, 26th April 1935.

67. 'On the Activity and Progress of the English Bolshevik–Leninists', in *Bulletin of the League of Communist-Internationalists*, no. 1, 1st May 1935, pp. 15ff.

68. 'The I.L.P. Conference', in *The New Leader*, vol. xxvii, new series, no. 67, 26th April 1935.

69. 'Communism — Live Issue at I.L.P. Conference', in the *Daily Worker*, 22nd April 1935.

70. See note 68 above; 'McGovern attacks the Communist International at I.L.P. Conference', in the *Daily Worker*, 22nd April 1935.

71. See note 68 above.

72. Ibid.

73. Fenner Brockway, 'Reflections after the I.L.P. Annual Conference', in *The New Leader*, new series, no. 68, 3rd May 1935.

74. L.D. Trotsky, 'Our Kind of Optimism', 27th April 1936, in *Writings of Leon Trotsky: Supplement, 1934–40*, p. 685.

75. 'Communism — Live Issue at I.L.P. Conference', in the *Daily Worker*, 22nd April 1935.

76. R.F. Andrews, 'Revolution or Reform Faces the I.L.P. at Derby', in *Labour Monthly*, vol. xxii, no. 4, April 1935, p. 223.

77. 'Discipline and Reorganisation Debates at Derby', in *The New Leader*, vol. xxviii, new series, no. 68, 3rd May 1935, p. 4.

78. H. Pollitt, 'Masks off those who Masqueraded as Marxists', in the *Daily Worker*, 24th April 1935.

79. W. Rust, 'The I.L.P. at Derby', in *Labour Monthly*, vol. xvii, no. 6, June 1935, p. 352.

80. 'Communist Statement on I.L.P. Conference', in the *Daily Worker*, 11th April 1936 (referring to 'the previous year').

81. F. Theodorson, Letter to the Editor, *Controversy*, March 1936; cf. C.K. Cullen, 'Why We Broke with the I.L.P.', in *Labour Monthly*, vol. xvii, no. 12, December 1935, pp. 741-6.

82. 'Young Socialists Debate Policy', in *The New Leader*, vol. xxvi, new series, no. 19, 25th May 1934, p. 4.

83. By 21 votes to eleven; cf. 'Young Socialists and the Communist International', in *The New Leader*, vol. xxvii, new series, no. 43, 9th November 1934.

84. *The New Leader*, 28th June 1935; cf. Bornstein and Richardson, *Two Steps Back*, pp. 16 and 18, nn. 23-5.

85. 'London I.L.P. Discuss War Situation', in the *Daily Worker*, 30th September 1935.

86. 'London I.L.P. on Elections', in the *Daily Worker*, 31st October 1935; C.K. Cullen, 'Why We Broke with the I.L.P.', in *Labour Monthly*, vol. xvii, no. 12, December 1935, pp. 741-6.

87. 'Left Wing Leave I.L.P. and Join C.P.', the *Daily Worker*, 1st November 1935.

88. Jack Gaster, 'Open Letter to Fenner Brockway', in the *Daily Worker*, 5th November 1934.

89. 'More Leave the I.L.P.', in the *Daily Worker*, 9th November 1935; 'Recruits to Communism', in the *Daily Worker*, 12th November 1935.

90. 'Goodbye!', in *The New Leader*, vol. xxix, new series, no. 95, 8th November 1934, p. 4.

91. Ibid. Cf. Bornstein and Richardson, *Two Steps Back*, pp. 16-17.

92. D.D. Harber, 'The Present Position in the I.L.P. and How We should React to It', Internal document of the Marxist Group (no date).

93. McNair, *James Maxton — The Beloved Rebel*, p. 237.

94. C.L.R. James, 'Is This Worth a War?', in *The New Leader*, vol. xxix, 4th October 1935.

95. C.L.R. James, 'The Game at Geneva: Behind the Scenes in the "Thieves' Kitchen" ', in *The New Leader*, 18th October 1935, p. 2.

96. C.L.R. James, 'The Workers and Sanctions; Why the I.L.P. and the Communists Take an Opposite View', in *The New Leader*, 25th October 1935, p. 4.

97. R.F. Andrews, 'War and Mr. James — the Muddle of the I.L.P.', in the *Daily Worker*, 28th October 1935.

98. L.D. Trotsky, 'The I.L.P. and the Fourth International: In the Middle of the Road', 18th September 1935, in *Writings of Leon Trotsky, 1934-5*, p. 607.

99. L.D. Trotsky, 'Nothing in Common with the Decadent Comintern', 18th September 1935, in *Writings of Leon Trotsky: Supplement, 1934-40*, p. 607.

100. *The New Leader*, 18th October and 1st November 1935, 27th March 1936; the *Daily Worker*, 26th October 1935, 19th March 1936; Percy Downey, Interview with Sam Bornstein, 26th November 1977.

101. L.D. Trotsky, 'The I.L.P. and the Fourth International', 18th September 1935, in *Writings of Leon Trotsky, 1935-6*, pp. 134-149.

102. L.D. Trotsky, 'Tactical Questions and Splits', 18th November 1935, in *Writings of Leon Trotsky, 1935-6*, p. 195.

103. 'Socialists Discuss Policy', in *The New Leader*, vol. xxix, new series, no. 108, 7th February 1936.

104. F. Theodorson, Letter to the Editor, *Controversy*, March 1936.

105. L.D. Trotsky, 'Once Again the I.L.P.', November 1935, in *Writings of Leon Trotsky, 1935-6*, pp. 197-208.

106. 'I.L.P. Meets in Glasgow', in the *Daily Worker*, 4th February 1936.

107. Brockway, *Inside the Left*, p. 263.

108. L.D. Trotsky, 'Some Advice to a British Group' (Letter to Hugo Dewar), 7th March 1936, in *Writings of Leon Trotsky, 1935-6*, pp. 264-6.

109. *Documents of the Fourth International*, New York, 1973, pp. 66-75.

110. L.D. Trotsky, 'The Open Letter and the I.L.P.', autumn 1935, in *Writings of Leon Trotsky: Supplement, 1934-40*, p. 616.

111. Editorial, 'Where Trotsky Goes Wrong', in *The New Leader*, vol. xxix, new series, no. 114, 20th March 1936, p. 2.

112. L.D. Trotsky, 'Open Letter to a British Comrade', 3rd April 1936, in *Writings of Leon Trotsky, 1935-6*, pp. 293-7.

113. I.L.P., 'Resolutions for 44th Annual Conference' (pamphlet), April 1936,

pp. 8 and 19.

114. F. Brockway, 'The I.L.P. in Conference', in *The New Leader*, vol. xxx, new series, no. 118, 17th April 1936, p. 4.

115. F. Brockway, 'The I.L.P. in Conference: International Unity', in *The New Leader*, vol. xxx, new series, no. 118, 17th April 1936, p. 5.

116. Ibid., p. 3.

117. Ibid., p. 5.

118. See note 113 above (p. 15 and final resolution).

119. I.L.P., *Resolutions for the 44th Annual Conference*, April 11th–14th 1936, p. 21; 'I.L.P. Speaker Objects to the Word "Revolution" ', in the *Daily Worker*, 15th April 1936.

120. Reg Bishop, 'I.L.P. Conference at Keighley', in the *Daily Worker*, 13th April 1936.

121. Brockway, *Inside the Left*, p. 326.

122. 'The Abyssinian Debate', in *The New Leader*, vol. xxx, no. 118, 17th April 1936, p. 4.

123. McNair, *James Maxton — The Beloved Rebel*, p. 252.

124. See note 119 above (p. 19).

125. See note 122 above (p. 5).

126. Ibid.

127. Brockway, *Inside the Left*, pp. 327-8.

128. See note 122 above.

129. L.D. Trotsky, 'The London Bureau and the Fourth International', July 1936, in *Writings of Leon Trotsky: Supplement, 1934-40*, p. 692.

130. *Italy and Abyssinia: Should the British Workers Take Sides?*, *Controversy*, Special Supplement, no. 1.

131. 'A Controversy about *Controversy*', in *The New Leader*, vol. xxx, new series, no. 124, 29th May 1936, p. 4.

132. C.L.R. James, 'Fighting for the Abyssinian Emperor' (letter), in *The New Leader*, vol. xxx, new series, no. 125, 5th June 1936, p. 2. Cf. ref. in note 130 above, p. 11.

133. *The New Leader*, vol. xxx, new series, no. 125, 5th June 1936, p. 3.

134. McNair, *James Maxton —The Beloved Rebel*, p. 254.

135. Op. cit., note 119 above, p. 17; and note 114, p. 4.

136. Ibid.

137. L.D. Trotsky, 'On Dictators and the Heights of Oslo', 22nd April 1936, in *Writings of Leon Trotsky, 1935-6*, pp. 317-20.

Chapter Seven

The Marxist League, 1934–38

The year 1934 was a difficult one for the Communist League, involving a change in basic orientation, a relative lack of success, factional disputes, and the loss of valuable members. The entry of Bradley, Gifford and Searle from the Chelsea Group gave a boost at the beginning of the year, for Bradley was able to provide them with their own press, upon which they slowly and painstakingly produced their own edition of *Red Flag*;[1] but soon this proved to be too difficult to set up in its larger format, and an announcement made later stated that in future it would appear in magazine size as a 'theoretical journal'.[2] An issue did indeed come out in this new format, and then *Red Flag* ceased publication for eighteen months.[3] Some of the difficulties involved factional disputes over the gradual change to placing more emphasis on Labour Party work. Among the comrades lost in the course of this were Stewart Purkis, who resigned and went back to his Christian origins in the Thaxted Movement in the middle of 1934; and later on, Arthur Cooper and others, who went over to the Marxist Group in the I.L.P.

The change was a natural development of the group's previous propaganda over the Leninist attitude of 'critical support' to Labour Party candidates in the by-elections and municipal elections of 1933–4,[4] and also a result of the revival in the fortunes of international Social Democracy inspired by the heroic opposition of the Viennese workers to Dollfüss' suppression of the Schutzbund. As Wicks later described,

> Then, in 1934, [came] the Vienna uprising of the Schutzbund. From that moment onwards the Labour Party captured the London County Council . . . It was the impact of the defeat of Austrian Social Democracy in the spring of 1934 that changed our orientation, and we entered the Labour Party and until 1939 we were in the Labour Party.[5]

There they plunged into the day-to-day activity in the movement with energy and determination. Classes were organised in basic socialist education, through which passed generations of future Labour councillors. As Groves describes,

> We were already in the Labour movement in the district, and being on the trades council, or unemployed delegates as some of us were, they allowed us representation! . . . We helped out when there was a by-election in the borough, we took over the committee rooms and ran them, stocked with our people, and managed to poll a slightly higher percentage than the other part of the borough — to the agent's annoyance — but in other words we were so much involved in the Labour movement that just signing a form as a member of the Labour Party — there was no need for documents or pronunciations.[6]

Locally, a further outlet for the group existed in the *Balham and Tooting Citizen*, a monthly paper put out by the Co-op in which the local Labour Parties were assigned some pages of their own, into which Groves got some articles. When the paper came out with the policy of 'Britain for the British', a leaflet was produced explaining that 'the future lies in the hands of the workers of the world, who must build a world economy, breaking down the barriers between the peoples of every country and colour, and using the productive resources of the world for the benefit of all.'[7] Groves and Wicks were on the General Management Committee of the local party, with Dewar on that of Balham, and Chalkley, Dewar and Wicks on their respective trades councils in Battersea and Wandsworth. They also intervened in the unemployment agitation. In 1930 the T.U.C. had set up 'Unemployed Associations' not as a national movement, but as purely local bodies,[8] and the group was anxious that the energies of the unemployed should not be dissipated outside the Labour movement into stunt politics, but should be directed inwards to make the maximum impact on the traditional organisations. For this reason they favoured the T.U.C.'s associations as 'a much wider and more permanent form of work for militants', to convert them into 'fighting instruments of the unemployed and a means of bridging the gulf between the employed and the unemployed.'[9] 'They themselves started organising the Tooting unemployed, under the banner of the Trade Union organisation,' recalls Chalkley:

> This was opposed to the Communist Party-inspired 'National Unemployed Workers' Movement', and they had some very big rallies. I remember one towards the Wandsworth Town Hall when there was a building job . . . This was officially sponsored by the T.U.C., so the bigwigs in the local Labour

> Party couldn't say anything about it, although I don't think they were always happy at its actions.[10]

The Labour League of Youth, suddenly expanding in the spring of 1934, offered another fruitful field of activity, and they helped to organise its branches in South-West London. They tried to give a class direction to its activities, an example being a leaflet given out at a rally for 'Peace, Freedom and Socialism' in June 1934. 'We propose the formation of a left-wing group within the League, working to effect its transformation into a really serious organisation of Socialist Youth', they announced, and repeated their conviction that the unemployed 'should be organised by the trade unions and given every assistance by the whole movement.' They went on to give a summary of their views and activity:

> We do not, like the Communist Party and the I.L.P., stand aside from the real workers' movement, making savage criticisms and offering nothing but make-believe movements and unrepresentative committees, we play our part in the day to day activities of the Labour, Trade Union and Co-operative movements maintaining our own viewpoint and helping to found the basis upon which British Labour will go forward through its greatest trials and to its final triumph.[11]

But results on the whole were not encouraging. Recruits were slow in coming in, and their isolation was made painfully clear by such actions as the ban on group affiliation by the Marx Memorial Library[12] and the drift away from the international movement. Stagnation, as always, provoked internal dissension and splits. In Trotsky's estimation,

> . . . the experience of the British Section, on a small scale, is highly instructive. The 'Majority' maintaining its 'organisational autonomy' actually finds itself in a state of constant internal strife and division. Certain leaders have left the organisation altogether. On the other hand, the 'Minority' that entered the I.L.P. has maintained its internal solidarity and its connection with the international Bolshevik–Leninists, has made large use of the publications of the League in America and has had a series of successes inside the I.L.P.[13]

The Balham comrades were taking stock of the situation also. 'It is now nearly two months since we began to discuss support for the Labour government and penetration into reformist organisations,' wrote Groves. 'Little opposition was expressed at the time of the change, save from those comrades who resigned. Even this was more evidence of a desire to retire from Communist League work than principled opposition to the new policy.' He expressed disappointment that comrades spent far more time on personal wrangles than on discussing problems met in Labour movement work, and that, whilst the Marxist classics were indispensable, 'It still remains true that present day policy must be constructed from present day materials.' He deplored the continuation of 'amateurish fraction work' and 'the old so-called "independent" work — street canvass, street meetings, picking up members anywhere and anyhow'. Then he dealt with the criticism that the group was not paying enough attention to the struggle for the new International. 'A glance over our leaflets and publications over the past three or four months will show that we express ourselves very guardedly on this matter,' he went on; 'in my opinion, we have not been guarded enough.' He moved on to international perspectives:

> During the last few days we have received — unofficially — statements to the effect that Comrade Trotsky is urging the French comrades to enter the French Socialist Party. If this is so then Comrade Trotsky has, on the basis of the French situation, reached conclusions similar to those we have reached on the British situation. A further report, also received unofficially, says that the I.S. is urging that the British Communist League should turn towards the Labour Party and that they should issue the call for the resignation of the National Government. This has, of course, been our policy for a long time and the fact that the I.S. has been forced to amend its ideas about the British situation, although a trifle belatedly, is a striking justification of the stand we made many months ago, and a tribute, although possibly unintended, to the political sense of the majority comrades. It is also necessary that members should know that the International Communist League is itself the victim of the present storm and stresses raging everywhere in the workers' movement . . .
>
> This need not alarm us: our own experiences of the I.S. showed us the limitations of the I.C.L. and how much it was at the mercy of unstable elements . . .
>
> The issue of the new parties and the new International will come forward as a live question. But first we must establish firm foundations.[14]

In the circumstances it is not surprising that the Majority comrades should have permitted themselves some feelings of superiority; and when the Labour Party tactic itself came, a year and a half later, there was a definite sense of 'I told you so'. 'What did Harber do in the I.L.P.?' asked Wicks of one of the authors. 'And how long did he stay? Almost a year later, he was out of the I.L.P. organising the Labour League of Youth. Now, the balance sheet of what the Harber Group did that split the Communist League to go into the I.L.P., that balance sheet I've never seen rendered, and I would like to see it.'[15]

All the same, their lukewarm attitude towards raising the issue of the Fourth International showed how, in a few months, they had drifted from the course of the rest of the movement, and how the pressures of operating in a purely Social Democratic milieu were beginning to tell. They had a fresh example of these pressures when the Labour Party Conference met in Southport in October 1934. Even though Groves had been elected to go as delegate from Balham and Tooting Constituency Labour Party, the standing orders committee had refused to accept his credentials, on the grounds that an organisation called the 'Communist League' came under the heading of organisations 'subsidiary' to the C.P., which was on the banned list. At the last minute they elected another member of the group less well known than Groves, J.N. Pyne, a part-time gravedigger. He was not able to make a great impact on Conference on his own, being unused to public speaking and rather nervous, but he did get to the rostrum to make a speech to refer back the standing orders report. He described how, three days before, Groves had been ready to go to Conference, nominated by a full G.M.C. on a practically unanimous decision as 'one of the chief workers in the constituency'. He described how the Communist League members 'had fought on every occasion for the Labour candidates', and how membership of the local party had gone up 300% due to their efforts. He was even able to get in a thumb-nail sketch of how the League came to be expelled from the C.P., and its history since, before his attempt to refer back was overwhelmingly defeated.[16]

This was a hurdle they had not encountered before, so an adjustment would have to be made. They changed their name to 'Marxist League', defined as 'an association of Labour Party members, Trade unionists and co-operators, organised together for the study of Marxism, the training of Marxist leadership, and the advocacy of Marxist policy and principles in the Labour movement.' This League intended to work 'loyally as an integral part of the Labour Party' in order to 'convince others of the correctness of its views, not by isolating itself from the mass of the organised workers.' Further to this, they affirmed that 'organisations which separate the groups of workers from the main movement today serve only to weaken and disintegrate the strength of the workers.'[17]

Here again they were departing further from the rest of the Trotskyist movement, whose main group was working inside the I.L.P., an organisation whose split from the Labour Party Trotsky himself had described as correct. Only a few months earlier he had expressed the opinion that 'calling these entry tactics a panacea (as some comrades have done) amounts to a declaration of bankruptcy for the political line followed up till now, means the liquidation of the independent organisations, is both a cause and effect of complete demoralisation, and must be categorically rejected.'[18]

Once established in the Labour Party, it was a natural step to associate with whatever bodies existed for making propaganda for Socialist ideas. Here the field was occupied by the Socialist League, which was founded in 1932 from a merger between the old Labour Party 'Society for Socialist Inquiry and Propaganda' of G.D.H. Cole, and the group of ex-I.L.P.ers led by Frank Wise, who had split from the I.L.P. when they disaffiliated from the Labour Party.[19] On Wise's death in November 1933 he was succeeded as chairman by Sir Stafford Cripps. With 2,000 members already in 1932, its numbers began to grow up to the 3,000 mark, though its class content remained basically middle-class, and it moved consistently in its brief period of existence towards being what Groves described as 'a consciously revolutionary socialist group'.[20]

By June 1935 Groves was already well enough established to lecture for them quite widely,[21] and was elected onto their executive at the annual aggregate meeting held in Caxton Hall on 21st September,[22] becoming chairman of their London area. This opened up for the group wider possibilities than their own discontinued newspaper had been able to provide, for not only did Groves contribute to almost every issue of the League paper from then onwards — on subjects such as Liebknecht, the Paris Commune, the 1936 Conference of the French socialists, etc. — but he was also able to get them to publish two pamphlets written by him.

Trades Councils in the Fight for Socialism was an attempt to show how these bodies spanned the various branches of the Labour movement in the localities, and during the General Strike functioned as the leadership at grass roots level. Groves described how in turn they could serve as the nucleus for wider bodies, 'Labour Councils', to unite all the class organisations of whatever type; and touched upon their potential role as Soviets:

> The ordinary machinery of government and administration will probably fail to function for Socialist purposes; or only to the extent to which the power of the movement, its firm direction and the loyalty of the masses in every locality renders hopeless counter-revolutionary sabotage or rebellion, and provides, where needed, alternative machinery.[23]

Arms and the Unions, on the other hand, was an attempt to look at the implications of the coming war for the working class and its organisations. He sketched out methods of industrial serfdom, dilution, and undermining of the trade unions, and conscription, both military and industrial, so that 'the entire resources of industry and government' should be mobilised for 'a "major" war'. 'Let the rank-and-file of labour create the conditions and the machinery under which we can drive ahead to the widest mobilisation of working class power against the National Government for its overthrow,' he concluded.[24]

In the meantime, the League made steady progress towards the left. During the Abyssinian affair it gathered meetings all over the country to oppose League of Nations sanctions and government war preparations, despite the pressure of the Communist Party assisted by its own National Secretary, J.T. Murphy.[25] But the growth of the League and the work of the group within it led to a revival of their fortunes and the attracting of new members, and they could now think of reorganising their structure and renewing their open propaganda again. In January 1936 Dewar put out a duplicated pamphlet of Trotsky's work to 're-establish contact with many of the readers of the old *Red Flag* as well as reaching many new contacts', and promised that the new edition of *Red Flag* would appear on May Day.[26] At the same time relations were renewed with the international movement. Dewar and Hilary Sumner-Boyd went across to Paris to see Lev Sedov, Trotsky's son, and contact was re-established with Trotsky, who wrote to ask whether they had lost members through 'opportunist adaption to the Party apparatus', and whether they thought 'it was more favourable' for comrades of the Marxist Group 'to leave the I.L.P. in order to enter the Labour Party'.[27] Their reply, whilst inviting Trotsky to write for the new series of *Red Flag*, expressed hostility to the Marxist Group and showed that its position of boycotting Labour candidates who supported League sanctions made it a liability in the Labour Party.

Trotsky's next letter expressed doubt over what would be the political basis for any such co-operation, for as far as he could see, the differences since the split had increased rather than lessened. He disagreed with their reluctance to raise the question of the Fourth International in the Labour Party, stating that he could only collaborate with them if they made the 'Open Letter for the Fourth International' their own programme, and that 'if one *renounces* the carrying on of this propaganda, then one surrenders directly to the Second International.' He described the mistake of the Marxist Group over the boycott of Labour candidates as a tactical one emerging from revolutionary principles, but stated that their own objection to working with them in the Labour Party originated in 'opportunist premises'. 'The question whether one should enter the

I.L.P. or the Labour Party was and remains for us *not a question of principle*, but a question of practical opportunity,' he explained. He made a strong criticism of the group's activity:

> As against this, your group appears only as the left wing of the Labour Party, i.e., as a vague centrist trend. You have recruited hardly any new elements. It would indeed be hard to do this without a programme, without a political banner. The fact that many comrades from your group occupy positions in the Labour Party or the trade unions is without revolutionary significance, because these comrades represent no definite programme, but have been elected only on the basis of their individual activity. All historical experience teaches us that this is the shortest way to get absorbed into the reformist bureaucracy.[28]

The group replied by accepting Trotsky's conditions, whilst reminding him of the dubious role played by Witte in the split of 1933–4. He then turned to examine their present orientation towards the Socialist League, describing Sir Stafford Cripps as 'an utterly confused eccentric', and the Socialist League, as 'a selection in the likeness of Mr. Cripps himself' and '*not a mass organisation* but a faction'. 'All experience indicates that one can work with success in a mass organisation as an independent group, opposing each and every centrist faction,' he wrote. 'But if one enters a *centrist* faction then one loses one's own physiognomy and deprives oneself of the power to carry on real revolutionary work among the masses.'[29]

A final letter expressed the hope that the three existing groups would 'find a way towards a common goal' by sending delegations to the forthcoming 'Geneva' Conference (actually held in Paris) of the International Trotskyist movement, whilst agreeing that in Britain trade union work was becoming a priority and the I.L.P. 'more of a handicap than an aid'. As to their deep suspicions towards the International Secretariat, he denied that the conference would 'attempt to impose upon the English comrades a rigid line of policy', and suggested that if they were unable to take upon themselves international discipline in its fullest sense, some sort of sympathetic affiliation could be envisaged.[30]

Although the new edition of *Red Flag* did indeed appear in May 1936, with an article by Trotsky in its first issue,[31] the group did not in the end work out a collaboration with the Marxist Group and the 'Youth Militant' Group in the Labour Party, and the international tensions remained. Although the Marxist Group and the 'Youth Militant' group sent along C.L.R. James and Denzil Harber, no representative of the Marxist League attended the 'Geneva' conference, apparently through lack of sufficient means. But the real reason remained the bad feeling engendered by the split of 1934–5, which was worsened by the equivocal behaviour of Hilary Sumner-Boyd:

> [When] he went to Turkey . . . he wrote to me about some documents he'd left, and would I pick them up? He'd written to the chap who'd got them that I should have them, you see, and he said, 'If you find anything in the material you regard as antagonistic to you, please forgive me for it!' Well, I know that he made one remark — it wasn't really anything political; I think it was more of a personal nature. We were very friendly, Hilary and I, but for some reason or another he became less friendly. I really didn't notice it myself, but only later on, as a result of this note that he sent me from Turkey, it occurred to me that he might have said some things about me which weren't complimentary. This would have been in connection with his connection with France, with Paris. I think he did give wrong information to the I.S., that would probably be through Trotsky's son, Sedov. We went over on one occasion to see Sedov, and probably it was then that Sedov asked him to keep him informed on the situation here. You see, in one of Trotsky's letters there is something about the Groves/Dewar Grouping, not 'the Groves/Dewar Group', but 'Groves/Dewar'. It wasn't very complimentary, though it wasn't very specific.[32]

Complicating all these considerations was the acute worsening of the international situation, with the Moscow Trials breaking the headlines every day, and the outbreak of the Spanish Civil War, which involved the group in a curious way. The Barcelona Olympiad, due to be held between 22nd and 25th July, was a response to the use made by Hitler of the Olympics as a German propaganda stunt — a working-class rejoinder, so to speak. The Workers' Sports Federation, a Stalinist front group, was issuing invitations for the British team, so Dewar accepted one, as a chess player:

> . . . we got there, and the next morning, hearing what I thought were mats being beaten, I went to the window, and when I looked down the road there were barricades . . . It was difficult to get out. They shut up the hotel, and wouldn't allow anyone out. Anyway, I decided to go out and have a stroll around. There wasn't anything there, for the fighting in Barcelona was rather brief — overnight. It was more or less finishing — I didn't see any fighting. I saw some mules that were already bloated in the streets. I can only recollect meeting a girl, who said to me 'What's all this about?', and I tried to explain in my

three or four words of Spanish what was going on, and a lorry-load of workers and Civil Guards . . . passing by, and from the lorry they threw three handfuls of cigarettes, packets of cigarettes. But later on I saw a couple of militiamen outside a tobacco shop stopping any looting. I think there was very little looting, except from churches. I didn't see any windows smashed, because the Anarchists were pretty strong in that area, and I think they were quick to take control. You see, it was pretty chaotic. I didn't really know any Spanish at that time (I know a little more now), and to get in contact with anyone was very difficult, unless you could speak the language. You were up against armed guards, and you couldn't explain anything. I didn't have any contacts. I only remember that I was given by some woman a photo to take back to London, and only a couple or so years ago, I turned over one of these photographs, and strangely enough — I'd never noticed it before — they were taken by Edith Bone . . .

What is surprising, of course, I do recollect a report in a British newspaper by some of the people who had returned from Spain whom we were with, describing shooting, bodies on the street, and all that, which wasn't true at all! . . .

I can remember, a group of us went out to the sports ground, and there was absolutely nothing in the street, and there was no shooting. There was a possibility of snipers, odd snipers — you might hear an odd shot — but the story they told — it gave me an example of war reporting!

. . . I was only there for a few days. All the trains had stopped. As I said, the only aspect of it was the armed guards that you might see outside shops, which would be, presumably, mostly Anarchist guards. They seemed to have the district. They'd got arms . . .

All the people were dishing out leaflets — Anarchist — some of them in Catalonian. I think that, as a matter of fact, my recollections are that most of them were in Catalan. I did get copies of papers and leaflets which I brought back and subsequently I was getting *La Batalla* (P.O.U.M.) — I got a complete run of *La Batalla*, which was originally in Chatham House Library, and then they shifted them over to the British Museum. That, probably, was the only complete collection that was available, at any rate, in this country, and I used to get *Independent News* from Spain (published in Paris).[33]

Armed with this information, the group were able to carry into the literature of the Socialist League the news of how a real revolution had happened behind the Republican lines in Spain, and how the 'Popular Front' of the Stalinists was attempting to strangle it. Repudiating the story that the P.O.U.M. was a 'Trotskyist' party, Jack Winnocour attacked the idea of the Popular Front:

> Even were the Spanish working-class not within the authentic shadow of its own revolution, there would be no justification for a coalition of working-class parties and bourgeois republicans in the government of a capitalist state, for such Spain remains until the final conquest of power by the workers.
>
> . . . The Socialist Party and the Communist Party have adopted a reformist position in a revolutionary situation. I do not think that History will deal lightly with an error of this magnitude.[34]

Defending the Spanish Revolution against the blanket propaganda of the Communists both inside the League and outside was no small task. Groves' draft of a League leaflet entitled 'A Workers' or a Fascist Spain' was tampered with so that it was made to support the Communist position of winning the war first, and of only afterwards thinking of the revolution,[35] though he did manage to get the representatives on the secret 'unity' committee to raise the question of the persecution of the P.O.U.M. with the C.P.[36] But with the immense barrage of Stalinist and Liberal propaganda it was very difficult to get over to ordinary people what was going on. Chalkley remembers passing out the leaflet at Colliers' Wood tube station. 'They didn't have a clue what we were talking about,' he recalled, 'It was just like talking about landing on the moon in those days, to talk about what was happening in Spain.' At the same time, when he protested about the treatment of the P.O.U.M. by the Communists in his E.T.U. branch, he was told by a Stalinist official that if ever they took power he would be 'put up against the wall'.[37] Inside the Socialist League they circulated Nin's paper, *The Spanish Revolution*, in an attempt to stop the League joining the Communists' Popular Front campaign, and at one point they had a third of the delegates on Wandsworth Trades Council voting for their resolutions on Spain.[38]

The Socialist League continued its progress towards the left, much to the embarrassment of the Communist Party. On 4th October came the Cable Street clash with Mosley's Fascists, and the London Area Committee distributed Groves' pamphlet with its pointedly anti-Popular Front tone. 'You can see for yourselves,' it ran, 'Mosley and his Blackshirts break up Labour, Socialist and Communist meetings, not Conservative meetings. It is we who are attacked, not businessmen.' Nothing could be further from the Popular Front line than the declaration that

> The days of propaganda and of purely electoral activity are over. All over the world labour is fighting for its life and for the future of humanity. Will you individually and collectively help us to raise again the banner of class struggle in Britain, to maintain the freedom of the streets for the working people, to overthrow the National Government, to place power in the hands of the organised workers?[39]

The Socialist League itself remained fairly solid against the policy of the People's Front. Its Annual Conference at Hanley in Whitsun 1936 supported the line of working-class unity against 'C.P.-style amendments and arguments for "Peace Fronts" and Popular Fronts and all the latest trappings of Communist policy'.[40] But at the top Cripps had already been meeting the Communist Party leaders, and the 'Unity Committee' was in session, with its attempt to substitute the Popular Front for the alliance of workers' parties.[41] Groves realised the implications of this, that it would mean the League becoming an auxiliary of Communist propaganda, that its defence of the Spanish revolution would end, and that it would join in other Stalinist causes. As he recalls:

> We had a minute in the Executive Minutes that the matter of the Moscow Trials was raised, and it was agreed that an enquiry should be asked for, and that was quite a triumph and a smack in the eye for the 'Unity' people. They were furious about that. Then the Executive, in a moment of desperation I think, accepted a resolution from me that they should join the International of Left Wing Socialist Parties, in which the I.L.P. was. They agreed to attend its meetings, but not affiliate to it at the moment. Obviously they would be chucked out of the Labour Party for that. I thought that we were getting on the right road at last, but this was chopped down by the 'Unity Committee' and the decision to wind up the Socialist League.[42]

The results of the 'Unity' Meetings of the Socialist League, I.L.P. and Communist Party leaders were announced to the National Council at its meeting on 7th and 8th November 1936. There the delegates from the provinces protested that the Executive had not secured the approval of the National Council before starting their negotiations; but no discussion took place on the merits of having such an agreement, and they were manoeuvred into an implied approval of it by a detailed discussion of the document itself. Cripps argued for signing it, backed by Brailsford, Mitchinson, Horrabin and other E.C. members: Mellor kept his previous reservations to himself. Groves and Wicks spoke against, securing the defeat of the platform on one issue,[43] but then the National Council sent out a circular to the branches, giving 'a false impression of unanimity'.[44]

The Trotskyists managed to set up an unofficial resistance committee in London, and Groves sent a circular around the branches stating that, not only was there no unanimity, but the serious problems of the agreement were yet to be debated. By this time Transport House was becoming more than a little disturbed that the Socialist League, one of its affiliated organisations, was coming under Stalinist influence, and an uproar was caused when someone sent a copy to the *Daily Herald*. 'It had nothing to do with me,' commented Groves, 'but people like Cripps do supply newspapers with stuff, and they assumed that I had done it.'[45] The Communist Party then retaliated by accusing Groves of attacking 'Unity' through the pages of the *Daily Herald*, describing him as expelled from the C.P. 'because of his disruptive activity and unreliability', and claiming that Trotskyists in the U.S.S.R. were acting as 'agents of the Secret Police and Fascism'.[46] Groves could only reply that their article was 'without an atom of truth', and that 'no copy of that letter was sent or handed to any but Secretaries of Socialist League branches'. He denied, moreover, that he was opposed to building up working-class unity; he had always supported the United Front, even including the Communist Party, and his opposition to this particular agreement was to those clauses which sacrificed the Socialist League's 'position in the organised Labour movement without sufficient advantage to the revolutionary left in return.'[47]

The Special Delegate Conference of the League meeting in London on 17th January 1937 ratified the agreement by 56 votes, though this was a minority when those cast against were added to the abstentions of the more confused delegates. The first 'Unity Campaign' meeting of the three bodies was held the day after. The Socialist League had now become 'involved in the erection of an unreal façade of unity, behind which the brutal realities of Russian government policy operated unseen and unchecked; and the Socialist League found itself recruited into a conspiracy of silence about the misdoings of the Russian government in which had already been enlisted an impressive array of British intellectuals — writers, publishers, academics, and politicians.'[48]

Transport House was just as pleased as the Communist Party to be rid of the Socialist League, and from 1st June declared that membership of the League and the Labour Party were incompatible. A Special Conference of the League at Whitsun in Leicester carried Cripps' proposal that the League dissolve by an overwhelming majority.[49] It has since transpired that this whole scenario had originated with Pollitt and the Communist Party — that the Socialist

League should be lured into a clash with Transport House by agreeing to 'Unity' with the C.P.G.B., and then dissolve in order to campaign for the Popular Front in the Labour Party at large. 'The C.P. wanted to be rid of the Socialist League, with its dangerous potential as a centre for revolutionary Socialist ideas,' concluded Groves.[50] More to the point, it is obvious that the 'Unity' agreement was meant to stifle criticism of the Soviet Union and of Stalinism at the height of the Moscow Trials:

> The agreement denies the right of free criticism; either of the parties concerned, or of their personnel or of the actions and policies of the Soviet Government. This clause does not stop the *Daily Worker* from attacking individuals in the Socialist League: neither does it prevent the C.P.G.B. from attempting to destroy their critics and opponents in the working-class movement by slander and by malicious falsehood, but it does hamper those so attacked from replying freely, *for to do so is to be accused of seeking to disrupt the unity agreement*.[51]

After the Socialist League dissolved itself, Groves and the others attempted to set up an organisation to keep in contact all those who had been against the dissolution at the Special Conference. In June 1936 it was announced that a new group, the 'Socialist Left Federation', had been set up.[52] It consisted of no more than a dozen comrades to begin with, some of whom represented old Socialist League branches, and some who did not.[53] As Groves described:

> . . . a few of us [the London Committee] tried really to hold some branches. At the final conference the vote for disbanding was a minority vote — we got a substantial vote against — and if you added the non-votes! I was slow on that, I should have got up and said 'Why not discuss it again?' They got it all through, and that was enough for them, and they disbanded promptly and hid all the records, and so on. We tried using the badge — they had a badge, 'The Socialist League', with S.L. on it. We called ourselves 'The Socialist Left Federation', and wrote round to branches who had voted against it, and said we proposed to form a Socialist Federation of left groups, ex Socialist Leaguers.[54]

The organisation was stillborn, for immediately disputes broke out with the 'Militant Group' of Harber and Jackson, who sought to enter the group whilst keeping their own paper and organisation. The Secretary of the S.L.F. wrote to them asking them to abandon their own paper 'to mobilise all forces behind the S.L.F. and its proposed organ', whilst Harber accused the S.L.F. of being bureaucratic, and of only holding onto their majority on the council by co-opting members to outvote branch delegates.[55] Feelings reached such a pitch that on one occasion Harber had to be escorted from a Council meeting which he had gatecrashed. 'He was also running a faction inside this Left Federation,' commented Groves: 'I think this was stupid — you are recruiting from your own buddies.'[56] A year afterwards the S.L.F. collapsed.[57]

The Marxist League itself was not long to follow. Years of fighting with minute success against impossible odds had taken their toll in demoralisation, and now, on top of everything else, came the Moscow Trials. As Wicks recalls:

> It was the feeling of frustration, the feeling of defeat, that the Trials gave one. I can remember vividly Reg Groves expressing it, that the Moscow Trials 'represents curtains for us' — that was his phrase. It was from those feelings and thoughts we felt 'We have got to get together, we have got to unify, to erect some defence.' It was in that process that differences developed between us and Groves in the Marxist League. Groves was quite content with the work that was being done on a local level in the Labour Party and in the Socialist League, and we felt unification would have been an extra strength in the Trotskyist movement . . .
>
> I worked at this time closely with James, because whilst James was writing his book *World Revolution* I participated. I gave him material, and I went through his manuscript and discussed things with him, and I think he made a reference in the 'Foreword' to that. So I was working with him closely, and I thought that all of us should be in that situation. I felt that all of us should line up in the Communist League, where we all started, and I took the initiative of bringing it to a head in the Marxist League. The minority were Reg and Daisy, Arthur Wimbush, Hugo Dewar and Vic Carpenter — they were the people who were opposed. Reg sincerely believed that one had to patiently work in the structure of the Labour Party, and that was when we broke.[58]

The Marxist League officially dissolved in October 1937, and *Red Flag* came out no longer. In April 1938 the Ad Hoc Committee of the Marxist League fused with the Marxist Group of C.L.R. James to produce the Revolutionary Socialist League.[59]

As for Groves himself, he felt that 'it would be a waste of energy, time and resources to spend your life arguing with other Trotskyists: I think this is hopeless, and it took me years to have the courage to leave it alone, and this we did.'[60]

Within months of breaking with the Trotskyists Groves was

involved in his greatest triumph of propaganda on behalf of the working-class movement, the Aylesbury by-election.

In January 1938 Groves had only just finished his history of the Chartist movement for Secker and Warburg[61] when he had to fight for Labour in Aylesbury, Mid-Buckinghamshire, where he had been selected as parliamentary candidate by the divisional Labour Party the previous April. When he had accepted the nomination he had not expected to be catapulted into the limelight in this manner:

> About 1934/5 I got a job which I liked, and I hadn't had a regular job for years. Then this group of Socialists in parts of the Aylesbury constituency wrote and asked if they could nominate me as candidate. Well, I looked at the details and saw that they never got more than 4,000 votes against two candidates with 20,000 apiece — they lost their deposit every time. So I thought this was safe. I was not likely to be elected, and it would get me out into the country to do some propaganda. It did me the world of good, actually, although it was a selfish attitude. But I went through the villages talking, and this breaks through the old jargon quicker than anything. It was a very big area, and I had no car . . . It had over 400 square miles, and over 120 villages and towns, not all of which were linked together by the railways. So I spent a year going round all of these places at odd times, got to know everybody, and then to my horror was confronted by this by-election, which I didn't want to do because of my job.[62]

The acceptance of a Trotskyist as Labour candidate in a crucial by-election in the middle of the Communist Party's campaign for Liberal allies in the Popular Front brought down a storm of abuse around his head, and span a web of intrigue behind his back. The *Daily Worker* described the 'Trotskyist, masquerading in the garb of Labour in Aylesbury' who intended to 'give new succour and encouragement to Chamberlain, Hitler and Mussolini',[63] and under the label of the 'Progressive Alliance' the Communists got some well-known Labour figures in the constituency to support Atholl Roberton, the Liberal candidate.[64] A *Daily Worker* article claiming that Trotskyism had been disruptive in the U.S.S.R., Spain, China, etc., circulated around the constituency in leaflet form,[65] while the Communists claimed that Groves' policy meant 'the break-up of the Labour movement from within'.[66]

Tremendous pressure was put on Transport House from all the Communist Party's fellow travellers in the Popular Front, and they began to feel that an overwhelming defeat would destroy Labour's morale for the coming election, so they in turn tried to get Groves to stand down:

> Then I got a letter from Transport House asking me to go and see Mr. Shepherd (he became Lord Shepherd), the National Agent. He greeted me warmly — he had forgotten he'd nearly expelled me — and said he knew I was loyal to the Party because of the fight in the Socialist League. I didn't say anything to that. He then went on that we had to be careful about this by-election because of the Popular Front Campaign. 'We really want to do well. The Party would like you to stand down. We've got another man in mind whom we think would be more suitable (he put it a little less bluntly). If you stand down we'll see that you get another and a better place.' So I said that I would let the Aylesbury Constituency that had selected me decide. He thanked me warmly, and shook me by the hand. He thought he had got it.[67]

The Executive of Mid-Buckinghamshire Labour Party met upstairs in Aylesbury Town Hall, with the ordinary delegates and Groves down below, whilst Shepherd's representative tried to persuade them to drop Groves in favour of 'a retired army colonel, who was out to learn the business before going into a safe seat'. His argument was taken up by some of the C.P.'s entrists on the E.C.:

> There were a number of Communists on the Executive Committee — 'concealed' — but you could recognise them because of the area. Only people with cars could sit on the Executive, which met in three parts of the Division over the year . . .
>
> There were two or three Communists there, and they pressed that we should withdraw. They didn't want me anyway, being a Trotskyist, but they reckoned that if they got rid of me the colonel would have it, and they wouldn't fight. What apparently happened was that this Transport House bloke in exasperation (the majority were absolutely solid — they wouldn't waste time arguing, they would just say 'no') said, 'Let me put this to you, comrades, How is Major Attlee going to feel speaking on the same platform as Reg Groves?' So one of the blokes said 'And how is Reg Groves going to feel, speaking on the same platform as Attlee?' At this stage the bloke said, 'All right, I give in, I give in.' Then they came down and reported the fight was on, and there were enthusiastic scenes.[68]

Nonetheless, Groves' support on the Executive had been whittled down from 21 votes to 8 to 15 to 10.[69] But once the fight was on, the Labour Party nationally decided to rally round. 'A big Labour vote in Aylesbury will be a national event,' proclaimed the *Daily Herald*, adding that the Communist policy of supporting their Liberal enemies was 'the voice of defeatism, retreat, surrender'.[70] National Labour figures appeared to support Groves, however reluctantly in the case of D.N. Pritt, a notorious fellow traveller and defender of the Moscow Trials.[71] Transport House was still cool:

> Once it was known that I was the candidate, finally, I was asked to go to the House of Commons, and in the gloomy light, under gloomy arches (it was night-time), Dalton, Morrison, and somebody else (three there were) stood on one end, talking, and I stood at the other. Presently Morrison came across, and wished me well. At least it showed he had the human touch.[72]

By contrast, at the constituency level people fervently rallied round, for there was an old Labour tradition in Aylesbury, where George Howe had stood on a Labour ticket as far back as 1874. On the eve of the poll Groves addressed no fewer than fifteen meetings, and was carried about the constituency in the car of Wilfred Wigham, a veteran member of the I.L.P. Groves' meetings drew large audiences,[73] to which he preached 'the entire Socialist doctrine',[74] in the I.L.P.'s opinion 'the most outspoken Socialist appeal that had been heard from the official Labour Party platform for a long time.'[75] 'Mr. Groves, the Labour candidate, is putting up a splendid fight,' reported *Reynolds News*, 'he is appealing to the electors on a clear-cut Socialist platform, and declares that there can be nothing in common between Labour and Liberal policy.'[76]

When the poll was announced both the Tory and the Liberal had shed votes, but Labour had gained 3,560 votes on its previous 1935 showing. In spite of a reduced turn-out, Groves was the only candidate to have increased his share of the poll.[77]

Whilst N.C.L.C. organiser J.P. Millar, publisher Frederick Warburg, and the I.L.P. warmly congratulated Groves, the Communist Party was less than enthusiastic about this success for the Socialist cause:

> . . . [there] will be loud cheers at the result in Transport House. The increase in the Labour vote will be taken as justification for their opposition to the United Peace Alliance.
>
> The money that was poured out in support of Groves was not used against the National Government but against a Peace Alliance. It supported the betrayal of Spain now being carried through by the Chamberlain Government. It was right to call Groves a friend of Franco when he was acting in a way that has aided the pro-Fascists here to carry out their plans . . .[78]

But the only Trotskyist contribution to Groves' campaign had been from W.G. Hanton, who cycled over from Wandsworth, took a thousand leaflets, found that it was a glorious day, and lay down on a river bank all afternoon![79] For whilst the existing groups naturally supported Labour in the by-election,[80] the R.S.L. did not approve of all Groves' conduct during it, making it clear that 'though in many quarters he was called a "Trotskyist", [he] is not a member of this organisation.' For on 12th May he had been asked, along with the Liberal candidate, a question about his support for the League of Nations by the Council of Action for Peace and Reconstruction, one of Lloyd George's creations, and, according to them, had answered 'satisfactorily'. In this way, according to the R.S.L., he had 'made his policy indistinguishable from that of the Liberal candidate and did not unequivocally give the revolutionary Socialist policy on war.'[81]

Groves never again joined a Trotskyist organisation (despite an offer to lead the United section made by James P. Cannon when he came over to unite the various groups in the summer of 1938), though he continued to inspire the movement in his books, and to join in such later campaigns as the Socialist Anti-War Front. In a way, his passing marked the end of the old Trotskyism, for the movement that emerged from the Second World War was of an entirely different character. Small revolutionary groupings are relentless devourers of human material, even of the very best, yet the movement continues to throw up fresh generations of activists. But the courage of the first generation of Trotskyists, who stood up with so little support against the slander machine of Stalinism and the imperialist drive to war, remains an inspiration still.

Notes

1. 'One Year of the Red Flag', in *Red Flag*, vol. i, no. 9, May/June 1934.
2. *Red Flag*, vol. 1, no. 11, October 1934, p. 4.
3. i.e. November 1934; the next to appear was 'New Series, no. 1', May 1936.
4. See pp. 115-118 above.
5. Harry Wicks, Interview with Al Richardson, 11th March and 1st April 1978. Cf. 'Vienna and the London Elections', in *Red Flag*, vol. i, no. 8, March/April 1934.
6. Reg Groves, Interview with Al Richardson, 2nd April 1978.
7. *To All Members of Wandsworth Trade Union, Labour and Co-operative Movement* (undated duplicated leaflet).
8. Wal Hannington, *Unemployed Struggles, 1918–36*, London, 1936, p. 326.
9. 'The National Conference of Action', in *Red Flag*, vol. i, no. 7, January 1934, p. 4.
10. David Chalkley, Interview with Al Richardson, 14th November 1978.

11. *Forward Against Fascism: A Thesis for Labour Youth* (printed leaflet), Communist League.

12. 'Trotskyists Excluded', in *The New Leader*, vol. xxv, new series, no. 1, 19th January 1934; cf. 'Marx Library and Trotsky', in *The New Leader*, vol. xxv, new series, no. 7, 2nd March 1934.

13. L.D. Trotsky, 'Summary of the Discussion', 6th August 1934, in *Writings of Leon Trotsky, 1934-5*, New York, 1971, p. 64.

14. Reg Groves, 'Statement to All Members Concerning the Present Policy of the League and Its International', 23rd August 1934 (Internal Document of the Communist League).

15. Harry Wicks, Interview with Al Richardson, 11th March and 1st April 1978.

16. The Labour Party, *Report of the 34th Annual Conference Held in the Garrick Theatre, Southport*, 1st to 5th October 1934, p. 135.

17. *Aims and Objects of the Marxist League* (Duplicated statement).

18. L.D. Trotsky, 'Tasks for the I.C.L.', 21st July 1934, in *Writings of Leon Trotsky: Supplement, 1934-40*, New York, 1979, p. 512.

19. See p. 127 above. On the League as a whole, cf. S. Bornstein and A. Richardson, *Two Steps Back*, London, 1982, pp. 27-32.

20. Reg Groves, *A Documentary History of the Socialist League* (unpublished MS.), p. 14.

21. 'What the S.L. is Doing', in *The Socialist Leaguer*, no. 12, June 1935, p. 196 and passim.

22. *The Socialist*, new series, no. 2, November 1935, p. 8.

23. R. Groves, *Trades Councils in the Fight for Socialism*, Socialist League pamphlet (undated).

24. R. Groves,*Arms and the Unions*, Socialist League pamphlet, April 1936.

25. Cf. Bornstein and Richardson, *Two Steps Back*, p. 28.

26. 'Leon Trotsky on the Popular Front and Revolutionary Terrorism', *Marxist Bulletin*, January/February 1936, published by Hugo Dewar, p. 1.

27. L.D. Trotsky, 'Questions of a British Group', 15th January 1936, in *Writings of Leon Trotsky, 1935-6*, New York, 1970, pp. 250-1.

28. L.D. Trotsky, 'Some Advice to a British Group', 7th March 1936, in *Writings of Leon Trotsky, 1935-6*, pp. 264-6.

29. L.D. Trotsky, 'A Good Omen for Joint Work in Britain', 9th April 1936, in *Writings of Leon Trotsky, 1935-6*, pp. 298-9. This letter is not, as is stated in note 332, p. 543, written to Jack Winnocour, but to Hugo Dewar, for the group had decided to use 'Jack' as his pseudonym, instead of Trotsky's suggestion of 'Edgar', which they did not regard as proletarian enough. Cf. Hugo Dewar, note to Al Richardson, ch. V, n. 95, p. 158 above.

30. L.D. Trotsky, 'For a Common Goal in Britain', 13th July 1936, in *Writings of Leon Trotsky, 1935-6*, p. 360.

31. 'Trotsky on the Stalin Interview', in *Red Flag*, new series, no. 1, May 1936, p. 3.

32. Hugo Dewar, Interview with Al Richardson, 7th April 1978. On the failure to send a delegate to the 'Geneva' Conference, cf. his remarks in the same interview: 'The basic reason would probably be, we didn't have any money. That would be a start, probably the most important thing. Second, our experiences in the I.L.P. business gave us no confidence in the International. That would have been another factor, which would probably be a major factor. It might also be a question of language, nobody knowing what it was all about.'

33. Hugo Dewar, Interview with Al Richardson, 7th April 1978.

34. Jack Winnocour, 'Spain Has Lighted a Torch', in *The Socialist*, new series, no. 11, October 1936, p. 5.

35. Groves, *A Documentary History of the Socialist League*, p. 14.

36. Reg Groves, Interview with Al Richardson, 2nd April 1978.

37. David Chalkley, Interview with Al Richardson, 14th November 1978.

38. Cf. n. 36 above.

39. Reg Groves, *East End Crisis! Socialism, the Jews and Fascism*, issued by the London Area Committee, Socialist League.

40. Groves, *A Documentary History of the Socialist League*, p. 13.

41. Bornstein and Richardson, *Two Steps Back*, p. 29.

42. Reg Groves, Interview with Al Richardson, 2nd April 1978.

43. Harry Wicks, Interview with Al Richardson, 11th March and 1st April 1978.

44. Groves, *A Documentary History of the Socialist League*, p. 13.

45. Reg Groves, Interview with Al Richardson, 2nd April 1978.

46. 'Attack on Unity by Trotskyist Through Columns of Daily Herald', in the *Daily Worker*, 18th January 1937.

47. Reg Groves, 'A Disclaimer', in *The Socialist Broadsheet*, no. 1, February 1937, p. 2.

48. Groves, *A Documentary History of the Socialist League*, p. 14.

49. Cf. Bornstein and Richardson, *Two Steps Back*, p. 31.

50. Groves, *A Documentary History of the Socialist League*, p. 14.

51. 'Reg Groves Replies', in *Red Flag*, new series, no. 6, February 1937, pp. 3-4.

52. 'Formation of New Left Group in Labour Party', in *The New Leader*, 18th June 1937.

53. A. Dean (D.D. Harber), 'S.L.F. Leaders Sabotage Left Wing', in *The Militant*, vol. i, no. 4, October 1937.

54. Reg Groves, Interview with Al Richardson, 2nd April 1978.

55. See ref. in note 53 above.

56. Reg Groves, Interview with Al Richardson, 2nd April 1978.

57. 'S.L.F. Stillborn', in *The Militant*, vol. i, no. 5, November 1937, p. 8.

58. Harry Wicks, Interview with Al Richardson, 11th March and 1st April 1978.

59. Minutes of the Fusion Conference, R.S.L., in *Internal Bulletin* no. 1, April 1938, p. 7.

60. Reg Groves, Interview with Al Richardson, 2nd April 1978.

61. R. Groves, *But We Shall Rise Again*, London, 1938.

62. Reg Groves, Interview with Al Richardson, 2nd April 1978. The account which follows is based on this, and more especially on M. Upham, *The Aylesbury By-Election of 1938*, the text (privately circulated) of an address to the Conference of the Society for the Study of the History of Trotsky and the Revolutionary Movement, 10th October 1981, to which all serious students of the subject should turn. Cf. the short account in Bornstein and Richardson, *Two Steps Back*, pp. 36-9.

63. R. Palme Dutt, 'The People's Front is the Door to Socialism', in the *Daily Worker*, 14th May 1938.

64. These included Lord Addison of Stallingborough, who had just finished writing *A Policy for British Agriculture* for the Left Book Club, London, 1939 (preface signed 19th April 1938). In view of the Club's well-known Stalinist connections this is hardly surprising. Addison, himself an ex-Liberal, had been Minister of Agriculture in the Second Labour Government.

65. *Daily Worker*, 13th May 1938.

66. *Daily Worker*, 11th May 1938.

67. Reg Groves, Interview with Al Richardson, 2nd April 1978.

68. Ibid.

69. *News Chronicle*, 9th May 1938, as quoted in Upham, op. cit. (note 62 above), p. 8, n. 3.

70. 16th May 1938; cf. 'Who are the Defeatists?', Editorial, the *Daily Worker*, 17th May 1938.

71. Cf. below, p. 217.

72. Reg Groves, Interview with Al Richardson, 2nd April 1978.

73. *Daily Herald*, 9th May 1938; cf. Upham, p. 9, n. 1.

74. *Manchester Guardian*, 18th May 1938, as quoted in Upham, op. cit., p. 12, n. 2.

75. 'Now for a Workers' Front!', in *The New Leader*, vol. xxxi, new series, no. 228, 27th May 1938. Cf. The N.A.C.'s goodwill message in *The New Leader*, vol. xxxi, no. 227, 20th May 1938.

76. *Reynolds News*, 15th May 1938, as quoted in Upham, op. cit., pp. 11-11a, n. 3.

77. Ibid., pp. 12-12a, nn. 3-4.

78. 'Aylesbury Result Free Gift to Government', in the *Daily Worker*, 21st May 1938.

79. Reg Groves, Interview with Al Richardson, 2nd April 1978.

80. 'Aylesbury Rebuffs the Traitors', in *The Militant*, vol. i, no. 12, June 1938; 'The Lesson of Aylesbury', in *Fight*, vol. i, no. 3, June 1938, p. 2.

81. 'The Lesson of Aylesbury', in *Fight*, vol. i, no. 3, June 1938, p. 2; cf. no. 4, August 1938, 'A Letter and an Answer' (to S. Purkis).

Chapter Eight

'Midnight in the Century': The Moscow Trials

On 1st December 1934 Sergei Kirov, sent by Stalin to clean out the supporters of Zinoviev and Kamenev from the Leningrad Communist Party, was shot by Nikolayev, in a bungled scenario designed by the G.P.U. to incriminate Stalin's enemies. Already by the end of the year Zinoviev and Kamenev were under arrest, and for the next three years an unprecedented series of public and secret trials — or, more usually, exterminations without trial — removed a frightening total of public and private figures from the Russian population, and from among émigré Communists in Moscow. The trials served to prostrate Russia under permanent Stalinist terror, as well as to advertise Stalin's 'Popular Front' to world opinion, with the logic that if Stalin's policy was not revolution, then he didn't need any revolutionaries. The method could then be extended to other countries — chiefly Spain, where the Moscow press announced another such purge behind the Republican lines — whilst accusations of 'Trotskyism' flung at the accused could be used to cover Stalin's left flank, exposed now that the Comintern was in full support of 'democracy' against Fascism.

At the same time the Comintern's sections were given instructions to open up a frightful propaganda barrage, not just for the purpose of justifying Stalin's regime, but to intimidate and browbeat any opposition from the working class to the policy of the Popular Front. Now that Trotskyists were to be identified as Fascist saboteurs, they could be isolated inside the working class and driven out of its institutions; anyone reluctant to accept the verdict of the Trials could be vilified as a Trotskyist himself, or as being under their influence; and any opposition to the Popular Front could be similarly explained. The Moscow Trials and anti-Trotskyism became an all-inclusive vehicle of Soviet propaganda, suiting all their preoccupations. Organising their fellow-travellers, advertising Russia's offers of defence pacts, intriguing against other working-class tendencies, offering alliance to bourgeois politicians —all could be justified by the drive against 'counter-revolutionary Trotskyism'.

As one of the least significant of the sections of the Communist International — and one of the more servile — the British Communist Party turned over its propaganda machine wholeheartedly to this activity — producing books, pamphlets, articles, meetings, conference resolutions, leaflets, etc., almost without end; and the *Daily Worker* let hardly a week slip by until the eve of the Second World War without some mention of the affair.

It is difficult after this interval in time to convey to the detached reader the obsessive violence of these accusations, their sectarian vulgarity, or their mendaciousness; all that can be done is to give a few examples, leaving the rest to historical imagination.

As the trial of Zinoviev and Kamenev drew to a close, and before the verdict was delivered, the *Daily Worker* expressed the Party's policy in an editorial: 'They are a "festering cankering sore" and we echo fervently the workers' verdict: Shoot the Reptiles.'[1] After the execution, the Central Committee ended a resolution hailing Zinoviev's 'well-merited death' with the words

DOWN WITH THE TROTSKYIST ALLIES OF HITLER!

LONG LIVE THE COMMUNIST PARTY OF THE SOVIET UNION

LONG LIVE COMRADE STALIN, ITS GREAT LEADER.[2]

It was the same after the Second Trial; Trotskyists now became 'a frightful menace' and Trotsky himself 'the vicious enemy of all mankind'.[3] By the time of the Party's 14th Congress in May 1937, Trotskyism had become a 'foul abortion' which 'attracts to itself all the weak and base elements in the movement'[4] and a 'tool and ally of counter-revolutionary Fascism'.[5] A fresh development of the dialectic at the 15th Congress made them into 'alien bodies', 'whitewashers of Fascism' and 'poisonous scum'.[6]

Meanwhile, a fugue of literature from all the party's organs played endlessly over the same theme: the Communist Party issued *The Moscow Trial*[7] and *Defeat of Trotskyism*;[8] The Anglo-Russian Parliamentary Committee, *The Moscow Trial*;[9] the Friends of the Soviet Union, *Eight Soviet Generals Who Plotted Against Peace*;[10] and the Left Book Club, *Soviet Justice and the Trial of Radek and Others*,[11] *Soviet Democracy*[12] and *Soviet Policy and its Critics*.[13]

None of these effusions was characterised by consistency, honesty or detachment, and only the widespread popularity of the Popular Front policy can explain why they were ever taken seriously at all.[14] The libretto designed for the Trials themselves did not raise much confidence in this regard, with its accusations of mixing glass with the people's butter, secret liaisons in Danish Hotels that no longer existed, Trotsky's choice of Jews to make contact with Nazi officials, and an alliance with the Gestapo at a time when it had not yet been set up. But the rapidity with which one layer of victims was replaced by another caught the British Communist Party by surprise every time. Stalin's utter destruction of the Polish Communist Party, described as 'the assault on the Polish virgin', was characterised as 'an easily detected forgery of the *Manchester Guardian* Trotskyist'.[15] Bubnov, described as one of 'the Leninist Old Guard' by R. Page Arnot when justifying the Second Trial, was arrested nine months later.[16] Lajos Magyar, put up to denounce 'Trotskyism' in *Labour Monthly*, himself fell a victim to the purges not long afterwards. The great purger himself, 'our Bolshevik comrade Yezhov',[17] went the way of his victims.

J.R. Campbell was struck off to make the witch-hunt his speciality, and after a while it began to amount to an obsession with him. His 'Answers to Questions', featured in the *Daily Worker*, dwelt on very little else for week after week, and his concern began to be pathological — 'Give him a Trotskyist, and he'll be happy for hours' was said of him.[18] It reached its greatest extent in a 374-page book written to prove that Trotsky had 'collected as his agents and dupes all the refuse rejected by the revolutionary and reformist movements alike' and was a 'political degenerate'.[19] This was somewhat restrained compared with his previous descriptions of Trotsky as a 'political degenerate, ally of Fascism, a vile maniacal enemy of Socialism and Peace',[20] and the assertion that his case before the Dewey Commission was a 'farrago of lies shot through with almost maniacal egoism'.[21] His attempts to assist in a witch-hunt of the British Trotskyists went to almost fantastic lengths, such as when he wrote that 'some of the frantic hysterical lying emanating from the Trotskyists and their group is not unconnected with the activities of Goebbels' propaganda office',[22] and that 'wherever in a working class organisation Fascists or Trotskyists have got even a foot in, there is danger of anti-working class espionage.'[23]

Communists obviously risked expulsion if they sympathised with the contrary view; but what are we to make of the broad span of liberal and intellectual opinion, subject to no party discipline, that performed invaluable service in lending credibility to these accusations in wider society? From the outset it should be said that the Trials were so fantastic that without the help of respectable fellow travellers no one would have accepted the word of the Communist Party outside its own ranks. The fact that a person was a poet or a philosopher did not, of course, mean necessarily that he had reached any level of sophistication in political affairs: but others were far-seeing enough in their own interests when it came to the Cold War, and it is difficult to believe that cynical calculations did not play a part in their behaviour. The fact that the Soviet Union was 'against Hitler' served to still the doubts of some; and the questionings of others could be silenced with the demonstration that alliance with Russia in the coming war was in the interests of Britain too.

The advantages of forensic authority were evident from the very beginning. D.N. Pritt, K.C., elected as Labour M.P. for Hammersmith North in 1935, had built up a reputation in various civil liberties cases. By 1936, when he visited the Soviet Union, he had already been chairman of the Society for Cultural Relations with the U.S.S.R. for two years. Whilst 'present at the whole of the trial of the Zinoviev faction of plotters',[24] he delivered it as his learned judgement that 'the case was genuine, the trial fair, and the accused as guilty as they themselves said.'[25] Moreover, 'he said he was "shocked" at the action of Sir Walter Citrine and others in requesting a "Fair defence" for them.'[26] He handed on the brief for the Second Trial to Dudley Collard, 'a distinguished member of the English bar',[27] 'whose ability and judgement were greatly valued by his many fellow-lawyers who have come into contact with him.'[28] The result of his investigations was the Left Book Club production above referred to. Take the following as an example of special pleading, when the Norwegian authorities had produced proof that no such aircraft as mentioned had landed near Oslo:

> I have read some statement to the effect that no aeroplanes flew from Germany to Norway in December 1935. It seems hard to believe that this is so, and one does not know, of course, whether 'special' aeroplanes are referred to, or only civil airliners. In any case, it is clear that everyone was interested in concealing this trip, and that highly placed persons were concerned in organising it. It may be, therefore, that no record exists of the flight.[29]

'There is no question of a fake in the Moscow Trial,' he concluded.[30]

Of course, lawyers could not be expected to carry the burden of proof far beyond the court-rooms, so weightier expert witness was called in. John Strachey had been a fellow traveller of the Communist Party for most of the thirties, and he was widely acclaimed as one of the most capable Socialist thinkers. His command of political science convinced him that 'all these Trotskyists are working in closest association with the Nazis',[31] and he went on the platform in Caxton Hall to explain this.[32] Even more astonishingly, he had inside information that the Moscow Trials had thwarted Hitler's drive for world domination: 'I have evidence that Hitler's whole world plans have had to be revised now that he has lost his agents in the Soviet Union.'[33]

Strachey had been closely associated with the Communists over a long time, but even more disarming for the working-class movement was the attitude of *Tribune*, which continued to spout unadulterated Stalinist propaganda well on into the war. Sir Stafford Cripps, who had founded and financed it, had been drawn into the 'Unity' manoeuvres at the time of the dissolution of the Socialist League, and had promptly replaced its editor, Mellor, with a more compliant figure, E.Y. Hartshorn. Apart from a continuous series of speeches from Stalin and his acolytes,[34] and fake Trotskyist slogans and statements as a clumsy attempt at humour,[35] readers were regaled with adulatory reviews of books justifying the Trials[36] and with articles explaining how the victims had 'involved themselves in a conspiracy to overthrow the regime'.[37] Even the secret trial of the generals was defined as 'very democratic'.[38] Pat Sloan was put up to discredit Trotsky's *Revolution Betrayed* and Alec Bernstein to do a similar job on Souvarine's *Stalin*.[39]

To appreciate the hostility of the atmosphere at the time, it is well to remember that supporters and fellow travellers were obliged to introduce genuflections towards the Trials into whatever else they were dealing with at the time. T.A. Jackson, grappling manfully with the dialectic, turned his pen to proving that Trotskyism was 'a phosphorescent miasma over a petty-bourgeois swamp',[40] whilst a psychiatrist was roped in to explain how Trotskyists were 'unstable, unhappy, neurotic types' suffering an 'inner misery of mind' and 'akin to Fascist leaders in the subjective factors which impelled them'.[41]

Whilst the capitalist press could not be dominated and manipulated in the same way, it was the task of the fellow travellers to get favourable publicity for the Trials and create a public opinion amenable to them in the salon and the board-room. Despite his alleged disbelief, Kingsley Martin defended the validity of the Trials in *The New Statesman*,[42] and came back from an interview with Trotsky 'less inclined to scout the possibility of Trotsky's complicity than I had before', as Trotsky's unstable judgement made 'the possibility of a crazy plot more credible'.[43] A similar stand was taken by *The Observer*. 'It is futile to think the trial was staged and the charges trumped up,' it asserted, 'the government case against the defendants is genuine.'[44] Victor Gollancz, whose 'Left Book Club' was bringing in a fortune, took the chair at a meeting laid on by the Friends of the Soviet Union to defend the Trials.[45]

But it was neither as political commentators, nor as publicists, that the reputations of these figures were required: any and every 'name' was of some use, no matter how irrelevant to the political arena, providing it had some pull on middle-class opinion, so vital for the success of the Popular Front campaign going on at the same time.

The unfortunate Sean O'Casey was made to declare in the pages of the *Daily Worker* how providential it was that 'the conspiracy to overthrow Socialism in Russia has been overthrown',[46] and poor Stephen Spender, having written a book that was 90% on the Communist line, found himself taken to task on that small part where he had permitted himself a moment of doubt on the Moscow Trials, and had to publish a self-criticism.[47]

In sum, it was an incessant barrage, kept up day after day, backed not only by reputable Labour movement figures but by the country's finest intellectuals, and it is not at all surprising that ordinary trade unionists and Labour supporters, with neither the time nor the resources to examine these accusations thoroughly, should have been taken in by them. Even the fantastic nature of the accusations seemed to lend them credibility — 'I believe because it is impossible', an old religious tag, seemed to hold good here. Wouldn't anyone making up a scenario have tried to make it more credible? No one believed that the country of Socialism, 'the most modern country in the world', harboured the mentality of the Medieval witch-hunter or of the Spanish Inquisition. Even Churchill, who found it difficult to believe that the Nazi government was financing the 'most subversive form' of Communism, Trotskyism, thought that 'the point ought to be discussed in public and cleared up one way or the other', and felt in a quandary when faced with the 'monstrous and fathomless intrigues' revealed in the Moscow Trials.[48]

Nonetheless, the position was maintained with some difficulty, for much of the establishment press, including the *Manchester Guardian*, and important organs of the Labour press, including the *Daily Herald*, *Reynolds News* and the Glasgow *Forward* had grave doubts about the Trials. The Communists on their part attempted to use all the weapons of censorship and distortion to prevent uncomfortable facts from damaging an already fragile case. They refused outright to debate with the I.L.P., on the excuse that, as the I.L.P. had 'nobody worth convincing', it was a waste of time, and refused the *News Chronicle* permission to republish John Reed's *Ten Days That Shook the World* on the grounds that it contained 'not too accurate reportage' and 'inaccuracies and legends'.[49] Whilst the *Daily Worker* refused even to accept an advertisement for C.L.R. James' *World Revolution*,[50] the Left Book Club went even further. A letter from Gollancz in *Left Book News* explained that

> There is room in the list of publications of the Club for every Left point of view, and for any book which will help in the fight against Fascism, but there is no room whatever for a book which, while appearing to be Left, sets out to help the enemy,

> or for a book which fights on the side of Fascism. A Trotskyite book falls as obviously outside the scope of the Club's publication as does a Nazi book or a Fascist book . . .
>
> I beg the local Groups not to be drawn into arguments at Group meetings with professional disruptors. They will no doubt be asked to do so on the grounds of democracy, free discussion, and all the rest; but time is far too precious to waste on sterile debates of this kind.[51]

When Gollancz took this view, the party needed no prompting for its own house magazines: *Left Review*, for example, in refusing an advertisement for *The Case of Leon Trotsky*, was unperturbed by Warburg's pointed remarks about 'Catholic Inquisition' and 'Fascist authoritarianism'.[52] And whilst simple censorship might be the way to discipline awkward publishers, more direct methods were used in meetings and in the street. John Archer remembers J.R. Campbell inciting a crowd against him in the Town Hall Square in Leeds, where an ugly incident was avoided only with some difficulty,[53] and John Robinson had an attack made on his platform by Y.C.L.ers, who began smashing it up with bits of wood.[54] The worst incident was an attack upon Gerry Bradley's platform in Hyde Park by about 500 C.P.ers outraged by the oratorical talent he displayed in his constant ridicule of them.[55]

Curiously enough, the mainstream opinion of the Labour movement was more immune to the attempts to justify the Moscow Trials than its own left wing, or the intellectuals. The Labour leaders had no intention of sharing office with Popular Front Liberals or 'democratic' Tories, and even less intention of allowing the Communist Party to make propaganda for them in their own ranks. Any inconsistencies in the Trials were ready meat to demonstrate that Russia was a totalitarian state, and the British Communists its obedient tools. Right at the start of the Trials the *Daily Herald* poked fun at the gap between these proceedings and the 'democratic ' pretensions of the regime, remarking to the effect that if the Stalin Constitution were to be taken at all seriously, then Trotsky would still be airing his views in the Soviet Union.[56] Adler's pamphlet blowing the Trials wide open was translated and published by the Labour Party,[57] and British representatives on the Executive of the Socialist International and the International Confederation of Trade Unions signed an appeal regretting the Trials and the lack of an independent defence for the victims.[58] A year later, the *Daily Herald* asked point blank why the Communist Party had said nothing about the mass wave of exterminations, reports of which were by now making their way to the West.

The Communist Party had no other shield than flat denial for this sort of challenge:

> Why have we not spoken about the 'terrible wave of executions', the 'astonishing extermination of leading Communist citizens of the Soviet Union', and 'firing squads that kill Stalin's opponents'? Is it not, asks the *Herald*, because this would show up 'the vast pretence that the Soviet Union is the most democratic country in the world'?
>
> The reason the Communists have not dealt with these events is that they have not taken place. Eight generals have been shot, 40 pro-Fascist wreckers have been executed in Siberia, leading Communists who have neglected their public duty have been removed from their posts, but to magnify these events into a 'terrible wave of executions and arrests', 'vast and astonishing extermination' is to be guilty of *Daily Mail* hysteria.
>
> We ask you to produce the facts and figures of this 'vast and astonishing extermination' . . .[59]

If all else failed they could always fall back upon the utopian picture that the Webbs and Sloan were touching up for the U.S.S.R. Citrine and Adler had no reason to 'indulge in cowardly clap trap about "judicial guarantees",' they reasoned, 'the Soviet Court is the one court in the world which is just and independent of the bourgeoisie, basing itself on the laws of the Soviet Union and expressing the opinion and will of the millions of workers in the U.S.S.R.'[60] Pritt contributed a leading article advising the *Herald* not to 'play the game of reaction',[61] whilst Arnot on a lower level described the paper as the 'Organ of Odham's millionaire press',[62] which had 'lashed up an Anti-Soviet campaign that outdid the *Daily Mail*'.[63] When the *Herald* implied that only torture could have produced the confessions made, he replied with unconscious irony that 'the only excuse the *Daily Herald* scribes could make is that they were writing to order'.[64]

Emrys Hughes, editor of the Glasgow *Forward*, took an even more iconoclastic line. He published several of Trotsky's articles on the Trials and on Spain, and gave publicity to the counter-trial of the Dewey Committee.[65] Communists and non-Communists alike took part in a free discussion in which the defenders of the Trials had decidedly the worst of the encounter. None of this was reproduced, with the sole exception of Tom Johnston's note that he knew 'of no shred of evidence for any assertion that the trial was bogus or the confessions of the accused extorted'.[66] The Communists' signal failure in this direction led to the solemn pronouncement that 'working class organs with a previous record of struggle like the Glasgow *Forward* have, under Trotskyist influence, ceased to be papers rallying the masses of the people for united struggle against the Government, but have become slander sheets spreading disruption and helping to confuse the issues of the struggle.'

Among the Labour movement's own intellectuals, M.N. Brailsford made the most complete demolition of the charges in a number of articles in *Reynolds News* showing, in Brockway's opinion at least, that 'these executions are utterly unjustified, that the charges on which they are carried out were false, and that the true explanation (or the nearest we can come to the truth in the fog that has been deliberately created around them) is that the men were sent to their death because they stood for a revolutionary Socialist policy and against the strange tangles into which Soviet foreign policy has led Soviet Russia.'[67] On its part, the Communist Party reacted to Brailsford's articles with mounting irritation. At first he drew sympathy for being 'bewildered, doubtful and miserable',[68] with the hope that he would awaken to the need 'to clear out every weakness and hesitation, every echo of Fascist and Trotskyist propaganda from our ranks'.[69] By the next year he had 'lost his head and is circulating pernicious nonsense',[70] which was 'faithful to the style of the Fascists, Trotskyists and capitalist hack writers'.[71] Particularly objectionable to them was his remark that in view of the number of Bolshevik veterans who had been purged, it seemed that all the Bolshevik leaders except two were 'carrion'.[72]

The response of the I.L.P. was a lamentable one, typical in its vacillation, in its willingness to pass on the responsibility, in its desire to 'have it both ways'. Its initial reaction to the shooting of Kirov and the arrest of Zinoviev and Kamenev was to regret 'that these recent events have seriously disturbed the minds of many Soviet sympathisers outside Russia',[73] whilst Aplin deplored the attempt of Barbusse's book on Stalin 'once again to make Trotsky responsible for the Kirov murder'.[74] Then Brockway began to hedge. 'We are not prepared to accept without an impartial investigation the statements made by Leon Trotsky regarding the "persecution" of Opposition Communists on Soviet Russia, but the method of the Communist International in replying to them is not reassuring,' he wrote. 'These statements are neither true or untrue, and Trotsky's revolutionary services require a more serious answer', whilst 'many sincere friends of Soviet Russia are disturbed and they, too, are entitled to know the facts.'[75]

Brockway's policy was to ignore the Dewey Commission set up as a counter-trial in Mexico, and to try to get the London Bureau to float one of their own. 'Only an impartial investigation can settle this question,' he wrote, whilst accompanying his remarks with an article of his own wondering whether a revolt had taken place in the Soviet Union that had been put down by the regime![76] By the time autumn came, Brockway's vacillations had become more marked, for the I.L.P. leaders were already involved in the secret talks with the Communist Party and the Socialist League leaders about their coming 'Unity' campaign. Caught between a rank-and-file that was increasingly suspicious, and a Communist Party that was trying to throttle all criticism, Brockway was obliged to raise a smokescreen by attacking Trotskyism:

> Take the Trotskyists. I believe they hold a truth. I share their criticism of the 'Socialism in one country' line and the foreign policy which reflects it, their recognition of the danger of a transitional revolutionary dictatorship becoming a continuing bureaucracy, their disbelief in the Moscow Trial charges and of the branding of Trotsky as an ally of Hitler's secret service.
>
> I believe these views are true, yet the Trotskyists are everywhere a source of mischief in the working-class movement. They destroy and do not build. They remain conspiratorial cliques in whatever party they attach themselves to, disintegrating it, making it less effective in the class struggle, antagonising other sections of the working class. Even in the midst of the crisis in Spain, that is the effect of their influence there at this moment.
>
> Is not the reason that they do not relate their truth to the whole truth? They appear to be unable to see anything else than the crimes of the Stalinist bureaucracy. Even if the full total of their charges were true, they must be seen in relation to the biggest fact of history — the Soviet revolution and all that it means. They must be seen at this moment in relation to the supreme necessity of mobilising the working-class movement of the world behind Soviet Russia in the course which it is taking in Spain and the consequences that may flow from it.[77]

The very next issue of the paper carried a plug for the 'Unity Campaign', showing what price had been paid for Brockway's principles on this occasion.[78]

But events in Spain were fast showing that the Moscow Trials and the smashing of the revolution behind the Republican lines were part and parcel of the same policy. At the same time as Brockway was explaining that 'recognising Soviet Russia as the first Workers' State, we are prepared to subordinate our criticism to the supreme necessity of mobilising support for Soviet Russia in the present international crisis', he also noticed the curious fact that the Catalan Stalinist Party was demanding that the I.L.P.'s sister party, the P.O.U.M., should be removed from the Catalan regional government![79]

Yet as the Stalinists in Spain turned to bloody repression of the P.O.U.M., Brockway continued to hold out the olive branch here, especially over the Moscow Trials. 'We are anxious that an impartial investigation should be made, and that the truth, whatever it is, should be made known,' Brockway wrote: 'We hope, therefore, that both the Second and Third Internationals will collaborate.'[80] Accordingly, the National Administrative Council of the I.L.P. passed a resolution continuing to suspend judgement:

> The evidence given before the Moscow Trial and the repudiation of the evidence by Leon Trotsky have raised issues which affect not only Soviet Russia, but the whole International Working-Class movement. It is imperative that there should be an impartial investigation by representative Socialists who have the confidence of the working class.
>
> The N.A.C. is exploring the possibility of securing an investigation by such international representatives, who should analyse both the detailed evidence given at the trial and the full reply which it is understood Leon Trotsky intends to publish shortly.
>
> Meanwhile the N.A.C. expresses no judgement on the matter at issue, and instructs the Party to refrain from doing so.[81]

Under a cloak of impartiality, a more dishonest statement could not have been issued. By describing the Dewey Commission's investigation as Trotsky's 'reply' they were implying that it carried as little weight as the Moscow Trial indictments; and by calling for another investigation by 'representative' Socialists they were asking for other political parties' judgements on the Trials, not a real investigation. Finally, whilst the I.L.P. N.A.C. might suspend judgement, Vyshinsky was certainly not following their example in his Moscow courtroom, nor the G.P.U. in their extermination camps.

Carmichael was able to get a substantial majority at the I.L.P. Easter Conference for this wilful dishonesty, explaining that the N.A.C. was not prepared 'to declare out of hand that the trials are frame-ups, or that the prisoners are duped or drugged', and that the evidence available was 'inadequate to reach a final judgement'.[82]

There can be little doubt now that this singularly dishonest stance (or lack of one) was due to the pressure of the Communist Party mediated through its 'Unity Committee'. For whilst the secret preliminaries were going on in Cripps' chambers, R. Page Arnot had seen fit to warn the I.L.P. that

> Trotskyism is now revealed as an ancillary of Fascism. There are still innocent members of the British I.L.P. who would be astounded by this statement . . .
>
> The I.L.P. is in great danger of falling into the hands of Trotskyists, and becoming a wing of Fascism. Let the members of the I.L.P. look to it.[83]

As the pressure mounted in Spain against the P.O.U.M. and the Anarchists, with daily provocations accompanied by loud threats from Moscow and echoes from its Spanish supporters, it became increasingly difficult to keep up this pretence at impartiality, and Brockway was obliged to go through some difficult contortions to justify it:

> The American Enquiry (i.e. the Dewey Commission) is not all that is desirable. In our view it was a mistake to set up an 'Impartial' Commission through a Committee 'for the *defence* of Leon Trotsky'. The report from such a Commission will inevitably be regarded by opponents as biased. Nor, so far as we have been informed, are the terms of enquiry sufficiently wide. As stated in the I.L.P. National Council Resolution (subsequently endorsed by the Party Annual Conference), we wanted an enquiry into the international implications of the Moscow Trial. Charges were brought against Trotsky and Trotskyism which had a significance far beyond Soviet Russia.[84]

In other words, not only the veracity of the Moscow Trials was to come under investigation, but the 'international implications' of charges against 'Trotskyism'.

A later article, couched in the form of a review of C.L.R. James' book *World Revolution*, explained just what he meant by the problem of 'Trotskyism':

> The fault of Trotsky and of his disciples is that they can see nothing else than the mistakes of Soviet Russia and the Communist International. This is understandable in Trotsky, who has a refugee psychology, and even the most philosophic of minds find it difficult to resist it. In the case of Trotsky it still remains to be seen how far his personal experience and obsession with the problems of Russia have imbalanced his general attitude and thrown out of perspective his attitude to Russia itself.
>
> There is less excuse for the Trotskyists. It is no accident that in every country they become a negative and destroying force. They cannot relate their intensities to the real situation. To them Communists become as hateful as Fascists.[85]

Trotsky showed his disgust for this sort of spinelessness:

> The Secretary of the Independent Labour Party of Great Britain, Fenner Brockway, runs to the aid of Pritt, the King's Counsellor, with a plan to save the Moscow falsifiers. Pritt Number One tried to resolve the task *juridically*. Pritt Number

> Two considers the task politically. An international inquiry into the Moscow Trials, according to Fenner Brockway's way of thinking, is impermissible because it might arouse 'prejudice in Russia and in Communist circles'. Fenner Brockway thus recognises beforehand that an impartial verification could not confirm the Moscow accusations and justify the executions. On the contrary, Brockway is convinced that an honest and open inquiry can only 'prejudice' Stalin's clique and 'Communist circles'. That is precisely why Pritt Number Two proposes to organise an 'inquiry into the role of Trotskyism in the Working Class Movement'. In other words: instead of establishing the objective truth regarding the monstrous, criminal accusations, Brockway proposes a partisan political trial against his ideological adversary . . .
>
> However, Brockway's plan takes on a manifestly *dishonest* character at the point where he tries to replace a juridical inquiry into the criminal accusations and the trials, more exactly, into the greatest frame-ups in the world, with a factional political intrigue to avoid the 'prejudice' of Stalin and his agents. Here the advanced workers will say: 'Stop! Brockway's fears, whatever may be their source, will not hinder the truth from triumphing over the lie'[86]

On 21st May, a fortnight after Stalinist provocation had precipitated the Barcelona uprising, Brockway wrote on behalf of the London Bureau that it was 'not able to endorse the American Commission of Inquiry or to be represented on it because it takes the view that a disastrous mistake has been made in initiating the enquiry through a Committee which describes itself as a "Committee for the Defence of Trotsky".' Brockway, of course, could not understand Trotsky's attitude. 'Perhaps the "old man" (as his followers call him) was suffering from nerves,' he mused charitably — 'certainly he had reason to do so.'[87]

Meanwhile, the I.L.P. contingent in Spain was also feeling a little nervous. After the 'May Days' in Barcelona came the murder of Nin and the ban on the P.O.U.M., with the mysterious death of Bob Smillie and the flight of George Orwell, John McNair and Staff Cottman. Confirmation of the suppression of the Spanish revolution was provided directly when Brockway went to Spain in person. A week after he had signed the London Bureau's refusal to back the Dewey Commission, Brockway was obliged to write another letter, this time to the Communist Party, to explain that 'our boys were not involved in stabbing in the back the cause of Spanish democracy', but in 'resisting a stab in the back for which unfortunately the C.P. has a large share of responsibility.'[88] When he returned to tax the

C.P. with their behaviour, and with capturing control of the Spanish police to apply the methods of the G.P.U., they replied that whilst they hoped that this was the case, unfortunately his picture was untrue.[89] Now the I.L.P. itself came in for the treatment of the Trial victims and the Trotskyists. *The New Leader* found its own views being linked to those of the Fascists. 'There are a lot of points of resemblance between the two sheets these days,' it was explained: 'yesterday's issues have this in common, *Action* devotes 50 per cent of its space to attacks on the U.S.S.R. and the Jews, while the *New Leader* devotes 50 per cent of its space to attacks on the U.S.S.R., the Spanish Government and the C.P. of Spain.'[90]

Brockway was finally in a position to make the link between what was going on in Spain and the Trials in Moscow. 'It is no accident,' he wrote, 'that the Spanish Communist Party press — like the Russian press in relation to the purge in the Soviet Union — has already prejudged the issue, has found the arrested men and women guilty of being agents of Fascism and has demanded the death penalty.'[91] Finally, it was the C.P. who broke off the 'Unity Campaign' on the pretext of I.L.P. 'propaganda of a Trotskyist type'.[92] When the I.L.P. M.P.s and Brockway got round to sending a protest telegram to Stalin on 9th March 1938, the *Daily Worker* described it with the words, 'degenerates appeal for degenerates'.[93]

At no point during these exchanges was the I.L.P. able to rise above the events as they encountered them, day by day, to make a proper explanation of what was happening. They were able to grope towards the idea that the Moscow Trials were false only because the same charges laid against their own comrades in Spain were false. They could understand the use of slander and provocation in Spain to reverse a revolution, because they had gone there and seen it for themselves. What they could not understand was that the Moscow Trials were also the result of a counter-revolution, albeit of a different social character. The ingenuousness and innocence with which the I.L.P. confronted this latter phenomenon is well illustrated by Maxton's review of Trotsky's *Revolution Betrayed*:

> I have often wished, as I am sure thousands of Socialists throughout the world have wished, that these two [Trotsky and Stalin] were working together as comrades in the world struggle of the workers, and in Socialist construction in Russia, rather than that Trotsky should be in exile and the most virulent critic of the work of Stalin as head of the Russian Government . . .
>
> [On 'betrayal'] I do not like the word: I do not like it as the title of this book . . . It should not be used against men who, with the best will in the world to serve the workers' cause, make

> mistakes which have the effect of producing a set-back in the struggle for socialism.
>
> In spite of the very penetrating criticism of the Stalin Government in Russia, and the masterly presentation of facts in this book, I do not think 'betrayal' in the sense defined above is proved. I have the feeling that if Lenin had lived during these latter years and been at the head of the Russian state, and had been compelled to make adjustments, modifications and compromises not dissimilar in kind to those that have been adopted, Trotsky would not have described them as betrayal . . .
>
> Stalin should weigh it carefully, and consider whether some part of the criticism is not justified.[94]

Brockway's understanding did not run much deeper. He was quite unable to see the links between the principle of 'Socialism in One Country', the degeneration of the Soviet regime, and its counter-revolutionary policy abroad:

> This is a negative, incomplete and misleading diagnosis. Its effect is to discourage the effort to achieve as much Socialism as possible in any given country.
>
> If workers win power over any part of the earth's surface where the raw materials are available to satisfy the needs of life, it is their duty to take advantage of such circumstances to establish the Socialist order of Society.
>
> . . . no criticism could be made if the Russian Communists strained every power to build the fullest Socialist state within their borders.[95]

In this way, Brockway remained fascinated by the power of the *fait accompli*. Stalin's apparatus controlled a vast state; so much was in existence; Stalinism was a power in the world, even in Spain. What had Trotsky got apart from his ideas? 'The groups which form the Fourth International are the merest trifling sects, without any relation to the mass movement of the workers,'[96] he noted, 'insignificant, divided among themselves, and a destructive influence wherever they go.'[97]

So whilst the I.L.P.'s material base was shrinking rapidly, they were all the more held in awe of Soviet power. For the I.L.P. had little cause for self-congratulation at the splits of the Trotskyists. 'If we survey the history of the I.L.P. since it left the Labour Party,' observed Trotsky, 'it is nothing but a history of splits, splinterings, resignations, desertions, etc.', with this difference: that no programmatic struggle had been the cause of them. 'Thus it *appears* to these stout gentlemen that they have shrunk from 25,000 members to 3,000 without any "splits".'[98]

The atmosphere was getting worse for the Trotskyists by the week. It did not help their cause that the right of the Labour movement was hostile to the Stalinists and the Trials, as the left was much influenced by them, and this was used by the C.P. to isolate them still further. But it was exceptionally hard to get a hearing. Until the end of 1936 the Marxist Group had no real press of its own, and was dependent on the goodwill of the I.L.P. for anything they got published. Even after that time *Fight*, a small quarto magazine, did not enjoy a high circulation, and *Red Flag* enjoyed no better success, being intermittent and finally coming to an end in 1937, at the height of the witch-hunt, *The Militant* and *Youth Militant* were not in a good position to carry much more information.

One way was to turn up at official Stalinist meetings. Harry Wicks recalls an extraordinary scene when the C.P. held a public meeting to defend the trial of Zinoviev and Kamenev:

> In the first trial the Conway Hall was packed to capacity, with Johnny Campbell as the speaker and John Mahon in the chair. There was an Indian journalist [Raj Hansa] . . . as the meeting was about to start, this Indian free-lance journalist jumped up and said 'Mr. Chairman, would it be in order, before the commencement of the meeting, if we were to ask everybody to rise in honour of the old companion of Lenin, Zinoviev?' (who had been shot). There was pandemonium — it was a most dramatic question, in a most tense atmosphere when they were waiting for the opening of the meeting, and so they were half rising, and the C.P. yelled. I can't repeat it, but it was a most dramatic intervention by that chap . . . There was a whole crowd of youngsters from the Labour League of Youth, and there was the S.P.G.B. There was a chap named Cash, an S.P.G.B. taxi driver, and there was another youngster with a loud voice, a good propagandist from the S.P.G.B. They were able to raise their voice, and as a result of the solidity of their protest, they were able to get me on to the C.P. platform — I was the one allowed onto the platform on that occasion.[99]

There was less success elsewhere, perhaps because the C.P. was prepared. Goffe intervened with questions and interruptions at a meeting addressed by D.N. Pritt and Dr. Edith Summerskill in Sheffield City Hall; but, as he recalls, 'I must say, as a highly skilled lawyer, he probably got the better of me.'[100]

There was always the device of writing letters to the newspapers — particularly *The New Leader*, which had to give some space to Trotsky and his supporters because of the balancing act Brockway was involved in. When Earle Birney had visited Trotsky in Norway in November 1935, he had been shown the original letters and photographs pertaining to the miraculous escape of the old Armenian Bolshevik Tarov from Siberia, and of course he passed on the information to *The New Leader* after he got back.[101] When Ralph Fox wrote in the following number to pick up minor slips in geography and translation, Birney wrote in again to correct the points and to show that 'one is still left waiting for a denial or admission of the charges made of persecution of Opposition Communists.'[102] Robert Williams in turn wrote in to put Brockway on the spot about the non-appearance of the impartial tribunal of investigation he had been talking about. 'There are many prominent figures of the Labour movement of this country who would certainly agree to examine the accusation and the defence,' he pointed out. Brockway could only reply that, since the London Bureau's appeal had fallen on deaf ears, 'the Secretariat of the Bureau has communicated to the affiliated parties proposals for other forms of action.'[103]

The policy of the International Trotskyist movement had been to try to set up bodies similar to the Dewey Commission in other countries, so the next step was to issue an appeal for such a committee. Late in 1936 they got H.N. Brailsford, J.F. Horrabin, Reg Groves, Conrad Noel, Stewart Purkis, Fred Shaw, Rowland Hill, Irene Rathbone and Gary Allighan to sign an appeal to the organisations of the Labour movement for 'an enquiry through an international commission set up by the International Labour movement' which would 'investigate the materials in the Commissariat of Justice in Moscow and also the material and statements of Leon Trotsky'.[104] That was about as much success as they got. The *Manchester Guardian* and the *Daily Herald* reproduced it, A.E. Reade wrote to the national press to whip up support, with little return, and an approach to George Bernard Shaw elicited the response that Trotsky needed no defence from him.

Worst of all was a visit to Brockway made on 27th November 1936.[105] As Wicks recalls it,

> We went over to Ludgate Circus, to Bride Street, where the I.L.P. had a bookshop and their premises. Stewart Purkis was on that deputation, and we went at the height of the Moscow Trials . . . The C.P. was running these campaigns of meetings where we were intervening, and we wrote to Brockway, and went to see him at his office. There was Henry Sara, Stewart Purkis, and myself, and he said 'Gentlemen, sit down. What was the question? The Moscow Trials? Oh, excuse me.' And he goes into this little office, and he comes out with an all-red

> grandee's velvet uniform, with gold braid hat, to show us. 'This is the Spanish Revolution. The Revolution is on in Spain. This is the grand Spanish struggle. Now the Moscow Trials — if the sky was clear, if the clouds weren't big in the sky, we would really do something about the Moscow Trials. We would call meetings, we would have discussions, we would counter. But the Spanish Revolution is on, and the Spanish Revolution is dependent on Russian arms, so there is nothing we could do in the matter.' Now that is still vivid in my recollection, and from that moment on Brockway to me was a nothing.[106]

A further attempt by the British Committee on May Day 1937 to get some straight answers from Brockway met with equal failure. The I.L.P. and the London Bureau were not prepared to send a delegate to the Commission, to collaborate with it, to accept the commission's collaboration in an investigation of their own, or to accept the verdict of the Dewey Commission. A final question as to whether Brockway would give any publicity to the Dewey Commission's findings failed to elicit any response at all. The Committee could only assume that it was the Unity Agreement of the I.L.P. and the C.P.G.B. which 'expressly forbade all criticism of the Soviet Union and the policy of its government'.[107]

Undeterred, the British Trotskyists went ahead. They set up their committee, elected Harry Wicks to begin with — and later Hilary Sumner Boyd — as its Secretary, and issued its magazine, as well as publishing Trotsky's *I Stake My Life* speech in pamphlet form. Then they arranged a series of public meetings. A meeting in the Essex Hall, Essex Street, off the Strand on 9th September 1936 was addressed by Henry Sara, Harry Wicks and C.L.R. James.[108] Even more impressive was a meeting held in the Memorial Hall in Farringdon on 10th February 1937, on the theme of 'Justice for Leon Trotsky!', at which spoke Sidney Silverman, Stewart Purkis, Henry Sara, C.L.R. James, Reg Groves and Harry Wicks.[109] On this occasion between five and six hundred people attended,[110] and Dewar, who was acting as a steward, remembers the interest aroused by it:

> . . . the meeting-place was full, and Ellen Wilkinson turned up, and I was a chief steward, and I wouldn't let her in. Because I said, 'We're full!' and shut the doors. She said, 'Don't you know who I am? I'm Ellen Wilkinson!' I said, 'What difference does that make? Unfortunately, the place is full, and as I've turned other people away, I've got to turn you away', which made her very annoyed. The only thing I recollect about that meeting is that we had the Communist Party members in there. At the close of the meeting there was one chap who got up with a collecting tin, collecting for the Communist Party. Well, I

> picked him up and walked out of the room with him. Although he was six feet tall, he was so astonished, that he didn't know what to do. And then I remember Jack Diamond . . . a local councillor for the Labour Party . . . a sort of contact . . . was most indignant with me that I was so brutal, but I didn't hurt the chap at all. I just picked him up, and walked out with him, and dumped him down outside.[111]

A further meeting in Battersea Town Hall where Groves took the chair and Wicks spoke was disrupted by the Communist Party, who came in with the intention of breaking it up.[112]

Great efforts were made to try and force the Communist Party to debate the issue, usually without success. A second meeting at the Essex Hall at which C.L.R. James and Karl Westwood were billed to speak on 26th February 1937 included in its advertising matter 'Pat Sloan, invited to voice Stalinist opposition',[113] but the Communists were very reluctant to be caught in debate, especially with James. He only managed to manoeuvre Andrew Rothstein into a debate by arranging it with someone else to begin with, then going along instead.[114] Pat Devine was cut to pieces in a similar encounter in Islington Public Library.[115] After these brushes the Stalinists refused to debate with the Trotskyist leaders, just as they did with the I.L.P. After all, from their point of view, they were defending the weaker case in front of an audience that they had provided. Some opportunities still existed for debating in the provinces and amongst the youth, but wider possibilities dwindled fast. The cause was an unpopular one, the war was looming up, the issues seemed far off, and even the class content of the Trotskyist movement could so easily be used against it. Goffe remembers how he debated in Sheffield before an audience of the Labour League of Youth, with a leading Y.C.L. spokesman who hadn't a clue what he was talking about, was soundly trounced, and could supply as his argument only that he was a worker and Goffe was an intellectual.[116]

Relations between the groups on the Defence Committee were very poor. Most of the hard organisational work was done by the Marxist League, and whilst the other groups came along, they took little part. The names of spokesmen from the Militant Group had been left off the publicity leaflet for the Memorial Hall meeting on 10th February, and they reported that the atmosphere of the Committee was bad, 'dominated by the Marxist League who dislike us violently, trying to freeze us out'.[117] The Stalinist attempt to isolate the Trotskyists from the mass movement of the workers had been all too successful, and stagnation and lack of perspective had led to renewed factional conflict within the groups, and worse relations between them. Disillusion with the failure of the Trotskyists to alert the working class to the full menace of Stalinism revealed in the Trials led to the loss of valuable comrades, such as Arthur Ballard and even Groves himself. Practically without any allies, the Trotskyists had been the only effective protest raised against the monstrous perversion of the revolution that Stalinism had become, their voices drowned in a sea of slander, swelled by the outpourings of a spineless intelligentsia, and directed into a tidal wave by a corrupt machine. The last word on this experience rests with Wicks:

> Years later I passed to the Revolutionary Communist Party the files of that voluminous correspondence between the Committee of which I was secretary and the 'Left' intellectuals of that day. It represented to me a pitiful picture of how even 'great' minds are intimidated by power.[118]

Notes

1. Editorial, 'Shoot the Reptiles', in the *Daily Worker*, 24th August 1936.
2. 'Well-Merited Death', in the *Daily Worker*, 27th August 1936, p. 3.
3. Editorial, 'Drive Them Out', in the *Daily Worker*, 10th February 1937.
4. *It Can Be Done*, Report of the 14th Congress of the C.P.G.B., Battersea, 29th–31st May 1937, p. 89.
5. Ibid., p. 92.
6. *For Peace and Plenty*, Report of the 15th Congress of the C.P.G.B., p. 102.
7. W.G. Shepherd, *The Moscow Trial* (Preface by D.N. Pritt), C.P.G.B., 1936. Cf. the *Daily Worker*, 18th January 1936.
8. Marjorie Pollitt, *Defeat of Trotskyism*, C.P.G.B. pamphlet, 22nd December 1937.
9. Shepherd, *The Moscow Trial*.
10. H.R. George, *Eight Soviet Generals Who Plotted Against Peace*, 'Friends of the Soviet Union', undated.
11. Dudley Collard, *Soviet Justice and the Trial of Radek and Others*, London, 1937.
12. Pat Sloan, *Soviet Democracy*, London, 1937.
13. J.R. Campbell, *Soviet Policy and Its Critics*, London, 1939.
14. Cf. S. Bornstein and A. Richardson, *Two Steps Back*, London, 1982, pp. 20–1.
15. R. Page Arnot, 'The Trotsky Trial', in *Labour Monthly*, vol. xix, no. 3, March 1937, p. 181.
16. Ibid., p. 185. Cf. B. Pearce, 'The British Stalinists and the Moscow Trials', in *Labour Review*, March/April 1958. This is a superb treatment of the whole question, and should not be neglected by any student of Communist history. He notes that R. Fox had added Krestinsky as well — n. 2.
17. C.C. Resolution on the Soviet Union, 5th March 1938, in *Report of the C.C. to the 15th Party Congress*, 1938, p. 115.

18. P. Bolsover, 'The Man Behind the Answers', in the *Daily Worker*, 2nd April 1938.

19. J.R. Campbell, *Soviet Policy and Its Critics*, p. 373. Cf. *Spain's Left Critics*, C.P.G.B. pamphlet, 16th March 1937.

20. J.R. Campbell, 'The Lying and Fantastic Case of Leon Trotsky', in the *Daily Worker*, 17th November 1937.

21. J.R. Campbell, 'Trotsky's "Explanations" ', in *Left Review*, December 1937, p. 688.

22. J.R. Campbell, 'The Trotskyist Danger', in *For Peace and Plenty*, p. 94.

23. *Daily Worker*, 18th July 1938.

24. 'A Worker's Notebook', 'More Democracy', in the *Daily Worker*, 28th August 1936.

25. D.N. Pritt, Introduction to D. Collard, *Soviet Justice and the Trial of Radek and Others*, p. 7.

26. Op. cit., note 24 above.

27. W. Gallacher, 'A British Lawyer Looks at the Moscow Trial', in the *Daily Worker*, 19th March 1937.

28. Op. cit., note 25 above.

29. Ibid.

30. *Daily Worker*, 1st February 1937. Cf. the *Daily Herald*, 28th January 1937. It was even repeated in *Pravda*, 29th January 1937.

31. J. Strachey, 'Looking at the News', in the *Daily Worker*, 22nd January 1937.

32. Advertisement in the *Daily Worker*, for meeting 8th February 1937.

33. J. Strachey, 'The Great Fascist Defeat', in the *Daily Worker*, 1st April 1938.

34. E.g. *Tribune*, 17th March 1939 ('Stalin Speaks'), 28th April 1939 ('Something the Others Haven't Got' — Stalin again), 1st September 1939 (Voroshilov and Zhdanov), 8th September 1939 (Molotov).

35. E.g. 'Beachcomber', 'An Interview with Trotsky', in *Tribune*, 3rd February 1939; 'More Trotskyist Slogans', in *Tribune*, 14th April 1939, p. 16.

36. Alec Bernstein, 'Book of the Week', *Tribune*, 24th February 1939.

37. K. Zilliacus, 'Peace Has Always Been the Aim of Soviet Policy', in *Tribune*, 14th April 1939, p. 10.

38. 'Pat Sloan Replies', in *Tribune*, 9th June 1939, p. 20.

39. Alec Bernstein, in *Tribune*, 6th October 1939, p. 9.

40. T.A. Jackson, *Dialectics: The Logic of Marxism*, London, 1936, p. 521.

41. R. Osborn (Reuben Osbert), *The Psychology of Reaction*, London, 1938, ch. xix, 'The Psychology of Trotskyism', pp. 260–80.

42. 10th May 1937.

43. *Daily Worker*, 10th April 1937.

44. *The Observer*, 23rd August 1936.

45. 'Workers' Notebook', in the *Daily Worker*, 17th February 1937.

46. S. O'Casey, 'The Sword of the Soviet', in the *Daily Worker*, 25th March 1938.

47. J.R. Campbell, 'Forward from Liberalism —But Whither?', in the *Daily Worker*, 1st February 1937; S. Spender, 'I Join the C.P.', in the *Daily Worker*, 19th February 1937. Cf. Bornstein and Richardson, *Two Steps Back*, p. 22 and p. 52, n. 6. The reference is to *Forward from Liberalism*, London, 1937, p. 206.

48. Winston Churchill, 'We Are Still Free', in the *Evening Standard*, 16th October 1936.

49. J.R. Campbell, 'Answers to Questions', in the *Daily Worker*, 11th April 1938. Contrast the latter statement with Lenin's recommendation in the preface of the book, Penguin edition, 1970, p. 7. What the C.P.G.B. disliked about the book was not so much the mentions of Trotsky as the fact that Stalin himself hardly appears in it.

50. *News Chronicle*, 8th May 1937; cf. *The New Leader*, vol. xxxi, new series, no. 174, 14th May 1937, p. 4; *Fight*, vol. i, no. 7, June 1937.

51. V. Gollancz, Letter to Left Book Club Convenors, as quoted in *The New Leader*, vol. xxxi, new series, no. 178, 11th June 1937. Cf. Ivor Montagu on the Trials in *Left Book News*, October 1936.

52. *Controversy*, October 1937, p. 57.

53. John Archer, Interview with Martin Upham, p. 22.

54. John Robinson, Interview with Al Richardson, 3rd June 1976.

55. Gerry Bradley, Letter to *The New Leader*, vol. xxxi, new series, no. 220, 1st April 1938. The editorial comment makes clear that this was not the sole incident of this type.

56. *Daily Herald*, 13th June 1936; cf. the *Daily Worker*, 15th June 1936.

57. F. Adler, *The Witchcraft Trial in Moscow*, Labour Publications Department.

58. 'Citrine Sides with Traitors', in the *Daily Worker*, 24th August 1936. Cf. Bornstein and Richardson, *Two Steps Back*, p. 25.

59. 'Reply to *Daily Herald* on Soviet Trials', 1st July 1937, in *Report of the C.C. to the 15th Party Congress*, 16th–19th September 1938, p. 60. Cf. 'C.P. Answers Herald', in the *Daily Worker*, 1st July 1937.

60. 'Citrine Sides with Traitors', in the *Daily Worker*, 24th August 1936.

61. D.N. Pritt, K.C.M.P., 'Advises "Daily Herald" — Do Not Play the Game of Reaction', in the *Daily Worker*, 19th July 1937.

62. R. Page Arnot, 'The Soviet Trial', in *Labour Monthly*, vol. xx, no. 5, May 1938, p. 304.

63. R. Page Arnot, 'The Soviet Trial', in *Labour Monthly*, vol. xviii, no. 10, October 1936, p. 614.

64. Ibid., p. 616.

65. Cf. L.D. Trotsky, 'Permission to Use Articles', 14th December 1937', in *Writings of Leon Trotsky 1937–8*, New York, 1976, p. 104; Frank Maitland, 'The Antics of "Forward" ', in *Fight*, vol. i, no. 4, August 1938.

66. 'Workers' Diary', in the *Daily Worker*, 14th April 1938. Contrast this with the statements in 28th March 1938, etc.

67. Editorial, 'Spain and the U.S.S.R.', in *The New Leader*, vol. xxxi, new series, no. 181, 2nd July 1937, p. 2.

68. 'Lessons of the Soviet Trial', in the *Daily Worker*, 8th February 1937.

69. R. Palme Dutt, in the *Daily Worker*, 28th June 1937.

70. J.R. Campbell, 'Answers to Questions', in the *Daily Worker*, 8th March 1938.

71. Editorial, 'Brailsford Again', in the *Daily Worker*, 7th March 1938.

72. R. Palme Dutt, in the *Daily Worker*, 28th June 1937.

73. Editorial, 'Two Policies', in *The New Leader*, vol. xxvii, new series, no. 51, 4th January 1935, p. 2.

74. 'J.A.', 'Stalin and Trotsky: Frank Review of Barbusse's Book', in *The New Leader*, vol. xxix, new series, no. 98, 29th November 1935.

75. Editorial, 'Trotsky's Statement', in *The New Leader*, vol. xxix, no. 113, 13th March 1936, p. 2.

76. Editorial, 'Trotsky and the Soviet Trial'; F. Brockway, 'Doubts Caused by the Moscow Trial', in *The New Leader*, vol. xxx, new series, no. 137, 28th August 1936.

77. Fenner Brockway, 'How Can We Get Unity?', in *The New Leader*, vol. xxxi, new series, no. 151, 4th December 1936, p. 3.

78. Fenner Brockway, 'The Demand for Unity', in *The New Leader*, vol. xxxi, new series, no. 152, 11th December 1936, p. 2.

79. *The New Leader*, vol. xxxi, new series, no. 154, 25th December 1936, pp.1&3.

80. 'Trotsky Trial', in *The New Leader*, vol. xxxi, new series, no. 157, 15th January 1937, p. 3.

81. 'The Moscow Trial', in the *Annual Report of the N.A.C. of the I.L.P. for Annual Conference*, Glasgow, 27th–30th March 1937, p. 5.

82. 'Soviet Russia: War: The Internationals', in 'The I.L.P. in Conference', in *The New Leader*, vol. xxxi, new series, no. 168, 2nd April 1937, p. 5.

83. R. Page Arnot, 'The Soviet Trial', in *Labour Monthly*, vol. xviii, no. 10, October 1936, pp. 617–8.

84. Fenner Brockway, 'A Socialist World Round-About', in *The New Leader*, vol. xxxi, new series, no. 169, 9th April 1937, p. 3.

85. Fenner Brockway, Review of C.L.R. James', *World Revolution*, in *The New Leader*, vol. xxxi, new series, no. 170, 16th April 1937, p. 2.

86. L.D. Trotsky, 'Fenner Brockway — Pritt Number Two', 6th March 1937, in *Writings of Leon Trotsky*, 1936–7, New York, p. 221. The reference to 'raising prejudice in Russian and Communist circles' is taken by Trotsky from a letter of Brockway's to the U.S. Socialist Devere Allen.

87. Fenner Brockway, *Inside the Left*, London, 1942, p. 259.

88. *Daily Worker*, 10th June 1937. Cf. the similar letter from John Aplin in the issue of 3rd June.

89. Main Article (unsigned), 'He Heard — and He Believed — But it's Not True', in the *Daily Worker*, 23rd July 1937.

90. 'Workers' Diary', 'Two of a Kind', in the *Daily Worker*, 13th August 1937.

91. Editorial, 'Spain and the U.S.S.R.', in *The New Leader*, vol. xxxi, new series, no. 181, 2nd July 1937, p. 2.

92. 'The Communists and Unity' (Editorial), in *The New Leader*, vol. xxxi, new series, no. 200, 12th November 1937, p. 2.

93. Editorial, 11th March 1938.

94. James Maxton, 'It is Not Betrayal', in *The New Leader*, vol. xxxi, new series, no. 178, 11th June 1937, p. 5.

95. Fenner Brockway, op. cit., note 85 above, p. 2.

96. Ibid.

97. Fenner Brockway, 'The Tragedy of Trotsky', in *The New Leader*, vol. xxxi, new series, no. 190, 3rd September 1937, p. 2.

98. L.D. Trotsky, 'Remarks for an English Comrade', 8th April 1936, in *Writings of Leon Trotsky: Supplement, 1934–40*, New York, 1979, p. 653.

99. Harry Wicks, Interview with Al Richardson, 11th March and 1st April 1978.

100. John Goffe, Interview with Al Richardson, 18th May 1978.

101. 'Is This True?', in *The New Leader*, vol. xxix, new series, no. 103, 3rd January 1936, p. 6.

102. E. Robertson (Earle Birney), Letter in *The New Leader*, vol. xxix, new series, no. 106, 24th January 1936, p. 2. Cf. the letter from Jack Hammond in the same issue.

103. 'The Trotsky Investigation', in *The New Leader*, vol. xxx, new series, no. 141, 29th September 1936, p. 5.

104. *Letter from the Provisional Committee for the Defence of Leon Trotsky* (printed leaflet). Cf. 'Leon Trotsky', in *The New Leader*, vol. xxxi, new series, no. 151, 4th December 1936, p. 6.

105. F. Brockway, 'How Can We Get Unity?', in *The New Leader*, vol. xxxi, new series, no. 151, 4th December 1936, p. 3. Stewart Purkis, 'What Price Unity?', in *Red Flag*, new series, no. 5, January 1937.

106. Harry Wicks, Interview with Al Richardson, 11th March and 1st April 1978.

107. C. Sumner (Hilary Sumner-Boyd), 'The Case of Fenner Brockway', in the *Information Bulletin of the British Committee for the Defence of Leon Trotsky*, no. 2, July 1937, pp. 9–12.

108. Advertisement in *The New Leader*, vol. xxx, new series, no. 138, 4th

September 1936; Harry Wicks, Interview with Al Richardson, 11th March and 1st April 1978.

109. Advertisement in *The New Leader*, vol. xxxi, new series, no. 160, 5th February 1937, p. 6; Wicks, Interview with Al Richardson, 11th March and 1st April 1978.

110. 'Trotsky Defence Meeting', in *Fight*, vol. i, no. 4, February 1937, p. 5.

111. Hugo Dewar, Interview with Al Richardson, 7th April 1978.

112. Harry Wicks, Interview with Al Richardson, 11th March and 1st April 1978.

113. Advertisement in *The New Leader*, vol. xxxi, new series, no. 163, 26th February 1937, p. 6.

114. Margaret Johns, Interview with Al richardson, 4th February 1978.

115. Bert Atkinson, Interview with Sam Bornstein and Al Richardson, 4th November 1977.

116. John Goffe, Interview with Al Richardson, 18th May 1978.

117. Minutes of the E.C. for the London Area, Militant Group, 20th February 1937.

118. Harry Wicks, 'British Trotskyism in the Thirties', in *International* (I.M.G.), vol. i, no. 4, p. 32 (undated, but issued in 1971).

Chapter Nine

'And Then There Were Three'

The defeats for the revolutionaries in the I.L.P. coincided with a catastrophic decline in its membership and its influence. The original split with the Labour Party, made worse by the refusal to pay the political levy, had cost it a whole layer of working-class militants; the flirtations with Stalinism alienated others; the humiliation of the Abyssinian affair had almost completed the party's ruin. The referendum carried on at that time showed that the party's real strength was hardly in excess of a thousand.[1] At the same time, the recovery registered by the Labour Party in the municipal elections of 1934 had continued with the General Election of 14th November 1935. Not only was the I.L.P. stagnating, but it was fast becoming a political irrelevance in working-class terms.

The fortunes of the Marxist Group could only be shaped by its I.L.P. environment, and the early successes and rapid growth had now changed into stagnation and loss of members. The disintegration of the I.L.P. left the group without perspective, its leadership split with factional conflict and its most dominant section, led by James, Cooper, Ballard and Marzillier, began to move in an ultra-leftist direction. Disillusioned with the I.L.P.'s lack of progress towards a revolutionary standpoint, C.L.R. James had been visiting South Wales, where he had been well received at a W.E.A. Conference of two to three hundred miners' delegates whom he had addressed.[2] Having witnessed a sit-down strike, he described it as 'the steps (on a larger scale) by which a revolutionary period suddenly boils over into a revolutionary situation',[3] whereas nationally he believed that 'the stage is set for a great mass swing to the left.'[4] At the same time, he considered that 'the ruling classes, broadly speaking, are pro-Fascist' and that 'if, as is quite likely, their attempts to escape their League commitments discredit them completely, then the ruling class will turn to their bands of organised hooligans and unemployed middle-class.'[5] 'Parliament is now dangerous for the Imperialists,' he explained: 'They will turn to Fascism. That is the next move, and we must be ready.'[6] Apart from being an erroneous assessment of the British situation, it was precisely the concept they had opposed in the I.L.P., that the ruling class 'advances' Fascism as a means of counteracting a movement to the Left. It was far from being Trotskyist, having more in common with the views expressed by F.A. Ridley, or of the Communist Party during their tragic 'Third Period' phase. In concrete terms, this movement towards 'leftist' positions expressed itself in extreme hostility towards the Labour Party in the context of the General Election of November 1935 — a hostility in which their position was indistinguishable from the rest of the I.L.P., and which in the end they could not carry through:

> It was necessary, facing the General Election, to have an attitude towards the Labour candidates, because there were so few I.L.P. candidates. We couldn't pretend we were supporting the I.L.P. and not the Labour Party, and the outstanding row, in fact I think it was the first big row in the group, occurred at this time. The group split on whether we should support the Labour candidates in the coming General Election. The split had been caused by a Labour Party decision to support the government on the matter of sanctions. I don't recall very clearly what the issue was, but I recall most vividly simply the effect on the group, that it split. I think it was Margaret Johns and myself, possibly one or two others, who recognised that the Labour Party's attitude was not the question at all, but that we had to support the Labour Party in its electoral fights. We were defeated. I myself was already committed in the Election to some activity (I can't remember quite how it came about). I was in Finchley at that time, and I felt that I can't follow the group in taking no part in the election, and I told them I would break politically, for which I was suspended. I remember shortly after this Comrade Robertson went to see the Old Man in Oslo where he was then, firmly believing that I would be very, very severely castigated for supporting the Labour Party. But before he had come back, the Election had occurred, and everyone except C.L.R. James had broken discipline and supported and voted in the Election for the Labour candidates. C.L.R. James I remember as the one person who stood out.[7]

Apart from the Marxist League, who were by now largely active in the Labour Party, a number of the younger Trotskyists, basically of the L.S.E. group, had begun to trickle over from the I.L.P. to the

Labour Party. From the first there had been much less logic in being active among the I.L.P. Guild of Youth, which was quite small, than in the Labour League of Youth, which at this time numbered some 15,000. For reasons that remain obscure, already by November 1934 Denzil Harber had left both the group and the I.L.P. and become active in the Labour League of Youth.[8] By June of the next year he had been elected as organiser of the sales of the newspaper of the Socialist League in the London area.[9] An invaluable asset already existed in the League of Youth in Roma Dewar, Hugo's sister, who was on its National Advisory Council, and had a job as a sales-demonstrator, which enabled her to travel around the country and make contacts with young people outside London.[10] At this time both Trotskyists and Stalinists were together in support of the unofficial paper *Advance*, in temporary alliance due to their opposition to the foreign policy of the Labour leaderhip,[11] but in October 1935 the Trotskyists produced the duplicated paper *Youth Militant*, which advertised itself in its first issue as 'the first result of a committee of young socialists in organised youth movements.'[12]

The new group grew up in the Labour League of Youth and the Socialist League, but without a worked-out perspective to begin with. 'There had already been a splintering-off of the people from the I.L.P. to the Labour Party before 1936,' explained Margaret Johns later: 'But already Harber had left and joined the Socialist League, I think he reckoned because there was nobody else in the I.L.P. in London to win. It might be possible to recruit outside, but as far as London was concerned everybody had made up their minds of where they stood, and that was it.'[13] Tony Doncaster left the I.L.P. group along with Harber, and to begin with, apart from Roma Dewar, they concentrated on the Socialist League, much to the irritation of Reg Groves, already active there. From it were recruited Mary Whittaker, later Harber's wife, and two others from Eastbourne. Roma Dewar shared the editing of *Youth Militant* with Haseler of the East Islington Labour League of Youth, and from the League they brought in Sid Bone and Fred Emmett, who was to play an important part in the Trotskyist agitation in the Engineering Union during the War. At the same time they recruited Sid Bidwell, who was to bring them much-needed support in the railway union.

Whilst their entry into the Labour Party took place in a totally unorganised and empirical manner, it was not without precedent in the thinking of the Trotskyist movement. Groves and the Marxist League had already shown that there were important gains to be made there, and at the time of the Labour successes in the municipal elections in the spring of 1934 the International Secretariat had pointed out that 'the I.L.P. can perform serious work only in case it becomes the revolutionary lever influencing the masses of the

Labour Party and of the trade unions', and enquired of the Trotskyists active in the I.L.P. 'as to what conclusions from the last municipal elections your organisation has drawn for its future activity.'[14] The group's reaction at the time had been to concentrate on reversing the I.L.P.'s decision to stop paying the political levy in the trade unions, and on trying to get the I.L.P. to turn its back on the Communist Party and face towards the Labour Party, as advised by Trotsky.[15] But Harber at least had looked beyond this:

> It must be remembered that we cannot guarantee winning the I.L.P. as a party to our position. It may be that under certain circumstances we may be forced to split, taking with us out of the I.L.P. as many comrades as we can. With this possibility in mind it is especially important to make all members of the fraction real Bolshevik–Leninists, so that in the event of a split becoming necessary comrades shall not let themselves be influenced [by] considerations of sentiment, etc., but should resolutely adopt the correct revolutionary line.[16]

The question of whether the group should support Labour Party candidates in the November 1935 General Election showed, indeed, that most of its members had become influenced by their I.L.P. milieu and 'considerations of sentiment', and brought the whole matter to a head. So the two Canadians, Earle Birney and Ken Johnson, travelled to Hönefoss to find out Trotsky's opinion on the matter, and to work out a policy for the future in the I.L.P. Whilst agreeing that the I.L.P. was correct to run as many candidates as it could, even at the risk of splitting the Labour vote, he denied that the I.L.P. should have refused support to Labour candidates in the other seats who supported military sanctions against Italy:

> It should have given critical support to ALL Labour Party candidates, that is, where the I.L.P. itself was not contesting . . . The Labour Party should have been critically supported not because it was for or against sanctions but because it represented the working masses . . . The war crisis does not alter the fact that the Labour Party leadership cannot fulfil its promises, that it will betray the confidence which the masses place in it. In peacetime the workers will, if they trust in Social Democracy, die of hunger; in war, for the same reason, they will die from bullets. Revolutionists never give critical support to reformism on the assumption that reformism, in power, could satisfy the fundamental needs of the workers.. . .
>
> No, in war as in peace, the I.L.P. must say to the workers: 'The Labour Party will deceive you and betray you, but you do not believe us. Very well, we will go through your experiences with

> you, but in no case do we identify ourselves with the Labour Party programme' . . .
>
> As a general principle, a revolutionary party has the right to boycott parliament only when it has the capacity to overthrow it, that is, when it can replace parliamentary action by general strike and insurrection, by direct struggle for power.

Whilst he denied that the total entry of the I.L.P. into the Labour Party was posed as yet, it was not ruled out for the future. The case was quite otherwise with the Labour League of Youth:

> Since the I.L.P. youth seem to be few and scattered, while the Labour Youth is the mass youth organisation, I would say: Do not build fractions — seek to enter. For here the danger of Stalinist devastation is extreme. The youth are all-important. Unlike the older generation they have little actual experience of war; it will be easier for the Stalinists and the other pseudo-revolutionary patriots to confuse the youth on the war issues than to confuse those who survived the last war. On the other hand, the willingness of the Stalinists to drive these same youth into another actual war will make the young workers properly suspicious. They will listen more easily to us — if we are there to speak to them. No time must be lost. Out of the new generation comes the new International, the only hope for the world revolution. The British Section will recruit its first cadres from the thirty thousand young workers in the Labour League of Youth. Their more advanced comrades in the I.L.P. youth must not allow themselves to be isolated from them, especially now at the very moment when war is a real danger.[17]

At the same time, Trotsky came to the conclusion that 'there isn't much to be done with the I.L.P.', and worked out a plan with Birney and Johnson to draw up a manifesto addressed to the I.L.P., collect signatures in support of it, and leave to join the Labour Party.[18] In order to investigate the problem in the meantime — for opinion was by no means unanimous on the International Secretariat — Peter Schmidt of the Dutch organisation, which had collaborated with the I.L.P. on the London Bureau, was sent to London in January 1936 to confer with the group. Although Schmidt was making his visit as Secretary of the International movement, Trotsky realised that he had been 'tied by long friendship' to Brockway, and had 'perhaps a certain uneasiness, not to say mistrust, toward our friends as "sectarians" '. For this reason Trotsky wrote to Earle Birney, not only to help Schmidt make contacts and gather information, but to warn the British comrades that 'he would perhaps rather be inclined to insist on the necessity of our comrades continuing their work in the I.L.P.'[19]

Trotsky's doubts were well-founded. Schmidt judged Trotsky's plan on the manifesto and the split to be incorrect, and advised the International Secretariat and the Marxist Group to delay their decision until the clash in the I.L.P. over the Abyssinian question was settled at the following Easter Conference of the I.L.P. Schmidt's intervention had the effect of postponing the decision to split, as well as strengthening the resolve of those who did not wish to leave the I.L.P. at all. Schmidt himself broke with the Trotskyists later in the year and went back to Social Democracy. 'To lose two or three months in a critical period is always a great loss,' commented Trotsky ruefully.[20]

The comrades inside the Labour League of Youth decided to go ahead, and in February they formally set up the 'Bolshevik–Leninist Group in the Labour Party' with six members and with Johnson (K.V. Alexander) as its secretary.[21] From these small beginnings they slowly began to pick up supporters. Among the first of these was Charles Van Gelderen, still a militant in the Trotskyist movement, who had been a member of one of the two Trotskyist groups in South Africa, the Communist League, and had come to England for experience in the Labour movement:

> . . . when I came to London in December 1935 I contacted the Marxist Group, through Grant and Frost (his name was Bosch, actually), and through them I came into contact with the group inside the I.L.P. By that time there was already a turn towards the Labour Party. Bert Matlow had already put forward the position of entry into the Labour Party, and Harber and Margaret Johns and a few others had already entered the Labour Party. People like Emmett were already in the Labour League of Youth, and Roma Dewar. They produced a paper called the *Youth Militant*, and Roma and a man called Haseler were the editors. So the Marxist Group immediately directed me to go into the Labour Party and the Labour League of Youth. I was living in Stepney at the time, and I joined the Stepney Labour League of Youth about two weeks before their annual general meeting, and two weeks later I was elected on to the management committee . . . I then came on to the editorial staff of *Youth Militant* and on the executive of the Youth Militant Group.[22]

Significant for the functioning of the group was the recruitment in March 1936 of the remarkable figure of E. Starkey Jackson. Although still young, Jackson was already a veteran of the Labour and revolutionary movement. Hailing from Birmingham, he had become active in the Labour League of Youth whilst still at Grammar school, from which he was expelled for smoking. He became one of the youngest ever secretaries of a local Labour Party, apparently at the age of fourteen or fifteen, and became a clerk on the London Underground. Active as a picket during the General Strike, he was victimised and lost his job. Within the Labour League of Youth he was prominent in the opposition to Barbara Best (now Barbara Castle), and was joint secretary of the first British Young Workers' delegation which visited Russia between 1st October and 15th November 1926,[23] where he appeared on the platform along with Stalin at an official function at Rostov-on-Don. On his return from the Soviet Union, he broke with the Labour Party and joined the Y.C.L., becoming editor of their youth journal, *The Young Worker*. Unable to get a job after 1926, he was active in the Unemployed Workers' Movement, and on one occasion spent six months in jail after one of their demonstrations had been assaulted by the police. By 1929 he had become openly critical of the Communist Party's ultra-leftism during its 'Third Period' phase, and they expelled him, claiming that he had misappropriated party funds. Ostracised from the movement to which he had given his whole life, and unable to get a job, he eked out a demoralised existence on the margins of society for many years, where at one time he was jailed again when reduced to forging florins to get cigarettes from slot machines. Harber met him, restored his morale, and gave him back his faith in the working-class movement, and he became active with Leigh Davis in the Willesden area, and shortly afterwards organiser of the Youth Militant Group itself. Jackson was dedicated and tireless, and brought to the group the invaluable asset of his long experience in the working-class movement. He and Harber worked as a team: 'He had a good deal of experience, more than many of us,' recalls Margaret Johns, 'he was a good speaker; he used to say that Harber made the bullets, and he fired them.'[24] As Van Gelderen described him:

> He really kept the organisation together in the pre-War days. He was absolutely indefatigable as a worker — writing an article, writing a pamphlet, hitch-hiking all over the country or cycling. He would bike from here to Glagow! We couldn't afford the fares in those days. He had no money, was living on the dole of fifteen shillings a week, comrades were feeding him and giving him clothes, and so on — but his whole life was devoted to the movement. He was also a thinker, thought in theoretical terms, and to my mind he was the corner-stone of the Trotskyist movement in Britain in the years before the War.[25]

Factional disputes were by now troubling the Marxist Group itself, for the I.L.P. Keighley Conference had shown that I.L.P. work was coming to a dead-end. 'The idea of turning the I.L.P. into a revolutionary party,' wrote Trotsky, 'must now be described as utopian. We must construct an independent perspective for the revolutionary party.'[26] At the same time the members of the Marxist Group began to vote with their feet, showing that the decision to postpone the split had been a mistaken one:

> . . . Gradually the Marxist Group started to crumble after the Keighley Conference. For one thing, organised factions were banned, which made the work difficult, and it was then that the whole organisation divided itself between people who had joined the Marxist Group but were still I.L.P. loyalists in a way, and the people who were looking for a more profitable field of work. So it was rather a disorganised exodus towards the Labour Party. But it was, in a way, a logical step from the idea of critical support to the Labour Party in elections, that this was the mass organisation of the workers, and that entry into the I.L.P. had inevitably been a temporary measure —one won the I.L.P., or one left the I.L.P. — it was not a place one stayed forever, particularly as it was a dwindling organisation. But there was a section who were just unwilling to leave, and others who took longer about it. It was, as I say, a rather disorganised departure and re-entry into the Labour Party.[27]

The case for leaving the I.L.P. and joining the Labour Party was put to the Marxist Group by Bert Matlow. He analysed a growth in production and trade union membership, and prophesied a strike wave, which would swing the working class to the left. Their pressure in turn would oblige the Labour bureaucrats to turn leftwards, which would bring increasing numbers of workers into the trade unions and the Labour Party. At the same time, betrayal of this movement by the Labour leaders would mean increased support for the Communist Party, which was already making great progress. Resolutions supporting its affiliation to the Labour Party showed the extent of its support, and the Communists in the *Advance* group in the Labour League of Youth were already preparing for a merger with the Y.C.L. 'In the situation as described above,' he concluded, 'the I.L.P. will have no attractive force for the masses. The recent plebiscite has shown that it has no more than 1,400 active members, and thus has ceased to be a party in any real sense of the word. In any case its roots in the unions are insignificant, and its isolation from the mass movement and its lack of a clear policy make it certain that any left turn will pass it by entirely.' The I.L.P., being 'a minute centrist "party" ', was bankrupt, work within it was 'entirely unproductive', and it was a block on the way to influencing the mass youth movement. In order to prevent the development of a Popular

Front the Trotskyists must go to the masses, accepting 'the necessity of our at once putting the whole of the forces at our disposal into the mass organisations — the trade unions, the Labour Party and the Labour League of Youth, the Co-operatives, etc. — in order to fight to win the left-moving workers from Stalinist influence and to lay the basis for the new party.' 'At the moment,' he added, 'the struggle is most acute inside the Labour League of Youth but the very near future may see it spread over a far wider field.'[28]

Opposition to leaving the I.L.P. immediately and joining the Labour Party was led by Arthur Cooper, supported by Ballard, Pawsey and Marzillier. Noting the threat of a Popular Front behind the Communist Party's campaign for affiliation to the Labour Party, they held that it 'must be opposed', because 'there it will be a thousand times more dangerous and difficult to crush.' But they intended to attempt to do this from outside, because 'the bureaucratic machinery and the electoral basis of the L.P. render utopian the question of open revolutionary entry', and 'the reformist leaders will willingly agree to a united front only if revolutionary principles are sacrificed, if not in words, at any rate in practice.' Instead of full entry, they advocated that members of the Marxist Group should be the 'most active I.L.P.ers', that they should utilise the I.L.P. platform for revolutionary propaganda, that 'the group must continue its associations within the I.L.P. with a short-term split perspective', with the Annual Conference — a year away — as 'the final point of struggle'. The only concession they would make to entry was that in view of the serious position inside the Labour League of Youth all available youth forces were to be sent in to stop the Stalinists lining it up behind the Popular Front.[29]

Cooper replied to Matlow by taking up in detail the points of his analysis. He said that neither his strike wave, nor his left-wing movement inside the Labour Party 'of any account' had materialised, but that 'an expulsion of left sections in the Labour Party is also a likelihood in the near future':

> Above all, the Group MUST avoid being used as a tool of the Labour bureaucracy in its fight against centrist elements . . . Entrenched with mints of money, defended by armies of careerists in a field where there are no rocks of theory to give us shelter; the L.P. need not fear us until the mass strike movement begins (if a war does not come first), and by that time outer isolation will have received us . . . Lastly, I believe that work in the L.P. can easily lead to the development in the group of opportunism. Groves and Harber are already travelling along that road. . . . our entry into the I.L.P. will be

> misunderstood by the leftward masses. We will either be 'politically dishonest' or 'moving to the right'.

He pointed out (as many opponents of entrism since have done) that unlike in France during 'the French Turn', there was not as yet in England a mass movement to the left, but that 'of political groupings the I.L.P. alone moves towards a correct revolutionary line.' Whilst he did not rule out the forming of fractions inside the Labour Party, Cooper felt that it was not impossible that the I.L.P. would revive again, if the P.O.U.M. in Spain refused to declare for the Fourth International, which would 'lead to the triumph of the London Bureau and the rescue of the I.L.P. leadership.' Leaving the I.L.P. in such circumstances would be a grave mistake:

> We must leave the I.L.P. only on the non-acceptance of a minimum programme at the next annual conference. This must follow a tearing campaign for acceptance throughout the country. If the group leaves an intact I.L.P. the rump will forever be a danger.[30]

In the meantime, Trotsky's opinion that immediate entry into the Labour Party was the correct tactic was hardening. He knew that Schmidt's intervention had delayed the necessary decision and lost valuable time, in view of the increased penetration of the Communists into the Labour League of Youth:

> To continue now with an effort to revive an illusion which has been shattered to bits would be nothing less than to inflict a bad service on the cause. In times of calm, one can live on illusions for a long period; in a period of crisis, if one does not take into account the hard facts — that is, the actual policy of centrism and pacifism, and consequently their deeds — but considers one's own wishes and sentiments, one courts the danger of becoming the shadow of the centrists and pacifists and of compromising and destroying one's own organisation. That is why I deem it absolutely necessary for our own comrades to break openly with the I.L.P. and to transfer to the Labour Party where, as is shown especially by the experience in the youth, much more can be accomplished.[31]

But as yet none of the groups in Britain was aware of Trotsky's return to this view, so Sam Collins of the Marxist Group, who had just saved up the money for his summer holidays, volunteered to go to Norway and find out. As Charles Van Gelderen recalls:

> I was living with the Collinses in Highbury. Collins was a political nonentity, a taxi-cab driver. At the meeting, which was a joint meeting of the Marxist Group with us, he suddenly

> got up and said that 'At the end of July, my wife and I will be going on holiday to Norway, and if you wish me to contact Trotsky, I will try and do so.' And that's how he became famous. He was supporting Cooper, who was very hostile to entering into the Labour Party, and Cooper drafted the questions for the interview . . . Collins came back an absolutely convinced entrist after his interview with Trotsky![32]

Marzillier similarly remembers Collins as 'a very dedicated and enthusiastic London worker with very little intellectual background of history', whose 'attachment to the group was based more on emotions than on reasoning.'[33]

But before Collins arrived in Hönefoss to submit his questions to Trotsky, the first International Conference for the Fourth International had met in Paris,[34] from 29th to 31st July. To it travelled Denzil Harber from the Bolshevik–Leninist Group in the Labour Party, and C.L.R. James from the Marxist Group, together with two more British observers. Harber submitted Matlow's paper to the Conference, and C.L.R. James a similar series of documents and a resolution from his organisation. His material described the I.L.P. as 'the only independent working-class party in Britain', and denied that it was 'half Stalinist'. As it was 'still possible to work within the Party by using democratic machinery which is non-existent in the Labour Party or the C.P.G.B.', the majority of the group had decided to 'continue to work in the I.L.P.' But an immediate split was ruled out:

> To endeavour to form in Britain a new revolutionary party without the participation of these leftward moving proletarians in the I.L.P. is a much more difficult task than to continue to work with the party in a faction and, by broadening our basis in the party, to create a skeleton organisation for the new revolutionary party. To leave our work unfinished by breaking with the I.L.P. at this stage would be looked upon by the comrades who have come half our way as an act of desertion, and the blame of breaking up the I.L.P., whom they still regard as a potentially revolutionary party, will be placed on us.[35]

The resolution that accompanied this held that 'possibilities of work in the I.L.P. are not yet exhausted', and asked other British Trotskyists 'not to indulge in activities outside or inside the I.L.P. which in the opinion of a majority of the group will compromise its work in the I.L.P.'[36]

But this resolution only received two votes — that of James himself and the Belgian comrade, whose own resolution, that the Marxist Group should work within the I.L.P. until excluded and then set up an independent party, fell by the same margin. After listening to reports from Britain, the Conference approved the famous 'Geneva Resolution' by a majority of delegate votes (ten) instructing the three existing British groups to unite behind a perspective of entry into the Labour Party. It demanded the unification of the groups as an 'urgent necessity to effect with the least possible delay', saw 'no principled reason for such a division of the forces', and demanded 'a fusion on a democratic basis'. Continuation of the Marxist Group in the I.L.P., even with their new-planned journal, was a waste of valuable time, and left it 'without a real or clear perspective for a long period'. For the urgent necessity was for an exit from the I.L.P. and a turn to the Labour Party:

> The Conference is further of the opinion that the experience of the Bolshevik–Leninists within the I.L.P. must be brought to an end and that the group which at this moment is working in that organisation must shift its field of work in the direction of the mass organisations, especially towards the Labour Party and the Labour League of Youth . . . Their membership of the I.L.P. rises like an impenetrable wall between the Bolshevik–Leninists and the mass movement of the youth, potential reservoir of revolutionaries, from which the British Section of the Fourth International will draw the greater part of its cadres — as well as the base of the Labour Party. It is necessary to know, not only the moment at which it is profitable for revolutionary Marxists to enter a reformist or centrist organisation, but also the moment when it is imperative to leave it, and to implant their movement and their ideas in another milieu. The I.L.P. today is nothing but a centrist sect in decline; further work within it can only condemn our forces to mark time and vegetate in a restricted arena. The Labour Party, the Trades Unions and in particular the reformist organisation of the youth offer much greater possibilities to strengthen our movement and speed the growth of the section of the Fourth International in Britain.[37]

A few days later Sam Collins arrived at Hönefoss and submitted his questions to Trotsky. On every principled question Trotsky agreed completely with Matlow's paper over against that of Cooper. He argued that the group should not oppose Communist affiliation to the Labour Party, as this would cut across the 'mass desire for unity', and in any case when the Communists came in they would immediately expose themselves by lining up with the right wing. However, the question was abstract in the first place unless the group itself was in the Labour Party to begin with. On this, Matlow was '100 per cent correct'. A strike wave in the near future would 'drive the last nail into the coffin of the I.L.P.' 'The idea of remaining inside the I.L.P. for a further period in order to win a few more wavering elements, while the C.P. is rapidly penetrating into the mass organisations, is ridiculous,' he remarked, and added that 'the suggestion of a time limit such a the next annual conference of the I.L.P. in April is incomprehensible to me.' Time was fast running out, and it was necessary to get into the Labour Party 'as rapidly as possible'. Cooper's document was described as rigid and formalistic, with 'no relationship to Marxism at all', and as showing a 'complete lack of comprehension of the class struggle'. His final remarks should have burned themselves into every 'Trotskyist' since:

> Q. Is it even possible to consider at this stage an independent existence outside the mass organisations?
>
> A. The fact that Lenin was not afraid to split from Plekhanov in 1905 and to remain as a small isolated group bears no weight, because the same Lenin remained inside the Social Democracy until 1912 and in 1920 urged the affiliation of the British C.P. to the Labour Party. While it is necessary for the revolutionary party to maintain its independence at all times, a revolutionary group of a few hundred comrades is not a revolutionary party and can work most effectively at present by opposition to the social patriots within the mass parties. In view of the increasing acuteness of the international situation, it is absolutely essential to be within the mass organisations while there is the possibility of doing revolutionary work within them. Any such sectarian, sterile, and formalistic interpretation of Marxism in the present situation would disgrace an intelligent child of ten.[38]

In Britain the problem was solving itself in a concrete manner, as the Marxist Group began to disintegrate throughout the summer, and its members drifted over to the Bolshevik–Leninist Group in the Labour Party. In Sheffield, Goffe resigned from the I.L.P. with half a dozen members and entered the Labour Party, and Leigh Davis and Starkey Jackson wrote to John Archer in Leeds, 'summing up the experiences of the I.L.P. entry, drawing the conclusion that this entry had served its purpose, should not be prolonged, and very strongly making the case for a Bolshevik organisation to work as a secret faction inside the Labour Party.'[39] He joined, as did Mary Archer three months later. One of the last to go over was John Robinson:

> With the failure of the I.L.P. to re-affiliate, turn its attention to the working class — the organised working class — the

> perspective in the I.L.P. was becoming dimmer and dimmer, and it was quite natural that we would think in terms of virtually affiliating ourselves by individually joining the Labour Party. However, we were in the I.L.P. and it was necessary to get all — or as many as possible — to do the same, and I was the one who seemed to have been told off to argue the case in the I.L.P. I think it was a post of honour, but it did lead to me being one of the last members of the group inside the I.L.P. Everyone else had already gone into the Labour Party, and I recall pleading with the group to let me join the Labour Party, because I was fed up with the sterile sort of work inside the I.L.P. Everyone who was worth anything had already gone.[40]

By August 1936 the group had recruited 30 members in London from the Marxist Group and inside the Labour League of Youth,[41] and at the same time they recruited the whole of the Marble Arch group around Jock Haston.[42] This was a discussion circle of thirteen people formed after he had broken his links with the Communist Party in 1934:

> When I first began to question the C.P. line I still sold the *Daily Worker*, but at Marble Arch I came into contact with the Socialist Party of Great Britain, and a guy who was then the Secretary of the S.P.G.B. called Cohn. He gave me a terrible hammering one night on my 'Leninism', and I spent the whole night reading, and when I went back the following night he gave me a bigger hammering. For some months after that I used to attend S.P.G.B. meetings, and learned a great deal from the S.P.G.B. over the course of the next eight or nine months. But then I came across Trotsky's pamphlet *What Next for Germany?* and then *The Only Road*, and these made a very profound impression on me. [There was] a bookseller in Red Lion Square at that time called Charlie Lahr. I used to spend hours in his basement going through old material, where he had a lot of American Trotskyist stuff. He had nothing of the British Trotskyist movement, so I didn't know there was a British Trotskyist movement at that time. But I then decided actually that this was the line, you know, that I wanted to follow, and I set up a discussion group in Hyde Park, with a number of people discussing Trotskyism. We started, actually, with *What Next?*, and then *The Only Road*, and eventually we started to read the *New International*, which was the American theoretical publication at that time, and that became the basis of our discussion group . . . In fact, it wasn't till a year, or a couple of years, in fact, before we learned that there were

> Trotskyist organisations in this country, and we learned that through the Americans . . . Before we met the Militant Group, we met the Balham Group, and had some discussions with the Balham Group. We then had some discussions with the group that were in the I.L.P., and then we met the Militant Group. So at that time we had discussions with three quite distinct groups. All of them were appealing to us that tactically they were doing what's right for the Trotskyist movement in this country. In the end, some time in 1936, we decided that the Militant Group had the perspective that we agreed with, and the Paddington Group went into the Militant Group.[43]

Collins had got back from Norway by this time, and the discussion around leaving the I.L.P. had revived again with equal force within the Marxist Group. Collins himself, and the Liverpool group of Don James, Henry Cund and Douglas Orton had now come over to the entrist point of view, and the International Secretariat had sent over Braun (Erwin Wolf) to try and press their case. Preparations were made to settle the question at a group conference on 10th October, to be followed by a conference of all the groups to implement the 'Geneva Resolution' on unification. At the same time the Marxist Group and the Militant Group decided to mark the occasion by having their new magazine, *Fight*, appear at the same time as the Conference, despite Wolf's warning that it would provoke 'coercive measures' from the I.L.P. leadership.[44] The appeal leaflet put out with the co-operation of the Youth Militant Group described the Trotskyists as 'fighting for the Fourth International, which aims at leading the united workers and those sympathetic to them against capitalism', whilst describing them as 'scattered in various parties'.[45] The first issue duly appeared, dated to the day of the Conference.[46]

Meanwhile the tendency supported by Cooper, Ballard, Pawsey and Marzillier could not believe the information that Collins was laying before the group from his recent meeting with Trotsky. 'Poor O(ld) M(an), how is he misrepresented', was the immediate reaction:

> I cannot believe that cde. O.M. said that we must make the issue of affiliation to the Labour Party a pretext for leaving the I.L.P. I am certain that he would see that we had not previously had a campaign throughout the party on this, and to suddenly bring it forward, and after a campaign which (if, again, the report can be taken as correct) would only be a matter of a few days — since we are told we must enter the Labour Party immediately — looks and would look to the ordinary member of the Labour Party as a deliberate move to make an excuse to leave the

> I.L.P., which of course, would be a correct view of our leaving.[47]

A suggestion was made that a campaign in the I.L.P. on the Moscow Trials would be a more valid issue on which to split.

The first session of the Conference of 16 delegates and 18 sympathisers on Saturday 10th October was to settle the points at issue inside the Marxist Group itself, the session on the following day being devoted to open discussion on relations with the two other groups. Bert Matlow, as group chairman, was allowed to vacate the chair, as he wished to defend the Labour Party perspective from the floor of the Conference. C.L.R. James began with a report of the Geneva Conference of the International Bureau, and introduced along with it a resolution of his own interpreting it in terms that would be acceptable for the Marxist Group. It proposed the fusion of all existing groups 'independent of any political party', doing 'fraction work in various political parties', with an independent press and meetings. This was, in effect, a return of the position adopted by the Communist League in the period up to 1934, and was far from a wholehearted adoption of the total entry demanded by the International movement. In this direction it admitted that 'at the present moment the main field of work of a new organisation should be the Labour Party and considers that the new organisation should take immediate steps to strengthen the present B[olshevik] L[eninist] position in the Labour Party.' But at the same time, it 'considers it inadmissible that all its members be asked to leave the I.L.P. at once or within a fixed time.'[48] It was a cleverly constructed resolution, designed to appeal both to those who wished to leave the I.L.P. and set up an open group and those who wished to stay in it, but it was a clear evasion of the full entry issue raised by the I.S., as James admitted when Harber, as observer from his group, asked him point-blank whether his resolution interpreted the Geneva Resolution 'in the sense that the I.S. meant it to be interpreted'.[49] The paper passed narrowly by thirteen to twelve delegate votes in its first part and eleven to ten in its second. Among those voting against was Don James, representing the view of the Liverpool Group of himself, Doug Orton and Henry Cund, who ranged himself alongside 'Harber, the I.S. and the Old Man'.

Collins spoke for the entry position. He began by pointing out that only if the group passed the Labour Party entry perspective could the Conference be accepted as solving all the problems of the group once and for all. 'As regards the perspective of the I.L.P. group,' he affirmed, 'we can do no better than repeat the unequivocal remarks of Comrade O[ld] M[an], during his talk with Collins, when he stated that the idea of remaining inside the disintegrating I.L.P. in order to win a few more wavering elements, whilst the C.P. is rapidly penetrating into the mass organisations, is ridiculous and shows a lack of comprehension of the dynamic of the present revolutionary resurgence of Europe.'[50] 'He enlarged on his interviews with Cde. O[ld] M[an] (which has been circulated) and stated that he found the O.M. better informed than himself on British affairs.' 'There was nothing in the Cooper paper to commit the Marxist Group to break at the Easter Conference of the I.L.P.,' he noted, and threatened that 'members of the Islington Group considered the matter so important that they were prepared to leave the group and enter the Labour Party.'[51] Speaking for Cooper's point of view, Arthur Ballard could only note that 'the Old Man had been wrong on a number of organisational and political questions', and Joe Pawsey, that Trotsky 'had never understood the organisational structure of the British Labour movement.' As far as the I.L.P. itself was concerned, C.L.R. James made the unfortunate remark that 'there was no evidence that the I.L.P. would collapse; the Old Man had prophesied that the P.O.U.M. would collapse, and it had not done so.'[52] Next, Cooper moved his paper to argue against a wholesale withdrawal from the I.L.P., which would rally the remaining good elements 'around the leadership and would leave in existence a potentially dangerous centrist party'. 'The I.L.P. still offers great freedom of speech and action to Bolshevik–Leninists and the opportunities to organise mass work,' he maintained, whereas 'membership of the Labour Party, on the other hand, imposes powerful restraints of advocacy.'[53] Cooper's paper was endorsed by the conference by 13 votes to 8 along with that of C.L.R. James, though the emphasis of the one was upon an essentially independent group operating fractions inside other organisations, and of the other on continued work inside the I.L.P.

The position was further complicated when they came to discuss amendments to resolutions. Don James proposed amending C.L.R. James' resolution by deleting all the qualifications that would enable I.L.P. and open work to continue in equal measure with Labour Party work, and substituting instead that the group 'therefore supports the line laid down in the resolution on Britain passed at the Geneva Conference, i.e. that the group as a whole should leave the I.L.P. immediately and join the Labour Party', whilst conceding that a fraction should be left to work in the I.L.P.[54] This suggestion fell by thirteen votes to eight, but so did Cooper's amendment that 'the Marxist Group insists that no forces should be withdrawn from the I.L.P. which might reduce the effectiveness of the political struggle inside the party', by a similar margin, thirteen votes to ten.[55] It was plain that the conference was divided among three different viewpoints, of which the one with the largest single following — for the Labour Party tactic — was being outvoted by a combination of the other two.

Even more confusing were the results of the open session on the following day, which included representatives from all three of the Trotskyist Groups to discuss the unity proposals of the 'Geneva' resolution. Here the Labour Party orientation should have come through easily, as the other two groups were both committed to it, and with their co-thinkers in the Marxist Group easily made up a majority of the British Trotskyists. But deep antagonisms separated the Marxist League from the 'Youth Militant', and in fact the philosophy and mode of operation of the Marxist League were closer to those of the supporters of C.L.R. James. A statement handed by their representative, Harry Wicks, to the joint session of 39 delegates from the Marxist Group, 26 from the Youth Militant and the three from the Marxist League recognised that 'the widest possible diffusion of Bolshevik–Leninist views was valuable preparatory work which it was necessary to carry on in as many organisations as possible in the period prior to the formation of an independent organisation.' For this reason they opposed 'a purely formal decision to leave the I.L.P. and enter the L[abour] P[arty]', but suggested instead that the comrades in the I.L.P. carry on propaganda there for unity of that organisation with the Labour Party, and that in any case making the issue of the Fourth International the main reason for leaving the I.L.P. 'would make them the laughing-stock of the left-wing workers'. Besides, they believed themselves that 'the period of exclusive work within the L[abour] P[arty] is drawing to a close' and that the struggle between its leaders and its rank-and-file would 'pose before the left-wing workers in the L.P. the question of a new revolutionary Socialist Party.'[56]

This was more than halfway towards the view of C.L.R. James, and left Harber and his group alone to defend the full Labour Party orientation. He pointed out that they had been approaching the Marxist League for several months, for joint meetings to discuss fusion, without success. With the Marxist Group they had set up a joint E.C. to co-operate with them in trade union work and in the exposure of the Moscow Trials, and developments were there for a complete fusion of all the groups — which, on the basis of the Geneva and James resolutions, they took to be in the context of the Labour Party tactic.[57]

In the end all the delegates accepted a resolution to set up a Central Co-ordinating Committee from a meeting of two representatives from each group to produce a common internal bulletin, to avoid overlap in published material and to act as 'a cohesive force to all groups with a view to organisational fusion'.[58]

But within a fortnight the whole situation was transformed completely. At the Marxist Group Conference, C.L.R. James had stated that 'we must immediately raise the banner of the Fourth International', and the first issues of *Fight* had pre-empted the decision, for the I.L.P. leaders declared that in selling it outside the party 'the Trotskyists were engaged in carrying on an activity hostile to the party'.[59] The threat was now discussed in the London Group on 15th November, and C.L.R. James moved a resolution committing the Marxist Group to an open group orientation:

> . . . The M[arxist] G[roup] realises the necessity for working in reformist and centrist organisations for certain [periods] with the greatest intensity, e.g. at the present time in the L[abour] L[eague] O[f] Y[outh], but the group considers that there is and can be no short cut to the building of a party capable of revolutionary struggle: that such a party can be built only by direct participation in the class struggle; that this task can best be performed and the desired political conclusions drawn by the workers on the basis of an independent political organisation . . . [The Marxist Group's] influence on the I.L.P. has so deteriorated in the last few months of factional struggle and consequent lessened activity, that its prospect of winning more adherents is today extremely small, the group decides to form an independent organisation as quickly as possible.[60]

This policy, passed by sixteen votes to six only five weeks after the conference, and that by a local group alone, threw the Marxist Group into confusion. As it came down so strongly against the entry tactic, and James was in touch with some of Field's supporters in Canada, it is not surprising that the Youth Militant Group described the policy as based on 'the arguments of Bauer, Oehler, Field, etc.', and rejected outright an offer to co-operate with them as being an embarrassment to their Labour Party work.[61] In this they were supported by the International Bureau, which refused to accept the validity of a decision taken in such a way, as well as pointing out its incompatibility with the Geneva Resolution on the unification of the groups as well as the Labour Party orientation:

> The proposal from the majority of the London group, to bring help to the Bolshevik–Leninists in the Labour Party from outside by 'combined work' can be inspired by the best of intentions. But the first people who should give their opinion on this help should be the comrades who are themselves in the Labour Party. But they are the sharpest opponents of the precipitate independence, and they declare that an independent group located outside can do them nothing but harm, for in that case they would be regarded as agents of an outside

> organisation, and a pretext could easily be found to expel them prematurely and without political grounds.

They proposed instead a constituent conference of those supporting the Geneva Resolution to decide on which was the best policy.[62]

The Marxist Group, however, went ahead. On 11th December *The New Leader* carried the announcement that 'perhaps thirty' members of the Marxist Group had resigned from the Party, proposing to lay 'the foundations of a revolutionary party' and support the 'Fourth International'.[63] The day after, the Marxist Group, having used their majority on the editorial board to take over *Fight* as their exclusive paper,[64] brought out a second issue containing an address to the N.A.C. of the I.L.P. which ended:

> The national and international situation steadily worsens. No Party in Britain gives a clear, comprehensive and resolute lead. Yet without the revolutionary party there can be no hope of success for the workers in Britain, without the revolutionary International no hope for the workers of the world. We therefore withdraw from the I.L.P. and call upon revolutionaries inside and outside to join us or collaborate with us in laying the foundation of a revolutionary party which will lead the workers to conquer fascism . . .[65]

An open meeting calling for the new party accordingly took place on 16th December.[66]

But this brave show concealed, in fact, an important political defeat for the Marxist Group. In six months it had lost more than half its members,[67] and the group was in sad disarray. Only Arthur Ballard, Jock Milligan and Karl Westwood of the old leadership fully supported James in the turn to the open group: although Cooper had voted for it at the London meeting on 15th November, he refused to leave the I.L.P., along with a large number of others, such as Marzillier and Ernie Patterson, who — in addition to being prevented by his personal circumstances — had just been elected onto the London Divisional Council at its sectional conference.[68]

Thus, whilst the groups had in theory accepted the Geneva Resolution, in fact the gap between them was wider than ever. The 'Youth Militant' Group wrote to the International Bureau asking them to withdraw any further international recognition from the other groups, and refusing its call for a constituent unification conference.[69] In view of their co-operation with the Marxist Group in launching the journal *Fight*, they were obliged to issue a statement dissociating themselves from it in future, thus bringing the deep differences between the groups once more before public notice:

> There has recently been formed an 'outside organisation'

under the title of 'The Marxist Group' (Trotskyists). While we agree in general with the basic political principles advocated by this group, we wish to state publicly that we, the Youth Militant Group of the Labour League of Youth, have no organisational connexion with it. However, believing as we do that the place of all revolutionaries at the present time is inside the mass party — the Labour Party — and the mass youth organisation — the L.L.O.Y. — we can only deplore the action of our comrades of the 'Marxist Group' in forming an independent organisation which has no real basis and which must lead to their isolation from the mass of the politically-conscious workers. We foresee the speedy collapse of this untimely experiment and meanwhile desire to inform all British workers that the 'Marxist Group' does not represent the majority of the British Bolshevik–Leninists (Trotskyists) and that the latter are in no way responsible for its actions. Furthermore, we are in no way connected with or responsible for the journal *Fight*.[70]

Notes

1. The Abyssinian referendum registered 740 votes for the position of the M.P.s and 555 against. Allowing for abstentions (and abstention was a way of life in the I.L.P.) we can still see that real membership was much less than the party figures claimed.
2. Percy Downey, Interview with Sam Bornstein, 26th November 1977. Local people still point to the house where he stayed and allegedly did some of the work on his book *World Revolution*, but as it only appeared the following year, and Harry Wicks helped with the research, it is more likely that most of the writing was done in London.
3. C.L.R. James, 'National Stay-In Strike?', in *The New Leader*, vol. xxix, new series, no. 94, 1st November 1935, p. 3.
4. C.L.R. James, '"Honest Stanley" in a Fix. What Next in the Abyssinian Dispute?', in *The New Leader*, vol. xxix, new series, no. 102, 27th December 1935, p. 3.
5. C.L.R. James, 'Baldwin's Next Move. Parliament Has Become a Nuisance to the Ruling Class. Look Out for Fascist Developments', in *The New Leader*, vol. xxix, new series, no. 103, 3rd January 1936, p. 2.
6. Op. cit., note 4 above.
7. John Robinson, Interview with Al Richardson, 3rd June 1978.
8. Cf. chapter six above, p. 167 and note 49.
9. 'What the S.L. is Doing', in *The Socialist Leaguer*, no 12, June 1935, p. 196.
10. Margaret Johns, Interview with Al Richardson, 4th February 1978.
11. John Archer, Statement made at the inaugural conference of the Group for

the Study of Leon Trotsky and the Revolutionary Movement, 20th September 1980.

12. *Youth Militant* (duplicated magazine), October 1935, p. 5.

13. Margaret Johns, Interview with Al Richardson, 4th February 1978. The same point is made by Ted Grant, Interview with Sam Bornstein, 22nd August 1982.

14. Undated letter of the International Secretariat to the British Section, Bolshevik–Leninists (on internal evidence, after March 1934); cf. chapter six above, p. 166 and note 38.

15. Cf. pp. 165-6 above.

16. D.D. Harber, 'The Present Position in the I.L.P. and How We Should React to It', p. 3 (undated, but after Easter 1934, on internal evidence).

17. L.D. Trotsky, 'Once Again the I.L.P.', November 1935, in *Writings of Leon Trotsky, 1935–6*, New York, 1977, pp. 198-203.

18. L.D. Trotsky, 'The Dutch Section and the International', 15th–16th July 1936, in *Writings of Leon Trotsky, 1935–6*, p. 365. Cf. p. 179 above.

19. L.D. Trotsky, 'Schmidt's Trip to England', 19th January 1936, in *Writings of Leon Trotsky: Supplement, 1934–40*, New York, 1979, p. 639.

20. Cf. note 18 above.

21. 'Declaration of the International Bureau for the Fourth International on the Subject of the English Marxist Group', 13th December 1936, p. 3; (D.D. Harber), 'The Present Situation and Our Tasks', 27th February 1943 (Internal Document of the R.S.L.).

22. Charles Van Gelderen, Interview with Al Richardson, 4th October 1979.

23. 'Youth in Red Russia: Official Report of the First British Young Workers' Delegation to Soviet Russia' (pamphlet).

24. Margaret Johns, Interview with Al Richardson, 4th February 1978.

25. Charles Van Gelderen, Interview with Al Richardson, 4th October 1979. Most of the preceding account of Jackson's life is drawn from the interview cited in note 10 above, further interviews given to Al Richardson by John Goffe (18th May 1978) and John Robinson (3rd June 1978) and a conversation that Sam Bornstein had with George Tasker (25th June 1983). Cf. 'British Trotskyist Lost at Sea', in *Socialist Appeal*, vol. v, no. 6, March 1943.

26. L.D. Trotsky, 'Remarks for an English Comrade', 8th April 1936, in *Writings of Leon Trotsky: Supplement, 1934–40*, p. 653.

27. Margaret Johns, Interview with Al Richardson, 4th February 1978.

28. (A. Matlow), 'British Perspectives: Statement to the International Conference from the B.L. Group in the Labour Party', in *For Discussion*, no. 1 (Internal Organ of the Bolshevik–Leninist Group in the Labour Party), pp. 1-3.

29. A.F.G. Cooper, A.A. Ballard, J. Pawsey and F. Marzillier, 'Unity and the C.P. Affiliation to the L.P.', internal document, Marxist Group.

30. 'Arthur Cooper', 'Bolshevik–Leninists and the I.L.P.' (unsigned internal document, Marxist Group).

31. L.D. Trotsky, 'The Dutch Section and the International', 15th–16th July 1936, in *Writings of Leon Trotsky, 1935–6*, pp. 365-6.

32. Charles Van Gelderen, Interview with Al Richardson, 4th October 1979.

33. Frederick Marzillier, Interview with Al Richardson, 2nd December 1978.

34. This was the 'Geneva' Conference, so-called for security reasons. The Marxist League did not attend (above, pp. 199-200, 211 note 32).

35. 'Material to International Conference from M.G. [Marxist Group]', in *For Discussion*, internal organ of the Bolshevik–Leninist Group in the Labour Party, pp. 3 and 8.

36. 'Resolution Moved by M.G. [Marxist Group] at International Conference', in ibid., p. 8.

37. 'Resolution on the Tasks of the Bolshevik–Leninists of England', Geneva, 31st

July 1936, in *International Internal Bulletin*, no. 1, April 1937.

38. L.D. Trotsky, 'Interview on British Problems', in *Writings of Leon Trotsky, 1935–6*, pp. 377-82.

39. John Archer, Interview with Martin Upham.

40. John Robinson, Interview with Al Richardson, 3rd June 1978.

41. Minutes of National Conference, Militant Group, August 1937, p. 1.

42. 'Report of the First National Meeting of British B[olshevik] L[eninists]', 28th November 1936, in *Internal Bulletin*, p. 3 (Harber).

43. Jock Haston, Interview with Al Richardson, 30th April 1978.

44. International Secretariat, Letter to the E.C. of the Marxist Group, 7th November 1936, p. 2, in *International Bulletin*, no. 1, April 1937.

45. *Fight! For the Fourth International!* (printed leaflet appealing for donations and subscriptions).

46. *Fight* for the Fourth International. Organ of the British Bolshevik–Leninists (Trotskyists), vol. i, no. 1, 10th October 1936, edited by C.L.R. James and published by Robert Williams.

47. 'The Group Perspective', internal discussion paper of the Marxist Group (single sheet, unsigned).

48. 'Resolution Submitted by Cde. James to be taken in Conjunction with Geneva Report'.

49. 'Report of the First National Meeting of the British B./L.s, 28th November 1936' (Internal Bulletin), p. 1.

50. Annex C., 'C . . . s', 'The Group Perspective and the October Conference', pp. 9-10.

51. Op. cit., note 49 above, p. 2.

52. Ibid. Cf. Felix Morrow, *Revolution and Counter-Revolution in Spain*, New Park edition, London, 1963, p. 113.

53. 'Tasks of British B.–L.s' (internal document of the Marxist Group), October 1936, p. 2.

54. Don James' Amendment, in 'Report of the First National Meeting of British B./L.s', November 1936.

55. 'Addendum Cooper', in ibid.

56. 'A Short Statement from the Marxist League to the Delegates from the Youth Militant Group and the Marxist Group Conference', 10th–11th October 1936.

57. 'Joint Session', and 'Statement Subsequently Submitted to Central Co-ordination Committee by Bolshevik–Leninist Group in the Labour Party', in 'Report of the First National Meetings of British B./L.s', November 1936, pp. 14-15.

58. Ibid.

59. International Secretariat, Letter to the E.C. of the Marxist Group, 7th November 1936.

60. 'Resolution Passed by London Marxist Group', 15th November 1936, in 'Report of the First National Meeting of the British B./L.s', pp. 17-18.

61. 'Statement to the Bureau for the Fourth International from the B.L. Group in the Labour Party Regarding the Fulfilment of the Geneva Resolution on the Question of the Unity of the British Groups', pp. 4-5.

62. 'Declaration of the International Bureau For the Fourth International On the Subject of the English Marxist Group', 13th December 1936, in *International Internal Bulletin*, no. 1, April 1937.

63. 'Trotskyists Resign', in *The New Leader*, vol. xxi, new series, no. 152, 11th December 1936, p. 6.

64. Op. cit., note 61 above, p. 3.

65. 'Towards the New Workers' Party: Statement to the N.A.C. of the I.L.P. from the Members of the Former Marxist Group', in *Fight*, vol. i, no. 2, 12th December 1936, p. 6.

66. Op. cit., note 61 above, p. 3.

67. Op. cit., note 62 above, p. 3.
68. He was caretaker of the New Morris Hall in Clapham.
69. Op. cit., note 61 above.
70. Statement of the Editorial Committee, 17th December 1936, in *Youth Militant*, vol. ii, no. 1, January 1937, p. 8.

Chapter Ten

The Labour Party, For and Against

The Trotskyist movement now consisted of three organisations confronting each other, two operating an entrist perspective and the other appealing to individuals to build an open group. 'A dozen scattered individuals joined together are not twelve times as strong as each one on his own,' they pleaded, 'but a hundred times as strong.'[1] But it was obvious that the Marxist Group could make little headway. As far as the Labour Party was concerned, they called for a Labour government — from outside its ranks — 'although opposed in every fundamental principle to the Labour Party',[2] and for a vote to its local government candidates because 'working on strictly orthodox capitalist lines, Labour has done a great deal for London', though a Labour L.C.C. 'will not have brought us one step nearer Socialism.'[3] At the same time as offering gratuitous advice from outside (hardly a rare commodity in politics), they described the entrist perspective as hiding behind 'the cowardly formula of leaving it to the "historic process" ',[4] and of concealing the revolutionary message in an opportunistic fashion:

> Fear of Transport House necessitates circumspection in approaching these 'masses'. Elementary Socialist principles are whispered into chosen ears. ('The Communists disdain to conceal their views and aims.') Thus the semi-legal, furtive band, prepare the toiling masses for the revolutionary struggles ahead . . . It is our task now to raise the red flag of International Socialism. The workers are searching for it; they will not find it hidden away in the rotten archives of the Labour Party.[5]

Inevitably, their own activity was thrust back upon the old methods of the street corner meeting and the issuing of appeals. One of those who recalls this clearly was Ajit Roy, a student of Law at the L.S.E. who was introduced, first of all to Trotsky's books, and then to

C.L.R. James, by B.L. Gupta, later a member of the Indian parliament:

> I had rarely come across a finer political polemicist than C.L.R. James. His attacks on Stalinism were absolutely devastating. He was then thinking in terms of building an independent Trotskyist Party. I joined him readily. There was no doubt in my mind that all we had to do was to start with a clean slate. We had the answer to all the problems, and that the few of us would grow in the course of time into a mighty party. Now when I think of my faith in those days, I feel very amused.
>
> James and I got together and we took a flat in Boundary Road, where James had another great devotee, a chap from the East End called Stanton. Our main task was to bring out the *Fight* and to make open propaganda in street corner meetings. We built a portable platform and the three of us, James, a tall West Indian, Stanton, a very Jewish-looking chap from the East End, and myself, an Indian, taking the portable platform to the shopping centres all over London, regarding ourselves as the vanguard of the British proletariat! It is all very amusing — but people did listen — probably the very strangeness of it gave us an audience. But once James started speaking he always got a crowd.[6]

Such appeals as were made to the mass organisations inevitably assumed an abstract character, directed as they were at the movement from outside. 'The Marxist Group will therefore not apply to join this bloc as outlined by the I.L.P. for its counter-revolutionary policy' was their criticism of the 'Unity' Campaign begun in January 1937,[7] for 'the logical way to unite on a reformist programme is within the Labour Party.'[8] Not surprising also was the fact that their concept of the United Front was closer to that of the German Communist Party during the 'Third Period' than to any Trotskyist formulation, that 'a United Front has to be in the first place against reactionary leadership in the Labour Party.'[9] But the fact that such statements were aimed at the movement from outside made it quite easy for their opponents to dismiss them. Thus an excellent suggestion for the formation of workers' defence corps at the time of the Cable Street anti-Fascist confrontation was easily dealt with in the *Daily Worker* of 9th October as 'provocative and disruptive'.[10]

Some notable recruits were gained, among them Ben (A.B.) Elsbury, a veteran revolutionary and founder member of the British Communist Party. He had been the writer of one of the first syndicalist pamphlets before the War — once referred to by Tom Mann in a public meeting in the North East as 'the founder of syndicalism in this country',[11] and his name appears in *The Industrial Syndicalist* as their spokesman in the London area as early as 1910.[12] He had joined the Communist Party and been among the early visitors to Russia and an enthusiastic supporter of the Soviet system.[13] Along with his more famous brother Sam, he was a tailor and had his own shop in Highbury. His brother was one of the victims of the 'Red union' policy of the Comintern, and had been first 'set up' and then expelled from the Communist Party at the time of the founding of the ill-named 'United Clothing Workers' Union'.[14] A.B. Elsbury's suspicions about Stalinism seemed further confirmed by the behaviour of the Communists in Spain, particularly the treatment of Andres Nin, about which the group made a public protest.[15]

During this time James was more preoccupied with the broader international questions and with his literary projects. Early in 1937[16] Secker and Warburg published the book on which he had been working for some time with the assistance of Harry Wicks — *World Revolution*. It deals with international events with a broad sweep, and it is difficult to understand why, among James' other books, it has never been republished. At the same time it reflects the influence of Field's ideas upon him, in placing the degeneration of the Comintern at an earlier stage than Trotskyists were prepared to admit. The German débâcle of 1923 is treated as though it were a result of deliberate policy, it predated the acceptance of the theory of 'Socialism in One Country', and deals with the coming to power of Hitler as if it were a deliberate plan on Stalin's behalf — a view that has since been taken up by others.[17] For this reason Trotsky regarded the book as undialectical: it treated as fixed and set processes that were still in flux. In particular Trotsky did not agree that it was Stalin's express wish and intention that Hitler should come to power in 1933,[18] an argument that was of course fastened upon by Stalinist apologists to discredit the book.[19] But apart from the odd virulent review,[20] the C.P. preferred to limit the impact of the book by refusing advertisements for it in all the propaganda outlets under their control — and at this period they were considerable.[21] A similar censorship was exercised by the British colonial authorities, who forbade the export of copies to India.[22] During this time James was more preoccupied with international events, and particularly the colonial revolution and his books, than with the particular problems of party-building here. As John Goffe recalls, 'after the collapse of the Marxist Group and the efforts in the I.L.P., he tended to move towards the colonial movement which I mentioned, worked fairly closely with George Padmore, and began not to be in the mainstream of British Trotskyism.'[23] This was not at all surprising in the circumstances as, with the Second World War looming up, foreign affairs assumed an over-riding importance, and the association with Padmore enabled James to influence a whole generation of leaders of the post-war colonial revolt with his broad propaganda. Among his literary projects with this aim were *Minty Alley*, a novel,[24] *Revolt*, a play on the life of Toussaint l'Ouverture put on by the Stage Society,[25] 'A History of Negro Revolt' and, of course, his superb *Black Jacobins*, the latter two of which appeared in 1938.[26] Their future significance was well gauged in a review by Arthur Ballard, when he wrote:

> In the coming war the ruling class will be forced to arm the subject peoples. They should turn this situation to their own advantage and not support one imperialist group against another, whether 'democratic' or Fascist.[27]

Nor were other areas of the world neglected. Harold Isaacs had already written on the progress of the Chinese revolution.[28] and Henry Sara reviewed his book[29] and wrote similarly, from his own deep experience, on China (and on Japan) in what outlets were afforded by the I.L.P.[30]

Although James' close links with Padmore helped to get his views still published in the I.L.P. press, such Trotskyist activity as continued there was not, in fact, largely under the auspices of the Marxist Group. When the group as a whole had broken with the Party, Ernie Patterson had refused to follow them, along with his supporters, such as C. Ross, a Scot, who once caused a furore when he refused to take the oath in court when on trial for selling *The New Leader* at Hyde Park,[31] a matter raised by Maxton in parliament. Patterson continued to maintain quite openly that Clapham was 'a Trotskyist branch',[32] and its day schools and meetings continued to be addressed on such subjects as France and 'Socialism in One Country' by such speakers as himself, Matlow, James and Sara.[33] Another such Trotskyist branch was Kirkdale in Liverpool, where Henry Cund, although a supporter of the 'Youth Militant' Group, was kept inside the I.L.P. to argue for its policy because of his personal position.[34]

Their first real opportunity came with the Forty-Fifth Easter Conference of the I.L.P. in the St Mungo Halls in Glagow on 27th and 28th March 1937. The conference was overshadowed by the events in Spain, where the Stalinists in their counter-revolution behind the Republican lines were beginning to put pressure upon the P.O.U.M., the sister party of the I.L.P. At the same time the I.L.P. leaders were involved in their own 'Unity Campaign' with the Communist Party leadership, involving as it did a stifling of the criticism of Stalinism by the other groups and the gradual strangulation of the Socialist League.[35] In Russia itself, the Moscow Trials were in full swing, and the great purge of the Soviet army was in preparation. Whilst the N.A.C. of the I.L.P. were in theory opposed to the Popular Front, they were unwittingly involved in the preparations for it, and Patterson sought to amend its resolution to the effect that 'under no circumstances' should the I.L.P. enter such a Front, nor any 'United Front agreement, unless complete freedom of criticism and action, both inside and outside the agreed programme, be allowed.' As far as he was concerned, the so-called 'Unity Campaign' was 'the first step on a slippery slope'.[36] Cund supported him by pointing out that 'while the Labour rank-and-file was being urged to shift its bureaucracy, the Communist 'under cover' men in the Labour Party were not supporting the 'Unity Campaign', and that, as far as he was concerned, he would not 'speak with or work with members of the Communist Party while it is conducting its campaign against the P.O.U.M.'[37] Although the debate was marked with 'virulence and a Trotskyist offensive against the Communist Party', according to the *Daily Worker*, the amendments fell and the main resolution passed through with only four votes against.[38]

But whilst the implications of 'Unity' with the Communists were as yet unclear in Britain, they were all too obvious in Spain. Patterson showed that the policy of the Soviet Union was 'no longer concerned with world revolution', and here most of the Conference agreed with him. Bob Edwards came out with a spirited defence of the P.O.U.M., and Tom Taylor — later to be the victim of Stalinist slanders himself during the Second World War — was sharp enough to see that 'the Communist drive against all forms of what it called Trotskyism would lead ultimately to an attack upon the I.L.P. similar to the attack on P.O.U.M.'[39] The whole affair was highly embarrassing for the I.L.P. leaders in their flirtations with the Communists, who alleged that the P.O.U.M.'s 'treacherous record in Spain has been so thoroughly exposed', and were claiming that it proved that 'Trotskyist influence was destroying the great name and traditions of the I.L.P.'[40]

The subject of the Moscow Trials was more easily dealt with, as most of the open supporters of Stalinism had already left the I.L.P., leaving only Brandler's followers to defend them. Patterson and Cund attacked the Trials as frame-ups, whilst declaring that despite the bureaucracy the U.S.S.R. was still a workers' state, and that it was 'the unconditional duty of socialists to defend Soviet Russia'. Patterson was also able to argue against Brockway's opposition to forming a new International since, although 'the mass base of the new International will arise only in a revolutionary crisis', the International itself 'must be formed in readiness'.[41]

Patterson continued, almost single-handed, to press the cause of Trotskyism within the I.L.P., and to keep its ideas before the party's notice. Trotsky's books continued to gain favourable reviews,[42] and some of his shorter articles were printed in their internal bulletin, at times under his own name and at others under a suitable pseudonym.[43] Patterson himself wrote for it, and secured also space for articles by C.L.R. James, Dr. Worrall and Harry Wicks.[44]

Whilst Cund left after a while, Patterson was reinforced when Arthur Ballard and Alf Rosen left the Marxist Group in October 1937, and rejoined the I.L.P. Ballard was a firm supporter of the colonial revolution, and became Secretary of 'The British Centre Against Imperialism' as well as having a regular column headed 'Round the Empire' in *The New Leader*. But opportunities were fast dwindling for work inside the party as it withered to a husk outside of Glasgow, and its ideas hardened into a philistine pacifist orthdoxy. Even when the occasional resolution could be got through annual conference, there was little point in doing so for the few people who would be influenced there. Thus Patterson was finally successful at the Conference of 1938 in committing the Party 'never to participate in a Popular Front'.[45] The lesson of Spain had finally come home to them — and Ballard equally succeeded in getting the Party to set up a colonial bureau at the 1939 Conference, 'to assist the liberation movement in the colonies'.[46] But on all other issues the I.L.P.'s policy stuck exactly where it was, or even got worse. Patterson's attempts to get the Party to withdraw from the London Bureau and support the Fourth International as a 'disciplined and active international body' and to renounce the theory of 'Socialism in One Country' both failed at the Easter Conference of 1938,[47] and his move to get the I.L.P. to reaffiliate to the Labour Party was lost at the Conference of 1939.[48] What was worse, his resolution for the defence of the Soviet Union at the same time was rejected by the Party on the eve of the Second World War,[49] and his own position was fast becoming precarious. After making a speech which C.A. Smith found particularly objectionable, he received a warning letter to which he did not bother to reply, and this was made grounds for his expulsion by the I.L.P. Executive for 'anti-party political conduct'. When the London Divisional Council refused to operate his expulsion, the Executive suspended the whole of the Council, and called a special conference of the London Division to ratify it. Even those hostile to Trotskyism, such as Jack Huntz, who supported Brandler, and the right wing, were outraged by this undemocratic conduct, and nine branches withdrew from the conference in protest.[50] That was the end of the I.L.P. in London as far as Trotskyism was concerned. As for Patterson himself, he drifted down to the West Country during the War, where he played an important part in expanding the membership of the Constructional Engineering Union, and later became its General Secretary. After his retirement, he still played a part in the Labour Party in South London, where he still lives.

Not only the I.L.P. was disintegrating. Differences arose in the Marxist Group over whether to support China in the war with Japan, on Spain and on the attitude to the I.L.P., in which a 'left' minority of Cooper, Bill Duncan, George Weston, Alex Acheson and Jim Wood stood in opposition to the leadership of C.L.R. James. Worn out with the faction fighting, and greatly disillusioned with the Moscow Trials and the lack of progress of the International movement, Arthur Ballard and Alf Rosen resigned on 13th October 1937, and joined the I.L.P. 'with no fractional perspective'.[51] At the same time Harry Wicks and the Majority of the now dissolved Marxist League had been moving closer to C.L.R. James, with whom they had been co-operating in opposition to the Moscow Trials and in gathering the material for *World Revolution*. On 27th February 1938 they held a fusion conference in London and founded the Revolutionary Socialist League from what was left of both disintegrating organisations. But, if anything, its political position was even more vague than previously. As Wicks showed, when presenting the political report:

> Up to now, comrades had been working in two different worlds — inside the Labour Party and outside the Labour Party. Our forces had been divided and isolated on this tactical question of the best milieu for our work. Was there a basis for overcoming this difference and uniting on a common platform of work for the Fourth International?
>
> Such a basis did exist. We were, in fact, setting out to reconcile what was correct in these two different tactics. We were setting out to build an independent organisation and at the same time to drive our fraction work still deeper into the mass organisations.

Thus there was no real convergence of politics, only an agreement that both were right — those who advocated 'open work' and those who carried on entrism. But even here the picture was indistinct. The ex-Marxist League comrades and the Majority leadership of the Marxist Group advocated continuing to work in and build up the Socialist Left Federation that had succeeded the old Socialist League. But the Minority of Arthur Cooper, Bill Duncan, Hilda Lane, George Weston and Sid Frost thought that fusion had been very poorly prepared, and great differences remained unresolved. As Cooper expressed it:

> . . . the method adopted to effect fusion was deplorable. There were vital differences, for example, with regard to work in the S.L.F., which were being concealed. This would lead the organisation into a number of stupid blunders. The Political Statement itself was loose and vague, and therefore weak. There should have been a series of preliminary aggregate meetings so that these questions could have been thoroughly discussed. The differences of viewpoint should have been resolved and a real agreement reached. The present document did not indicate such agreement, and it was necessary to give a warning.[52]

Many years later, Wicks was to recognise the truth of this assessment. 'I can remember Cooper's contribution — I can remember it vividly,' he explained. 'It [the fusion] was not politically prepared, and in subsequent history I can look back and say that Cooper was more knowledgeable than I in that setting.'[53] It emerged almost immediately when the S.L.F. promptly collapsed, and the Cooper–Duncan Minority, who regarded it in any case as 'a Centrist organisation on a third class ticket', felt completely justified. The fusion proved utterly barren as, despite the increased numbers, fraction work in the mass organisations 'almost disappeared', the paper lapsed, general activity fell, and apathy and grumbling announced 'an impending paroxysm and loss of members'.[54] But the crisis sprang not only from a poorly prepared unification, or an assessment of work in the S.L.F., but from a mistaken assumption about the whole method of revolutionary entry in the first place. As Jackson, attending as observer from the Militant Group, pointed out:

> The Labour Party was the mass political party of the working class. It was possible to win the leadership of the left-wing of the Labour Party and in this way to build a real basis for the revolutionary party. All our energies should be devoted to this work, which was the most productive.[55]

Nonetheless, the new group was announced in *Fight* as a 'great blow' struck for unity by 'the fusion of the two oldest Trotskyist groups in the country'.[56]

For a while the fortunes of the other organisation, the Bolshevik–Leninist Group in the Labour Party, looked much brighter. After months wasted discussing fusion with the other groups following the October Conference of the Marxist Group, they settled down to entrist work, particularly within the Labour League of Youth. Their first task — that of working out a political perspective — took them some time to elaborate, but documents issued later enable us to reconstruct its main lines:

> . . . the Group believes that the best method of fighting for the revolutionary party is by working as a strictly disciplined faction in the mass party of the working class, the Labour Party and its auxiliary organisations, in order to fight for the leadership of the developing leftward movement. It intends to break away at the appropriate moment with the best elements of all the left wing to form the new revolutionary Party.[57]

The immediate perspective, then, was for the development of a mass left-wing tendency inside the Labour Party, which they must be in a position to influence, and then split away:

> This party can never be captured by us owing to the tremendous strength of the reformist bureaucracy, but with the decline of capitalism and the consequent undermining of the social basis of reformism, a growing left-wing tendency must develop inside it. It is our task to struggle inside the Labour Party for the leadership of this left-wing movement in order to break away the best elements at the appropriate time. Until this has been done, the bulk of our forces must be concentrated upon work inside the Labour Party.[58]

The method of their work followed logically on from this:

> Our ostensible aim is to build up the Labour Party, to strengthen the Socialist convictions and to purge it of anti-working-class elements. Although our perspective does not permit us to consider the possibility of our replacing the present Labour Party leadership, nevertheless our practical activity is carried on as if the Labour Party could become a revolutionary party. Any other kind of activity would completely invalidate our membership of the Labour Party. The rank and file whom we wish to win, but who still seek socialism through the Labour Party, would be driven from us if they did not think that we shared their elementary desires, to strengthen the Labour Party both numerically and politically. The Labour Party tactic recognises that we must accommodate ourselves to this necessity, and it is because of this that we do not . . . advance our 'split' perspective.[59]

Logically, then, membership of the group was only open to those accepting its platform who already were, or were willing to become, members of the Labour Party.[60]

Of course, none of these broad formulations was of direct use in working out the lines of a concrete approach. Here a paper was issued within the group as early as September 1936 which laid out the problems, recognised the pitfalls, and sketched out techniques of work. Firstly, a paper was necessary, together with study circles and readers' discussion groups, to overcome the contempt for theory that was almost universal in the Labour Party. The post of Literature Secretary was thus an important one for the propagation of the group's literature and ideas. The maze of bureaucratic and constitutional procedure also made the post of Party Chairman a strategic one. Preparation for Annual Conference must take place well in advance, in co-operation with militant elements in other Labour Parties. Topicality, and the avoidance of vague slogans, were essential, as was the constant promotion of 'the democratic initiative of members'. Even questions of tone and approach were discussed in a serious and illuminating manner:

> To deal with reformist ideology, it is important to know when to approach the minds of reformist workers 'obliquely', that is in a tactful manner, and when to employ 'shock tactics' with a blunt presentation of a problem. Only experience and some psychological understanding can tell what line of approach to take. There are two dangers here . . . One is that too much tact takes the edge off our argument, and our opinion is respected or tolerated without having much influence upon others. The other danger is that too blunt or too aggressive a presentation of our argument repels reformist workers irrationally, and closes their minds to our ideas. Both these dangers can be minimised — if we recognise their existence . . .
>
> Our success depends largely on how we present our point of view. If we announce our future exit from the house-tops as soon as we join; if we act as wise strangers who have condescended to pay the Party dues for the time being; if we exercise no care regarding the conditions of membership of the Party (for example regarding the paper), then we shall leave the Labour Party far, far sooner than we wish. If, on the other hand, we push tact to the point of diplomatic evasions of crucial issues, and aim primarily at toleration by the party authorities, then we shall remain an ineffective group. We can and must find our way between these two pitfalls, using whatever aids seem advisable.[61]

Finally, all this was envisaged in terms of a very short-term perspective. A minimum requirement was that within a year some hundreds of Labour Party workers should be ready to join the group to set up an independent party, to be able, if necessary, to 'declare independence'. 'If a year's work by a group reaches less than this,' the document affirmed, 'then the step of joining the Labour Party has failed to bring the necessary result.'

Unfortunately, the way they undertook to encourage the birth of a mass centrist current was to set it up themselves. They revived the 'inner circle' concept that they first floated when discussing their entry into the I.L.P. — of an outside group, controlled by an inner Bolshevik élite. At the first annual conference of the Bolshevik–Leninists in the Labour Party on 1st August 1937, Harber proposed that the best way to work for the creation of a revolutionary party was by 'the formation, inside the Labour Party, of an open organisation based upon a partial programme.' This partial programme was to be the group position, minus the demand for a new party and an international. Then he went on:

> Since the whole object of such a partial programme is the recruitment into the new organisation of workers who do not accept the full B.L. position (i.e. Left Centrists), and since the workers may, and in fact should, outnumber the Bolshevik–Leninists, there is always a danger that such a body may degenerate into an ordinary centrist organisation like the I.L.P. or the Socialist League. This danger can be obviated only if the Bolshevik–Leninists provide the political leadership of the new organisation, and consciously lead it towards a split from the Labour Party and the formation of the British Section of the IVth International.
>
> The Bolshevik–Leninists can only carry out this new task if they remain together as a disciplined group inside the new organisation . . .[62]

This unwise policy, which was to prove the Achilles' Heel of the new grouping, only prevailed against much opposition, by 38 votes to 20. The Liverpool Group in particular couldn't see the necessity for the inner group, and John Archer, the point of having a 'new left centrist organisation'. The Islington Group agreed with Liverpool, and Jock Haston thought that the paper was only putting over a partial programme as it was.

The formation of the new organisation, the 'Militant Labour League', was duly announced, in November 1937, with just such a programme.[63] The sterility of the whole approach was once more clearly revealed when the new body held its first annual conference on 6th November 1938. With the exception of two names alone, all those mentioned in the minutes were Trotskyists, members of the group; and every one of the speakers went through the charade of running a 'centrist' organisation.[64] In such a way the group tried to build 'a strong revolutionary left within the working class movement'.

It was all the more peculiar because such a centrist organisation already existed within the Labour Party, having arisen out of the conditions of struggle within it, rather than as an artificial creation — the Socialist Left Federation of Groves and his old allies from the collapsed Socialist League. Harber had already attempted to merge with the 'Centrists' inside that body — McCarthy, Gary Allighan, etc., even though Margaret Johns had opposed it because it would 'mean liquidation of our programme'.[65] In the end it became a dead issue in view of Groves' hostility and the decline of the S.L.F. to almost nothing; but even when it was breathing its last, Starkey Jackson was still proposing a fusion with the hardly existent Militant Labour League.[66] The chimera of the 'centrist current' was pursued to the very end, in conditions that came to resemble the less convincing of the Communist Party's 'Front' operations.

But the age of the Trotskyists, and the urgency of the situation, meant that the main thrust of their activity was inside the Labour League of Youth, which was rapidly being penetrated by the Communist Party. Although they had started off here with several advantages, the delay in breaking with the I.L.P. and the failure to set up a clear factional organisation from the beginning cost them dear. To begin with they had made a bloc with the Communists in opposition to the foreign policy of the Labour Party, and had helped to found the paper *Advance*, which soon fell under complete Stalinist influence. At the beginning of 1936 they had a majority on the London Advisory Committee of the League of Youth, but at the following conference rapid Stalinist penetration cost them all but one seat on it.[67] Superior organisation, professional organisers and generous funds made Stalinist success in the League of Youth a certainty. The League's Annual Conference in Manchester in Easter 1936 carried the Communist Party policy on the 'United Front' (sic!) of youth organisations, and the Labour Party's representatives complained that Y.C.L. members maintained contact with the delegates (including Advisory Committee members) on the floor of the Conference, since their messages were placed upon chairs before sessions began, 'undoubtedly with the knowledge' of some of the Advisory Committee's members.[68] As a result, the N.E.C. decided to disband the League N.A.C. and take steps to suspend its annual conference. By September 1936 the League was so penetrated by Stalinism that bitter personal attacks were being made on the last surviving Trotskyist on the London Advisory Committee, Roma Dewar, on the grounds that she hadn't 'the confidence and backing of the membership' and had united 'with reactionary elements within the London executive'.[69]

The atmosphere inevitably worsened inside the League of Youth; but since it maintained its associations with the Labour Party, the *Advance* faction was obliged to debate with the Trotskyists, and could not subject them to the extremes of hooliganism and censorship that they practised outside. As John Goffe recalls:

> I was at the time in the Whitechapel Branch Labour League of Youth; which was again totally dominated by the Stalinists. I don't think there was a member in it who was not either a Stalinist or a Trotskyist. I don't think there was anybody else at all . . .
>
> They could not adopt the same attitude as the members of the Young Communist League, who of course took the view that Trotskyism is Fascism, and attempted to make a complete break and a refusal to discuss on those grounds, and even then they couldn't do that inside the Labour League of Youth. So we were able to discuss on policy, on facts and on arguments, and they were, in that sense, on the defensive; although, having an overwhelming majority in the organisation, they didn't have to worry unduly about the gnats stinging them from the small number of young Trotskyists.[70]

Since Willis and his supporters were incapable of answering the arguments, the Communist Party was forced to intervene, and pay more attention to the Bolshevik–Leninists in the Labour League of Youth. John Gollan's speech to the 9th Congress of the Y.C.L. in June 1937 described the 'small group of Trotskyists in the Labour League of Youth' as 'provocateurs, alien elements', who were 'pursuing wrecking tactics', 'disrupting the League of Youth' and 'blocking every movement towards practical work'.[71] The adult Party showed equally generous concern for the Labour Youth when it complained that 'branch after branch of the Labour League of Youth had been ruined by sterile arguments; keen working-class youths have been driven away from the struggle by the efforts of these people', whose aim was 'not to construct, build up and unify, but to destroy.'[72] Gollan was struck off to debate with the Youth Militant Group at a crowded meeting of the Labour League of Youth and the Y.C.L. at Finsbury Town Hall in July 1936. Although Ken Alexander, speaking for the group, showed that war could not be prevented by joining 'Peace Councils' along with the bourgeoisie (and war came in any case in 1939, with or without Peace Councils), Gollan claimed that because the Economic League had circulated a pamphlet against Peace Councils, that proved that the Trotskyists were 'assisting the Economic League'. As the meeting was so obviously packed against them, the Communist Party was able to claim that they 'had been met in open debate and have been clearly exposed', and Willis that they had been 'annihilated'.[73]

Annihilated or not, the Y.C.L. was obliged to organise two

lectures by Gollan at St. George's Town Hall in the East End a year and a half later,to expose 'the wrecking aims and activities of the Trotskyists' and 'take the lid off their methods and manoeuvres', at which one of the authors witnessed a 'roughing up' of Jock Haston in the audience.[74]

Strangely, the venom with which the Stalinists attacked the Trotskyists in the Labour League of Youth gained them sympathy, and even converts, from their own ranks. Paddington Y.C.L. had to be totally disbanded 'owing to Trotskyist influence', and the same was threatened of Bethnal Green.[75] Converts were gained from the C.P. in Leeds;[76] and in London, Charlie Orwell and others came from Limehouse Y.C.L., and Gerry Healy from Hyde Park Corner. This most important convert was won over directly as a result of Stalinist violence, as Jock Haston remembers:

> I was selling the *Militant* outside the toilets in Hyde Park, Marble Arch, which was quite differently constructed then than it is today, and I got into an argument (we used to be beaten up, incidentally, every weekend for selling there). I got into an argument with Healy and two others who were putting the Stalinist line, and this led to a fracas. So my first contact with Healy was there, at a fracas at Hyde Park Corner, at Marble Arch Corner. Subsequently, in discussion with Healy some months later — you know, because he came back, again and again, and argued — I won Healy over to the Trotskyist movement.[77]

Healy immediately showed his tremendous energy by moving up to the West Riding and assisting John Archer in selling the paper, in running open-air meetings in Bradford, and in generally building up the group in industrial Yorkshire. He was accepted as a full member of the group at its National Conference in August 1937 on the proposal of Denzil Harber and John Archer.[78]

Stalinist pressure inside the Labour League of Youth was more subtle, and less violent, and here the Trotskyists also had to contend with the bureaucratism of Transport House. The 1936 Labour Party Conference had ratified a report seeking to ban the L.L.O.Y. Conference, close down its paper, and in general throttle its activities. The *Advance* leadership had no intention of opposing this, since they feared that they would be removed from the Party completely, and they wanted to use the Labour League of Youth as a lever to obtain Communist affiliation to the Labour Party and promote a Popular Front. Naturally the Trotskyists opposed both the attempt to choke off League democracy, and the lack of opposition to this by Willis and his friends. Here they made the mistake of suggesting that the League should separate itself from the

Party, run itself independently, and then afterwards reapply for affiliation; as Sid Bone put it, 'now before it is too late, the League must cut the throttling control of the parent body, and organise itself into an independent Socialist Youth movement.'[79] This was a grave tactical error, as it enabled the Stalinists to pose as Labour Party loyalists and supporters of unity, and brand the Trotskyists as splitters. 'The people who want us to split from the Labour Party,' wrote F.L. Brown, 'are the same people who oppose the Unity Campaign.'[80] They were accused of wanting to 'throw up the sponge by breaking away from the Labour Party and forming an impotent, nominally independent youth organisation',[81] and then, 'proudly, in its matured wisdom and power, to demand affiliation'.[82]

Not that the *Advance* group were themselves great partisans of League democracy. When 'two Trotskyist disruptionists' opposed Willis' policy at the National Advisory Committee on 7th February 1937, he came out with the following remarks:

> . . . for the last year or two we have been blessed (is that the right word?) with a tiny group of people in the League who style themselves Trotskyists and who, true to style, busy themselves with obstruction of work and destruction of organisation . . .
>
> In the paper that is issued by this group — the *Youth Militant* — no opportunity is lost to attack the Soviet Union . . . the *Youth Militant* rushes to defend the terrorists and plotters who seek to destroy that which has been built up so self-sacrificingly and joyfully since the revolution.
>
> In the February issue of *Youth Militant* even the lick-spittle, fawning, professional hacks of the yellow gutter press are outdone in venom by these self-styled 'Bolshevik–Leninists' . . .
>
> Like all other Trotskyist groups they are a tiny minority, entirely divorced from the rank-and-file and the masses. Mainly middle-class types their record is one of disruption, cleverly taking advantage of the weaknesses of the League to insinuate themselves into its organisation. They are dangerous, precisely because the League is weak and because they hide their light under a bushel of fine Marxist phrases which might fool some young people, who with good reason are disgruntled with the party . . .
>
> We, in the League of Youth, must finish with this group of Trotskyists who only spread confusion and doubt . . . There is no place for Trotskyists in a live movement, just as there is no place for boils on a healthy human . . . Expose them as

> splitters, and creators only of dissension! Turn them lock, stock and barrel out of the Labour movement![83]

Where Willis led the way, the rest were bound to follow, and the Youth Militant Group began to be the victims of gross bureaucratic procedure. A Conference of the London Leagues of Youth, on 6th April 1937, passed a resolution against *Youth Militant* by a large majority, whilst Willis abused his position in the chair to dismiss their protests as 'cynicism and slander'.[84]

> This Conference views with disgust and dismay the growing disruption inside the League of Youth, particularly at conferences, due in no small measure to the activities of *Youth Militant* sympathisers, feeling that a conference is an occasion for planning constructive activity and not for indulging in wrangling and internal strife and knowing that were it not for the introduction of such extraneous subjects as Trotsky & Co., this atmosphere would not prevail.[85]

The whole machine now swung into operation among the branches to prepare a rough reception for *Youth Militant* speakers at the forthcoming special conference of the Leagues. 'One word before I close,' ran a letter from Lancashire: 'Let me add my voice to the cry of all the decent London comrades: "Out the Trotskies, the sooner the better",'[86] whilst one of these decent comrades, Alec Bernstein, was hard at work explaining why the method of the purge trial and the amalgam was desirable for the Labour Party's youth. 'Young Socialists in the provinces who have very little experience of these so-called "Trotskyists" wonder what all the fuss is about,' he explained. 'They say, "After all, what does it matter if they do talk bilge, they've a right to, and no-one ever listens to them" '. Bernstein explained patiently that the Trotskyists created rowdyism, and tried to shout down speakers and the chair. 'Isn't it rather drastic to clear them out?' asked his imaginary companion. 'The Spanish and Belgian Young Socialists were driven to take this step,' he replied: 'There's room in the League for all who are willing to work for Socialism, but not for the enemies of our fight, whatever their guise.'[87]

Such an atmosphere was created that the Special League Conference on 8th and 9th May 1937 in the Central Library, Holloway Road, was a foregone conclusion. The draft resolution placed before the 172 delegates from 121 branches had been prepared by the Communist Party in advance.[88] No resolutions apart from that of the N.A.C. were allowed, and only one amendment per branch.[89] The main resolution stated more or less crudely that Fascism was the enemy, that youth should rally to the Labour Party to defend democracy, and that youth should be won to the cause of Socialism and Peace.[90] The branches supporting the Trotskyist case, East and West Islington, Peckham,Paddington and Golder's Green, were only able to rally twelve votes to their whole series of amendments, and when Willis from the platform threatened that 'it was time the *Youth Militant* Group were expelled' as 'enemies of the youth movement', there was cheering in the hall.[91] Even this weak opposition could not be tolerated by the Stalinists, accustomed as they were to a mechanical unanimity in their own proceedings, so Alec Bernstein even appealed to the branches putting the minority view to remove the Trotskyists from them:

> Their leaders are Van Gelderen, Roma Dewar, Emmett, Alexander and Bone, with a few misled and misguided followers. Their activities are inspired by the Trotskyist centre in this country.
>
> How about it Stoke, East Islington, Peckham and Golder's Green? The League looks to you to clear out the wreckers![92]

While all these unedifying proceedings were in train, the news came through of the 'May Days' in Barcelona, where the workers had erected barricades to defend their revolution against the provocations of the Stalinists. The Trotskyists from East Islington had already tried to raise the issue of the Popular Front in Spain by protesting at the banning of the Internationale and the shouting of working-class slogans by the Spanish Food-ship Committee at its Trafalgar Square Demonstration three weeks earlier.[93] Now Sid Bone and Charlie Van Gelderen introduced an emergency resolution supporting the workers' uprising, to the 'interruption of the assembled delegates, who were infuriated by this insult to Socialism'. Willis, Rigg and Bernstein in reply urged the 'fullest support to the democratic government of the Spanish people' against the 'treasonable role of the Barcelona insurgents'. 'In the self-governing League of Youth that we're fighting for, there'll be no room for people who've exposed themselves as traitors to the working class,' concluded Willis.[94]

Now that the Islington comrades had brought the news of the Barcelona 'May Days' before the provincial delegates, the *Advance* group realised that they had some explaining to do, and that they would have to give some space to the Trotskyists as well. The same issue of *Advance* that carried the conference report also included a long article by Y.C.L. leader John Gollan, explaining how the Trotskyists by supporting the Spanish workers had 'lost the right to belong to the working-class movement, and should be flung out' of the 'too hospitable ranks of the Labour League of Youth.' The next issue contained a long article from Robert Ellis, explaining how

Spain was a 'People's Democracy' (shades of Eastern Europe!) and not a 'government of "capitalist" democracy, reformism and betrayal of the workers.'[95] Then it was Charlie Van Gelderen's turn. He described in as short a space as possible how the revolution had developed in the Republican zone, and how the Assault Guards under the Stalinist Rodriguez Salas had provoked the Barcelona revolt by attacking the C.N.T.-held Telefonica in support of the Popular Front government.[96] Next to the article was an editorial reply almost as long, calling the Barcelona workers a 'few hundred isolated provocateurs'.[97] This was as much as could be done by the Trotskyists with their small forces to help the Spanish Revolution, apart from Alex Rudling being able to offer hospitality to Emma Goldman when she visited Norwich to address a defence meeting arranged by the Trotskyists, the I.L.P. and the Anarchists.[98]

As the League of Youth slid deeper into Stalinism, chances for the Trotskyists became slimmer and slimmer, bureaucratic manipulation became worse, free speech became less, and Socialism hardly spoken of at all. A further quarterly conference of the London Leagues witnessed a speaker from East Islington about to move his motion, when the chair accepted a motion of 'next business' that was promptly voted through by the *Advance* supporters and which deprived him of his chance even to be heard.[99] The next such gathering was rather more evenly balanced, with the *Youth Militant* comrades gaining up to 26 votes against the 37 for the *Advance* slate, and winning over three people; but numbers in the Youth Leagues were declining fast, and the political level was dropping accordingly. 'Another disturbing feature was the frequency with which the words "bloody revolution" was used in a derogatory sense by the *Advance* crowd,' commented the *Militant*,[100] and the I.L.P. was even more scathing:

> There was little said that could raise any hopes that the League of Youth might move in a revolutionary direction, except that which came from the very small, hopelessly outnumbered *Militant* youth section. It was obvious that very few, if any, were prepared to listen to their arguments. They were 'Trotskyists', and so condemned before they spoke.[101]

The last public conferences registered the depressing progress of the Labour League of Youth towards being a Stalinist Front organisation. Support for the Duchess of Atholl in the Perth by-election went along with obsessive Trotsky-hunting, to the point at which Mr. Dawes of the London Labour Party warned them 'against continuing the discussions on "Trotskyism" which are going on in the branches.' That did not seem to deter Willis and his friends from then moving a resolution denouncing 'Trotskyist disruption', demanding the expulsion of supporters of *Youth Militant* from the Leagues, and then moving 'next business' again to rob them of their right to reply.[102] But even when Willis called an unofficial conference, at which only a third of the Leagues put in an appearance, the Trotskyists fought him to the end, rallying two-fifths of the votes against him.[103]

By this time the Labour League of Youth was fast shrinking, as it moved closer to the Communist Party, and the latter moved closer to war. The Leagues had been openly associating with the Y.C.L. in 'Coronation Hikes' as early as June 1937,[104] and several branches were present at the 1939 Y.C.L. Bermondsey Conference.[105] Willis himself joined the Y.C.L. in July 1939, claiming that the decisions of the Labour Party Conference at Southport had finally decided him.[106] Mournfully, the comrades of the *Youth Militant* drew the balance sheet of the entire experience:

> We warned the League of Youth three years ago that the Young Communist League was trying to get control for their own purposes, and not for the good of the League or of the young workers. Helped by their paper, *Advance*, and big amounts of money, the Communist elements got control of the League of Youth. They used it to advocate the 'Popular Front' and all their other stunts of that sort.
>
> The Communists called for a war against Germany, and got a lot of League of Youth members to join the Territorials 'to hold back Hitler'.[107]

Associated with the *Advance* group for much of this period was the late General Secretary of the Labour Party, Jim Mortimer. His enthusiasm for Trotskyist-baiting seems to have survived his change of political allegiance.

Opportunities were even fewer in the adult Labour Party, for to be able to operate there it is necessary to become established over a period. Nonetheless, the Liverpool comrades succeeded in getting a group resolution on Spain for the Bournemouth Party Conference of 1937 through Fairfield Division of the Labour Party, and the North London Group a similar one through East Islington. As the group's press describes it:

> . . . a resolution from the Fairfield (Liverpool) Labour Party calls for an international working class embargo on all goods and arms going to the rebels. This demand is repeated by East Islington who emphasise that we must assist the Spanish workers to extend the struggle for a workers' republic and not simply for capitalist 'democracy'. Both these resolutions

> contain a vigorous working class policy and are worthy of the support of all militants.[108]

The conference was attended by Starkey Jackson and Jimmy Deane, the only two of the group's representatives to be selected as delegates.

Nor did the group neglect the struggle in the streets. Before the Long Lane affair, the group showed that 'through their organisations the workers must form their own defence corps which can organise the mass hostility against Fascism and drive the blackshirts off the streets.'[109] 'How much more could have been achieved if the resistance had been organised,' they went on: 'Long Lane has demonstrated yet again the necessity for a Workers' Defence Corps which can lead the workers against the Fascist provocations, lead the resistance to all attempts of the capitalist police to force the bosses' lackeys through the Labour strongholds.'[110] Ted Grant was particularly to the fore in this activity,[111] and a photograph still exists of him on the barricades in Bermondsey.[112]

The group made good progress throughout 1937, given that it was not at all rooted in the working class to begin with. They were proud of their theoretical level and, with one exception, were essentially the group that had split off from the Communist League at the end of 1933.[113] As Goffe remembers:

> The *Militant* Group was primarily what we might say the L.S.E. leadership — Harber, Stewart Kirby, John Archer and Margaret Johns, who were of that particular group, and one or two others, and therefore very much had intellectual origins, and only later began to collect any working-class support. This was partly due to John Archer and myself, who quite consciously and deliberately went into the provinces, he to Leeds and I to Sheffield. I only stayed in Sheffield about eighteen months, I think, to try to build up, or get, some kind of working-class base for the *Militant* Group, which we succeeded in doing, and therefore their contribution, I think, was quite important. Although the leadership of the *Militant* Group was still mainly intellectual, people like Starkey Jackson, who had a working-class background, and was in the leadership in the latter part, was an indication of this, that it seemed to be moving in the right direction of trying to get a working-class base for the predominantly middle-class leadership, and was making a good deal of progress, which of course was halted by the outbreak of war.[114]

Slowly, recruits, both working-class and middle-class, began to come in. Early in 1937 joined Hilda Pratt, the daughter of an old member of the S.P.G.B., Andy Sharfe, son of an old Russian Menshevik, and Harry Ratner.[115] An even greater breakthrough came later in the year in Liverpool, where the group recruited Gertie Deane and her son Jimmy, and his friends Harry Matthews, Tommy Birchall and Eric Brewer. The Deane family was a direct link with the oldest revolutionary traditions of the British working class. Gertie's father had been a member of the S.D.F., and the first Labour councillor in Liverpool. Jim Larkin and H.M. Hyndman were frequent visitors to their house, and Gertie remembers clearly the day when Hyndman spoke in the Sun Hall in Kensington. She herself was an active suffragette, and a close friend of the suffragette leader Mary Bamber. She remains a staunch revolutionary to this day.[116]

This same link with the oldest revolutionary families was made with the recruitment of Rose Carson (Rosa Selner):

> My father came from Russia. He was a Bundist, and a follower of Kropotkin. They left Russia because of the pogroms, under the scheme of a Baron Hirsch. He was a wealthy man. He hired a ship and [took] a lot of people who were hiding from the pogromists to South America, to the Argentine. It was a complete and utter failure. He took them there, unloaded them off the ship onto the Pampas, [and] gave them a few coppers in their pockets. Then he gave them a candle and some sugar. My father would often repeat the story. He left them there and went off. They had no contacts, they had nothing, they couldn't do anything. They wanted to start some agriculture, as they did in Israel. But they couldn't — it was quite impossible . . .
>
> He was a baker by trade, by profession. But he couldn't do anything. Everything they tried to create came to nothing. They didn't have any money, so they couldn't buy any tools. Nobody gave them anything, nobody instructed them. It was quite impossible. They tried to create a Kibbutz-type of organisation but there was nothing there at all. So eventually my father and my eldest brother, who was born in Russia, went to a famous port, Bahia Blanca, and he got a job as a baker. He did very well. He was an attractive man, very intelligent and charming, had marvellous ideas, and could speak. He worked for a general baker. This same general baker wanted to adopt my father and his family. He stayed there for a while, and formed a union. In Russia they had started to set up unions, and he did set up the first Bakers' Union in this famous port. Of course, nobody knew what a trade union was there. And they heard that he was a Jew, so they thought he had horns.

They said, 'Good gracious, you haven't any horns.' But they made his life such a misery that he couldn't stand it. I was born in this port, and my sister was born in Buenos Aires a couple of years later . . .

When we went to Buenos Aires his reputation as a trade unionist followed him, and he was prosecuted. After a couple of years they deported him. He wanted to go to Israel (it was called Palestine then). He wanted to be with Jewish people. But my mother had an uncle living in London, and when he heard that we were coming to Europe he persuaded them to come and stay and continue the journey to Palestine later on. When he left Buenos Aires, he later showed me documents signed by a number of workers he had been trying to organise. They also swore and cut their blood-brotherhood, that sort of thing. Anyhow, we came on a boat . . . We came to England about 1912 or 1913, when I was six or seven years old, and my brother was four years older than me. My sister was just born, she was a little baby. When we got to London there was a Jewish shelter in Mansell Street off Leman Street. We went there until we found my uncle, or rather my father's uncle . . . A lot of his friends were collecting together to go to a Kibbutz in Palestine . . . Before he could get himself and his children together and arrange to go, the war started. By the time the war broke out he had become very much involved in the trade union movement. He helped set up some small craft trade unions like the Waistcoat Makers' Union, the Trouser Makers' Union, the Jewish Bakers' Union — all very small unions — and he was a member of the Workers' Circle.

He was involved in the working-class movement and after that he didn't want to go to Palestine . . . My father learned English, and he became a journalist. He still did baking, but not exclusively. He worked on the *Jewish Times* and the *Jewish Evening News* . . . My father became ill, and there was a 'benefit' for him. They collected some money and bought him a little shop . . . in the Commercial Road . . . But he couldn't keep the business going. It was a cut-throat business — you remember, cut-price cigarettes — but he couldn't maintain the business. Around that time I met my husband, and he said he would take over the shop. He was a barber, and we made the back into a hairdressing shop, and we sold cigarettes and papers in the front so my father could carry on. He bought a baker's shop in Hanbury Street in the East End. He didn't do baking, he had someone else for that, but he travelled around covering meetings as a journalist, and making reports. He wrote under

> the name of 'A Wanderer'. He wrote at least two articles a week, and he used to write in the militant press, and in the *Tukunt* and the *Frei Arbeiter Stimme*, which was the Anarchist paper. My father was actually an Anarchist, and active in the Anarchist movement. I was their protégé. I would go to all their meetings and take part in discussions . . . I can't remember his name now, but somebody brought the *Militant* into the shop, and he would stand outside and sell it. All kinds of people came down to buy the *Militant* — Michael Tippett, for instance, and other famous people came in. I can't remember names now. And eventually Harber came down to see us, and the South African, Van Gelderen . . .
>
> Andy Sharff and Jack Warman came along and sold the paper, and some Communists would come along, and there would be fights with them. And we would have discussions, and in that way we got to know all about it . . . We held meetings in the shop, and then we got very interested, and I would write articles for the paper.[117]

By the group's National conference in August 1937, membership numbers stood at just under a hundred[118] and sales of the group's newspapers rose to about 1,600 when the *Youth Militant*, which had come out duplicated but with a printed cover, for a long time, went into print, and *The Militant* came out as a large format printed paper as the year progressed.

Yet, by the end of the year, the group was beginning to stagnate. Group minutes reported the decline in the Labour League of Youth, and admitted that there was 'very little to be done' there.[119] Considering the fact that this had been the major focus of the group's activity, it was a major blow. The International Secretariat itself criticised its work as 'ineffective, not only on account of the unfavourable objective situation, but also owing to their organisational inefficiency.'[120] By the criteria that they had set themselves at the beginning, of several hundreds of workers ready to leave the Labour Party in a year for open activity, they had manifestly failed. In the teeth of vicious Stalinist opposition in the League of Youth they had struggled manfully, but their wrong policy on splitting from the Labour Party in the spring of 1937 had done them deep damage.

Nor had any real progress been made on unification with the other groups under the terms of the 'Geneva' Resolution of the International Conference. The Marxist League continued to reject even joint discussions of the members of the two Labour Party organisations, and the Militant Group supported by the International Bureau felt that joint work with the Marxist Group, a body outside the Labour Party, would prejudice their entry work and lay them open to expulsion by the Labour Party leadership. By the end of December 1936, only two meetings of the co-ordinating committee of the three groups had taken place since it had been set up on 11th October, and the Bolshevik–Leninist Group in the Labour Party was complaining that 'far too much of our time of late has been devoted to discussion on relations with other groups instead of getting on with our own work in the Labour Party and the Labour League of Youth.' They therefore refused the request of the International Bureau for further joint meetings — at least with the Marxist Group — and asked for International recognition to be withdrawn from the other two groups and solely conferred upon themselves.[121]

The International movement made one last attempt, and sent the International Secretary himself, Erwin Wolf, to attend a joint meeting on 14th February 1937. To begin with, the Militant Group wished only to discuss with the Marxist League, which shared their perspective of Labour Party work, but the latter refused to do so unless the Marxist Group were also present. Since the Marxist League put forward the perspective of an early split from the Labour Party, and agreed with the continuation of I.L.P. work, the Militant Group were unable to get agreement on joint work, and their tactic of ignoring the Marxist Group also failed.[122] For this reason they decided from then on to ignore the existence of the other two groups, and concentrate upon their work in the Labour Party, an approach that also won the approval of Erwin Wolf.[123]

The truth was that differences between the Militant Group and the other two organisations were widening all the time, whereas to a certain extent a majority of the Marxist League was moving closer to the position of the Marxist Group.

This seems surprising at first, since the Marxist League and the Militant Group were both organisations working almost exclusively in the Labour Party, but this similarity concealed great differences in activity, philosophy, and approach. In fact, the Marxist League, even before it had dropped its previous name of 'Communist League', had operated as a group with fractions in organisations other than the Labour Party, and shared much of the old British Marxist tradition of propaganda by 'street work' that the Marxist Group was now taking up. Disillusioned with the poor results of long years of work in the Socialist League, Wicks and the majority were putting forward a perspective of an early split from the Labour Party; and there was bad feeling between the leaderships of the Marxist League and the Militant Group, who complained that on the joint co-ordinating committee the contribution of the Marxist League delegate was 'confined to stirring up factional disputes',[124] and that at the joint members' meeting they were trying to play off the other two groups against each other.[125]

The Militant Group, in fact, were of the opinion that the Marxist League had ceased to be a Trotskyist organisation at all. Because the League distributed copies of the P.O.U.M. English language newspaper to show what was really happening in Spain, they were accused of actually supporting 'the opportunistic policy of that body', and it was said that they could 'in no way be considered a Bolshevik–Leninist organisation'.[126] Differences of age, of class background, of activity and outlook were far wider than the simple common feature of holding a Labour Party card. As Goffe expressed it:

> I think we tended to regard them as a group which had lost its drive and initiative, and rather getting settled into a kind of softer left-wing group which wasn't really challenging in the same sense as we were for the effective leadership of the left wing of the Labour Party and to build up a disciplined organisation, and we regarded them therefore as a looser left-wing grouping.[127]

On the other hand the Marxist Group were convinced that as the Marxist League were moving towards their position they could get unity on their own terms, if they only stuck fast to their position. Their perspective was to continue as an open group, with the addition of the other two organisations as its fractions in the Labour Party, and perhaps another small fraction in the I.L.P. There would thus be no unity of policy at all, but just two small fractions subordinated to an open group. They made constant overtures to the other two groups for joint work between those outside the Labour Party and those within. 'The methods of a fused group,' they maintained, 'can be no other than the maintenance of an independent platform and propaganda allied to correct fraction work in the mass organisations', and they criticised the other two groups for 'confining the perspective for activity to the reformist Labour Party'.[128] To accept this would mean, in effect, a return to the old Majority view about entry when it was first discussed in the context of the I.L.P. in 1933. Effective entry means total entry, there must be no public links with any outside body to arouse suspicions of disloyalty among the mass party's rank-and-file, or premature expulsions from its bureaucracy. 'The Militant Group is not prepared to send speakers to meetings held under the direct auspices of the Marxist Group,' they replied to another such overture in August 1937; 'to do so would be to provide an excuse for our premature expulsion from the Labour Party and would, in our opinion, do far more harm than good.'[129] The public attack made upon entry work in *Fight* was a confirmation of this, and the International Bureau supported the Militant Group, citing examples from other countries in their support. As was later remembered by Harber:

> ... in any case the connection with an outside body known to L[abour] P[arty] members inevitably alienates them from us — at least in the vast majority of cases ... Should we inside the L.P. openly co-operate with ... [other groups] ... we might just as well have an outside group of our own for we should be identified by the L.P. members with other outside groups and be regarded as working for them. This is the reason why, in the past, we systematically rejected such offers of 'joint work in the Labour Party' when they were made by the old R.S.L. headed by C.L.R. J[ames] which had an outside organisation, and this is why the I.S. always supported us in such refusals.[130]

Relations, in fact, worsened consistently over the whole period. At one encounter, according to the Militant Group representative:

> The Marxist Group spent most of its time attacking our group, accusing us of 'intrigue', 'playing off one group with another', 'plotting with the I.S.', and generally revealed themselves as hopelessly bankrupt.[131]

Here again, ideological differences had widened. The Militant Group believed that the Marxist Group's policy of an open group showed 'principled differences with the policy of our international organisation', an objection to entry work as giving up the revolutionary independence of the Marxist Party along the lines of 'the arguments of Bauer, Oehler, Field, etc.', and that James in particular was 'completely under the ideological influence of the Field Group'.[132]

So by autumn 1937 there was a malaise common to all three groups, a stagnation in growth (and even a drop in membership in the Marxist Group and League), a sense of common defeat and failure, and an outbreak of factional conflict in all of them. Valuable cadres, such as Roma Dewar and Bert Matlow had left the movement. Gaps were widening between Groves and Wicks in the Marxist League, between James and Cooper and Duncan in the Marxist Group, and between the provincial branches (especially Liverpool and Glasgow) and the leadership of the Militant Group. And this crisis in the ranks of the British Marxists was only the local expression of the world crisis that was about to break out in the Second World War.

Notes

1. 'A Call to Revolutionaries' (Editorial), in *Fight*, vol. i, no. 5, April 1937, p. 3.

2. 'A Revolutionary Policy for the British Workers', in *Fight*, vol. i, no. 11, November 1937, p. 14.

3. 'The L.C.C. Elections in March', in *Fight*, vol. i, no. 4, February 1937, p. 3.

4. 'For Revolutionary Independence', in *Fight*, vol. i, no. 9, August 1937, p. 1.

5. Ibid., p. 3.

6. Ajit Roy, Statement for this book, Calcutta, November 1975.

7. 'The Meaning of the New "Left Bloc" ', in *Fight*, vol. i, no. 3, January 1937, p. 3. Cf. S. Bornstein and A. Richardson, *Two Steps Back*, London, 1982, p. 30.

8. 'The Bournemouth Conference', in *Fight*, vol. i, no. 11, November 1937, p. 13.

9. Ibid.

10. 'The Popular Front in Britain', in *Fight*, vol. i, no. 2, 12th December 1936, p. 1.

11. W. Kendall, Conversation with Sam Bornstein, 22nd February 1984 (from Elsbury). Cf. A. Elsbury, *Industrial Unionism*, Bradford, 1909 (pamphlet).

12. 'List of Persons Willing to Speak as Advocates of Industrial Syndicalism in Their Respective Districts', in *The Industrial Syndicalist*, vol. i, no. 3, September 1910, reprint, Nottingham, 1974, pp. 94-5.

13. A.B. Elsbury, 'How a House Soviet Does its Work', in the *Sunday Worker*, no. 84, 17th October 1926.

14. 'Sam Elsbury's Expulsion', in *Workers Life* no. 152, 20th December 1929; J. Mahon, 'Strike Experiences of the British Minority Movement', in *Labour Monthly*, vol. xxi, no. 6, June 1930, p. 437; A.B. Elsbury, 'Stalinist Corruption Exposed', in *Fight*, vol. i, no. 2, May 1938; Bornstein & Richardson, *Two Steps Back*, pp. 2-3; S.W. Lerner, *Breakaway Unions and the Small Trade Union*, London, 1961, pp. 102-36. During the First World War, A.B. Elsbury had been wrongly suspected of being a police spy: having a stutter, he had to be defended by his brother Sam before the unofficial tribunal, and was declared innocent. Cf. K. Weller, *Don't Be A Soldier!*, London, 1985, p. 64. This book is also very valuable for an account of the war resistance of Henry Sara and Dick Beech, but came out too recently to be utilised in this volume.

15. Cf. the Letter of the C.C. of the Marxist Group to the Spanish Ambassador on the Arrest of Nin, 26th June 1937, in *Fight*, vol. i, no. 8, July 1937, p. 11. On Elsbury's interest in Spain, cf. his later pamphlet —*Alibi: Arms for Spain*, R.S.L. pamphlet, 1939.

16. The first advertisement for the book appears in *Fight*, vol. i, no. 5, April 1937.

17. *Writings of Leon Trotsky, 1938–39*, New York, 1974, pp. 260-6.

18. Ibid.

19. J.R. Campbell, in *Controversy*, vol. i, no. 8, May 1937, p. 36.

20. R.F. Andrews (Andrew Rothstein), 'Leninism Trotskified', in *Left News*, June 1937, pp. 291-8.

21. Martin Secker & Warburg, 'Letter to the Editor', 30th April 1937, in *Fight*, vol. i, no. 7, June 1937.

22. George Padmore, Letter to *Tribune*, 10th September 1937, p. 13.

23. John Goffe, Interview with Al Richardson, 18th May 1978.

24. First reviewed in *The New Leader*, 13th November 1936.

25. Reviewed in *The New Leader*, vol. xxix, new series, no. 114, 20th March 1936, p. 3.

26. C.L.R. James, 'A History of Negro Revolt', in *Fact*, September 1938; *The Black Jacobins*, London, 1938.

27. A. Ballard, 'The Greatest Slave Revolt in History', in *The New Leader*, vol. xxxi, new series, no. 256, 9th December 1938, p. 6.

28. Letter in *The New Leader*, vol. xxix, new series, no. 114, 20th March 1936, p. 4; 'Popular Front of the East: Where it is Leading China', in *The New Leader*, vol. xxx, new series, no. 123, 22nd May 1936, p. 2.

29. H. Sara, *The New Leader*, vol. xxxi, new series, no. 249, 21st October 1938, p. 7.

30. H. Sara, 'China and the Comintern', in *Controversy*, October 1937, pp. 54-6; 'Japan: Weakest Link in the Chain', in *Controversy*, no. 23, August 1938, pp. 218-20.

31. *The New Leader*, 3rd December 1937.

32. 'The Easter Conference of the I.L.P. at Glasgow', in the *Daily Worker*, 30th March 1937.

33. Cf. the advertisements in *The New Leader*, 5th March 1937.

34. Minutes of the National Conference, Militant Group, August 1937, p. 1.

35. Cf. Bornstein and Richardson, *Two Steps Back*, pp. 27-33.

36. 'The I.L.P. in Conference', in *The New Leader*, vol. xxxi, new series, no. 168, 2nd April 1937, p. 5.

37. Ibid.

38. 'Easter Conference of the I.L.P. at Glasgow', in the *Daily Worker*, 30th March 1937.

39. Op. cit., note 36 above; cf. Bornstein and Richardson, *Two Steps Back*, pp. 81-2.

40. R. Bishop, 'Is the I.L.P. Destroying Its Name and Traditions?', in the *Daily Worker*, 6th April 1937.

41. Op. cit., note 36 above.

42. E.g. 'Terrorism and Communism', in *The New Leader*, vol. xxi, new series, no. 233, 1st June 1938. Cf. also C.A. Smith's similar review of Groves' *We Shall Rise Again* in vol. xxxi, new series, no. 227, 20th May, p. 7.

43. 'Statistician', 'The End of the Old Guard', in *Controversy*, vol. ii, no. 13, October 1937; '90 Years of the Communist Manifesto', *Controversy*, no. 19, April 1938.

44. E. Patterson, 'The Series on Socialism', in *Controversy*, vol. i, no. 10, July 1937, pp. 83-4; 'Mosley Marches', vol. i, no. 11, August 1937, p. 98; C.L.R. James, 'Trotskyism', in *Controversy*, vol. ii, no. 13, October 1937; 'Six Questions of Trotskyists — And Their Answers', vol. ii, no. 17, February 1938. For Sara's articles, see above, p. 66; and for E.L. Worrall, *Controversy*, vol. i, no. 8, May 1937, pp. 36-7.

45. 'Conference Supplement', in *The New Leader*, vol. xxxi, new series, no. 223, 22nd April 1938, p. iii.

46. 'The 47th Annual Conference of the I.L.P.', in *The New Leader*, vol. xxxi, new series, no. 274, 14th April 1939, p. 3.

47. Op. cit., note 45 above, pp. ii and iv.

48. Op. cit., note 46 above, p. 6.

49. Ibid.

50. 'No Split in London I.L.P.', in *The New Leader*, vol. xxxi, new series, no 288, 21st July 1939, p. 7. C.A. Smith himself left the Party shortly afterwards over the same issue.

51. A.A. Ballard and A. Rosen, 'Statement to the Marxist Group', 13th October 1937.

52. Minutes of the Founding Conference of the R.S.L., *Internal Bulletin*, April 1938, pp. 8 and 10.

53. Harry Wicks, Interview with Al Richardson, 1st April 1978.

54. W. Duncan, 'Fusion and C.C. Muddle', Internal Document of the R.S.L., 14th July 1938, pp. 2-3.

55. Op. cit., note 52 above, p. 12 (our emphasis).
56. C.L.R. James, 'Revolutionary Socialist League', in *Fight*, vol. i, no. 1, new series, April 1938.
57. Point 10, 'Platform of the Militant Group'.
58. 'Draft Programme of the R.S.L.' (Conference Document, 1939), p. 10.
59. J.L.R[obinson], 'Once Again — the Labour Party Tactic', March 1942, p. 2.
60. 'Constitution of the Militant Group'.
61. 'R.W.' ('Robert Williams'), 'On the Work of Bolshevik–Leninists in the Labour Party', September 1936, pp. 1-3.
62. Minutes of the National Conference of the Militant Group, 1st and 2nd August 1937, p. 3.
63. 'Our Programme For Left Wing', in *The Militant*, vol. i, no. 5, November 1937, p. 2.
64. 'Report of the First National Conference of the Militant Labour League'.
65. Bolshevik–Leninist Group, 'Minutes London E.C.', 20th February 1937, p. 3. Cf. above, pp. 205-6.
66. Minutes of the Fusion Conference of the R.S.L., 27th February 1938, p. 14.
67. Ted Willis, 'Clear Them Out!', in *Advance*, vol. i, no. 10, April 1937, p. 2.
68. 'The League of Youth', in 'Report of the 36th Annual Conference of the Labour Party, Edinburgh, 1936', p. 75.
69. E.S. Harrison, Letter to *Advance*, new series, vol. i, no. 3, p. 13.
70. John Goffe, Interview with Al Richardson, 18th May 1978.
71. Cf. R. Black, *Stalinism in Britain*, London, 1970, p. 475 (quoted from *Youth of Britain, Advance!*).
72. *For Peace and Plenty*, Report of the 15th Congress of the C.P.G.B., 16th–19th September 1938, pp. 70-1.
73. 'Trotskyists Beaten in Open Debate', in the *Daily Worker*, 24th July 1936, p. 3; Ted Willis, 'Clear Them Out!', in *Advance*, vol. i, no. 10, April 1937, p. 2.
74. 'Workers' Notebook', in the *Daily Worker*, 5th February 1938; cf. Black, *Stalinism in Britain*, p. 110 (quoted from *What Will London's Youth Do?*, Y.C.L. pamphlet, 1938).
75. Militant Group, Minutes of General Members' Meeting, 12th September 1937, p. 2.
76. Minutes of the National Conference of the Militant Group, 1st and 2nd August 1937, p. 2.
77. Jock Haston, Interview with Al Richardson, 30th April 1978.
78. Minutes, National Conference of the Militant Group, 1st & 2nd August 1937, p. 2; cf. Mary and John Archer, 'Notes on Healy's Role in Early Days of the British Trotskyist Movement', in *Healy's Big Lie*, New York, 1976, p. 30; J. Archer, 'On the "Reply" of Sam Bornstein to Our Article "Healy's Early Days in the British Trotskyist Movement" ', undated, p. 1.
79. Sid Bone, Peckham L.O.Y., Letter to *Advance*, February 1937, p. 6; *Youth Militant*, April 1937, p. 1.
80. F.L. Brown, Organiser, Stoke Newington L.O.Y. to *Advance*, vol. i, no. 9, March 1937, p. 13.
81. Editorial, 'The Future is Ours', in *Advance*, vol. i, no. 10, April 1937, p. 3.
82. R.H. Hartman, Charlton L.O.Y., 'The Debate Continues', in *Advance*, vol. i, no. 10, April 1937, p. 12.
83. Ted Willis, 'We Have Our Wreckers Too', in *Advance*, vol. i, no. 9, March 1937, pp. 9-10; cf. 'National Committee Meets', p. 3.
84. 'London Leagues in Conference', in *Youth Militant*, vol. ii, no. 3, April 1937, p. 3.

85. A. Bernstein, 'See How They Run!', in *Advance*, vol. i, no. 11, May 1937, p. 14.

86. A. Fisher, Letter to *Advance*, vol. i, no. 10, April 1937, p. 8 (emphasis as in original).

87. Op. cit., note 85 above.

88. 'Labour League of Youth Conference', in *Fight*, vol. i, no. 7, June 1937, p. 13.

89. E. Haseler, Motion from East Islington League of Youth, in *Advance*, vol. i, no. 11, May 1937, p. 13.

90. Op. cit., note 88 above.

91. Ibid. Cf. A. Bernstein, 'Enemies of Socialism', in *Advance*, vol. i, no. 12, June 1937, p. 14. 'L.A.C. Conference Fiasco', in *The Militant*, vol. i, no. 2, August 1937, p. 4.

92. Bernstein, op. cit., note 91 above.

93. Op. cit., note 89 above.

94. Frank Budd, 'The National Conference', in *Advance*, vol. i, no. 12, June 1937, p. 3.

95. John Gollan, 'What Next For Youth Unity?', in *Advance*, vol. i, no. 12, June 1937, p. 13; R. Ellis, 'Spain — A People's Democracy', in *Advance*, July 1937, p. 16.

96. C. Van Gelderen, 'Spain — A Trotskyist View', in *Advance*, vol. ii, no. 2, August 1937, pp. 12-13.

97. 'The Editor Replies', in ibid.

98. Minutes of the National Conference of the Militant Group, 1st and 2nd August 1937, p. 3; Alex Rudling, Letter to *Dissent*, winter, 1984, p. 143.

99. 'Youth League Bans Democracy', in *The Militant*, vol. i, no. 4, October 1937.

100. 'Militants Progress in Youth League', in *The Militant*, vol. i, no. 7, January 1938, p. 3.

101. 'Labour League of Youth Forgets About Socialism', in *The New Leader*, vol. xxxi, new series, no. 217, 11th March 1938, p. 3.

102. 'Labour Youth Meets', in *The Militant*, vol. ii, no. 6, January 1939. Cf. Bornstein and Richardson, *Two Steps Back*, pp. 34-5.

103. 'When Will the League Have Its National Conference?', Editorial, *Youth Militant*, new series, no. 5, June 1940, p. 2.

104. *Advance*, vol. i, no. 12, June 1937, p. 15.

105. Bob Home, 'National Chairman Speaks', in *Advance*, vol. ii, no. 1, July 1939, p. 10.

106. 'Ted Willis Joins Young Communists', in the *Daily Worker*, 14th July 1939.

107. 'Who Publishes Youth Militant and Why?', in *Youth Militant*, new series, no. 1, December 1939.

108. 'The Bournemouth Conference', in *The Militant*, vol. i, no. 2, August 1937, p. 3.

109. *Militant*, August 1937; cf. *Spartacist Britain*, no. 12, June 1979, p. 4.

110. 'A Barricade Builder', 'Barricades Bar Blackshirts', in *The Militant*, vol. i, no. 5, November 1937, p. 7.

111. Jock Haston, Interview with Al Richardson, 30th April 1978.

112. Ted Grant, *The Menace of Fascism*, R.C.P., 1948, p. 43 (pamphlet).

113. 'Statement to the Bureau for the Fourth International from the B.L. Group in the Labour Party Regarding the Fulfilment of the Geneva Resolution on the Question of Unity of the British Groups', p. 4.

114. John Goffe, Interview with Al Richardson, 18th May 1978.

115. Minutes, London E.C., Militant Group, 20th February 1937.

116. Gertrude Deane, Interview with Sam Bornstein, Liverpool, 8th July 1980.

117. Rose Selner, Interview with Sam Bornstein, 23rd June 1984.

118. Minutes of the Annual Conference, Militant Group, 1st–2nd August 1937, pp. 1-3; Minutes, London E.C., Militant Group, 20th February 1937; Letter to all Groups, Editorial Board, *The Militant* (undated, but on internal evidence, September 1937); Conference Minutes, p. 12.

119. Minutes of the Secretariat, Militant Group, 12th September 1937.

120. 'Resolution on the English Youth Movement as Amended by Gould'.

121. 'Statement to the Bureau for the Fourth International from the B.L. Group in the Labour Party Regarding the Fulfilment of the Geneva Resolution on the Question of the Unity of the British Groups'.

122. 'Report to Provincial Branch on Joint Meeting, 14th February 1937' (Internal document of the Militant Group).

123. 'Statement of the E.C. of the Militant Group on Inter-Group Relations', 20th August 1937.

124. Op. cit., note 121 above.

125. Op. cit., note 122 above.

126. Op. cit., note 121 above.

127. John Goffe, Interview with Al Richardson, 8th May 1978.

128. 'Resolution and Theses of the Marxist Group', Half yearly Conference, 11th July 1937.

129. 'Interim Reply of the E.C. of the Militant Group', 5th August 1937.

130. 'Letter of Secretary, R.S.L.', 18th July 1943.

131. 'Report to Provincial Branch on Joint Meeting, 14th February 1937' (Internal Bulletin of Bolshevik–Leninist Group in the Labour Party).

132. Op. cit., note 121 above.

Appendix One

The thanks we owe to the following who granted us interviews must be obvious to all who have read this book:

BERT ATKINSON Interviewed by Sam Bornstein and Al Richardson, 4th November 1977.

EVE BROWN (FINCH) Interviewed by Sam Bornstein, 21st January 1984.

FRED BUNBY Interviewed by Sam Bornstein, 26th March 1978.

JOHN BYRNE Interviewed by Al Richardson, September 1976.

DAVID CHALKLEY Interviewed by Al Richardson, 14th November 1978.

GERTRUDE DEANE Interviewed by Sam Bornstein, 8th July 1980.

HUGO DEWAR Interviewed by Al Richardson, 7th April 1978.

STEVE DOWDALL and DAISY GROVES Interviewed by Al Richardson.

PERCY DOWNEY Interviewed by Sam Bornstein, 26th November 1977.

SID FROST (MAX BOSCH) Interviewed by Sam Bornstein and Al Richardson, 14th June 1983.

JOHN GOFFE Interviewed by Al Richardson, 18th May 1978.

MILDRED GORDON (FALLERMAN) Interviewed by Al Richardson, 13th February 1981.

SAM GORDON Interviewed by Sam Bornstein, 17th October 1977.

DAVE GRANICK Interviewed by Sam Bornstein, August 1976.

TED GRANT Interviewed by Sam Bornstein, 22nd August 1982.

REG GROVES Interviewed by Al Richardson, 2nd April 1978.

GEORGE HANSEN Interviewed by Sam Bornstein, 3rd April 1978.

JOCK HASTON and MILLIE HASTON (LEE) Interviewed by Al Richardson, 30th April 1978.

ELLIS HILLMAN Interviewed by Sam Bornstein and Al Richardson, 19th June 1978.

JIM HINCHCLIFFE Interviewed by Sam Bornstein, 31st December 1977.

MARGARET JOHNS Interviewed by Al Richardson, 4th February 1978.

ANN KEEN Interviewed by Sam Bornstein, 10th February 1974.

GEORGE LESLIE Interviewed by Sam Bornstein and Al Richardson, 20th May 1974.

SHEILA LESLIE (LAHR) Interviewed by Sam Bornstein and Al Richardson, 20th May 1974.

SAM LEVY Interviewed by Sam Bornstein and Al Richardson, 20th May 1973.

PAT McVEIGH Interviewed by Sam Bornstein, September 1973.

FRANK MAITLAND Interviewed by Sam Bornstein, August 1976.

FREDERICK MARZILLIER Interviewed by Al Richardson, 2nd December 1978.

MATTY MERRIGAN Interviewed by Sam Bornstein, 15th April 1974.

ALEX MURIE Interviewed by Sam Bornstein, 17th August 1984.

MAX NICHOLLS Interviewed by Sam Bornstein, 15th December 1979.

DAISY RAWLINGS Interviewed by Sam Bornstein, 7th September 1976.

JACK RAWLINGS Interviewed by Sam Bornstein, September 1973.

FRANK RIDLEY Interviewed by Al Richardson, 10th September 1977.

JOHN ROBINSON Interviewed by Al Richardson, 30th June 1978.

AJIT ROY Tape done for Sam Bornstein, September 1979.

ROSE SELNER (CARSON) Interviewed by Sam Bornstein, 23rd June 1984.

T. DAN SMITH Interviewed by Sam Bornstein, 5th June 1985.

ROY TEARSE Interviewed by Al Richardson, 6th July 1978.

CHARLIE VAN GELDEREN Interviewed by Al Richardson, 4th October 1979.

FRANK WARD Interviewed by Sam Bornstein and Al Richardson, 27th September 1980.

HARRY WICKS Interviewed by Al Richardson, 11th March and 1st April 1978.

BOB WILSKER Interviewed by Al Richardson, 10th November 1984.

RYAN WORRALL Interviewed by Al Richardson, 26th November 1978.

We have also profited greatly from the following interviews, kindly loaned to us:

JOHN ARCHER Interviewed by Martin Upham (no date).

NILS DAHL Interviewed by Mildred Gordon, 27th December 1983.

Appendix Two

Michael Tippett and the Trotskyist Movement

The latest biography of Michael Tippett[1] notes that Tippett was attracted to the Trotskyist position as a result of reading the propaganda of the Communist League; and Reg Groves recalls that he came along to several of their meetings and took part in their discussions, but that he was not a dues-paying member, or an activist, as far as he was aware.[2] However, the statement that he 'never joined a Trotskyist Party'[3] is certainly incorrect. An earlier account by Meirion Bowen is far more accurate when it describes Tippett as joining the Communist Party for a few months in 1935 but leaving 'when he failed to convert his party branch to Trotskyism'.[4] He was part of the Musicians' Group of the Bolshevik/Leninist Group in the Labour Party (the *Militant* Group), and his anti-militarist play, *War Ramp*, was performed at various Labour Party rallies. On 8th January 1938 he wrote a letter protesting about the handling of the 'Lee Affair' to the leadership of the *Militant* Group,[5] and according to Ted Grant[6] he was a supporter of the W.I.L. for a short time, recruited by Betty Hamilton, who had been a pupil of Isadora Duncan. But in 1940, despairing of the ability of Trotskyism to halt 'the barbarities of Nazism and Stalinism', he joined the Peace Pledge Union and registered as a conscientious objector. He spent three months in prison for resisting the terms of registration.[7]

Notes

1. I. Kemp, *Tippett: The Composer and His Music*, London, 1984, pp. 31–3.
2. Reg Groves, Conversation with Al Richardson, 30th June 1985.
3. Kemp, *Tippett*, p. 33.
4. M. Bowen, *Michael Tippett*, London, 1981, p. 21.
5. To be dealt with in our next volume.
6. Interview with Sam Bornstein, 22nd August 1982.
7. Bowen, *Michael Tippett*, p. 23.

Index

Printed in the United Kingdom
by Lightning Source UK Ltd.
119873UK00001B/379-384